5 Ingredient favorites

Better Homes and Gardens.

5 Ingredient favorites

700 Favorite Recipes with Five Ingredients or Less

Better Homes and Gardens® Books
Des Moines, Iowa

Better Homes and Gardens® 5-Ingredient Favorites
Editor: Alrica Goldstein
Contributing Project Editor: Spectrum Communication
  Services, Inc.
Contributing Graphic Designer: Diana Van Winkle
Copy Chief: Doug Kouma
Copy Editor: Kevin Cox
Publishing Operations Manager: Karen Schirm
Edit and Design Production Coordinator: Mary Lee Gavin
Editorial Assistant: Sheri Cord
Book Production Managers: Marjorie J. Schenkelberg,
  Mark Weaver
Contributing Proofreaders: Karen Fraley, Stephan Maras
Contributing Indexer: Elizabeth Parson
Test Kitchen Director: Lynn Blanchard
Test Kitchen Product Supervisor: Marilyn Cornelius
Test Kitchen Culinary Specialists: Marilyn Cornelius,
  Juliana Hale, Maryellyn Krantz, Jill Moberly, Colleen
  Weeden, Lori Wilson
Test Kitchen Nutrition Specialists: Elizabeth Burt,
  R.D.,L.D.; Laura Marzen, R.D., L.D.

Meredith® Books
Editorial Director: John Riha
Managing Editor: Kathleen Armentrout
Deputy Editor: Jennifer Darling
Brand Manager: Janell Pittman
Group Editor: Jan Miller
Senior Associate Design Director: Mick Schnepf

Director, Marketing and Publicity: Amy Nichols
Executive Director, Sales: Ken Zagor
Director, Operations: George A. Susral
Director, Production: Douglas M. Johnston
Business Director: Janice Croat

Vice President and General Manager, SIM: Jeff Myers

Better Homes and Gardens® Magazine
Editor in Chief: Gayle Goodson Butler
Deputy Editor, Food and Entertaining: Nancy Hopkins

Meredith Publishing Group
President: Jack Griffin
Executive Vice President: Doug Olson

Meredith Corporation
Chairman of the Board: William T. Kerr
President and Chief Executive Officer: Stephen M. Lacy

In Memoriam: E. T. Meredith III (1933–2003)

All of us at Meredith® Books are dedicated to providing
you with the information and ideas you need to create
delicious foods. We welcome your comments and
suggestions. Write to us at: Meredith Books, Cookbook
Editorial Department, 1716 Locust St., Des Moines, IA
50309-3023.

Our seal assures you that every recipe in *5-Ingredient
Favorites* has been tested in the Better Homes and
Gardens® Test Kitchen. This means that each recipe is
practical and reliable and meets our high standards of
taste appeal. We guarantee your satisfaction with this
book for as long as you own it.

Pictured on front cover: Barbecued Pork Chop
Sandwich, page 84; Fresh Corn and Tomato Salad,
page 236; Strawberry-Chocolate Cake, page 302;
Cranberry Chicken, page 19

contents

Introduction 4

Savory Chicken & Turkey 5

Hearty Beef, Pork & Lamb 41

Fast-Fixin' Fish, Shellfish & Meatless 127

Warming Soups & Stews 165

Serve-Along Sides 187
  Seasonal Vegetables 188
  Robust Pastas, Grains & Breads 215
  No-Fuss Salads 229
  Simple Sauces, Salsas & Rubs 249

Delectable Desserts 279
  Tempting Cobblers & Fruit Delights 280
  Easy Anytime Cakes 302
  Homestyle Pies & Puddings 316
  Ever-Popular Cookies & Candies 329

Take Five for Fun 341
  Party Snacks & Appetizers 342
  Refreshing Drinks & Sippers 369
  Perfect for Kids 379

Index 399

Metric Measurements 414

introduction

In today's busy world it's hard enough finding time to cook, let alone shop for the ingredients to stock your pantry. *5-Ingredient Favorites* is the perfect cookbook for on the go families.

Inside this book you will find delectable yet easy recipes to create a healthy meal. Everything is included, from main entrées to sides to desserts. Who wants to spend hours shopping for all of the ingredients and then another hour in the kitchen cooking? The short prep time for these recipes helps you produce a delicious meal that's ready when you are.

How do we count ingredients? Each recipe in this book uses five ingredients or fewer. The following are not counted:

- water
- nonstick cooking spray
- any ingredients listed as optional

Salt and pepper are counted as one ingredient.

Easy cooking techniques contribute to the simplicity. Many recipes in this book have a grilling or slow cooker designation. Consider these options when you are pressed for time or looking for a new experience. All of the slow cooker recipes in this book were tested with a continuous slow cooker/crockery cooker appliance. This appliance has two fixed settings—low and high—and a ceramic liner that may or may not be removable. The recipes will not cook properly in an intermittent slow cooker that has a dial indicating temperatures in degrees and cycles on and off during operation. Grilling recipes include instructions for both a gas and a charcoal grill.

Every recipe in this book was tested and approved by the Better Homes and Gardens® Test Kitchen, which guarantees success every time you make the recipe.

Happy cooking!

savory
chicken & turkey

Roast Chicken with Fruit and Pesto

PREP: 20 minutes **ROAST:** 1¾ hours **STAND:** 15 minutes
MAKES: 8 to 10 servings

1   cup apricot or peach preserves

½   cup snipped dried apricots or peaches

¼   teaspoon ground ginger

⅔   cup purchased basil pesto

1   5- to 6-pound whole roasting chicken

one In a medium bowl stir together preserves, dried apricots, and ginger. Remove ⅓ cup of the mixture; place in a small bowl. Stir in pesto; set aside. Set aside the remaining preserve mixture for sauce.

two Remove neck and giblets from chicken. Rinse inside of chicken; pat dry with paper towels. Slip your fingers between the skin and breast meat, loosening the skin.

three Spoon some of the pesto mixture under the skin and spread over breast meat. Spread some of the pesto mixture into the neck cavity. Skewer neck skin to back. Spread some of the pesto mixture into the body cavity. Rub the remaining pesto mixture over outside of chicken. Tie drumsticks to tail. Twist wing tips under back. If desired, insert a meat thermometer into the center of an inside thigh muscle without touching bone.

four Place chicken, breast side up, on a rack in a shallow roasting pan. Roast, uncovered, in a 325°F oven for 1¾ to 2½ hours or until drumsticks move easily in their sockets and juices run clear (180°F), cutting string between drumsticks during the last 45 minutes of roasting. Transfer chicken to a serving platter. Cover with foil and let stand for 15 minutes before carving.

five Meanwhile, for sauce, in a small saucepan heat the reserved preserve mixture over low heat until preserves melt and mixture is heated through. Serve sauce with chicken.

NUTRITION FACTS PER SERVING: 873 cal., 57 g total fat (12 g sat. fat), 208 mg chol., 323 mg sodium, 36 g carbo., 1 g fiber, 52 g pro.

Garlicky Grilled Chicken

PREP: 15 minutes **GRILL:** 1 hour **STAND:** 10 minutes
MAKES: 4 servings

1	2½- to 3-pound whole broiler-fryer chicken
1	tablespoon cooking oil
2	cloves garlic, minced
1	teaspoon dark roast ground coffee
	Salt and black pepper

one Remove neck and giblets from chicken. Skewer neck skin to back. Tie drumsticks to tail. Twist wing tips under back. In a small bowl combine oil and garlic. Brush garlic mixture over chicken; sprinkle with coffee, salt, and pepper. If desired, insert a meat thermometer into the center of an inside thigh muscle without touching bone.

two For a charcoal grill, arrange medium-hot coals around a drip pan. Test for medium heat above pan. Place chicken, breast side up, on grill rack over drip pan. Cover and grill for 1 to 1¼ hours or until drumsticks move easily in their sockets and juices run clear (180°F). (For a gas grill, preheat grill. Reduce heat to medium. Adjust for indirect cooking. Grill as above.)

three Remove chicken from grill. Cover with foil and let stand for 10 minutes before carving.

NUTRITION FACTS PER SERVING: 462 cal., 34 g total fat (9 g sat. fat), 148 mg chol., 402 mg sodium, 1 g carbo., 0 g fiber, 35 g pro.

Honey-Mustard Baked Chicken

PREP: 5 minutes **BAKE:** 35 minutes **MAKES:** 6 servings

2½	to 3 pounds meaty chicken pieces (breast halves, thighs, and drumsticks)
⅓	cup brown mustard
1	to 2 tablespoons honey
1	tablespoon cooking oil
1	tablespoon soy sauce

one If desired, skin chicken. Place chicken pieces in a lightly greased shallow baking pan. Bake, uncovered, in a 425°F oven for 15 minutes. Meanwhile, in a small bowl stir together brown mustard, honey, oil, and soy sauce. Brush mixture generously over chicken.

two Bake, uncovered, for 20 to 25 minutes more or until chicken is tender and no longer pink (170°F for breasts; 180°F for thighs and drumsticks), brushing frequently with mustard mixture.

NUTRITION FACTS PER SERVING: 259 cal., 14 g total fat (3 g sat. fat), 86 mg chol., 409 mg sodium, 4 g carbo., 0 g fiber, 29 g pro.

Kickin' Chicken

PREP: 20 minutes **GRILL:** 50 minutes **MAKES:** 6 servings

2½   to 3 pounds meaty chicken pieces (breast halves, thighs, and drumsticks)

     Salt and black pepper

⅔   cup orange marmalade

¼   cup bottled chili sauce

2   tablespoons soy sauce

1   tablespoon ground coriander (optional)

¼   teaspoon bottled hot pepper sauce

one If desired, skin chicken. Sprinkle the chicken with salt and pepper.

two For sauce, in a small saucepan combine marmalade, chili sauce, soy sauce, coriander (if desired), and hot pepper sauce. Cook over medium heat just until bubbly, stirring occasionally. Remove ⅓ cup of the sauce to use for basting. Set aside the remaining sauce until ready to serve.

three For a charcoal grill, arrange medium-hot coals around a drip pan. Test for medium heat above pan. Place chicken, bone sides up, on grill rack over drip pan.

four Cover and grill for 50 to 60 minutes or until chicken is tender and no longer pink (170°F for breasts; 180°F for thighs and drumsticks), turning once halfway through grilling and brushing with the ⅓ cup sauce during the last 10 minutes. (For a gas grill, preheat grill. Reduce heat to medium. Adjust for indirect cooking. Grill as above.) Serve chicken pieces with reserved sauce.

NUTRITION FACTS PER SERVING: 316 cal., 11 g total fat (3 g sat. fat), 87 mg chol., 635 mg sodium, 26 g carbo., 1 g fiber, 29 g pro.

Tuscan Chicken

PREP: 20 minutes **COOK:** 30 minutes **MAKES:** 4 servings

2   to 2½ pounds meaty chicken pieces (breast halves, thighs, and drumsticks)

2   tablespoons olive oil

1¼   teaspoons pesto seasoning

½   cup whole kalamata olives

½   cup dry white wine or chicken broth

one In a 12-inch skillet cook chicken pieces in hot oil over medium heat for 15 minutes, turning to brown evenly. Reduce heat. Drain off fat. Sprinkle pesto seasoning evenly over chicken. Add olives and white wine.

two Cover tightly; cook for 25 minutes. Cook, uncovered, for 5 to 10 minutes more or until chicken is tender and no longer pink (170°F for breasts; 180°F for thighs and drumsticks).

NUTRITION FACTS PER SERVING: 334 cal., 18 g total fat (4 g sat. fat), 104 mg chol., 280 mg sodium, 2 g carbo., 1 g fiber, 34 g pro.

Sweet and Spicy Chicken

PREP: 15 minutes **COOK:** 45 minutes **MAKES:** 6 servings

3   pounds meaty chicken pieces (breast halves, thighs, and drumsticks)

3   cloves garlic, minced

2   tablespoons cooking oil

¾   cup bottled sweet-and-sour sauce

¾   cup bottled hot-style barbecue sauce

one If desired, skin chicken; set aside. For sauce, in a 12-inch skillet cook and stir garlic in 1 tablespoon of the oil over medium heat for 1 minute. Using a slotted spoon, transfer garlic to a medium bowl. Stir sweet-and-sour sauce and barbecue sauce into garlic in bowl; set sauce aside.

two Add the remaining 1 tablespoon oil to skillet; add chicken pieces. Cook over medium heat for 10 minutes, turning to brown evenly. Add more oil if necessary. Reduce heat. Cover tightly and cook for 25 minutes.

three Pour sauce over chicken. Bring to boiling over medium heat. Cook, uncovered, about 10 minutes more or until chicken is tender and no longer pink (170°F for breasts; 180°F for thighs and drumsticks), spooning sauce over chicken occasionally. Transfer chicken to a serving platter. Stir sauce and spoon over chicken.

NUTRITION FACTS PER SERVING: 399 cal., 18 g total fat (4 g sat. fat), 104 mg chol., 606 mg sodium, 21 g carbo., 0 g fiber, 33 g pro.

Oven-Fried Coconut Chicken

PREP: 10 minutes **BAKE:** 45 minutes **MAKES:** 6 servings

½   cup flaked coconut

¼   cup seasoned fine dry bread crumbs

2½   to 3 pounds meaty chicken pieces (breast halves, thighs, and drumsticks)

¼   cup butter or margarine, melted

one In a shallow bowl stir together coconut and bread crumbs; set aside. Brush chicken pieces with melted butter. Roll chicken pieces in coconut mixture to coat all sides. In a 15×10×1- or a 13×9×2-inch baking pan arrange chicken, skin sides up, so pieces don't touch. Drizzle any remaining melted butter over chicken.

two Bake, uncovered, in a 375°F oven for 45 to 50 minutes or until chicken is tender and no longer pink (170°F for breasts; 180°F for thighs and drumsticks). Do not turn.

NUTRITION FACTS PER SERVING: 332 cal., 21 g total fat (10 g sat. fat), 108 mg chol., 284 mg sodium, 6 g carbo., 0 g fiber, 29 g pro.

Chicken with Pineapple-Hoisin Glaze

PREP: 25 minutes **GRILL:** 12 minutes **MAKES:** 4 servings

1	20-ounce can pineapple slices (juice pack), drained
3	tablespoons bottled hoisin sauce
1/8	to 1/4 teaspoon crushed red pepper
4	skinless, boneless chicken breast halves (about 1 1/4 pounds)
2	tablespoons snipped fresh cilantro

Food Safety The very best way to prevent foodborne illness is to cook meats and poultry to a minimum internal temperature, as directed in the recipes. Also practice the following:

- Keep raw meats separate from cooked foods.
- Wash your hands and cutting boards frequently.
- Don't use the same plates or utensils for raw meats and cooked foods.
- Always marinate meats, poultry, or seafood in the refrigerator. Discard any leftover marinade or bring it to a full boil before use.
- Keep hot foods hot and cold foods cold. Don't let any cooked food sit out at room temperature for more than 2 hours.

one For glaze, remove and reserve 4 slices of pineapple. Chop the remaining pineapple slices (you should have about 1 1/4 cups). In a blender or small food processor combine the chopped pineapple, hoisin sauce, and crushed red pepper. Cover and blend until nearly smooth.

two For a charcoal grill, grill chicken on the rack of an uncovered grill directly over medium coals for 12 to 15 minutes or until chicken is tender and no longer pink (170°F), turning once and brushing with half of the glaze halfway through grilling.

three After 6 minutes of grilling, add pineapple slices to grill rack; turn once and brush with more of the glaze during grilling. (For a gas grill, preheat grill. Reduce heat to medium. Place chicken, then pineapple on grill rack over heat. Cover and grill as above.)

four Reheat the remaining glaze until bubbly; serve with chicken and pineapple. Sprinkle with cilantro.

NUTRITION FACTS PER SERVING: 268 cal., 3 g total fat (1 g sat. fat), 82 mg chol., 235 mg sodium, 27 g carbo., 2 g fiber, 34 g pro.

Tangy Lemon Chicken *See photo on page 111.*

PREP: 10 minutes **MARINATE:** 2 to 4 hours **GRILL:** 12 minutes
MAKES: 4 servings

4	skinless, boneless chicken breast halves (about 1¼ pounds)
½	cup bottled creamy Italian salad dressing
1	tablespoon finely shredded lemon peel
¼	cup lemon juice
	Dash black pepper

one Place chicken in a resealable plastic bag set in a shallow dish. For marinade, in a small bowl stir together salad dressing, lemon peel, lemon juice, and pepper. Pour over chicken; seal bag. Marinate in the refrigerator for 2 to 4 hours, turning bag occasionally. Drain chicken, reserving marinade.

two For a charcoal grill, grill chicken on the rack of an uncovered grill directly over medium coals for 12 to 15 minutes or until chicken is tender and no longer pink (170°F), turning once and brushing with marinade halfway through grilling. (For a gas grill, preheat grill. Reduce heat to medium. Place chicken on grill rack over heat. Cover and grill as above.) Discard any remaining marinade.

NUTRITION FACTS PER SERVING: 177 cal., 6 g total fat (1 g sat. fat), 66 mg chol., 179 mg sodium, 2 g carbo., 0 g fiber, 26 g pro.

> **Why Marinate?** Marinades tenderize and flavor poultry, meats, and seafood. They usually consist of an acid (such as vinegar, lemon juice, or wine), seasonings, and cooking or olive oil. Because marinades contain acid, always marinate in a ceramic, glass, or stainless steel container—never aluminum. Better yet, use a resealable plastic bag to simplify cleanup. Turn the bag occasionally to ensure that the marinade is evenly distributed.

Pepper and Peach Fajita Chicken

START TO FINISH: 30 minutes **MAKES:** 4 servings

4	skinless, boneless chicken breast halves (about 1¼ pounds)
1½	teaspoons fajita seasoning
2	tablespoons olive oil or butter
1½	cups sweet pepper strips
1	medium fresh peach or nectarine, cut into thin slices, or 1 cup frozen unsweetened peach slices, thawed

one Sprinkle both sides of chicken with fajita seasoning. In a large skillet cook chicken in 1 tablespoon of the oil over medium heat for 12 to 14 minutes or until chicken is tender and no longer pink (170°F), turning once. Transfer chicken to a serving platter; cover and keep warm.

two Add the remaining 1 tablespoon oil to skillet; add pepper strips. Cook and stir about 3 minutes or until pepper strips are crisp-tender. Gently stir in peach slices. Cook for 1 to 2 minutes more or until heated through. Spoon over chicken.

NUTRITION FACTS PER SERVING: 243 cal., 9 g total fat (1 g sat. fat), 82 mg chol., 150 mg sodium, 7 g carbo., 2 g fiber, 33 g pro.

Florentine Chicken

PREP: 20 minutes **BAKE:** 25 minutes **MAKES:** 4 servings

- 1 12-ounce package frozen spinach soufflé
- 4 skinless, boneless chicken breast halves (about 1¼ pounds)
- 1 4½-ounce can (drained weight) sliced mushrooms, drained
- ½ cup shredded cheddar cheese (2 ounces)

one Run warm water over spinach soufflé for a few seconds to loosen it from the pan. Remove soufflé from pan and divide into 4 squares. Place each chicken breast half, boned side up, between 2 pieces of plastic wrap. Pound the chicken lightly until ¼ inch thick. Discard plastic wrap.

two Place chicken pieces in a greased 3-quart rectangular baking dish. Top each piece with some of the mushrooms and one portion of soufflé.

three Bake, uncovered, in a 400°F oven for 20 minutes. Sprinkle shredded cheese on top of each piece. Bake about 5 minutes more or until chicken is tender and no longer pink and cheese melts.

NUTRITION FACTS PER SERVING: 331 cal., 14 g total fat (5 g sat. fat), 187 mg chol., 642 mg sodium, 8 g carbo., 1 g fiber, 41 g pro.

GRILLING

Chicken Burgundy

PREP: 10 minutes **GRILL:** 12 minutes **MAKES:** 4 servings

- ⅓ cup orange marmalade
- ¼ cup Burgundy or other dry red wine
- ¼ teaspoon salt
- 4 skinless, boneless chicken breast halves (about 1¼ pounds)

one For sauce, in a small saucepan combine orange marmalade, Burgundy, and salt. Cook and stir over low heat until marmalade melts. Remove from heat.

two For a charcoal grill, grill chicken on the rack of an uncovered grill directly over medium coals for 12 to 15 minutes or until chicken is tender and no longer pink (170°), turning once halfway through grilling and brushing with some of the sauce during the last 5 minutes of grilling. (For a gas grill, preheat grill. Reduce heat to medium. Place chicken on grill rack over heat. Cover and grill as above.)

three To serve, reheat the remaining sauce until bubbly; serve with chicken.

NUTRITION FACTS PER SERVING: 239 cal., 2 g total fat (1 g sat. fat), 82 mg chol., 237 mg sodium, 18 g carbo., 0 g fiber, 33 g pro.

Apricot-Cranberry Chicken

PREP: 35 minutesr **BAKE:** 25 minutes **MAKES:** 6 servings

6   skinless, boneless chicken breast halves (about 2 pounds)

1½ cups herb-seasoned stuffing mix

½   cup apricot jam

⅓   cup dried cranberries

¼   cup butter or margarine, melted

one Place each chicken breast half, boned side up, between 2 pieces of plastic wrap. Pound chicken lightly until about ⅛ inch thick. Discard plastic wrap. Set chicken aside.

two In a medium bowl combine stuffing mix, ⅓ cup of the jam, ¼ cup of the dried cranberries, and 3 tablespoons of the melted butter. Stir until moistened; set aside.

three For glaze, in a small bowl stir together the remaining jam, remaining dried cranberries, and remaining melted butter. Set aside. Place some of stuffing mixture on each chicken piece. Fold in sides and roll up. Secure with toothpicks. Place chicken rolls in a greased 3-quart rectangular baking dish.

four Bake, uncovered, in a 400°F oven for 15 minutes. Brush chicken with glaze. Bake, uncovered, for 10 to 15 minutes more or until chicken is tender and no longer pink.

NUTRITION FACTS PER SERVING: 393 cal., 11 g total fat (6 g sat. fat), 109 mg chol., 374 mg sodium, 35 g carbo., 2 g fiber, 37 g pro.

Skillet Chicken Alfredo

START TO FINISH: 20 minutes **MAKES:** 4 servings

1   10-ounce package frozen broccoli or asparagus spears

12 ounces skinless, boneless chicken breast halves or turkey breast tenderloin

1   tablespoon cooking oil

1   10-ounce container refrigerated Alfredo pasta sauce

4   English muffins or bagels, split and toasted

one Cook broccoli according to package directions; drain. Cover and keep warm. Meanwhile, cut chicken crosswise into ½-inch strips.

two In a large skillet cook chicken in hot oil over medium-high heat for 3 to 4 minutes or until tender and no longer pink (170°F). Drain off fat. Stir in pasta sauce. Cook for 2 to 3 minutes more or until sauce is heated through.

three Place toasted muffin or bagel halves on 4 dinner plates. Arrange broccoli spears on top. Spoon chicken and sauce over all.

NUTRITION FACTS PER SERVING: 497 cal., 28 g total fat (1 g sat. fat), 85 mg chol., 573 mg sodium, 33 g carbo., 4 g fiber, 30 g pro.

Chicken Kabobs with Thai Brushing Sauce

See photo on page 112.

PREP: 15 minutes **GRILL:** 10 minutes **MAKES:** 4 servings

1	small fresh pineapple (3 to 3½ pounds) (optional)
	Nonstick cooking spray (optional)
⅔	cup bottled sweet-and-sour sauce
2	tablespoons snipped fresh basil
1	teaspoon Thai seasoning or five-spice powder
1	clove garlic, minced
1	pound skinless, boneless chicken breast halves, cut into 1-inch pieces
	Fresh basil sprigs (optional)
	Fresh red chile peppers (optional)

one If using pineapple, cut off the ends. Halve pineapple lengthwise; cut each half crosswise into 4 slices. Lightly coat pineapple slices with cooking spray. Set aside.

two For sauce, in a small bowl combine sweet-and-sour sauce, the 2 tablespoons basil, the Thai seasoning, and garlic. Set sauce aside.

three Thread chicken pieces onto 4 long metal skewers, leaving ¼ inch between pieces.

four For a charcoal grill, grill chicken on the rack of an uncovered grill directly over medium coals for 10 to 12 minutes or until chicken is tender and no longer pink, turning once and brushing with ¼ cup of the sauce halfway through grilling.

five If using pineapple, add slices to grill rack after 5 minutes of grilling; turn once during grilling. (For a gas grill, preheat grill. Reduce heat to medium. Place kabobs, then pineapple, if using, on grill rack over heat. Cover and grill as above.)

six Reheat remaining sauce until bubbly; serve with chicken and pineapple. If desired, garnish with additional fresh basil and red chile peppers.

NUTRITION FACTS PER SERVING: 177 cal., 2 g total fat (0 g sat. fat), 66 mg chol., 396 mg sodium, 12 g carbo., 0 g fiber, 26 g pro.

Sweet Ginger Stir-Fry *See photo on page 111.*

START TO FINISH: 20 minutes **MAKES:** 4 servings

12	ounces skinless, boneless chicken breast halves or skinless, boneless chicken thighs
2	tablespoons cooking oil
2	cups desired frozen stir-fry vegetables
½	cup bottled sweet ginger or teriyaki stir-fry sauce
2	cups hot cooked rice

one Cut chicken into 1-inch pieces; set aside. In a wok or large skillet heat oil over medium-high heat. Add frozen vegetables. Cook and stir about 3 minutes or until vegetables are crisp-tender. Remove vegetables from wok.

two Add chicken to hot wok. (Add more oil if necessary.) Cook and stir for 3 to 4 minutes or until chicken is tender and no longer pink. Push chicken from center of the wok.

three Add sauce to center of the wok. Cook and stir until bubbly. Return cooked vegetables to wok; stir to coat ingredients with sauce. Cook and stir about 1 minute more or until heated through. Serve over hot cooked rice.

NUTRITION FACTS PER SERVING: 382 cal., 9 g total fat (1 g sat. fat), 49 mg chol., 879 mg sodium, 50 g carbo., 3 g fiber, 24 g pro.

SLOW COOKER

Greek Chicken with Couscous

PREP: 15 minutes **COOK:** Low 5 hours, High 2½ hours
STAND: 5 minutes **MAKES:** 8 servings

2	pounds skinless, boneless chicken breast halves
2	14½-ounce cans diced tomatoes with basil, garlic, and oregano, undrained
1½	cups water
2	5.6-ounce packages toasted pine nut-flavor couscous mix
1	cup crumbled feta cheese (4 ounces)
½	cup pitted kalamata olives, coarsely chopped

one Cut chicken into ½-inch pieces. Place chicken in a 3½- or 4-quart slow cooker. Pour undrained tomatoes and water over chicken.

two Cover and cook on low-heat setting for 5 to 6 hours or on high-heat setting for 2½ to 3 hours. Stir in couscous mixes. Cover and let stand for 5 minutes. Fluff couscous with a fork.

three To serve, spoon chicken mixture onto 8 dinner plates. Sprinkle with feta cheese and olives.

NUTRITION FACTS PER SERVING: 377 cal., 8 g total fat (4 g sat. fat), 82 mg chol., 1,226 mg sodium, 41 g carbo., 3 g fiber, 36 g pro.

Chicken and Bean Burritos

PREP: 20 minutes **COOK:** Low 5 hours, High 2½ hours
MAKES: 8 servings

- 2 pounds skinless, boneless chicken breast halves
- 1 15-ounce can chili beans in chili gravy, undrained
- 1 16-ounce bottle (1⅔ cups) salsa with chipotle peppers
- 8 10-inch flour tortillas, warmed (see tip, below)
- 1½ cups shredded Monterey Jack cheese (6 ounces)

  Shredded lettuce, chopped tomato, and/or dairy sour cream (optional)

one In a 3½-quart slow cooker place chicken and undrained beans. Pour salsa over chicken and beans.

two Cover and cook on low-heat setting for 5 to 6 hours or on high-heat setting for 2½ to 3 hours.

three Remove chicken from cooker. On a cutting board, use 2 forks to shred chicken into bite-size pieces. Using a potato masher, mash beans slightly in slow cooker. Return chicken to cooker, stirring to combine.

four Divide chicken mixture evenly among the warmed tortillas. Top with cheese. Fold up bottom edge of each tortilla over filling. Fold in opposite sides just until they meet. Roll up from the bottom. If necessary, secure with toothpicks. If desired, pass lettuce, tomato, and/or sour cream.

NUTRITION FACTS PER SERVING: 400 cal., 12 g total fat (5 g sat. fat), 84 mg chol., 662 mg sodium, 34 g carbo., 5 g fiber, 38 g pro.

Warming Tortillas When you want to warm flour tortillas, wrap the tortillas in foil and heat them in a 350°F oven for about 10 minutes. Or warm them in a microwave oven by stacking the tortillas between paper towels and heating them on 100 percent power (high). For two to four tortillas, allow 20 to 30 seconds; for six or more tortillas, allow 30 to 45 seconds.

Fast Chicken Fettuccine

START TO FINISH: 20 minutes **MAKES:** 4 servings

1	9-ounce package refrigerated red sweet pepper fettuccine
¼	of a 7-ounce jar (¼ cup) oil-packed dried tomato strips or pieces, undrained
1	large zucchini or yellow summer squash, halved lengthwise and sliced (about 2 cups)
8	ounces packaged chicken stir-fry strips
½	cup finely shredded Parmesan, Romano, or Asiago cheese (2 ounces)

one Cut pasta in half. Cook according to package directions; drain. Return pasta to hot pan.

two Meanwhile, drain tomato strips, reserving 2 tablespoons oil from jar; set aside. In a large skillet cook and stir zucchini in 1 tablespoon of the reserved oil over medium-high heat for 2 to 3 minutes or until crisp-tender. Remove from skillet.

three Add remaining 1 tablespoon reserved oil to skillet. Add chicken; cook and stir for 2 to 3 minutes or until tender and no longer pink. Add zucchini, chicken, tomato strips, and cheese to cooked pasta; toss gently to combine.

NUTRITION FACTS PER SERVING: 394 cal., 15 g total fat (5 g sat. fat), 113 mg chol., 231 mg sodium, 39 g carbo., 3 g fiber, 26 g pro.

Ranch-Style Chicken Strips

PREP: 15 minutes **BAKE:** 12 minutes **MAKES:** 4 servings

	Nonstick cooking spray
2	cups crushed cornflakes
2	tablespoons snipped fresh basil or 1 teaspoon dried basil, crushed
1	8-ounce bottle buttermilk ranch salad dressing
12	ounces skinless, boneless chicken breast halves, cut into thin strips

one Lightly coat a 15×10×1-inch baking pan with cooking spray; set aside. In a shallow dish combine the cornflakes and basil. In another dish place ½ cup of the dressing. Dip chicken strips into dressing; roll in crumb mixture to coat. Arrange strips in the prepared pan.

two Bake, uncovered, in a 425°F oven for 12 to 15 minutes or until chicken is tender and no longer pink. Serve chicken strips with the remaining dressing.

NUTRITION FACTS PER SERVING: 543 cal., 32 g total fat (5 g sat. fat), 54 mg chol., 928 mg sodium, 38 g carbo., 0 g fiber, 24 g pro.

Honey-Glazed Chicken Drumsticks

PREP: 10 minutes **BAKE:** 45 minutes **MAKES:** 4 servings

3   tablespoons honey
3   tablespoons Dijon-style mustard
1   teaspoon lemon juice
1   teaspoon finely shredded orange peel
8   chicken drumsticks

one For sauce, in a small bowl stir together honey, mustard, lemon juice, and orange peel. Set aside.

two Place drumsticks on a rack in a shallow roasting pan. Bake, uncovered, in a 375°F oven for 45 to 55 minutes or until chicken is tender and no longer pink (180°F), brushing with sauce during the last half of baking.

NUTRITION FACTS PER SERVING: 241 cal., 9 g total fat (2 g sat. fat), 87 mg chol., 370 mg sodium, 14 g carbo., 0 g fiber, 26 g pro.

GRILLING

Chipotle-Peach-Glazed Chicken Thighs

PREP: 20 minutes **GRILL:** 50 minutes **MAKES:** 4 servings

8   chicken thighs
½   teaspoon salt
¼   teaspoon black pepper
¼   teaspoon ground nutmeg
⅓   cup peach preserves
2   tablespoons white wine vinegar
2   to 3 teaspoons chopped canned chipotle peppers in adobo sauce

one Skin chicken. For rub, in a small bowl combine salt, black pepper, and ⅛ teaspoon of the nutmeg. Sprinkle rub evenly over chicken thighs; rub in with your fingers.

two For glaze, in a small saucepan combine the remaining ⅛ teaspoon nutmeg, the preserves, vinegar, and chipotle peppers. Cook and stir just until preserves melt. Set aside.

three For a charcoal grill, arrange medium-hot coals around a drip pan. Test for medium heat above pan. Place chicken, bone sides up, on grill rack over drip pan. Cover and grill for 50 to 60 minutes or until chicken is tender and no longer pink (180°F), brushing with glaze during the last 10 minutes of grilling. (For a gas grill, preheat grill. Reduce heat to medium. Adjust for indirect cooking. Grill as above.)

NUTRITION FACTS PER SERVING: 462 cal., 27 g total fat (8 g sat. fat), 157 mg chol., 426 mg sodium, 18 g carbo., 0 g fiber, 33 g pro.

Cranberry Chicken *See photo on page 113.*

PREP: 15 minutes **COOK:** Low 5 hours, High 2½ hours
MAKES: 6 servings

2½   to 3 pounds chicken thighs and/or drumsticks
1   16-ounce can whole cranberry sauce
2   tablespoons onion soup mix
2   tablespoons quick-cooking tapioca
3   cups hot cooked rice

one Skin chicken. Place chicken in a 3½- or 4-quart slow cooker. In a small bowl combine cranberry sauce, dry soup mix, and tapioca. Pour over chicken.

two Cover and cook on low-heat setting for 5 to 6 hours or on high-heat setting for 2½ to 3 hours. Serve chicken and sauce over hot cooked rice.

NUTRITION FACTS PER SERVING: 357 cal., 4 g total fat (1 g sat. fat), 89 mg chol., 268 mg sodium, 55 g carbo., 1 g fiber, 23 g pro.

Asian Chicken and Vegetables

PREP: 10 minutes **BAKE:** 40 minutes **MAKES:** 4 servings

8   chicken drumsticks and/or thighs
1   tablespoon cooking oil
1½   teaspoons five-spice powder
⅓   cup bottled plum sauce or sweet-and-sour sauce
1   14-ounce package frozen baby potatoes, broccoli, carrots, baby corn, and red peppers or one 16-ounce package frozen desired stir-fry vegetables

one Skin chicken. Arrange chicken pieces in a 13×9×2-inch baking pan. Brush chicken with oil; sprinkle with 1 teaspoon of the five-spice powder. Bake, uncovered, in a 400°F oven for 25 minutes.

two Meanwhile, in a large bowl combine the remaining ½ teaspoon five-spice powder and the plum sauce. Add frozen vegetables; toss to coat. Push chicken to one side of baking pan. Add vegetable mixture to other side of pan.

three Bake, uncovered, for 15 to 20 minutes more or until chicken is tender and no longer pink (180°F), stirring vegetables once during baking. Using a slotted spoon, transfer chicken and vegetables to a serving platter.

NUTRITION FACTS PER SERVING: 277 cal., 9 g total fat (2 g sat. fat), 98 mg chol., 124 mg sodium, 21 g carbo., 2 g fiber, 30 g pro.

French-Onion Baked Chicken

PREP: 20 minutes **BAKE:** 35 minutes **MAKES:** 4 servings

- 2 pounds chicken thighs or drumsticks
- ⅓ cup bottled creamy ranch salad dressing or French salad dressing
- ¼ teaspoon bottled hot pepper sauce
- 1 2.8-ounce can French-fried onions, crumbled
- ½ cup crushed cornflakes

one Skin chicken; set aside. In a shallow bowl stir together salad dressing and hot pepper sauce. In another bowl combine French-fried onions and cornflakes.

two Place chicken pieces, meaty sides up, on a rack in a 3-quart rectangular baking dish. Brush chicken with salad dressing mixture. Sprinkle with onion mixture, pressing mixture onto chicken.

three Bake, uncovered, in a 425°F oven for 35 to 40 minutes or until chicken is tender and no longer pink (180°F). If necessary, cover loosely with foil during the last 10 minutes to prevent overbrowning.

NUTRITION FACTS PER SERVING: 408 cal., 24 g total fat (3 g sat. fat), 108 mg chol., 558 mg sodium, 18 g carbo., 0 g fiber, 28 g pro.

SLOW COOKER

Honey-Mustard Chicken with Sweet Potatoes

PREP: 20 minutes **COOK:** Low 7 hours, High 3½ hours
MAKES: 6 servings

- 2 to 2½ pounds chicken thighs and/or drumsticks
- 6 medium sweet potatoes (about 2½ pounds), peeled and quartered
- 1 small onion, cut into thin wedges
- ¾ cup bottled honey-mustard salad dressing
- ½ teaspoon dried rosemary, crushed

one Skin chicken; set aside. In a 4½- to 6-quart slow cooker place sweet potatoes and onion wedges. Place chicken on top of vegetables.

two In a small bowl stir together salad dressing and rosemary. Pour over chicken.

three Cover and cook on low-heat setting for 7 to 9 hours or on high-heat setting for 3½ to 4½ hours.

four Using a slotted spoon, transfer chicken and vegetables to a serving platter. Whisk cooking liquid until smooth; pass cooking liquid with chicken and vegetables.

NUTRITION FACTS PER SERVING: 378 cal., 16 g total fat (2 g sat. fat), 71 mg chol., 186 mg sodium, 40 g carbo., 4 g fiber, 19 g pro.

SLOW COOKER

Finger Lickin' Barbecue Chicken

PREP: 10 minutes **COOK:** Low 6 hours, High 3 hours
MAKES: 4 to 6 servings

2½ to 3 pounds chicken drumsticks
1 cup bottled barbecue sauce
⅓ cup apricot or peach preserves
2 teaspoons yellow mustard

one If desired, skin chicken. Place chicken in a 3½- or 4-quart slow cooker. In a small bowl stir together the barbecue sauce, preserves, and mustard. Pour over chicken.

two Cover and cook on low-heat setting for 6 to 8 hours or on high-heat setting for 3 to 4 hours. Transfer chicken to a serving dish; cover and keep warm.

three If desired, transfer sauce from cooker to a medium saucepan. Bring to boiling; reduce heat. Simmer, uncovered, about 10 minutes or until desired consistency. Pass sauce with chicken.

NUTRITION FACTS PER SERVING: 456 cal., 17 g total fat (4 g sat. fat), 154 mg chol., 963 mg sodium, 37 g carbo., 2 g fiber, 38 g pro.

SLOW COOKER

Cherried Chicken

PREP: 20 minutes **COOK:** Low 5 hours, High 2½ hours
MAKES: 4 servings

2½ to 3 pounds chicken drumsticks, skinned
1 teaspoon herb-pepper seasoning
1 15- to 17-ounce can pitted dark sweet cherries, drained
1 12-ounce bottle chili sauce
½ cup packed brown sugar

one Skin chicken. Sprinkle chicken evenly with herb-pepper seasoning. Place chicken in a 3½- or 4-quart slow cooker. In a medium bowl combine cherries, chili sauce, and brown sugar. Pour mixture over chicken.

two Cover and cook on low-heat setting for 5 to 6 hours or on high-heat setting for 2½ to 3 hours.

three Transfer chicken to a serving platter. Skim fat from sauce. Spoon some of the sauce over chicken; pass the remaining sauce.

NUTRITION FACTS PER SERVING: 410 cal., 5 g total fat (1 g sat. fat), 105 mg chol., 1,539 mg sodium, 63 g carbo., 7 g fiber, 31 g pro.

Southwest Chicken Burgers

PREP: 20 minutes **GRILL:** 15 minutes **MAKES:** 4 servings

3   tablespoons finely chopped green sweet pepper

¾   teaspoon chili powder

¼   teaspoon salt

¼   teaspoon black pepper

1   pound uncooked ground chicken

1   cup shredded Monterey Jack cheese with jalapeño
     peppers (4 ounces)

4   kaiser rolls, split and toasted

1   medium avocado, seeded, peeled, and sliced (optional)

     Bottled salsa (optional)

Burger Doneness Don't rely on the meat's color to gauge whether a burger is completely cooked. A chicken or turkey patty cooked to 165°F and a beef, veal, lamb, or pork patty cooked to 160°F is safe, regardless of color. To determine whether a burger is done, insert an instant-read thermometer through the side of the patty to a depth of 2 to 3 inches.

one In a large bowl combine sweet pepper, chili powder, salt, and black pepper. Add ground chicken; mix well. Shape chicken mixture into four ¾-inch-thick patties.

two For a charcoal grill, grill burgers on the rack of an uncovered grill directly over medium coals for 14 to 18 minutes or until no longer pink (165°F), turning once halfway through grilling.

three Sprinkle each burger with cheese. Grill for 1 to 2 minutes more or until cheese melts. (For a gas grill, preheat grill. Reduce heat to medium. Place burgers on grill rack over heat. Cover and grill as above.)

four Serve burgers on kaiser rolls. If desired, top with avocado and salsa.

NUTRITION FACTS PER SERVING: 497 cal., 26 g total fat (6 g sat. fat), 25 mg chol., 683 mg sodium, 31 g carbo., 2 g fiber, 32 g pro.

Coconut-Chicken Pasta

START TO FINISH: 20 minutes **MAKES:** 4 servings

8   ounces dried angel hair pasta

3   cups frozen cooked chicken breast strips, thawed

1   14-ounce can unsweetened coconut milk

1   teaspoon Thai seasoning

¼   cup roasted peanuts

one Cook pasta according to package directions; drain. Return pasta to hot pan; cover and keep warm.

two Meanwhile, in a large skillet combine chicken strips, coconut milk, and Thai seasoning. Cook and stir over medium heat until mixture is heated through.

three Pour hot chicken mixture over cooked pasta; toss gently to coat. Transfer to a serving platter or bowl. Sprinkle with peanuts.

NUTRITION FACTS PER SERVING: 644 cal., 31 g total fat (19 g sat. fat), 93 mg chol., 236 mg sodium, 47 g carbo., 2 g fiber, 42 g pro.

Quick Chicken Tortilla Bake

PREP: 15 minutes **BAKE:** 45 minutes **MAKES:** 8 servings

2   10¾-ounce cans reduced-fat and reduced-sodium condensed cream of chicken soup

1   10-ounce can diced tomatoes and green chiles, undrained

12   6-inch corn tortillas, cut into thin bite-size strips

3   cups cubed cooked chicken

1   cup shredded Mexican cheese blend (4 ounces)

one In a medium bowl combine soup and undrained tomatoes. Set aside.

two Sprinkle one-third of the tortilla strips onto the bottom of an ungreased 3-quart rectangular baking dish. Layer half of the chicken over tortilla strips; spoon half of the soup mixture on top. Repeat layers. Top with the remaining tortilla strips.

three Bake, covered, in a 350°F oven about 40 minutes or until edges are bubbly and center is hot. Sprinkle with cheese. Bake, uncovered, about 5 minutes more or until cheese melts.

NUTRITION FACTS PER SERVING: 291 cal., 10 g total fat (4 g sat. fat), 64 mg chol., 658 mg sodium, 28 g carbo., 2 g fiber, 22 g pro.

Sweet Chicken Tostadas

START TO FINISH: 20 minutes **MAKES:** 4 servings

- 8 tostada shells
- ½ cup dairy sour cream
- 1 cup bottled fruit salsa
- 1½ cups chopped cooked chicken
- 1 cup shredded Monterey Jack cheese with jalapeño peppers (4 ounces)

one Spread one side of each tostada shell with sour cream, spreading to edges. Spread salsa evenly on top of sour cream. Top the tostadas with chicken and cheese.

two Place 4 of the tostadas on a large baking sheet. Place on a broiler rack 4 to 5 inches from the heat. Broil for 1 to 1½ minutes or until cheese melts. Repeat with the remaining tostadas. Serve warm.

NUTRITION FACTS PER SERVING: 511 cal., 26 g total fat (12 g sat. fat), 89 mg chol., 488 mg sodium, 42 g carbo., 4 g fiber, 27 g pro.

SLOW COOKER

Homestyle Chicken and Stuffing

PREP: 15 minutes **COOK:** Low 5 hours, High 2½ hours
MAKES: 6 servings

- 1 10¾-ounce can reduced-fat and reduced-sodium condensed cream of chicken soup or cream of mushroom soup
- ¼ cup butter or margarine, melted
- ¼ cup water
- 1 16-ounce package frozen broccoli, corn, and red peppers
- 2½ cups cubed cooked chicken
- 1 8-ounce package corn bread stuffing mix

one In a very large bowl stir together soup, melted butter, and water. Add frozen vegetables, chicken, and corn bread stuffing mix; stir until combined. Transfer mixture to a 3½- or 4-quart slow cooker.

two Cover and cook on low-heat setting for 5 to 6 hours or on high-heat setting for 2½ to 3 hours.

NUTRITION FACTS PER SERVING: 393 cal., 14 g total fat (6 g sat. fat), 76 mg chol., 1,041 mg sodium, 40 g carbo., 3 g fiber, 24 g pro.

Chicken Alfredo Potpies

PREP: 20 minutes **BAKE:** 12 minutes **MAKES:** 4 servings

- ½ of a 15-ounce package (1 crust) rolled refrigerated unbaked piecrust
- 3 cups frozen mixed vegetables
- 3 cups cubed cooked chicken
- 1 10-ounce container refrigerated Alfredo pasta sauce
- ½ teaspoon dried sage, marjoram, or thyme, crushed

one Let piecrust stand according to package directions. In a large skillet cook vegetables in a small amount of boiling water for 5 minutes; drain. Return to skillet. Stir in chicken, pasta sauce, and sage. Cook and stir until bubbly. Divide mixture among four 10-ounce casseroles or custard cups.

two On a lightly floured surface, roll piecrust into a 13-inch circle. Cut four 5-inch circles and place on top of the casseroles. Press edges of pastry firmly against sides of casseroles. Cut slits in the tops for steam to escape.

three Place casseroles in a foil-lined shallow baking pan. Bake, uncovered, in a 450°F oven for 12 to 15 minutes or until pastry is golden brown.

NUTRITION FACTS PER SERVING: 709 cal., 41 g total fat (19 g sat. fat), 143 mg chol., 596 mg sodium, 45 g carbo., 4 g fiber, 38 g pro.

Chicken Taco Salad

PREP: 10 minutes **COOK:** 10 minutes **MAKES:** 4 servings

- 1 9-ounce package frozen cooked Southwestern-style chicken breast strips
- 1 15-ounce can pinto beans, rinsed and drained
- 1 cup frozen whole kernel corn
- ¾ cup bottled salsa

  Crushed tortilla chips

one In a medium saucepan stir together chicken, pinto beans, frozen corn, and salsa.

two Bring to boiling; reduce heat. Simmer, covered, about 10 minutes or until heated through, stirring occasionally. Serve on top of tortilla chips.

NUTRITION FACTS PER SERVING: 320 cal., 9 g total fat (2 g sat. fat), 30 mg chol., 1,066 mg sodium, 42 g carbo., 8 g fiber, 23 g pro.

Mandarin Chicken Salad *See photo on page 113.*

START TO FINISH: 15 minutes MAKES: 4 servings

1 10-ounce package torn mixed salad greens

8 ounces cooked chicken, cut into bite-size pieces

⅓ cup bottled oriental salad dressing

1 11- or 15-ounce can mandarin orange sections, drained

3 tablespoons sliced almonds, toasted (see tip, page 280)

one In a large bowl combine salad greens and chicken. Add salad dressing; toss gently to coat.

two Divide greens mixture among 4 dinner plates. Top with mandarin orange sections and almonds.

NUTRITION FACTS PER SERVING: 218 cal., 9 g total fat (1 g sat. fat), 50 mg chol., 502 mg sodium, 15 g carbo., 2 g fiber, 19 g pro.

SLOW COOKER

Smoky Chicken and Cheesy Potato Casserole

PREP: 20 minutes COOK: Low 5 hours MAKES: 6 servings

Nonstick cooking spray

1 28-ounce package frozen diced hash brown potatoes with onions and peppers, thawed

3 cups chopped smoked or roasted chicken or turkey

1½ cups shredded smoked cheddar cheese (6 ounces)

1 10¾-ounce can condensed cream of chicken with herbs soup

1 8-ounce carton dairy sour cream

Crushed croutons (optional)

one Lightly coat a 3½- or 4-quart slow cooker with cooking spray. In the prepared cooker combine hash brown potatoes, chicken, cheese, soup, and sour cream.

two Cover and cook on low-heat setting for 5 to 6 hours. If desired, top each serving with crushed croutons.

NUTRITION FACTS PER SERVING: 399 cal., 20 g total fat (12 g sat. fat), 80 mg chol., 1,313 mg sodium, 31 g carbo., 3 g fiber, 25 g pro.

Quick Chicken Fajitas *See photo on page 113.*

START TO FINISH: 20 minutes **MAKES:** 4 servings

- ¼ cup bottled clear Italian salad dressing (not reduced-fat dressing)
- 2 medium red and/or green sweet peppers, cut into strips
- 1 medium onion, halved lengthwise and sliced
- 2 6-ounce packages refrigerated cooked plain or Southwestern-style chicken breast strips
- 8 7- to 8-inch flour tortillas, warmed (see tip, page 16)

  Purchased guacamole, bottled salsa, and/or dairy sour cream (optional)

one In a large skillet heat 2 tablespoons of the salad dressing over medium-high heat. Add sweet peppers and onion to skillet; cook and stir for 2 to 3 minutes or until vegetables are crisp-tender. Add chicken strips and the remaining 2 tablespoons salad dressing; cook and stir for 2 to 3 minutes or until heated through.

two Spoon mixture onto warmed tortillas; roll up tortillas. If desired, top with guacamole, salsa, and/or sour cream.

NUTRITION FACTS PER SERVING: 399 cal., 15 g total fat (2 g sat. fat), 55 mg chol., 1,048 mg sodium, 34 g carbo., 2 g fiber, 26 g pro.

Mushroom-Tomato-Pesto Pizza

PREP: 15 minutes **BAKE:** 10 minutes **MAKES:** 4 servings

- 1 12-inch Italian bread shell (such as Boboli brand)
- ½ cup purchased dried tomato pesto
- 1 cup shredded pizza cheese blend (4 ounces)
- 1 6-ounce package refrigerated cooked Italian-style chicken breast strips
- 1½ cups sliced fresh mushrooms

one Place bread shell in a 12-inch pizza pan. Spread pesto over bread shell. Sprinkle with half of the cheese. Top with the chicken pieces and mushrooms. Sprinkle with the remaining cheese.

two Bake, uncovered, in a 400°F oven for 10 to 15 minutes or until cheese is golden and bubbly.

NUTRITION FACTS PER SERVING: 585 cal., 24 g total fat (8 g sat. fat), 55 mg chol., 1,382 mg sodium, 64 g carbo., 4 g fiber, 33 g pro.

Turkey on the Grill

PREP: 20 minutes **GRILL:** 2½ hours **STAND:** 15 minutes
MAKES: 8 to 10 servings

- 1   8- to 10-pound whole turkey
- 2   teaspoons dried Italian seasoning, basil, or oregano, crushed
- 1   teaspoon poultry seasoning
- ½   teaspoon salt
- ½   teaspoon black pepper
- 1   tablespoon cooking oil

one Thaw turkey, if frozen. Remove neck and giblets from turkey. Rinse inside of turkey; pat dry with paper towels. In a small bowl combine Italian seasoning, poultry seasoning, salt, and pepper; set aside.

two Starting at the neck on one side of the breast, slip your fingers between skin and meat, loosening the skin as you work toward the tail end. Once your entire hand is under the skin, free the skin around the top of the thigh and leg area up to, but not around, the tip of the drumstick. Repeat on the other side of the breast.

three Rub seasonings under the skin directly on meat. Skewer neck skin to back. Tuck drumsticks under band of skin or tie to tail. Twist wing tips under back. If desired, insert a meat thermometer into the center of an inside thigh muscle without touching bone. Brush turkey with oil.

four For a charcoal grill, arrange medium-hot coals around a drip pan. Test for medium heat above the pan. Place turkey, breast side up, on grill rack over drip pan. Cover and grill for 2½ to 3 hours or until drumsticks move easily in their sockets and juices run clear (180°F), adding fresh coals every 45 to 60 minutes and cutting band of skin or string during the last 1 hour of grilling. (For a gas grill, preheat grill. Reduce heat to medium. Adjust for indirect cooking. Grill as above.)

five Remove turkey from grill. Cover with foil and let stand for 15 minutes before carving.

NUTRITION FACTS PER SERVING: 723 cal., 36 g total fat (10 g sat. fat), 306 mg chol., 367 mg sodium, 0 g carbo., 0 g fiber, 93 g pro.

Turkey with Dried Tomato Pesto *See photo on page 114.*

PREP: 15 minutes **GRILL:** 1¼ hours **STAND:** 10 minutes
MAKES: 8 servings

⅓   cup purchased basil pesto

3   tablespoons oil-packed dried tomatoes, drained and chopped

1   2- to 2½-pound turkey breast half with bone
    Salt and black pepper

12 ounces dried fettuccine, cooked and drained
    Fresh basil sprigs (optional)

one In a small bowl combine pesto and dried tomatoes; set aside. Starting at the breast bone, slip your fingers between the skin and turkey meat to loosen skin, leaving skin attached at one side to make a pocket.

two Spoon half of the pesto mixture under the skin and spread over breast meat. Fold skin back over meat, covering as much as possible. Sprinkle turkey breast with salt and pepper. If desired, insert a meat thermometer into the thickest part of the turkey breast without touching bone.

three For a charcoal grill, arrange medium-hot coals around a drip pan. Test for medium heat above the pan. Place turkey breast, bone side down, on grill rack over drip pan. Cover and grill for 1¼ to 2 hours or until juices run clear (170°F). (For a gas grill, preheat grill. Reduce heat to medium. Adjust for indirect cooking. Grill as above.)

four Remove turkey from grill. Cover with foil and let stand for 10 minutes before carving.

five Meanwhile, toss the remaining pesto mixture with the hot cooked fettuccine. Slice turkey; serve with fettuccine. If desired, garnish with fresh basil.

NUTRITION FACTS PER SERVING: 328 cal., 9 g total fat (1 g sat. fat), 50 mg chol., 196 mg sodium, 34 g carbo., 1 g fiber, 26 g pro.

A Spoonful of Pesto Pesto is the perfect condiment for adding flavor in a hurry. Try these simple ideas to finish off that partial container:

- Spread a spoonful on top of grilled meat, fish, or poultry.
- Slather some on the toasted bun of a grilled or broiled hamburger or chicken sandwich.
- Mix a bit into a ranch-style dressing for a green salad.
- Toss some with your favorite cooked vegetable.
- Swirl a little into a serving of hot soup.

Turkey Breast with Raspberry Salsa

PREP: 10 minutes **GRILL:** 1¼ hours **STAND:** 10 minutes
MAKES: 8 servings

⅓ cup seedless raspberry jam

1 tablespoon Dijon-style mustard

1 teaspoon finely shredded orange peel

½ cup bottled mild salsa

1 2- to 2½-pound turkey breast half with bone

one In a small bowl combine raspberry jam, mustard, and orange peel. Stir 3 tablespoons of the jam mixture into the salsa. Cover and chill both mixtures.

two If desired, insert a meat thermometer into the thickest part of the turkey breast without touching bone.

three For a charcoal grill, arrange medium-hot coals around a drip pan. Test for medium heat above pan. Place turkey breast, bone side down, on grill rack over drip pan. Cover and grill for 1¼ to 2 hours or until juices run clear (170°F), brushing occasionally with jam mixture during the last 15 minutes of grilling. (For a gas grill, preheat grill. Reduce heat to medium. Adjust for indirect cooking. Grill as above.)

four Remove turkey from grill. Cover with foil and let stand 10 minutes before carving. Serve turkey with salsa mixture.

NUTRITION FACTS PER SERVING: 143 cal., 1 g total fat (0 g sat. fat), 55 mg chol., 192 mg sodium, 11 g carbo., 0 g fiber, 22 g pro.

Nutty Turkey Tenderloins

PREP: 15 minutes **BAKE:** 18 minutes **MAKES:** 4 servings

2 turkey breast tenderloins (about 1 pound), halved horizontally

¼ cup creamy Dijon-style mustard blend

1 cup corn bread stuffing mix

½ cup finely chopped pecans

2 tablespoons butter or margarine, melted

one Brush turkey generously with the mustard blend. In a shallow dish combine the stuffing mix and pecans; dip turkey into stuffing mixture to coat both sides. Place in a shallow baking pan. Drizzle with melted butter.

two Bake, uncovered, in a 375°F oven for 18 to 20 minutes or until turkey is tender and no longer pink (170°).

NUTRITION FACTS PER SERVING: 395 cal., 21 g total fat (5 g sat. fat), 84 mg chol., 566 mg sodium, 21 g carbo., 1 g fiber, 30 g pro.

Turkey Tenderloin with Black Bean and Corn Salsa

START TO FINISH: 25 minutes **MAKES:** 4 servings

  2 turkey breast tenderloins (about 1 pound), halved horizontally

     Salt and black pepper

  ¼ cup red jalapeño jelly

1¼ cups bottled black bean and corn salsa

  2 tablespoons snipped fresh cilantro

one Place turkey on the unheated rack of a broiler pan. Sprinkle with salt and pepper. Broil 4 to 5 inches from heat for 5 minutes.

two Meanwhile, in a small saucepan melt jelly. Remove 2 tablespoons of the jelly. Turn turkey and brush with the 2 tablespoons jelly. Broil for 4 to 6 minutes more or until turkey is tender and no longer pink (170°F).

three Transfer turkey to a serving plate. Spoon remaining jelly over turkey; cover and keep warm. In a small saucepan heat salsa; spoon over turkey. Sprinkle with cilantro.

NUTRITION FACTS PER SERVING: 196 cal., 2 g total fat (1 g sat. fat), 66 mg chol., 377 mg sodium, 16 g carbo., 1 g fiber, 27 g pro.

SLOW COOKER

Turkey and Pasta Primavera

PREP: 15 minutes **COOK:** Low 4 hours, High 2 hours
MAKES: 8 servings

  2 pounds turkey breast tenderloins or skinless, boneless chicken breast halves

  1 16-ounce package frozen sugar snap stir-fry vegetables (carrots, sugar snap peas, onions, and mushrooms)

  2 teaspoons dried basil, oregano, or Italian seasoning, crushed

  1 16-ounce jar Alfredo pasta sauce

 12 ounces dried spaghetti or linguine, broken

     Shredded Parmesan cheese (optional)

one Cut turkey into 1-inch pieces. In a 4½- to 6-quart slow cooker combine turkey and frozen vegetables. Sprinkle with basil. Stir in Alfredo sauce.

two Cover and cook on low-heat setting for 4 to 5 hours or on high-heat setting for 2 to 2½ hours.

three Cook pasta according to package directions; drain. Stir pasta into mixture in slow cooker. To serve, spoon pasta mixture into shallow bowls. If desired, sprinkle with Parmesan cheese.

NUTRITION FACTS PER SERVING: 407 cal., 11 g total fat (5 g sat. fat), 103 mg chol., 447 mg sodium, 39 g carbo., 2 g fiber, 36 g pro.

Turkey Nuggets and Sweet Potatoes

PREP: 15 minutes **ROAST:** 20 minutes **MAKES:** 4 servings

- 3 tablespoons olive oil
- 2 teaspoons snipped fresh rosemary
- 2 medium sweet potatoes, peeled and cut into bite-size pieces (3 cups)
- 12 ounces turkey breast tenderloin, cut into bite-size pieces
- ⅓ cup finely crushed stone-ground wheat crackers (8 to 10 crackers)

one In a medium bowl combine oil and rosemary. Add sweet potatoes; toss to coat. Using a slotted spoon, transfer sweet potatoes to a 15×10×1-inch baking pan.

two Add turkey to the remaining oil mixture in bowl; toss to coat. Add crushed crackers to turkey; toss to coat. Add to potatoes in pan. Arrange in a single layer.

three Roast, uncovered, in a 400°F oven about 20 minutes or until turkey and sweet potatoes are tender and turkey is no longer pink.

NUTRITION FACTS PER SERVING: 327 cal., 13 g total fat (2 g sat. fat), 51 mg chol., 102 mg sodium, 30 g carbo., 4 g fiber, 22 g pro.

GRILLING

Barbecued Turkey
Tenderloin Sandwiches *See photo on page 114.*

PREP: 20 minutes **GRILL:** 16 minutes **MAKES:** 4 servings

- ½ cup bottled hickory-flavor barbecue sauce
- 1 tablespoon tahini (sesame seed paste)
- 1 small fresh jalapeño chile pepper, seeded and finely chopped (see tip, page 59)
- 2 turkey breast tenderloins (about 1 pound)
- 4 French-style rolls, split and toasted
   Fresh spinach (optional)
   Bottled green salsa (optional)

one In a small bowl combine barbecue sauce, tahini, and jalapeño pepper. Set aside half of the sauce to use for basting. Reserve remaining sauce until ready to serve.

two Brush both sides of each turkey tenderloin with basting sauce. For a charcoal grill, grill turkey on the greased rack of an uncovered grill directly over medium coals for 16 to 20 minutes or until turkey is tender and no longer pink (170°F), turning once halfway through grilling. (For a gas grill, preheat grill. Reduce heat to medium. Place turkey on greased grill rack over heat. Cover and grill as above.)

three Thinly slice turkey. Serve on rolls with reserved sauce and, if desired, spinach and salsa.

NUTRITION FACTS PER SERVING: 512 cal., 9 g total fat (2 g sat. fat), 68 mg chol., 1,039 mg sodium, 69 g carbo., 5 g fiber, 37 g pro.

Sesame-Ginger Turkey Wraps *See photo on page 115.*

PREP: 20 minutes **COOK:** Low 6 hours, High 3 hours
STAND: 5 minutes **MAKES:** 12 servings

    Nonstick cooking spray

3½ to 4 pounds turkey thighs (about 3 thighs)

1 cup bottled sesame-ginger stir-fry sauce

¼ cup water

1 16-ounce package shredded broccoli
    (broccoli slaw mix)

12 8-inch flour tortillas, warmed (see tip, page 16)

¾ cup sliced green onion

one Lightly coat a 3½- or 4-quart slow cooker with cooking spray. Skin turkey thighs. Place turkey in prepared cooker. In a small bowl combine stir-fry sauce and water. Pour over turkey.

two Cover and cook on low-heat setting for 6 to 7 hours or on high-heat setting for 3 to 3½ hours.

three Remove turkey from cooker; cool slightly. Remove turkey from bones; discard bones. Using 2 forks, shred turkey into bite-size pieces. Return to mixture in cooker. Add broccoli slaw mix; stir to coat. Cover and let stand for 5 minutes. Using a slotted spoon, remove turkey and broccoli from cooker.

four Divide turkey mixture among warmed tortillas. Top with green onion. If desired, spoon some of the sauce from cooker on top of green onion. Roll up and serve immediately.

NUTRITION FACTS PER SERVING: 207 cal., 5 g total fat (1 g sat. fat), 67 mg chol., 422 mg sodium, 20 g carbo., 2 g fiber, 20 g pro.

Plan Ahead Because you'll want to start many slow-cooker recipes early in the day, you can eliminate some breakfast-time hassles by preparing ingredients the night before. Here are some dos and don'ts:

- Chop vegetables and refrigerate them in separate containers. (You can keep cut-up potatoes from turning brown by covering them with water.) Or if your cooker has a removable liner, place the vegetables in the liner, cover it, and keep it in the refrigerator until the next morning.
- Assemble, cover, and chill liquid ingredients or sauces separately from the solids.
- If you'd like to brown ground meat or poultry and bulk sausage the night before, be sure to cook it completely. Then store it tightly covered in the refrigerator. Don't brown roasts, cubed meat, or poultry pieces ahead because browning doesn't cook the meat or poultry completely through.

Maple- and Mustard-Sauced
Turkey Thighs

PREP: 20 minutes **COOK:** Low 6 hours, High 3 hours
MAKES: 4 servings

1   pound tiny new potatoes, quartered
2   to 2½ pounds turkey thighs (about 2 thighs)
⅓   cup coarse-grain brown mustard
¼   cup maple syrup
1   tablespoon quick-cooking tapioca

one Place potatoes in a 3½- or 4-quart slow cooker. Skin turkey thighs. Place turkey on top of potatoes. In a small bowl stir together mustard, maple syrup, and tapioca. Pour over turkey.

two Cover and cook on low-heat setting for 6 to 7 hours or on high-heat setting for 3 to 3½ hours.

NUTRITION FACTS PER SERVING: 377 cal., 10 g total fat (3 g sat. fat), 93 mg chol., 369 mg sodium, 36 g carbo., 2 g fiber, 36 g pro.

Easy Turkey-Pesto Potpies

PREP: 15 minutes **BAKE:** 15 minutes **MAKES:** 6 servings

1   18-ounce jar turkey gravy
¼   cup purchased basil or dried tomato pesto
3   cups cubed cooked turkey
1   16-ounce package frozen peas and carrots
½   of an 11-ounce package (6) refrigerated
      breadsticks

one In a large saucepan combine gravy and pesto; stir in turkey and vegetables. Bring to boiling, stirring frequently. Divide mixture evenly among six 8-ounce au gratin dishes.

two Unroll and separate breadsticks. Arrange a breadstick on top of each dish; reserve the remaining breadsticks for another use.

three Bake, uncovered, in a 375°F oven about 15 minutes or until breadsticks are golden brown.

NUTRITION FACTS PER SERVING: 372 cal., 14 g total fat (2 g sat. fat), 59 mg chol., 988 mg sodium, 30 g carbo., 3 g fiber, 30 g pro.

Polenta with Turkey Sausage Florentine

START TO FINISH: 25 minutes **MAKES:** 2 servings

1   9- or 10-ounce package frozen
     creamed spinach

8   ounces uncooked bulk turkey sausage

½   of a 16-ounce tube refrigerated cooked polenta with
     wild mushrooms, cut into ¾-inch slices

1   tablespoon olive oil

2   tablespoons sliced almonds or pine nuts,
     toasted (see tip, page 280)

one Cook spinach according to package directions. Meanwhile, in a medium skillet cook sausage until brown. Drain sausage in a colander.

two In the same skillet cook polenta slices in hot oil about 6 minutes or until golden brown, turning once. Transfer polenta to 2 dinner plates.

three Stir cooked sausage into hot creamed spinach; heat through. Spoon over polenta. Sprinkle with nuts.

NUTRITION FACTS PER SERVING: 607 cal., 41 g total fat (8 g sat. fat), 119 mg chol., 1,586 mg sodium, 33 g carbo., 6 g fiber, 28 g pro.

SLOW COOKER

Country-Style Smoked Sausage and Sauerkraut

PREP: 15 minutes **COOK:** Low 6 hours, High 3 hours
MAKES: 4 servings

10   to 12 tiny new potatoes (about 1 pound), quartered

1   medium onion, cut into thin wedges

1   pound smoked turkey sausage, cut into 1-inch pieces

1   14- to 15-ounce can Bavarian-style sauerkraut
     (with caraway seeds),* undrained

⅓   cup water

1   tablespoon Dijon-style mustard

one In a 3½- or 4-quart slow cooker place potatoes and onion wedges. Top with sausage and undrained sauerkraut. In a small bowl whisk together water and mustard; pour over sauerkraut.

two Cover and cook on low-heat setting for 6 to 8 hours or on high-heat setting for 3 to 4 hours.

*Note: *If Bavarian-style sauerkraut is not available, substitute one 14½-ounce can sauerkraut, undrained, plus 2 tablespoons packed brown sugar and ½ teaspoon caraway seeds.*

NUTRITION FACTS PER SERVING: 317 cal., 10 g total fat (2 g sat. fat), 76 mg chol., 3,472 mg sodium, 37 g carbo., 2 g fiber, 21 g pro.

Barbecue Beans and Hot Dogs over Corn Bread

PREP: 10 minutes **COOK:** Low 5 hours, High 2½ hours
MAKES: 6 servings

2   15-ounce cans pork and beans in tomato sauce, undrained

2   15-ounce cans black beans and/or pinto beans, rinsed and drained

⅔   cup bottled barbecue sauce

16 ounces cooked turkey hot dogs, cut crosswise into fourths

Purchased corn bread

one In a 3½- or 4-quart slow cooker combine undrained pork and beans, black beans and/or pinto beans, and barbecue sauce. Stir in turkey hot dogs.

two Cover and cook on low-heat setting for 5 to 6 hours or on high-heat setting for 2½ to 3 hours.

three To serve, cut corn bread into 6 pieces. Place a corn bread piece in each of 6 shallow bowls. Spoon bean mixture over corn bread pieces.

NUTRITION FACTS PER SERVING: 596 cal., 21 g total fat (6 g sat. fat), 112 mg chol., 2,541 mg sodium, 78 g carbo., 15 g fiber, 30 g pro.

Turkey and Spinach Muffins with Hollandaise

START TO FINISH: 20 minutes **MAKES:** 4 servings

1   10-ounce package frozen chopped spinach

1   0.9-ounce envelope hollandaise sauce mix

4   English muffins, split and toasted

8   ounces sliced cooked smoked turkey or chicken breast

1   tablespoon cooking oil

one Cook spinach according to package directions; drain well. Prepare hollandaise sauce according to package directions; cover and keep warm. Place 2 muffin halves on each of 4 dinner plates.

two In a large skillet cook turkey slices in hot oil over medium heat about 1 minute or until heated through. Spoon spinach over muffin halves; top with turkey slices. Spoon hollandaise sauce over turkey.

NUTRITION FACTS PER SERVING: 267 cal., 7 g total fat (1 g sat. fat), 29 mg chol., 1,117 mg sodium, 34 g carbo., 4 g fiber, 17 g pro.

Quick Turkey Tetrazzini

PREP: 20 minutes **BAKE:** 12 minutes **MAKES:** 4 servings

    Nonstick cooking spray

6   ounces dried spaghetti

1   18.8-ounce can ready-to-serve chicken Alfredo soup

6   ounces cooked turkey breast, chopped (about 1 cup)

½   cup finely shredded Parmesan cheese (2 ounces)

2   tablespoons sliced almonds

one Lightly coat a 2-quart square baking dish with cooking spray; set aside. Cook spaghetti according to package directions; drain and return to pan. Stir in soup, turkey, and ¼ cup of the Parmesan cheese; heat through.

two Transfer spaghetti mixture to prepared baking dish. Sprinkle with the remaining ¼ cup Parmesan cheese and the almonds. Bake, uncovered, in a 425°F oven for 12 to 15 minutes or until top is golden.

NUTRITION FACTS PER SERVING: 413 cal., 13 g total fat (5 g sat. fat), 59 mg chol., 752 mg sodium, 43 g carbo., 2 g fiber, 28 g pro.

Turkey-Avocado Quesadillas

START TO FINISH: 15 minutes **MAKES:** 3 servings

3   7- to 8-inch flour tortillas

3   tablespoons bottled peppercorn ranch salad dressing

1   cup bite-size pieces cooked turkey breast or one 5-ounce can chunk-style turkey, drained

1   medium avocado, seeded, peeled, and sliced

¾   cup shredded Monterey Jack cheese (3 ounces)

one Spread one side of each tortilla with salad dressing. Arrange turkey and avocado slices over half of each tortilla; sprinkle with cheese. Fold tortilla in half, pressing gently (tortilla will be full).

two On a large nonstick griddle cook quesadillas over medium heat about 4 minutes or until lightly browned and cheese melts, turning once.

NUTRITION FACTS PER SERVING: 437 cal., 29 g total fat (9 g sat. fat), 69 mg chol., 481 mg sodium, 20 g carbo., 3 g fiber, 26 g pro.

Turkey Calzones

PREP: 30 minutes **BAKE:** 18 minutes **MAKES:** 6 servings

12 ounces cooked turkey breast, chopped
    (about 2¼ cups)

2 cups chopped fresh spinach

1 cup shredded pizza cheese blend
   (4 ounces)

1 8-ounce can pizza sauce

2 13.8-ounce packages refrigerated pizza dough

one In a large bowl combine turkey, spinach, cheese, and ½ cup of the sauce. On a lightly floured surface, roll or pat 1 package of pizza dough into a 12×10-inch rectangle. Cut into three 10×4-inch rectangles.

two Divide turkey mixture among rectangles, placing mixture on half of each and spreading to within 1 inch of the edges. Moisten edges of dough with water. Fold dough over turkey mixture to opposite edge. Press edges with a fork to seal. Place calzones on a lightly greased baking sheet. Prick tops to allow steam to escape.

three Bake, uncovered, in a 375°F oven about 18 minutes or until golden brown. Serve with remaining ½ cup pizza sauce.

NUTRITION FACTS PER SERVING: 344 cal., 10 g total fat (3 g sat. fat), 57 mg chol., 1,338 mg sodium, 41 g carbo., 2 g fiber, 23 g pro.

Raspberry-Smoked Turkey Pockets

START TO FINISH: 15 minutes **MAKES:** 4 servings

8 ounces cooked smoked turkey breast,
   cut into thin strips

2 cups shredded romaine lettuce or spinach

¾ cup raspberries or sliced strawberries

¼ cup bottled raspberry vinaigrette salad dressing

2 large pita bread rounds, halved crosswise

one In a large bowl gently toss together turkey strips, romaine lettuce, raspberries, and vinaigrette dressing.

two Fill pita halves with turkey mixture.

NUTRITION FACTS PER SERVING: 192 cal., 6 g total fat (1 g sat. fat), 25 mg chol., 935 mg sodium, 24 g carbo., 3 g fiber, 13 g pro.

Turkey Subs with Orange Mayonnaise

START TO FINISH: 15 minutes **MAKES:** 4 servings

1   orange

½   cup mayonnaise or salad dressing

4   sourdough rolls or one 8-ounce loaf baguette-style
    French bread, cut crosswise into quarters

8   to 12 ounces thinly sliced cooked peppered turkey or
    cooked smoked turkey

4   slices Swiss or provolone cheese (3 or 4 ounces)

one Finely shred 1 teaspoon of peel from the orange. Cut the orange in half; squeeze 2 tablespoons juice from orange halves. Discard seeds and remaining orange. For orange mayonnaise, in a small bowl stir together mayonnaise, the 2 tablespoons orange juice, and the 1 teaspoon orange peel.

two Split rolls in half horizontally; toast, if desired. Spread orange mayonnaise on cut sides of rolls. Place bottom halves of rolls on a serving platter, mayonnaise sides up. Layer turkey and cheese on rolls. Replace top halves of rolls, mayonnaise sides down. Cover and store any remaining orange mayonnaise in the refrigerator for up to 3 days.

NUTRITION FACTS PER SERVING: 436 cal., 30 g total fat (7 g sat. fat), 61 mg chol., 1,123 mg sodium, 21 g carbo., 1 g fiber, 21 g pro.

Quick and Crunchy Turkey Salad

START TO FINISH: 10 minutes **MAKES:** 4 servings

1   16-ounce package shredded cabbage with carrot
    (coleslaw mix)

6   ounces cooked turkey breast, cubed (1¼ cups)

1   3-ounce package ramen noodles

⅔   cup bottled red wine vinaigrette salad dressing

1   11- or 15-ounce can mandarin orange sections,
    drained

one In a large bowl combine coleslaw mix and turkey. Remove seasoning packet from noodles; reserve for another use. Crumble noodles; add to turkey mixture.

two Pour vinaigrette dressing over turkey mixture; toss gently to coat. Gently stir in mandarin orange sections.

NUTRITION FACTS PER SERVING: 527 cal., 23 g total fat (1 g sat. fat), 15 mg chol., 1,552 mg sodium, 67 g carbo., 3 g fiber, 17 g pro.

Maple-Cranberry Game Hens

PREP: 30 minutes **MARINATE:** 4 hours **GRILL:** 50 minutes
STAND: 10 minutes **MAKES:** 2 servings

2   1¼- to 1½-pound Cornish game hens
6   cups white cranberry juice or white grape juice
½   cup maple-flavor syrup
¼   cup coarse salt

one Remove giblets from game hens, if present. Rinse insides of hens. For brine, in a stainless-steel or enamel stockpot or plastic container combine cranberry juice, maple syrup, and salt; stir to dissolve salt.

two Carefully add game hens to brine. Cover and marinate in the refrigerator for 4 hours, turning hens occasionally.

three Remove game hens from brine; discard brine. Rinse hens; pat dry with paper towels. Tie drumsticks to tails. Twist wing tips under backs.

four For a charcoal grill, arrange medium-hot coals around a drip pan. Test for medium heat above pan. Place the game hens, breast sides up, on grill rack over drip pan. Cover and grill for 50 to 60 minutes or until hens are no longer pink (180°F). (For a gas grill, preheat grill. Reduce heat to medium. Adjust for indirect cooking.Grill as above.)

five Remove game hens from grill. Cover with foil and let stand for 10 minutes before carving.

NUTRITION FACTS PER SERVING: 807 cal., 45 g total fat (12 g sat. fat), 346 mg chol., 1,180 mg sodium, 36 g carbo., 0 g fiber, 59 g pro.

Hoisin-Sauced Cornish Hens

PREP: 15 minutes **BAKE:** 1¼ hours **MAKES:** 4 servings

2   1- to 1½-pound Cornish game hens
½   cup bottled hoisin sauce
¼   cup raspberry vinegar or red wine vinegar
¼   cup orange juice
1   to 2 teaspoons red chili paste

one Remove giblets from game hens, if present. Rinse insides of hens; pat dry with paper towels. Using a sharp knife or kitchen shears, halve hens lengthwise. Place game hens, breast sides up, on a rack in a shallow roasting pan. Cover loosely with foil. Roast in a 375°F oven for 30 minutes.

two Meanwhile, in a small bowl stir together hoisin sauce, vinegar, orange juice, and chili paste. Brush some of the mixture over hens.

three Roast, uncovered, for 45 to 60 minutes more or until hens are no longer pink (180°F), brushing occasionally with the remaining hoisin mixture.

NUTRITION FACTS PER SERVING: 371 cal., 23 g total fat (5 g sat. fat), 120 mg chol., 2,223 mg sodium, 6 g carbo., 0 g fiber, 38 g pro.

hearty
beef, pork & lamb

Chili-Rubbed Prime Rib

PREP: 20 minutes **GRILL:** 2 hours **STAND:** 15 minutes
MAKES: 10 to 12 servings

1	4- to 5-pound beef rib roast
2	tablespoons hot Mexican-style chili powder or chili powder
1	tablespoon unsweetened cocoa powder
½	teaspoon coarse salt
½	teaspoon black pepper
1	tablespoon olive oil
1	recipe Citrus Butter (see recipe, page 262) (optional)

one Trim fat from meat. For rub, in a small bowl combine chili powder, cocoa powder, salt, and pepper. Brush meat with oil. Sprinkle rub evenly over meat; rub in with your fingers.

two For a charcoal grill, arrange medium coals around a drip pan. Test for medium-low heat above pan. Place meat, bone side down, on grill rack over drip pan. Cover and grill for 2 to 2¾ hours for medium-rare (135°F) or 2½ to 3¼ hours for medium (150°F). (For a gas grill, preheat grill. Reduce heat to medium-low. Adjust for indirect cooking. Place meat, bone side down, on grill rack. Grill as above.)

three Remove meat from grill. Cover with foil and let stand for 15 minutes before slicing. (The meat's temperature will rise 10°F during standing.) If desired, serve with Citrus Butter.

NUTRITION FACTS PER SERVING: 226 cal., 15 g total fat (6 g sat. fat), 61 mg chol., 168 mg sodium, 1 g carbo., 1 g fiber, 21 g pro.

Basil-Beef Sirloin

PREP: 15 minutes **ROAST:** 50 minutes **STAND:** 15 minutes
MAKES: 10 to 12 servings

1	3- to 3½-pound boneless beef sirloin roast, cut 1¾ inches thick
¼	teaspoon salt
¼	teaspoon black pepper
2	cups lightly packed fresh basil leaves, snipped
8	cloves garlic, minced
2	teaspoons olive oil

one Trim fat from meat. Make five or six 5-inch-long slits along top of meat, cutting almost through it. Sprinkle with salt and pepper. In a medium bowl combine basil and garlic; stuff mixture into slits in meat. Tie meat with 100-percent-cotton kitchen string to hold slits closed. Drizzle with oil.

two Place meat on a rack in a shallow roasting pan. Roast, uncovered, in a 425°F oven for 15 minutes. Reduce oven temperature to 350°F.

three Roast, uncovered, for 35 to 45 minutes more or until desired doneness (150°F for medium). Cover with foil and let stand for 15 minutes before slicing. (The meat's temperature will rise 10°F during standing.)

NUTRITION FACTS PER SERVING: 255 cal., 13 g total fat (5 g sat. fat), 91 mg chol., 121 mg sodium, 1 g carbo., 0 g fiber, 31 g pro.

German-Style Beef Roast

PREP: 30 minutes **BAKE:** 2½ hours **MAKES:** 8 to 10 servings

1	3-pound boneless beef round rump roast
1	12-ounce can beer
1	cup ketchup
1	tablespoon packed brown sugar
¼	teaspoon black pepper

one Trim fat from meat. Place meat in a 4-quart Dutch oven. In a medium bowl combine beer and ketchup; pour over meat.

two Bake, covered, in a 325°F oven about 2½ hours or until tender. Remove meat from Dutch oven. Cover with foil and let stand while finishing sauce.

three For sauce, stir brown sugar and pepper into mixture in Dutch oven. Bring to boiling; reduce heat. Simmer, uncovered, about 10 minutes or until slightly thickened. Slice meat. Skim fat from sauce. Serve meat with sauce.

NUTRITION FACTS PER SERVING: 278 cal., 7 g total fat (2 g sat. fat), 89 mg chol., 470 mg sodium, 11 g carbo., 1 g fiber, 39 g pro.

Stroganoff-Sauced Beef Roast

PREP: 15 minutes **COOK:** 15 minutes **MAKES:** 3 or 4 servings

1	16-ounce package refrigerated cooked beef pot roast with juices
2	cups fresh shiitake, crimini, or button mushrooms
½	cup dairy sour cream French onion-flavor dip
2	cups hot cooked noodles

one Transfer beef with juices to a large skillet (leave meat whole). Remove stems from shiitake mushrooms, if using. Halve or quarter mushrooms. Add mushrooms to skillet.

two Cook, covered, over medium-low heat about 15 minutes or until meat is heated through, stirring mushrooms and turning meat once.

three Break meat into bite-size pieces. Stir onion dip into meat mixture; heat through (do not boil). Stir in noodles.

NUTRITION FACTS PER SERVING: 542 cal., 7 g total fat (11 g sat. fat), 99 mg chol., 787 mg sodium, 46 g carbo., 4 g fiber, 8 g pro.

Five-Spice Tri-Tip Roast

PREP: 10 minutes **MARINATE:** 2 to 4 hours **GRILL:** 35 minutes
STAND: 15 minutes **MAKES:** 6 servings

1   1½- to 2-pound boneless beef bottom sirloin
      (tri-tip) roast
1   tablespoon toasted sesame oil
2   teaspoons five-spice powder
½   teaspoon salt

one Trim fat from meat. In a small bowl combine sesame oil, five-spice powder, and salt. Rub oil mixture evenly over meat with your fingers. Place meat in a resealable plastic bag; seal bag. Marinate in the refrigerator for 2 to 4 hours.

two For a charcoal grill, arrange medium-hot coals around a drip pan. Test for medium heat above the pan. Place meat on grill rack over drip pan. Cover and grill for 35 to 40 minutes for medium-rare (135°F) or 40 to 45 minutes for medium (150°F). (For a gas grill, preheat grill. Reduce heat to medium. Adjust grill for indirect cooking. Grill as above.)

three Remove meat from grill. Cover with foil and let stand for 15 minutes before slicing. (The meat's temperature will rise 10°F during standing.)

NUTRITION FACTS PER SERVING: 211 cal., 12 g total fat (4 g sat. fat), 74 mg chol., 253 mg sodium, 1 g carbo., 0 g fiber, 24 g pro.

Homestyle Beef and Vegetables

PREP: 20 minutes **COOK:** Low 8 hours, High 4 hours; plus 30 minutes on High **MAKES:** 6 servings

      Nonstick cooking spray
1   3- to 3½-pound boneless beef chuck pot roast
1   0.6-ounce envelope Italian dry salad dressing mix
3   tablespoons quick-cooking tapioca
1   14-ounce can onion-flavor beef broth
1   16-ounce package frozen Italian-blend
      vegetables (cauliflower, broccoli, zucchini,
      and Italian green beans)

one Lightly coat a 3½- or 4-quart slow cooker with cooking spray; set aside. Trim fat from meat. Lightly coat a large skillet with cooking spray; heat over medium heat. Cook meat in hot skillet until brown on all sides.

two Place meat in the prepared cooker. Sprinkle with salad dressing mix and tapioca. Pour broth over all.

three Cover and cook on low-heat setting for 8 to 9 hours or on high-heat setting for 4 to 4½ hours. If using low-heat setting, turn to high-heat setting. Add frozen vegetables to cooker. Cover and cook about 30 minutes more or until vegetables are tender.

NUTRITION FACTS PER SERVING: 338 cal., 8 g total fat (3 g sat. fat), 134 mg chol., 787 mg sodium, 11 g carbo., 2 g fiber, 50 g pro.

Pot Roast with Mushroom Sauce

PREP: 15 minutes **COOK:** Low 10 hours, High 5 hours
MAKES: 5 servings

1	1½-pound boneless beef eye round roast or rump roast
	Nonstick cooking spray
4	medium potatoes, quartered
1	16-ounce package peeled baby carrots
1	10¾-ounce can condensed golden mushroom soup
½	teaspoon dried tarragon or basil, crushed

one Trim fat from meat. Lightly coat a large skillet with cooking spray; heat over medium heat. Cook meat in hot skillet until brown on all sides.

two In a 3½- or 4-quart slow cooker place potatoes and carrots. Place meat on top of vegetables. Pour soup over meat; sprinkle with tarragon.

three Cover and cook on low-heat setting for 10 to 12 hours or on high-heat setting for 5 to 6 hours. Transfer meat and vegetables to a serving platter. Stir sauce; spoon over meat and vegetables.

NUTRITION FACTS PER SERVING: 391 cal., 13 g total fat (5 g sat. fat), 79 mg chol., 567 mg sodium, 33 g carbo., 5 g fiber, 33 g pro.

Cola Pot Roast

PREP: 15 minutes **COOK:** Low 7 hours, High 3½ hours
MAKES: 6 servings

1	2½- to 3-pound boneless beef chuck pot roast
	Nonstick cooking spray
2	16-ounce packages frozen stew vegetables
1	12-ounce can cola
1	envelope (half of a 2-ounce package) onion soup mix
2	tablespoons quick-cooking tapioca

one Trim fat from meat. Lightly coat a large skillet with cooking spray; heat over medium heat. Cook meat in hot skillet until brown on all sides.

two Place meat in a 4½- or 5-quart slow cooker. Top with frozen vegetables. In a medium bowl stir together cola, soup mix, and tapioca. Pour over meat and vegetables.

three Cover and cook on low-heat setting for 7 to 8 hours or on high-heat setting for 3½ to 4 hours.

NUTRITION FACTS PER SERVING: 278 cal., 5 g total fat (2 g sat. fat), 75 mg chol., 582 mg sodium, 28 g carbo., 2 g fiber, 29 g pro.

HEARTY BEEF, PORK & LAMB

Pot Roast with
Chipotle-Fruit Sauce

PREP: 20 minutes **COOK:** Low 10 hours, High 5 hours
MAKES: 6 to 8 servings

- 1 3-pound boneless beef chuck pot roast
- 2 teaspoons garlic-pepper seasoning
- 1 7-ounce package mixed dried fruit
- ½ cup water
- 1 tablespoon finely chopped canned chipotle peppers in adobo sauce
- 1 tablespoon cold water
- 2 teaspoons cornstarch

one Trim fat from meat. Sprinkle both sides of meat with garlic-pepper seasoning. If necessary, cut meat to fit into a 3½- or 4-quart slow cooker. Place meat in cooker. Add dried fruit, the ½ cup water, and chipotle peppers.

two Cover and cook on low-heat setting for 10 to 11 hours or on high-heat setting for 5 to 5½ hours. Transfer meat and fruit to a serving platter. Cover and keep warm.

three Pour cooking liquid into a glass measuring cup; skim off fat. In a medium saucepan combine the 1 tablespoon water and the cornstarch; add cooking liquid. Cook and stir until thickened and bubbly. Cook and stir for 2 minutes more.

four Thinly slice meat. Spoon sauce over meat and fruit.

NUTRITION FACTS PER SERVING: 576 cal., 19 g total fat (7 g sat. fat), 229 mg chol., 502 mg sodium, 23 g carbo., 1 g fiber, 76 g pro.

Grass-Fed Beef Rapidly growing in popularity, grass-fed beef is prized by many as a healthful, sustainably grown, and delicious alternative to grain-fed beef.

Because grass-fed cattle feed only on grass or hay, their flavor is often said to be heartier than that of mild grain-fed beef. Grass-fed beef may also be lower in fat while, at the same time, higher in healthful beta-carotene and omega-3 fatty acids. To give it a try, ask around for local sources of high-quality grass-fed beef that is not "finished" on grain.

Oven-Barbecued Beef Sandwiches

PREP: 10 minutes **BAKE:** 2 hours **MAKES:** 6 to 8 servings

1	4- to 6-pound boneless beef round roast or chuck roast
1	10¾-ounce can condensed cream of chicken or cream of mushroom soup
1¼	cups bottled barbecue sauce
1	envelope (half of a 2-ounce package) dry onion soup mix
6	to 8 onion buns or kaiser rolls, toasted

one Trim fat from meat. Place meat in a shallow roasting pan. Pour canned soup and barbecue sauce over meat. Sprinkle with dry soup mix.

two Bake, covered, in a 350°F oven about 2 hours or until meat is tender enough to slice. (For shredded meat, bake about 3 hours or until very tender.)

three Slice or shred the meat and serve on buns. Skim fat off sauce and spoon over meat.

NUTRITION FACTS PER SERVING: 887 cal., 53 g total fat (20 g sat. fat), 179 mg chol., 1,446 mg sodium, 42 g carbo., 2 g fiber, 56 g pro.

SLOW COOKER

French Dips with Mushrooms

PREP: 25 minutes **COOK:** Low 8 hours, High 4 hours
STAND: 10 minutes **MAKES:** 8 servings

1	3- to 3½-pound boneless beef bottom round roast or rump roast
	Nonstick cooking spray
4	fresh portobello mushrooms (3 to 4 inches in diameter)
1	14-ounce can onion-flavor beef broth
1	large red onion, cut into ½-inch slices
8	hoagie buns, split and toasted

one Trim fat from meat. If necessary, cut meat to fit into a 3½- to 6-quart slow cooker. Lightly coat a large skillet with cooking spray; heat over medium heat. Cook meat in hot skillet until brown on all sides. Place meat in prepared cooker.

two Remove and discard stems from mushrooms. Cut mushrooms into ¼-inch slices. Add to meat in cooker. Pour broth over meat and mushrooms.

three Cover and cook on low-heat setting for 8 to 9 hours or on high-heat setting for 4 to 4½ hours. Remove meat from cooker; cover and let stand for 10 minutes.

four Meanwhile, using a slotted spoon, remove mushrooms and set aside. Thinly slice meat. Arrange meat, mushroom slices, and onion slices on toasted buns. Pour cooking liquid into a measuring cup; skim off fat. Drizzle a little of the liquid onto each sandwich and pour the remaining liquid into 8 small bowls to serve with sandwiches for dipping.

NUTRITION FACTS PER SERVING: 780 cal., 33 g total fat (11 g sat. fat), 106 mg chol., 955 mg sodium, 73 g carbo., 4 g fiber, 47 g pro.

Corned Beef and Cabbage

PREP: 15 minutes **COOK:** Low 10 hours, High 5 hours
MAKES: 6 servings

- 1   3- to 4-pound corned beef brisket with spice packet
- ½   of a small head cabbage, cut into 3 wedges
- 4   medium carrots, cut into 2-inch pieces
- 2   medium yellow potatoes, cut into 2-inch pieces
- 1   medium onion, quartered
- ½   cup water

one Trim fat from meat. If necessary, cut meat to fit into a 5- to 6-quart slow cooker. Sprinkle spices from packet evenly over meat; rub in with your fingers.

two Place cabbage, carrots, potatoes, and onion in the cooker. Pour water over vegetables. Top with meat.

three Cover and cook on low-heat setting for 10 to 12 hours or on high-heat setting for 5 to 6 hours. Remove meat from cooker. Thinly slice meat across the grain; arrange slices on a serving platter. Using a slotted spoon, transfer vegetables to serving platter. Discard cooking liquid.

NUTRITION FACTS PER SERVING: 457 cal., 27 g total fat (7 g sat. fat), 115 mg chol., 1,543 mg sodium, 16 g carbo., 3 g fiber, 35 g pro.

SLOW COOKER

Reubens from a Crock

PREP: 15 minutes **COOK:** Low 4 hours, High 2 hours
MAKES: 8 servings

- 1   2- to 3-pound corned beef brisket with spice packet
- 1   16-ounce jar sauerkraut, drained
- ½   cup bottled Thousand Island salad dressing
- 16   slices rye swirl bread, toasted
- 8   ounces sliced Swiss cheese
     Bottled Thousand Island salad dressing (optional)

one Trim fat from meat. If necessary, cut meat to fit into a 3½- or 4-quart slow cooker. Place meat in cooker. Sprinkle spices from packet evenly over meat. Spread sauerkraut over meat. Drizzle with the ½ cup salad dressing.

two Cover and cook on low-heat setting for 4 to 6 hours or on high-heat setting for 2 to 3 hours. Remove meat from cooker. Thinly slice meat across the grain. Return sliced meat to the cooker and stir to combine with the cooking liquid.

three Using a slotted spoon, spoon corned beef mixture onto 8 of the toasted bread slices. Top with cheese, additiona salad dressing (if desired), and the remaining bread slices.

NUTRITION FACTS PER SERVING: 564 cal., 34 g total fat (10 g sat. fat), 89 mg chol., 2,101 mg sodium, 35 g carbo., 4 g fiber, 29 g pro.

Honey-Bourbon Steaks

PREP: 15 minutes **MARINATE:** 6 to 8 hours **GRILL:** 10 minutes
MAKES: 6 servings

2½	cups water
½	cup bourbon
⅓	cup honey
8	sprigs fresh lemon thyme
3	tablespoons coarse salt
1	teaspoon black pepper
6	boneless beef top loin steaks, cut 1 inch thick

one For brine, in a large bowl combine water, ⅓ cup of the bourbon, ¼ cup of the honey, the lemon thyme, salt, and pepper; stir to dissolve salt.

two Trim fat from meat. Place meat in a resealable plastic bag set in a shallow dish. Pour brine over meat; seal bag.

Marinate in the refrigerator for 6 to 8 hours, turning bag occasionally. In a small bowl combine the remaining bourbon and the remaining honey; cover and chill.

three Drain meat, discarding brine. Rinse meat and pat dry with paper towels. Remove the reserved bourbon mixture from refrigerator.

four For a charcoal grill, grill meat on the rack of an uncovered grill directly over medium coals for 10 to 12 minutes for medium-rare (145°F) or 12 to 15 minutes for medium (160°F), turning once halfway through grilling. (For a gas grill, preheat grill. Reduce heat to medium. Place meat on grill rack over heat. Cover and grill as above.)

five Drizzle the meat with the reserved bourbon mixture.

NUTRITION FACTS PER SERVING: 375 cal., 12 g total fat (4 g sat. fat), 133 mg chol., 436 mg sodium, 8 g carbo., 0 g fiber, 49 g pro.

Steak and Mushrooms

START TO FINISH: 20 minutes **MAKES:** 4 servings

4	beef tenderloin steaks (about 1 pound), cut 1 inch thick
1	tablespoon olive oil
8	ounces fresh crimini, shiitake, baby portobello, and/or button mushrooms, sliced (3 cups)
¼	cup onion-flavor beef broth
¼	cup whipping cream

one Trim fat from meat. In a large skillet cook meat in hot oil over medium heat for 10 to 13 minutes for medium-rare to medium, turning once. Transfer meat to a serving platter; cover and keep warm.

two In the same skillet cook and stir mushrooms over medium heat for 4 to 5 minutes or until tender. Stir in broth and whipping cream. Cook and stir about 2 minutes or until slightly thickened. Spoon mushroom mixture over meat.

NUTRITION FACTS PER SERVING: 271 cal., 18 g total fat (7 g sat. fat), 90 mg chol., 116 mg sodium, 2 g carbo., 0 g fiber, 26 g pro.

BLT Steaks

PREP: 15 minutes **GRILL:** 13 minutes **MAKES:** 4 servings

- 2 12-ounce boneless beef top loin steaks, cut 1¼ inches thick
- 8 slices bacon
- ½ cup bottled balsamic vinaigrette salad dressing
- 8 slices red and/or yellow tomatoes
  Torn mixed baby salad greens

one Trim fat from meat. For a charcoal grill, grill meat on the rack of an uncovered grill directly over medium coals for 13 to 17 minutes for medium-rare (145°F) or 17 to 21 minutes for medium (160°F), turning once halfway through grilling. (For a gas grill, preheat grill. Reduce heat to medium. Place meat on grill rack over heat. Cover and grill as above.)

two Meanwhile, in a large skillet cook bacon over medium heat until crisp. Drain bacon on paper towels, reserving 1 tablespoon drippings in skillet. Add salad dressing to the reserved drippings. Cook and stir over high heat for 1 minute, scraping up any browned bits. Remove skillet from heat.

three To serve, halve each steak. Top each steak piece with 2 tomato slices, 2 bacon slices, salad greens, and a splash of the hot dressing from skillet.

NUTRITION FACTS PER SERVING: 556 cal., 42 g total fat (14 g sat. fat), 122 mg chol., 636 mg sodium, 5 g carbo., 1 g fiber, 38 g pro.

Saucy Strip Steaks

PREP: 15 minutes **GRILL:** 10 minutes **MAKES:** 4 servings

- ⅔ cup orange marmalade
- 2 tablespoons butter or margarine
- 1 teaspoon snipped fresh rosemary or ¼ teaspoon dried rosemary, crushed
- 4 8-ounce boneless beef top loin steaks, cut about 1 inch thick
  Salt and black pepper

one In a small saucepan combine marmalade, butter, and rosemary. Cook and stir over low heat until butter melts. Set aside. Trim fat from meat. Sprinkle both sides of meat with salt and pepper.

two For a charcoal grill, grill meat on the rack of an uncovered grill directly over medium coals for 10 to 12 minutes for medium-rare (145°F) or 12 to 15 minutes for medium (160°F), turning once halfway through grilling and brushing occasionally with marmalade mixture during the last 5 minutes of grilling.

three Transfer meat to a serving platter. Spoon any remaining marmalade mixture over meat.

NUTRITION FACTS PER SERVING: 464 cal., 14 g total fat (7 g sat. fat), 123 mg chol., 357 mg sodium, 35 g carbo., 0 g fiber, 49 g pro.

Prosciutto-Wrapped Tenderloin

PREP: 15 minutes **BROIL:** 12 minutes **MAKES:** 4 servings

1   ounce sliced prosciutto, chopped

1   small carrot, shredded

1   green onion, sliced

4   beef tenderloin steaks (about 1 pound),
       cut 1 inch thick

4   thin slices prosciutto

one For stuffing, in a small bowl combine chopped prosciutto, carrot, and green onion.

two Trim fat from meat. Cut a horizontal slit in each steak to form a pocket. Fill pockets with stuffing. Cut sliced prosciutto into 1-inch strips. Wrap prosciutto around each steak; secure with toothpicks.

three Place meat on the unheated rack of a broiler pan. Broil 3 to 4 inches from the heat for 12 to 14 minutes for medium-rare (145°F) or 15 to 18 minutes for medium (160°F), turning once.

NUTRITION FACTS PER SERVING: 296 cal., 13 g total fat (5 g sat. fat), 115 mg chol., 516 mg sodium, 1 g carbo., 0 g fiber, 40 g pro.

Spinach-Stuffed Flank Steak

PREP: 20 minutes **BROIL:** 10 minutes **MAKES:** 4 servings

¼   cup dried tomatoes (not oil-packed)

1   1-pound beef flank steak or top round steak

1   10-ounce package frozen chopped spinach, thawed
       and well drained

2   tablespoons grated Parmesan cheese

2   tablespoons snipped fresh basil

one In a small bowl soak dried tomatoes in enough hot water to cover for 10 minutes; drain. Snip into small pieces.

two Meanwhile, trim fat from meat. Score both sides of meat in a diamond pattern by making shallow diagonal cuts at 1-inch intervals. Place meat between 2 pieces of plastic wrap. Pound into a 12×8-inch rectangle. Discard plastic wrap.

three Spread spinach over meat. Sprinkle with tomatoes, cheese, and basil. Starting from a short side, roll up meat. Secure with toothpicks at 1-inch intervals, starting ½ inch from one end. Cut between toothpicks into eight 1-inch slices.

four Place slices, cut sides down, on the unheated rack of a broiler pan. Broil 3 to 4 inches from the heat for 10 to 12 minutes for medium-rare or 12 to 16 minutes for medium, turning once. Remove toothpicks.

NUTRITION FACTS PER SERVING: 281 cal., 9 g total fat (4 g sat. fat), 45 mg chol., 521 mg sodium, 18 g carbo., 12 g fiber, 37 g pro.

Deviled Steaks

PREP: 10 minutes **GRILL:** 10 minutes **MAKES:** 4 servings

1	tablespoon ketchup
1	tablespoon water
1	tablespoon Worcestershire sauce
1	teaspoon dry mustard
¼	teaspoon salt
	Dash black pepper
4	beef tenderloin steaks (about 1 pound), cut 1 inch thick

one For sauce, in a small bowl combine ketchup, water, Worcestershire sauce, mustard, salt, and pepper. Set aside.

two Trim fat from meat. For a charcoal grill, grill meat on the rack of an uncovered grill directly over medium coals for 10 to 12 minutes for medium-rare (145°F) or 12 to 15 minutes for medium (160°F), turning once and brushing with sauce halfway through grilling. (For a gas grill, preheat grill. Place meat on grill rack over heat. Cover and grill as above.)

three Brush meat with any remaining sauce before serving.

NUTRITION FACTS PER SERVING: 186 cal., 9 g total fat (3 g sat. fat), 70 mg chol., 288 mg sodium, 2 g carbo., 0 g fiber, 24 g pro.

Flat-Iron Steaks *See photo on page 117.*

PREP: 10 minutes **GRILL:** 7 minutes **MAKES:** 6 servings

4	boneless beef chuck top blade (flat-iron) steaks, cut ¾ inch thick
1	tablespoon dried marjoram, crushed
½	teaspoon garlic salt
½	teaspoon black pepper

one Trim fat from meat. For rub, in a small bowl combine marjoram, garlic salt, and pepper. Sprinkle rub evenly over both sides of meat; rub in with your fingers. If desired, cover and chill for 2 to 24 hours.

two For a charcoal grill, grill meat on the rack of an uncovered grill directly over medium coals for 7 to 9 minutes for medium-rare (145°F) or 10 to 12 minutes for medium (160°F), turning once halfway through grilling. (For a gas grill, preheat grill. Reduce heat to medium. Place meat on grill rack over heat. Cover and grill as above.)

NUTRITION FACTS PER SERVING: 132 cal., 5 g total fat (2 g sat. fat), 53 mg chol., 129 mg sodium, 1 g carbo., 0 g fiber, 20 g pro.

> **Flat-Iron Steaks** Not only are flat-iron steaks one of the most tender cuts around, but they contain plenty of flavorful marbling and are often cheaper than more popular steaks such as ribeye and T-bone. If you don't see steaks labeled "flat-iron" in your butcher's case, don't panic. They may also be marketed as "beef chuck top blade steaks."

Beef Tenderloin with Blue Cheese

PREP: 10 minutes **COOK:** 10 minutes **MAKES:** 4 servings

4	beef tenderloin steaks (about 1 pound), cut 1 inch thick
½	teaspoon garlic salt
	Nonstick cooking spray
⅓	cup dairy sour cream
3	tablespoons crumbled blue cheese
3	tablespoons chopped walnuts, toasted (see tip, page 280)

one Trim fat from meat. Sprinkle both sides of meat with garlic salt. Lightly coat a large skillet with cooking spray; heat over medium-high heat.

two Add meat to hot skillet; reduce heat to medium. Cook for 10 to 13 minutes for medium-rare to medium, turning once. Transfer meat to a serving platter.

three Meanwhile, in a small bowl stir together sour cream and blue cheese. Spoon sour cream mixture on top of meat. Sprinkle with walnuts.

NUTRITION FACTS PER SERVING: 264 cal., 17 g total fat (6 g sat. fat), 81 mg chol., 255 mg sodium, 2 g carbo., 0 g fiber, 26 g pro.

SLOW COOKER

Steak with Tuscan Tomato Sauce *See photo on page 118.*

PREP: 25 minutes **COOK:** Low 8 hours, High 4 hours
MAKES: 4 servings

1	1-pound boneless beef round steak, cut 1 inch thick
	Nonstick cooking spray
1	medium onion, sliced and separated into rings
2	tablespoons quick-cooking tapioca
1	teaspoon dried thyme, crushed
¼	teaspoon black pepper
⅛	teaspoon salt
1	14½-ounce can diced tomatoes with basil, garlic, and oregano, undrained
2	cups hot cooked noodles or rice (optional)

one Trim fat from meat. Cut meat into 4 serving-size pieces. Lightly coat a large skillet with cooking spray; heat over medium heat. Cook meat in hot skillet until brown on both sides.

two Place onion in a 3½- or 4-quart slow cooker. Sprinkle with tapioca, thyme, pepper, and salt. Pour the undrained tomatoes over onion. Top with meat.

three Cover and cook on low-heat setting for 8 to 10 hours or on high-heat setting for 4 to 5 hours. If desired, serve with hot cooked noodles.

NUTRITION FACTS PER SERVING: 205 cal., 2 g total fat (1 g sat. fat), 49 mg chol., 667 mg sodium, 16 g carbo., 1 g fiber, 28 g pro.

Bloody Mary Steak *See photo on page 116.*

PREP: 20 minutes **COOK:** Low 8 hours, High 4 hours
MAKES: 6 servings

2   1-pound boneless beef round steaks, cut ¾ inch thick
    Nonstick cooking spray
¾   cup hot-style tomato juice
¼   cup water
2   cloves garlic, minced
2   tablespoons cold water
4   teaspoons cornstarch
2   teaspoons prepared horseradish
    Salt and black pepper

one Trim fat from meat. Cut meat into 6 serving-size pieces. Lightly coat a large skillet with cooking spray; heat over medium-high heat. Cook meat in hot skillet until brown on both sides. Place meat in a 2½- to 3½-quart slow cooker. Add tomato juice, the ¼ cup water, and the garlic.

two Cover and cook on low-heat setting for 8 to 9 hours or on high-heat setting for 4 to 4½ hours. Transfer meat to a serving platter, reserving cooking liquid. Cover meat and keep warm.

three For gravy, pour cooking liquid into a 2-cup glass measuring cup; skim off fat. Measure liquid; if necessary, add water to equal 1½ cups total.

four In a small saucepan combine the 2 tablespoons cold water and the cornstarch; stir in cooking liquid. Cook and stir over medium heat until thickened and bubbly. Cook and stir for 2 minutes more. Stir in horseradish. Season to taste with salt and pepper. Slice meat. Serve meat with gravy.

NUTRITION FACTS PER SERVING: 196 cal., 4 g total fat (1 g sat. fat), 85 mg chol., 292 mg sodium, 3 g carbo., 0 g fiber, 35 g pro.

Steaks with Tarragon Butter

PREP: 10 minutes **BROIL:** 20 minutes **MAKES:** 6 servings

¼   cup butter, softened
1   teaspoon lemon juice
½   teaspoon dried tarragon, crushed
1   clove garlic, minced
2   1-pound beef porterhouse, T-bone, or sirloin steaks, cut 1½ inches thick

one In a small bowl stir together butter, lemon juice, tarragon, and garlic. Chill butter mixture while preparing meat.

two Trim fat from meat. Place meat on the unheated rack of a broiler pan. Broil 3 to 4 inches from the heat for 20 to 25 minutes for medium-rare (145°F) or 25 to 30 minutes for medium (160°F), turning once.

three Cut meat into 6 serving-size pieces. Serve meat with butter mixture.

NUTRITION FACTS PER SERVING: 207 cal., 14 g total fat (7 g sat. fat), 64 mg chol., 128 mg sodium, 0 g carbo., 0 g fiber, 20 g pro.

Mustard-Marinated Flank Steak

PREP: 20 minutes **MARINATE:** 2 to 24 hours **GRILL:** 17 minutes
MAKES: 4 to 6 servings

1	1¼- to 1½-pound beef flank steak
½	teaspoon black pepper
1	cup bottled Italian salad dressing
½	cup yellow mustard

one Trim fat from meat. Score both sides of meat in a diamond pattern by making shallow diagonal cuts at 1-inch intervals. Rub pepper onto both sides of meat.

two Place meat in a resealable plastic bag set in a shallow dish. For marinade, in a small bowl stir together salad dressing and mustard. Pour over meat; seal bag. Marinate in the refrigerator for 2 to 24 hours, turning bag occasionally.

three Drain meat, reserving marinade. For a charcoal grill, grill meat on the rack of an uncovered grill directly over medium coals for 17 to 21 minutes for medium (160°F), turning and brushing once with marinade halfway through grilling. (For a gas grill, preheat grill. Reduce heat to medium. Place meat on grill rack over heat. Cover and grill as above.) Thinly slice meat diagonally across the grain.

NUTRITION FACTS PER SERVING: 290 cal., 16 g total fat (4 g sat. fat), 48 mg chol., 730 mg sodium, 4 g carbo., 1 g fiber, 31 g pro.

Pepper Steak *See photo on page 117.*

PREP: 15 minutes **COOK:** Low 10 hours, High 5 hours
MAKES: 4 servings

1	1-pound boneless beef round steak, cut ¾ to 1 inch thick
¼	teaspoon salt
¼	teaspoon black pepper
	Nonstick cooking spray
1	14½-ounce can Italian-style stewed tomatoes, undrained
3	tablespoons Italian-style tomato paste
1	teaspoon Worcestershire sauce
1	16-ounce package frozen pepper stir-fry vegetables (green, red, and yellow peppers and onions)

one Trim fat from meat. Cut meat into 4 serving-size pieces. Sprinkle meat with salt and black pepper. Lightly coat a large skillet with cooking spray; heat over medium-high heat. Cook meat in hot skillet until brown on both sides. Transfer meat to a 3½- or 4-quart slow cooker.

two In a medium bowl stir together undrained tomatoes, tomato paste, and Worcestershire sauce; pour over meat in cooker. Top with frozen vegetables.

three Cover and cook on low-heat setting for 10 to 12 hours or on high-heat setting for 5 to 6 hours.

NUTRITION FACTS PER SERVING: 344 cal., 18 g total fat (6 g sat. fat), 71 mg chol., 496 mg sodium, 17 g carbo., 4 g fiber, 25 g pro.

Asian Beef Short Ribs

PREP: 25 minutes **COOK:** Low 6 hours, High 3 hours
MAKES: 6 servings

- 3 pounds boneless beef short ribs
- 1 7.6-ounce jar plum sauce
- ⅔ cup ketchup
- 1 tablespoon rice vinegar
- 2 teaspoons grated fresh ginger

one In a large nonstick skillet cook meat over medium-high heat until brown on both sides. Drain off fat. Place meat in a 3½- or 4-quart slow cooker. In a medium bowl stir together plum sauce, ketchup, vinegar, and ginger. Pour over meat.

two Cover and cook on low-heat setting for 6 to 8 hours or on high-heat setting for 3 to 4 hours.

three Using a slotted spoon, transfer meat to a serving platter. Skim fat from cooking liquid. Spoon some of the cooking liquid over meat; discard the remaining liquid.

NUTRITION FACTS PER SERVING: 245 cal., 8 g total fat (3 g sat. fat), 53 mg chol., 538 mg sodium, 25 g carbo., 0 g fiber, 18 g pro.

Thai Beef Stir-Fry

START TO FINISH: 15 minutes **MAKES:** 4 servings

- 4 ounces rice noodles
- 2 tablespoons cooking oil
- 1 16-ounce package frozen pepper stir-fry vegetables (green, red, and yellow peppers and onions)
- 12 ounces packaged beef stir-fry strips
- ½ cup bottled peanut stir-fry sauce

one Prepare noodles according to package directions; drain and set aside. In a large skillet heat 1 tablespoon of the oil over medium-high heat. Add frozen vegetables. Cook and stir for 2 to 3 minutes or until vegetables are crisp-tender. Drain and remove vegetables from skillet.

two Add the remaining 1 tablespoon oil to hot skillet; add meat. Cook and stir for 2 to 3 minutes or until meat is slightly pink in center. Push meat from center of skillet.

three Add sauce to center of skillet. Cook and stir until bubbly. Return cooked vegetables to skillet; stir to coat ingredients with sauce. Cook and stir about 1 minute more or until heated through. Serve over noodles.

NUTRITION FACTS PER SERVING: 404 cal., 16 g total fat (4 g sat. fat), 50 mg chol., 597 mg sodium, 39 g carbo., 3 g fiber, 23 g pro.

Stir-Fry Time-Saver Stir-fries are quick and convenient one-dish meals. You can get dinner on the table even more quickly when you use meats and poultry that are precut by your supermarket's butcher. If you must cut your own beef strips for the recipe above, the task is easier if you partially freeze the meat first. Place it in the freezer for 30 minutes before cooking time, then thinly slice across the grain.

Beef in Red Wine Gravy

PREP: 15 minutes **COOK:** Low 10 hours, High 5 hours
MAKES: 6 servings

1½	pounds beef stew meat, cut into 1-inch pieces
2	medium onions, cut up
3	tablespoons cornstarch
2	teaspoons instant beef bouillon granules or 1 envelope (half of a 2-ounce package) onion soup mix
	Salt and black pepper
1½	cups dry red wine
3	cups hot cooked noodles (optional)

one In a 3½- or 4-quart slow cooker combine meat and onions. Sprinkle with cornstarch, bouillon granules, salt, and pepper. Pour red wine over mixture in cooker.

two Cover and cook on low-heat setting for 10 to 12 hours or on high-heat setting for 5 to 6 hours. If desired, serve over hot cooked noodles.

NUTRITION FACTS PER SERVING: 211 cal., 4 g total fat (1 g sat. fat), 67 mg chol., 430 mg sodium, 8 g carbo., 0 g fiber, 24 g pro.

Round Steak with Herbs

PREP: 20 minutes **COOK:** Low 10 hours, High 5 hours
MAKES: 6 servings

2	1-pound boneless beef round steaks, cut ¾ inch thick
1	medium onion, sliced
1	10¾-ounce can condensed cream of celery soup
¾	teaspoon dried Italian seasoning, crushed
¼	teaspoon black pepper
4	cups hot cooked noodles

one Trim fat from meat. If necessary, cut meat to fit into a 3½- or 4-quart slow cooker. Place onion in cooker; place meat on top of onion. Pour soup over meat and onion; sprinkle with Italian seasoning and pepper.

two Cover and cook on low-heat setting for 10 to 12 hours or on high-heat setting for 5 to 6 hours.

three Remove meat from cooker. Cut meat into bite-size pieces. Toss meat and soup mixture with hot cooked noodles.

NUTRITION FACTS PER SERVING: 392 cal., 11 g total fat (3 g sat. fat), 113 mg chol., 483 mg sodium, 32 g carbo., 2 g fiber, 39 g pro.

HEARTY BEEF, PORK & LAMB

Thai Beef

PREP: 15 minutes **COOK:** Low 8 hours, High 4 hours
MAKES: 6 servings

1   1½- to 2-pound beef flank steak
1   16-ounce package peeled baby carrots
1   11½-ounce bottle peanut stir-fry sauce
1   cup unsweetened coconut milk
¼   cup chopped dry roasted peanuts

one Trim fat from meat. Thinly slice meat across the grain into bite-size strips. In a 3½- or 4-quart slow cooker place meat and carrots. Pour peanut sauce over all.

two Cover and cook on low-heat setting for 8 to 10 hours or on high-heat setting for 4 to 5 hours. Stir in coconut milk. Sprinkle each serving with peanuts.

NUTRITION FACTS PER SERVING: 449 cal., 25 g total fat (12 g sat. fat), 46 mg chol., 814 mg sodium, 23 g carbo., 6 g fiber, 31 g pro.

GRILLING

Beef Kabobs with Blue Cheese Dipping Sauce

PREP: 20 minutes **GRILL:** 8 minutes **MAKES:** 4 servings

1   1-pound boneless beef sirloin steak, cut 1 inch thick
2   teaspoons steak seasoning
12 fresh cremini mushrooms, halved
6   green onions, cut into 2-inch pieces
1   cup bottled blue cheese salad dressing

one Trim fat from meat. Cut meat into 1-inch pieces. In a medium bowl combine meat and steak seasoning; toss to coat. On eight 8-inch metal skewers, alternately thread meat pieces, mushrooms, and green onions, leaving ¼ inch between pieces.

two For a charcoal grill, grill kabobs on the rack of an uncovered grill directly over medium coals for 8 to 12 minutes for medium (160°F), turning once halfway through grilling. (For a gas grill, preheat grill. Reduce heat to medium. Place kabobs on grill rack over heat. Cover and grill as above.)

three Serve kabobs with salad dressing.

NUTRITION FACTS PER SERVING: 475 cal., 38 g total fat (8 g sat. fat), 79 mg chol., 1,071 mg sodium, 8 g carbo., 1 g fiber, 29 g pro.

Southwestern Steak Roll-Ups

PREP: 15 minutes **COOK:** Low 7 hours, High 3½ hours
MAKES: 4 servings

1   16-ounce package frozen pepper stir-fry vegetables (green, red, and yellow peppers and onions)

1   1-pound beef flank steak

1   14½-ounce can Mexican-style stewed tomatoes, undrained

2   teaspoons chili powder

1   small jalapeño chile pepper, seeded and finely chopped (see tip, below) (optional)

4   9- to 10-inch flour tortillas, warmed (see tip, page 16)

one Place frozen vegetables in a 3½- or 4-quart slow cooker. Trim fat from meat. If necessary, cut meat to fit into cooker. Place meat on top of vegetables. In a medium bowl stir together undrained tomatoes, chili powder, and, if desired, jalapeño pepper. Pour over meat in cooker.

two Cover and cook on low-heat setting for 7 to 8 hours or on high-heat setting for 3½ to 4 hours.

three Remove meat from cooker. Slice meat across the grain. Using a slotted spoon, remove vegetables from cooker. Divide meat and vegetables among warmed tortillas; roll up tortillas.

NUTRITION FACTS PER SERVING: 389 cal., 12 g total fat (5 g sat. fat), 46 mg chol., 647 mg sodium, 36 g carbo., 4 g fiber, 32 g pro.

Working with Hot Chile Peppers Hot chiles contain oils that will burn not only your tongue but your skin and eyes too if you're not careful. The best way to avoid burns is to wear rubber gloves or disposable plastic gloves. If you don't have gloves, simply cover your hands with small plastic bags.

If you do happen to get chile oil on your hands, wash them thoroughly with hot, soapy water. Flush your eyes with cool water if they become affected. Finally, clean your knives and cutting boards to keep from transferring the hot chile oil to other foods.

HEARTY BEEF, PORK & LAMB

Vegetable and Pastrami Panini

START TO FINISH: 15 minutes **MAKES:** 4 servings

- 4 thin slices provolone cheese (2 ounces)
- 8 ½-inch slices sourdough or Vienna bread
- 1 cup roasted or grilled vegetables from the deli or deli-marinated vegetables, coarsely chopped
- 4 thin slices pastrami (3 ounces)
- 1 tablespoon olive oil

one Place a cheese slice on 4 of the bread slices. Spread vegetables evenly over cheese. Top with pastrami and the remaining bread slices. Brush outsides of sandwiches with oil

two Heat a large nonstick skillet or griddle over medium heat. Cook sandwiches in hot skillet for 4 to 6 minutes or unt bread is golden brown and cheese melts, turning once. Cut each sandwich in half.

NUTRITION FACTS PER SERVING: 254 cal., 9 g total fat (3 g sat. fat), 30 mg chol., 658 mg sodium, 30 g carbo., 1 g fiber, 13 g pro.

Deli Roast Beef Sandwiches

START TO FINISH: 10 minutes **MAKES:** 2 servings

- 8 ounces thinly sliced deli roast beef
- 4 slices pumpernickel, rye, or whole wheat bread
- ½ cup deli coleslaw
    Herb-pepper seasoning

one Arrange the roast beef on 2 of the bread slices.

two Spread coleslaw evenly over roast beef; sprinkle with herb-pepper seasoning. Top with the remaining bread slices. Cut each sandwich in half.

NUTRITION FACTS PER SERVING: 369 cal., 8 g total fat (2 g sat. fat), 80 mg chol., 507 mg sodium, 34 g carbo., 5 g fiber, 39 g pro.

Reuben Loaves

PREP: 30 minutes **RISE:** 30 minutes **BAKE:** 25 minutes
MAKES: 10 servings

- 1 16-ounce package hot roll mix
- 1 cup bottled Thousand Island salad dressing
- 1 pound sliced cooked corned beef
- 2 cups shredded Swiss cheese (8 ounces)
- 1 14- to 16-ounce jar or can sauerkraut, rinsed
    and drained

one Prepare the hot roll mix according to package directions. Let rest for 5 minutes. Meanwhile, line a very large baking sheet with foil; grease foil. Set aside.

two Divide dough in half; roll each portion into a 12×8-inch rectangle. Spread ¼ cup of the dressing over each dough portion. Layer half of the corned beef, half of the cheese, and half of the sauerkraut on each dough portion to within 1 inch of the edges. Starting from a long side, roll each portion into a loaf. Brush edges with water; press to seal.

three Place loaves, seam sides down, on prepared baking sheet. Cover and let rise in a warm place for 30 minutes. Make 4 diagonal slits, ¼ inch deep, in the top of each loaf. Bake, uncovered, in a 375°F oven for 25 to 30 minutes or until golden brown. Serve with the remaining ¾ cup dressing.

NUTRITION FACTS PER SERVING: 492 cal., 27 g total fat (8 g sat. fat), 91 mg chol., 1,305 mg sodium, 41 g carbo., 1 g fiber, 22 g pro.

Middle Eastern Pitas

START TO FINISH: 10 minutes **MAKES:** 4 servings

- 1 7- or 8-ounce container roasted garlic-flavor hummus
- 4 pita bread rounds, halved crosswise
- 12 ounces thinly sliced deli roast beef
- ½ cup plain yogurt
- ½ cup chopped cucumber

one Spread hummus inside the pita bread halves. Fill pita halves with roast beef.

two In a small bowl stir together yogurt and cucumber. Spoon the yogurt mixture over roast beef in pita halves.

NUTRITION FACTS PER SERVING: 463 cal., 18 g total fat (5 g sat. fat), 70 mg chol., 735 mg sodium, 44 g carbo., 3 g fiber, 34 g pro.

Greek-Style Pitas

PREP: 15 minutes **CHILL:** 1 hour **MAKES:** 4 servings

- 1   cup deli creamy cucumber and onion salad
- ½   cup chopped tomato
- 1   teaspoon snipped fresh dill
- 4   whole wheat or white pita bread rounds, halved crosswise
- 12   ounces thinly sliced deli roast beef

one In a small bowl combine cucumber and onion salad, tomato, and dill. Cover and chill for 1 hour.

two Fill pita bread halves with roast beef. Spoon the salad mixture over roast beef in pita halves.

NUTRITION FACTS PER SERVING: 380 cal., 10 g total fat (3 g sat. fat), 82 mg chol., 427 mg sodium, 39 g carbo., 1 g fiber, 34 g pro.

Cheesy Reuben Potatoes

START TO FINISH: 25 minutes **MAKES:** 4 servings

- 1   8-ounce can sauerkraut, rinsed and drained (about 1 cup)
- 1   cup bottled Thousand Island salad dressing
- 4   medium baking potatoes (6 to 8 ounces each)
- 4   ounces sliced process Swiss cheese, halved diagonally
- 1   6-ounce package sliced cooked corned beef, cut into bite-size pieces (about 1 cup)

one In a medium bowl combine sauerkraut and salad dressing; set aside.

two Scrub potatoes and pierce with a fork. Arrange about 1 inch apart on a large microwave-safe plate. Microwave on 100 percent power (high) for 12 to 18 minutes or until tender, turning the potatoes after 6 minutes. Remove from oven. Cover with foil; let stand for 6 minutes. Cut each potato open.

three Top potatoes with half of the cheese, the sauerkraut mixture, and corned beef. Top with the remaining cheese. Microwave, uncovered, for 3 to 4 minutes more or until cheese melts, giving the dish a half-turn once.

NUTRITION FACTS PER SERVING: 566 cal., 36 g total fat (11 g sat. fat), 80 mg chol., 1,262 mg sodium, 39 g carbo., 4 g fiber, 25 g pro.

Hamburgers with Squished Tomato Topper

PREP: 10 minutes **GRILL:** 14 minutes **MAKES:** 4 servings

1½	pounds lean ground beef
2	ripe tomatoes, peeled and seeded
2	teaspoons olive oil
2	teaspoons balsamic vinegar
	Salt and black pepper
4	hamburger buns, split and toasted
	Lettuce leaves (optional)

one Shape ground beef into four ¾-inch-thick patties.

two For a charcoal grill, grill burgers on the rack of an uncovered grill directly over medium coals for 14 to 18 minutes or until done (160°F), turning once halfway through grilling. (For a gas grill, preheat grill. Reduce heat to medium. Place burgers on grill rack over heat. Cover and grill as above.)

three Meanwhile, for tomato topper, in a medium bowl mash tomatoes with a fork. Stir in olive oil and vinegar. Season to taste with salt and pepper. If desired, line buns with lettuce leaves. Serve burgers on buns with tomato topper.

NUTRITION FACTS PER SERVING: 429 cal., 20 g total fat (7 g sat. fat), 107 mg chol., 416 mg sodium, 25 g carbo., 2 g fiber, 35 g pro.

Bunless Burgers *See photo on page 115.*

PREP: 20 minutes **GRILL:** 18 minutes **MAKES:** 6 servings

2	pounds lean ground beef
8	ounces mild or hot bulk Italian sausage
12	1-inch pieces bottled roasted red sweet peppers
3	ounces Parmesan cheese, cut into 1×¼-inch slices
	Salt and black pepper
	Iceberg lettuce leaves
6	pear or cherry tomatoes (optional)

one In a large bowl combine ground beef and sausage. Shape meat mixture into 12 balls. On waxed paper, pat each ball into a 4-inch-diameter patty. Place a piece of roasted pepper in the center of 6 of the patties; top with Parmesan cheese slices and the remaining roasted pepper pieces. Top with the remaining meat patties; press gently to seal edges. Sprinkle with salt and black pepper.

two For a charcoal grill, arrange medium-hot coals around a drip pan. Test for medium heat above pan. Place burgers on grill rack over drip pan. Cover and grill for 18 to 22 minutes or until meat is done (160°F). (For a gas grill, preheat grill. Reduce heat to medium. Adjust for indirect cooking. Grill as above.)

three To serve, place each burger between a few lettuce leaves. If desired, use toothpicks to attach a tomato to each.

NUTRITION FACTS PER SERVING: 391 cal., 26 g total fat (11 g sat. fat), 107 mg chol., 604 mg sodium, 2 g carbo., 0 g fiber, 33 g pro.

Beer and Pretzel Burgers

PREP: 20 minutes **GRILL:** 14 minutes **MAKES:** 8 servings

⅔	cup beer or tomato juice
½	cup crushed pretzels
2	to 4 tablespoons finely chopped onion
2	tablespoons pickle relish (optional)
½	teaspoon salt
2½	pounds lean ground beef
8	hamburger buns, split and toasted

one In a large bowl combine beer, pretzels, onion, relish (if desired), and salt. Add ground beef; mix well. Shape meat mixture into eight ¾-inch-thick patties.

two For a charcoal grill, grill burgers on the rack of an uncovered grill directly over medium coals for 14 to 18 minutes or until done (160°F), turning once halfway through grilling. (For a gas grill, preheat grill. Reduce heat to medium. Place burgers on grill rack over heat. Cover and grill as above.) Serve burgers on buns.

NUTRITION FACTS PER SERVING: 379 cal., 15 g total fat (6 g sat. fat), 89 mg chol., 21 mg sodium, 26 g carbo., 1 g fiber, 30 g pro.

Gorgonzola- and Garlic-Stuffed Burgers

PREP: 20 minutes **GRILL:** 14 minutes **MAKES:** 4 servings

½	cup crumbled Gorgonzola cheese or other blue cheese
¼	cup snipped fresh basil
1	clove garlic, minced
1¼	pounds lean ground beef
	Salt and black pepper
4	kaiser rolls, split and toasted
1½	cups arugula or fresh spinach leaves (optional)
1	large tomato, sliced (optional)

one In a small bowl combine Gorgonzola cheese, basil, and garlic; shape into 4 slightly flattened mounds. Shape ground beef into eight ¼-inch-thick patties. Place a cheese mound in the center of 4 of the patties. Top with the remaining patties; press gently to seal edges. Sprinkle with salt and pepper.

two For a charcoal grill, grill burgers on the rack of an uncovered grill directly over medium coals for 14 to 18 minutes or until meat is done (160°F), turning once halfway through grilling. (For a gas grill, preheat grill. Reduce heat to medium. Place burgers on grill rack over heat. Cover and grill as above.)

three Serve burgers on kaiser rolls with, if desired, arugula and tomato.

NUTRITION FACTS PER SERVING: 448 cal., 20 g total fat (8 g sat. fat), 100 mg chol., 704 mg sodium, 31 g carbo., 1 g fiber, 34 g pro.

Bacon Cheeseburgers

PREP: 15 minutes **BROIL:** 11 minutes **MAKES:** 4 servings

1¼	pounds lean ground beef
8	thin slices co-jack or cheddar cheese (4 ounces)
4	slices bacon, crisp-cooked and crumbled
4	hamburger buns, split and toasted
¼	cup dairy sour cream French onion-flavor dip

one Shape ground beef into eight ¼-inch-thick patties. Place a cheese slice on 4 of the patties; sprinkle with crumbled bacon. Top with the remaining patties; press gently to seal edges.

two Place burgers on the unheated rack of a broiler pan. Broil 3 to 4 inches from the heat for 10 to 12 minutes or until done (160°F), turning once. Place the remaining cheese slices on top of burgers. Broil for 1 minute more.

three Meanwhile, spread cut sides of buns with onion dip. Serve burgers on buns.

NUTRITION FACTS PER SERVING: 635 cal., 41 g total fat (19 g sat. fat), 133 mg chol., 691 mg sodium, 25 g carbo., 1 g fiber, 37 g pro.

SLOW COOKER

Easy Goulash

PREP: 20 minutes **COOK:** Low 6 hours, High 3 hours
STAND: 5 minutes **MAKES:** 4 servings

1	pound lean ground beef
½	of a 28-ounce package (about 3½ cups) frozen diced hash brown potatoes with onions and peppers
1	15-ounce can tomato sauce
1	14½-ounce can diced tomatoes with basil, garlic, and oregano, undrained
½	cup shredded cheddar cheese (2 ounces)

one In a large skillet cook ground beef over medium-high heat until brown. Drain off fat.

two In a 3½- or 4-quart slow cooker combine meat, frozen potatoes, tomato sauce, and undrained tomatoes.

three Cover and cook on low-heat setting for 6 to 8 hours or on high-heat setting for 3 to 4 hours. Remove liner from cooker or turn off cooker. Sprinkle meat mixture with cheese. Let stand, covered, about 5 minutes or until cheese melts.

NUTRITION FACTS PER SERVING: 535 cal., 33 g total fat (14 g sat. fat), 109 mg chol., 1,371 mg sodium, 34 g carbo., 4 g fiber, 27 g pro.

Upside-Down Pizza Casserole

PREP: 20 minutes **BAKE:** 15 minutes **MAKES:** 5 servings

1½ pounds lean ground beef

1 15-ounce can Italian-style tomato sauce

1½ cups shredded mozzarella cheese
      (6 ounces)

1 10-ounce package (10) refrigerated biscuits

one In a large skillet cook ground beef over medium-high heat until brown. Drain off fat. Stir in tomato sauce; heat through.

two Transfer mixture to an ungreased 2-quart rectangular baking dish. Sprinkle with cheese. Flatten each biscuit with your hands; arrange the biscuits on top of casserole.

three Bake, uncovered, in a 400°F oven about 15 minutes or until biscuits are golden brown.

NUTRITION FACTS PER SERVING: 642 cal., 40 g total fat (16 g sat. fat), 116 mg chol., 1,102 mg sodium, 30 g carbo., 2 g fiber, 34 g pro.

SLOW COOKER

Tostadas

PREP: 15 minutes **COOK:** Low 3 hours, High 1½ hours
MAKES: 10 servings

2 pounds lean ground beef

2 1¼-ounce envelopes taco seasoning mix

1 16-ounce can refried beans

1 10¾-ounce can condensed fiesta nacho
      cheese soup

10 tostada shells

      Shredded lettuce, chopped tomatoes, dairy sour
      cream, and/or bottled salsa (optional)

one In a large skillet cook ground beef over medium-high heat until brown. Drain off fat. Add taco seasoning mix to meat and continue preparing according to package directions.

two Transfer seasoned meat mixture to a 3½- or 4-quart slow cooker. Stir in refried beans and soup.

three Cover and cook on low-heat setting for 3 to 4 hours or on high-heat setting for 1½ to 2 hours. Serve meat mixture on tostada shells. If desired, top with lettuce, tomatoes, sour cream, and/or salsa.

NUTRITION FACTS PER SERVING: 347 cal., 20 g total fat (6 g sat. fat), 65 mg chol., 1,198 mg sodium, 21 g carbo., 4 g fiber, 24 g pro.

Beefy Shepherd's Pie

PREP: 20 minutes **COOK:** Low 6 hours, High 3 hours
MAKES: 8 servings

- 2   pounds lean ground beef
- 1   cup chopped onion
- 1   16-ounce package frozen mixed vegetables
- 2   10¾-ounce cans condensed tomato soup
- 8   servings refrigerated or frozen mashed potatoes

Avoid Lid Lifting Savory aroma wafting through the kitchen has tempted many to lift the lid of a slow cooker for a closer scent. Resist! Lost low heat isn't quickly regained. If stirring or adding an ingredient requires lid lifting, get the cover back on ASAP. And if you lift the lid without the recipe telling you to do so, extend the cooking time by about 30 minutes..

one In a large skillet cook ground beef and onion over medium-high heat until meat is brown and onion is tender. Drain off fat.

two In a 3½- or 4-quart slow cooker combine meat mixture, frozen mixed vegetables, and soup.

three Cover and cook on low-heat setting for 6 to 8 hours or on high-heat setting for 3 to 4 hours.

four Meanwhile, prepare mashed potatoes according to package directions. Serve meat mixture with potatoes.

NUTRITION FACTS PER SERVING: 575 cal., 27 g total fat (13 g sat. fat), 106 mg chol., 836 mg sodium, 51 g carbo., 7 g fiber, 32 g pro.

Cacciatore-Style Penne

START TO FINISH: 30 minutes **MAKES:** 6 servings

- 1   pound dried penne pasta
- 8   ounces lean ground beef or bulk Italian sausage
- ¾   cup chopped green sweet pepper
- 1   14-ounce jar pasta sauce
- 1   4½-ounce can (drained weight) sliced mushrooms, drained

one Cook pasta according to package directions; drain. Return to hot pan; cover and keep warm.

two Meanwhile, in a large skillet cook ground beef and sweet pepper over medium-high heat until meat is brown and pepper is tender. Drain off fat. Stir in pasta sauce and mushrooms; heat through.

three In a large serving bowl toss meat mixture with hot cooked pasta.

NUTRITION FACTS PER SERVING: 420 cal., 10 g total fat (3 g sat. fat), 27 mg chol., 580 mg sodium, 63 g carbo., 4 g fiber, 18 g pro.

Mexican-Stuffed Sweet Peppers

PREP: 25 minutes **COOK:** Low 6 hours, High 3 hours
MAKES: 4 servings

4	medium green, red, and/or yellow sweet peppers
1	pound lean ground beef or ground pork
1	16-ounce jar bottled black bean salsa or chunky salsa
1½	cups shredded Monterey Jack cheese with jalapeño peppers or Monterey Jack cheese (6 ounces)
1	cup uncooked instant white rice
1	cup water

one Remove tops of sweet peppers; scoop out membranes and seeds. Set aside.

two For filling, in a large skillet cook ground meat over medium-high heat until brown. Drain off fat. Stir in salsa, 1 cup of the cheese, and the rice. Spoon filling into peppers, mounding as needed.

three Pour the water into a 4½- or 5-quart slow cooker. Arrange stuffed peppers, filling sides up, in cooker.

four Cover and cook on low-heat setting for 6 to 7 hours or on high-heat setting for 3 to 3½ hours. Transfer peppers to a serving platter. Sprinkle with the remaining ½ cup cheese.

NUTRITION FACTS PER SERVING: 513 cal., 24 g total fat (12 g sat. fat), 109 mg chol., 1,060 mg sodium, 38 g carbo., 2 g fiber, 37 g pro.

Cheesy Sloppy Joes

PREP: 20 minutes **COOK:** Low 4½ hours, High 2½ hours
MAKES: 16 servings

2½	pounds lean ground beef
1	cup chopped onion
2	10¾-ounce cans condensed fiesta nacho cheese soup
¾	cup ketchup
16	hamburger buns, split and toasted

one In a 12-inch skillet cook ground beef and onion over medium-high heat until meat is brown and onion is tender. Drain off fat.

two In a 3½- or 4-quart slow cooker combine meat mixture, soup, and ketchup.

three Cover and cook on low-heat setting for 4½ to 5 hours or on high-heat setting for 2½ to 3 hours. Serve meat mixture on toasted buns.

NUTRITION FACTS PER SERVING: 389 cal., 22 g total fat (9 g sat. fat), 63 mg chol., 680 mg sodium, 29 g carbo., 2 g fiber, 17 g pro.

Saucy Meatball Sandwiches *See photo on page 115.*

START TO FINISH: 20 minutes **MAKES:** 6 servings

1	16-ounce package (32) frozen cooked Italian-style meatballs
1	26- to 28-ounce jar red pasta sauce
½	cup coarsely chopped green sweet pepper
6	French-style rolls, split and toasted
1	cup shredded Italian cheese blend (4 ounces)

one In a large saucepan combine frozen meatballs, pasta sauce, and sweet pepper. Bring to boiling; reduce heat. Simmer, covered, about 10 minutes or until meatballs are heated through, stirring occasionally.

two Spoon hot meatball mixture onto bottom halves of rolls. Spoon any remaining sauce over the meatballs. Sprinkle with cheese. Replace tops of rolls.

NUTRITION FACTS PER SERVING: 467 cal., 26 g total fat (12 g sat. fat), 68 mg chol., 1,359 mg sodium, 34 g carbo., 6 g fiber, 24 g pro.

Taco Pizza

PREP: 15 minutes **BAKE:** 20 minutes **MAKES:** 6 servings

8	ounces lean ground beef and/or bulk pork sausage
¾	cup chopped green sweet pepper
1	11½-ounce package refrigerated corn bread twists
½	cup bottled salsa
3	cups shredded taco cheese blend (12 ounces)

one In a medium skillet cook ground meat and sweet pepper over medium-high heat until meat is brown and pepper is tender. Drain off fat. Set aside.

two Unroll corn bread dough (do not separate into strips). Press dough into the bottom and up the side of a greased 12-inch pizza pan. Spread salsa over dough. Sprinkle with meat mixture and cheese.

three Bake, uncovered, in a 400°F oven about 20 minutes or until bottom of crust is golden brown. Cut into wedges.

NUTRITION FACTS PER SERVING: 465 cal., 30 g total fat (15 g sat. fat), 73 mg chol., 870 mg sodium, 27 g carbo., 1 g fiber, 22 g pro.

Veal Rolls Stuffed with Herb Cheese *See photo on page 118.*

PREP: 25 minutes   **GRILL:** 20 minutes   **MAKES:** 4 servings

- 1   1-pound boneless veal round steak
- 4   ounces haricots verts or tiny young green beans, trimmed
- 4   tablespoons semisoft cheese with garlic and herbs
- 4   slices prosciutto (about 2½ ounces)
- 2   tablespoons butter or margarine, melted

one Trim fat from meat. Cut meat into 4 serving-size pieces. Place each between 2 pieces of plastic wrap. Working from center to edges, use the flat side of a meat mallet to pound meat to ¼-inch thickness. Remove plastic wrap.

two In a covered small saucepan cook beans in a small amount of boiling, lightly salted water for 4 minutes; drain.

three Spread each piece of meat with 1 tablespoon of the cheese. Top with one-fourth of the beans and a slice of prosciutto (trim beans and fold prosciutto to fit if necessary). Fold in sides; roll up meat. Secure with wooden toothpicks or small metal skewers. Brush rolls with melted butter.

four For a charcoal grill, arrange medium-hot coals around a drip pan. Test for medium heat above the pan. Place meat rolls on grill rack over drip pan. Cover and grill for 20 to 24 minutes for medium (160°F), turning once halfway through grilling. (For a gas grill, preheat grill. Reduce heat to medium. Adjust for indirect cooking. Grill as above.)

five To serve, remove toothpicks or skewers from meat rolls.

NUTRITION FACTS PER SERVING: 245 cal., 12 g total fat (7 g sat. fat), 117 mg chol., 641 mg sodium, 2 g carbo., 1 g fiber, 30 g pro.

Charcoal Grill Features Large, kettle-type charcoal grills are often less expensive than gas grills, are able to cook hotter, and do a super job with a wide range of foods. That's why they're a popular choice with many backyard grillmeisters. When looking for a charcoal grill, avoid the small, portable, lidless type because those are designed mainly for direct grilling, not barbecuing with indirect heat.

In a kettle-type grill, look for vents on both top and bottom, which are crucial for controlling the cooking temperature. Also, favor a grill with a heavy, tight-fitting lid and solid construction.

Veal Chops with Apples

PREP: 10 minutes **MARINATE:** 6 to 24 hours
GRILL: 10 minutes **MAKES:** 4 servings

- 4 boneless veal top loin chops, cut ¾ inch thick
- ½ cup dry white wine
- 2 tablespoons cooking oil
- 2 teaspoons dried sage, crushed
- ½ teaspoon salt
- ½ teaspoon black pepper
- 2 medium tart cooking apples

one Trim fat from chops. Place chops in a resealable plastic bag set in a shallow dish. For marinade, in a small bowl combine wine, oil, sage, salt, and pepper. Pour over chops; seal bag. Marinate in the refrigerator for 6 to 24 hours, turning bag occasionally.

two Drain chops, reserving marinade. Just before grilling, core apples; cut crosswise into 1-inch slices.

three For a charcoal grill, grill chops and apple slices on the rack of an uncovered grill directly over medium coals for 10 to 12 minutes for medium (160°F), turning and brushing chops and apple slices once with marinade halfway through grilling. (For a gas grill, preheat grill. Reduce heat to medium. Place chops and apple slices on grill rack over heat. Cover and grill as above.) Discard any remaining marinade.

NUTRITION FACTS PER SERVING: 271 cal., 13 g total fat (3 g sat. fat), 95 mg chol., 354 mg sodium, 9 g carbo., 1 g fiber, 24 g pro.

Veal Chops with Ginger Butter

PREP: 15 minutes **GRILL:** 12 minutes **MAKES:** 4 servings

- ¼ cup butter, softened
- 2 tablespoons chopped crystallized ginger
- 1 tablespoon chopped shallot
- 1 tablespoon snipped fresh tarragon
- 4 veal loin chops, cut about 1 inch thick
  Salt and black pepper

one In a small bowl combine butter, ginger, shallot, and tarragon; set butter mixture aside.

two Trim fat from chops. Sprinkle chops with salt and pepper. For a charcoal grill, grill chops on the rack of an uncovered grill directly over medium coals for 12 to 15 minutes for medium (160°F), turning once halfway through grilling. (For a gas grill, preheat grill. Reduce heat to medium. Place chops on grill rack over heat. Cover and grill as above.)

three To serve, top each chop with 1 tablespoon of the butter mixture.

NUTRITION FACTS PER SERVING: 251 cal., 16 g total fat (9 g sat. fat), 123 mg chol., 358 mg sodium, 3 g carbo., 0 g fiber, 23 g pro.

Veal Osso Buco

PREP: 20 minutes **COOK:** Low 8 hours, High 4 hours
MAKES: 4 to 6 servings

- 4   to 6 veal shank cross cuts (2½ to 3 pounds)
    Salt and black pepper (optional)
- ¼   cup all-purpose flour
- 2   tablespoons cooking oil
- 2   14½-ounce cans diced tomatoes with basil, garlic, and oregano, undrained
- ½   cup dry red wine
- 1   recipe Gremolata (optional)
- 2   to 3 cups hot cooked rice (optional)

one If desired, sprinkle meat with salt and pepper. Place flour in a shallow dish. Dip meat into flour to coat. In a large skillet cook meat, half at a time, in hot oil over medium-high heat until brown, turning to cook evenly. Drain off fat.

two Place meat in a 3½- or 4-quart slow cooker. Pour undrained tomatoes and red wine over meat. Cover and cook on low-heat setting for 8 to 9 hours or on high-heat setting for 4 to 4½ hours.

three Using a slotted spoon, transfer meat and tomatoes to a serving dish. Discard cooking liquid. If desired, sprinkle with Gremolata and serve with hot cooked rice.

NUTRITION FACTS PER SERVING: 397 cal., 9 g total fat (2 g sat. fat), 163 mg chol., 1,249 mg sodium, 25 g carbo., 2 g fiber, 46 g pro.

Gremolata: In a small bowl stir together ½ cup snipped fresh parsley, 2 teaspoons finely shredded lemon peel, and 2 cloves garlic, minced.

Pork with Cider and Cream

START TO FINISH: 25 minutes **MAKES:** 4 servings

- 1   12-ounce pork tenderloin
- 2   tablespoons butter or margarine
- ½   cup whipping cream
- 1   4½-ounce can (drained weight) whole mushrooms, drained
- 2   tablespoons Calvados, applejack, brandy, or apple juice

one Trim fat from meat. Cut meat into 1-inch slices. Place each slice between 2 pieces of plastic wrap. Using the heel of your hand, press meat until ½ inch thick. Remove plastic wrap.

two In a large skillet cook meat in melted butter over medium-high heat for 6 to 8 minutes or until meat is slightly pink in center and juices run clear, turning once. Transfer to a serving platter; cover and keep warm.

three For sauce, stir whipping cream, mushrooms, and Calvados into drippings in skillet. Bring to boiling; reduce heat. Simmer, uncovered, for 3 to 5 minutes or until slightly thickened. Serve sauce over meat.

NUTRITION FACTS PER SERVING: 279 cal., 20 g total fat (12 g sat. fat), 112 mg chol., 183 mg sodium, 2 g carbo., 0 g fiber, 19 g pro.

Peachy Pork Tenderloin

PREP: 10 minutes **MARINATE:** 4 to 24 hours **GRILL:** 30 minutes
STAND: 10 minutes **MAKES:** 4 servings

1 12-ounce pork tenderloin
⅓ cup peach nectar
3 tablespoons teriyaki sauce
2 tablespoons snipped fresh rosemary or
   2 teaspoons dried rosemary, crushed
1 tablespoon olive oil

one Trim fat from meat. Place meat in a resealable plastic bag set in a shallow dish. For marinade, in a small bowl combine peach nectar, teriyaki sauce, rosemary, and oil. Pour marinade over meat; seal bag. Marinate in the refrigerator for 4 to 24 hours, turning bag occasionally.

two Drain meat, discarding marinade. For a charcoal grill, arrange hot coals around a drip pan. Test for medium-hot heat above pan. Place meat on grill rack over pan. Cover and grill for 30 to 35 minutes or until a meat thermometer registers 155°F. (For a gas grill, preheat grill. Reduce heat to medium-high. Adjust for indirect cooking. Grill as above.)

three Remove meat from grill. Cover with foil and let stand for 10 minutes before slicing. (The meat's temperature will rise 5°F during standing.)

NUTRITION FACTS PER SERVING: 162 cal., 7 g total fat (2 g sat. fat), 60 mg chol., 285 mg sodium, 6 g carbo., 0 g fiber, 19 g pro.

Soy and Sesame Pork

PREP: 10 minutes **MARINATE:** 4 to 24 hours **ROAST:** 45 minutes
MAKES: 4 servings

1 1-pound pork tenderloin
¼ cup reduced-sodium soy sauce
1 tablespoon ketchup
¼ teaspoon garlic powder
2 to 3 tablespoons sesame seeds, toasted
   (see tip, page 280)

one Trim fat from meat. Place meat in a resealable plastic bag set in a shallow dish. For marinade, in a small bowl combine soy sauce, ketchup, and garlic powder. Pour marinade over meat; seal bag. Marinate in the refrigerator for 4 to 24 hours, turning bag occasionally.

two Drain meat, discarding marinade. Place meat on a rack in a shallow roasting pan. Roast, uncovered, in a 325°F oven for 45 to 60 minutes or until a thermometer registers 155°F. Cover meat with foil and let stand for 10 minutes. (The meat's temperature will rise 5°F during standing.)

three Sprinkle sesame seeds onto a piece of foil. Carefully roll meat in sesame seeds. Cut meat into thin slices.

NUTRITION FACTS PER SERVING: 162 cal., 5 g total fat (1 g sat. fat), 73 mg chol., 357 mg sodium, 2 g carbo., 1 g fiber, 25 g pro.

Pork Medallions with Cherry Sauce

START TO FINISH: 20 minutes   **MAKES:** 4 servings

- 1 1-pound pork tenderloin
  Salt and black pepper
  Nonstick cooking spray
- ¾ cup cranberry juice or apple juice
- 2 teaspoons spicy brown mustard
- 1 teaspoon cornstarch
- 1 cup sweet cherries (such as Rainier or Bing), halved and pitted, or 1 cup frozen unsweetened pitted dark sweet cherries, thawed

one Trim fat from meat. Cut meat into 1-inch slices. Place each slice between 2 pieces of plastic wrap. Using the heel of your hand, press meat until ½ inch thick. Remove plastic wrap. Sprinkle meat with salt and pepper.

two Coat a large nonstick skillet with cooking spray; heat over medium-high heat. Cook meat in hot skillet for 6 to 8 minutes or until meat is slightly pink in center and juices run clear, turning once. Transfer to a serving platter; cover and keep warm.

three For sauce, in a small bowl combine cranberry juice, mustard, and cornstarch; add to skillet. Cook and stir until thickened and bubbly. Cook and stir for 2 minutes more. Stir in cherries. Serve meat with sauce.

NUTRITION FACTS PER SERVING: 197 cal., 5 g total fat (2 g sat. fat), 81 mg chol., 127 mg sodium, 12 g carbo., 0 g fiber, 26 g pro.

Pork Tenderloin with Sweet Potatoes

START TO FINISH: 25 minutes **MAKES:** 4 servings

- 1 12-ounce pork tenderloin
- 1 large onion, cut into wedges
- 1 tablespoon cooking oil
- 1 20-ounce package frozen candied sweet potatoes, thawed
- 1 tablespoon snipped fresh thyme or ½ teaspoon dried thyme, crushed

one Trim fat from meat. Cut meat into ½-inch slices. In a large skillet cook meat and onion in hot oil over medium-high heat for 6 to 8 minutes or until meat is slightly pink in center and juices run clear, turning once. Remove meat from skillet; set aside.

two Add sweet potatoes with sauce and dried thyme, if using, to onion in skillet. Bring to boiling; reduce heat. Cook, covered, over medium heat about 10 minutes or until potatoes are tender. Return meat to skillet; heat through. Stir in fresh thyme, if using.

NUTRITION FACTS PER SERVING: 386 cal., 13 g total fat (2 g sat. fat), 55 mg chol., 484 mg sodium, 44 g carbo., 4 g fiber, 20 g pro.

Pork Loin with Vegetables

PREP: 15 minutes **ROAST:** 35 minutes **STAND:** 10 minutes
MAKES: 4 servings

2½ cups packaged peeled baby carrots
12 ounces tiny new potatoes, quartered
1 12- to 16-ounce pork tenderloin
⅔ cup apricot preserves
¼ cup white wine vinegar or white vinegar

one In a medium saucepan cook carrots and potatoes in a small amount of boiling water for 4 minutes; drain. Meanwhile, trim fat from meat. Place meat in a 13×9×2-inch baking pan. Arrange carrots and potatoes around meat. Roast, uncovered, in a 425°F oven for 20 minutes.

two In a small bowl stir together preserves and vinegar; brush some of the mixture over meat. Drizzle the remaining preserves mixture over vegetables; toss to coat. Roast, uncovered, about 15 minutes more or until a thermometer inserted in meat registers 155°F and vegetables are tender. Stir vegetable mixture.

three Cover meat and vegetables and let stand for 10 minutes. (The meat's temperature will rise 5°F during standing.) Slice meat; arrange slices on a serving platter. Using a slotted spoon, transfer vegetables to the serving platter. Drizzle pan juices over meat and vegetables.

NUTRITION FACTS PER SERVING: 365 cal., 2 g total fat (1 g sat. fat), 50 mg chol., 84 mg sodium, 62 g carbo., 5 g fiber, 23 g pro.

Pork Medallions with Apples

START TO FINISH: 15 minutes **MAKES:** 4 servings

1 1-pound pork tenderloin
2 cloves garlic, minced
2 tablespoons olive oil or butter
1 20-ounce can sliced apples, drained
2 teaspoons fresh snipped thyme or
   ½ teaspoon dried thyme, crushed

one Trim fat from meat. Cut meat into ½-inch slices. In a 12-inch skillet cook and stir garlic in hot oil over medium-high heat for 15 seconds.

two Add meat to skillet. Cook for 6 to 8 minutes or until meat is slightly pink in center and juices run clear, turning once. Add sliced apples and thyme. Cook, covered, about 1 minute more or until apples are heated through.

NUTRITION FACTS PER SERVING: 292 cal., 11 g total fat (2 g sat. fat), 73 mg chol., 61 mg sodium, 24 g carbo., 2 g fiber, 24 g pro.

Rhubarb-Glazed Pork Roast

PREP: 15 minutes **COOK:** 20 minutes **GRILL:** 1¼ hours
STAND: 15 minutes **MAKES:** 6 servings

- 2 cups fresh or frozen sliced rhubarb
- 1 6-ounce can (⅔ cup) frozen apple juice concentrate
  Several drops red food coloring (optional)
- 2 tablespoons honey
- 1 3- to 4-pound pork loin center rib roast (4 ribs), backbone loosened

one For glaze, in a medium saucepan combine rhubarb, juice concentrate, and, if desired, food coloring. Bring to boiling; reduce heat. Simmer, covered, for 15 to 20 minutes or until rhubarb is very tender.

two Strain mixture into a small bowl, pressing out liquid with the back of a spoon; discard pulp. Return rhubarb liquid to saucepan. Bring to boiling; reduce heat. Simmer, uncovered, about 5 minutes or until reduced to ½ cup. Remove saucepan from heat; stir in honey. Set aside ¼ cup of the glaze to use for basting. Reserve the remaining glaze until ready to serve.

three Meanwhile, trim fat from meat. Insert a meat thermometer into center of meat without touching bone.

four For a charcoal grill, arrange medium coals around a drip pan. Test for medium-low heat above pan. Place meat, bone side down, on grill rack over pan. Cover and grill for 1¼ to 2 hours or until thermometer registers 150°F, brushing occasionally with the ¼ cup glaze during the last 15 minutes of grilling. (For a gas grill, preheat grill. Reduce heat to medium-low. Adjust for indirect cooking. Grill as above.)

five Remove meat from grill. Cover with foil and let stand for 15 minutes before slicing. (The meat's temperature will rise 10°F during standing.) Reheat and pass the remaining glaze.

NUTRITION FACTS PER SERVING: 266 cal., 7 g total fat (3 g sat. fat), 71 mg chol., 56 mg sodium, 19 g carbo., 0 g fiber, 29 g pro.

Types of Thermometers In the quest for roasted or grilled meat perfection, there's no handier tool than a good meat thermometer. Two common, useful types are the oven-/grill-safe thermometer and the instant-read thermometer.

Oven-/grill-safe thermometers are meant to remain in the food the entire time it cooks. They work best with large items such as roasts or whole poultry.

Instant-read thermometers are available in both digital and dial versions and are not designed to remain in food while it cooks. But because they can measure temperatures in just 10 to 20 seconds, they're easy to remove and reinsert as needed. This type of thermometer is particularly nice to use for thin foods, when it's necessary to insert the thermometer sideways.

For the most accurate reading, always insert any meat thermometer into the thickest part of the meat and away from any bones or fat.

Cranberry Pork Roast

PREP: 35 minutes **COOK:** Low 8 hours, High 4 hours
MAKES: 6 servings

1   2½- to 3-pound boneless pork shoulder roast
    Nonstick cooking spray
1   16-ounce package frozen stew vegetables
1   16-ounce can whole cranberry sauce
½   cup bottled chili sauce

one Trim fat from meat. Lightly coat a large skillet with cooking spray; heat over medium heat. Cook meat in hot skillet until brown on all sides.

two Place meat in a 3½- or 4-quart slow cooker. Top with frozen vegetables. In a small bowl stir together cranberry sauce and chili sauce. Pour over meat and vegetables.

three Cover and cook on low-heat setting for 8 to 9 hours or on high-heat setting for 4 to 4½ hours. Transfer meat and vegetables to a serving platter; cover and keep warm.

four Strain cooking liquid and skim off fat. In a medium saucepan bring cooking liquid to boiling; reduce heat. Simmer, uncovered, about 20 minutes or until thickened and the volume is reduced by half. Pass with meat and vegetables.

NUTRITION FACTS PER SERVING: 494 cal., 16 g total fat (5 g sat. fat), 140 mg chol., 833 mg sodium, 44 g carbo., 2 g fiber, 41 g pro.

Pork Roast with Apricot Glaze

PREP: 15 minutes **COOK:** Low 10 hours, High 5 hours
MAKES: 6 to 8 servings

1   3- to 3½-pound boneless pork shoulder roast
1   18-ounce jar apricot preserves
1   cup chopped onion
¼   cup chicken broth
2   tablespoons Dijon-style mustard

one Trim fat from meat. If necessary, cut meat to fit into a 3½- or 4-quart slow cooker. Place meat in cooker. For glaze, in a small bowl combine apricot preserves, onion, broth, and mustard. Pour over meat.

two Cover and cook on low-heat setting for 10 to 12 hours or on high-heat setting for 5 to 6 hours. Transfer meat to a serving platter. Skim fat from glaze. Spoon some of the glaze over the meat. Discard any remaining glaze.

NUTRITION FACTS PER SERVING: 456 cal., 10 g total fat (3 g sat. fat), 93 mg chol., 184 mg sodium, 61 g carbo., 2 g fiber, 29 g pro.

HEARTY BEEF, PORK & LAMB

Italian Rolled Pork Roast

PREP: 25 minutes **GRILL:** 1½ hours **STAND:** 15 minutes
MAKES: 10 to 12 servings

- 1   3- to 4-pound boneless pork shoulder blade roast (rolled and tied)
- ½   cup snipped fresh parsley
- 1½   teaspoons fennel seeds, crushed
- 1½   teaspoons cracked black pepper
- 2   cloves garlic, minced
- ¾   teaspoon salt

one Untie meat. Trim fat from meat. Using a sharp knife, cut several 1-inch slits all over the meat.

two For rub, in a small bowl combine parsley, fennel seeds, pepper, garlic, and salt. Press some of the rub into the slits with your fingers. Sprinkle the remaining rub evenly over the entire meat; rub in with your fingers. Retie meat with 100-percent-cotton kitchen string. Insert a meat thermometer into center of meat.

three For a charcoal grill, arrange medium coals around a drip pan. Test for medium-low heat above pan. Place meat on grill rack over pan. Cover and grill for 1½ to 2¼ hours or until meat thermometer registers 155°F. (For a gas grill, preheat grill. Reduce heat to medium-low. Adjust for indirect cooking. Grill as above.)

four Remove meat from grill. Cover with foil and let stand for 15 minutes before slicing. (The meat's temperature will rise 5°F during standing.)

NUTRITION FACTS PER SERVING: 208 cal., 10 g total fat (3 g sat. fat), 92 mg chol., 253 mg sodium, 1 g carbo., 0 g fiber, 27 g pro.

Gas Grill Safety Check In addition to periodically reviewing your grill's safety manual, be vigilant about the following:

- Watch for gas leaks. Brush soapy water on all joints and fittings—bubbles indicate a leak. Don't light the grill until the leak is fixed.
- Check hoses for cracks and brittleness—replace hoses that show either. Keep hoses away from heat and hot surfaces.
- Follow the safe transport and storage directions on your propane tank. Always remember that tanks can leak or explode if not handled properly.

Ranch Pork Roast

PREP: 15 minutes **COOK:** Low 9 hours, High 4½ hours
MAKES: 6 servings

1 2½- to 3-pound boneless pork shoulder roast
   Nonstick cooking spray
1 pound tiny new potatoes, halved
1 10¾-ounce can condensed cream of chicken soup
1 8-ounce package cream cheese, cubed and softened
1 0.4-ounce envelope ranch dry salad dressing mix

one Trim fat from meat. Lightly coat a large skillet with cooking spray; heat over medium heat. Cook meat in hot skillet until brown on all sides.

two Place potatoes in a 3½- or 4-quart slow cooker. Place meat on top of potatoes. In a medium bowl whisk together soup, cream cheese, and salad dressing mix. Pour over meat and potatoes in cooker.

three Cover and cook on low-heat setting for 9 to 10 hours or on high-heat setting for 4½ to 5 hours.

NUTRITION FACTS PER SERVING: 521 cal., 31 g total fat (15 g sat. fat), 173 mg chol., 757 mg sodium, 16 g carbo., 1 g fiber, 42 g pro.

Apricot Pulled Pork

PREP: 20 minutes **COOK:** Low 8 hours, High 4 hours
MAKES: 6 to 8 servings

   Nonstick cooking spray
1 3- to 3½-pound boneless pork shoulder roast
1 10-ounce jar apricot spreadable fruit
1 cup bottled hot-style barbecue sauce
½ cup chopped sweet onion
½ cup snipped dried apricots

one Lightly coat a 3½- or 4-quart slow cooker with cooking spray. Trim fat from meat. If necessary, cut meat to fit into cooker. Place meat in the prepared cooker. For sauce, in a medium bowl combine spreadable fruit, barbecue sauce, onion, and dried apricots. Pour over meat in cooker.

two Cover and cook on low-heat setting for 8 to 10 hours or on high-heat setting for 4 to 5 hours.

three Transfer meat to a cutting board. Using 2 forks, shred meat into bite-size pieces. In a large bowl combine meat and enough of the sauce to moisten. Pass the remaining sauce.

NUTRITION FACTS PER SERVING: 535 cal., 19 g total fat (7 g sat. fat), 166 mg chol., 513 mg sodium, 42 g carbo., 2 g fiber, 49 g pro.

Shredded Pork Barbecue Rolls *See photo on page 121.*

PREP: 10 minutes **COOK:** Low 10 hours, High 5 hours
MAKES: 16 servings

- 1   4- to 5-pound pork shoulder blade roast
- ¾   cup cider vinegar
- 2   tablespoons packed brown sugar
- ½   teaspoon salt
- ½   teaspoon crushed red pepper
- ¼   teaspoon black pepper
- 16 kaiser rolls, split and toasted
     Deli coleslaw (optional)

one Trim fat from meat. Cut meat to fit into a 4- to 6-quart slow cooker. Place meat in cooker. In a small bowl combine vinegar, brown sugar, salt, crushed red pepper, and black pepper. Pour over meat.

two Cover and cook on low-heat setting for 10 to 12 hours or on high-heat setting for 5 to 6 hours.

three Transfer meat to a cutting board, reserving cooking liquid. When cool enough to handle, cut meat off bones. Using 2 forks, shred meat into bite-size pieces. In a medium bowl combine meat and enough of the cooking liquid to moisten. Spoon meat onto bottoms of rolls. If desired, top with coleslaw. Replace tops of rolls.

NUTRITION FACTS PER SERVING: 324 cal., 9 g total fat (3 g sat. fat), 68 mg chol., 458 mg sodium, 32 g carbo., 1 g fiber, 27 g pro.

Honey-Mustard Pork Tenderloin Sandwiches

PREP: 10 minutes **GRILL:** 7 minutes **MAKES:** 4 servings

- 1   1-pound pork tenderloin
     Black pepper
- 2   tablespoons honey
- 2   tablespoons Dijon-style mustard
- 4   kaiser rolls or hamburger buns, split and toasted
- ¼   cup mayonnaise or salad dressing
- 4   tomato slices (optional)

one Trim fat from meat. Cut meat into ¾-inch slices. Sprinkle meat with pepper. For glaze, in a small bowl combine honey and mustard; set aside.

two For a charcoal grill, grill meat slices on the rack of an uncovered grill directly over medium coals for 7 to 9 minutes or until slightly pink in center and juices run clear (160°F), turning and brushing once with glaze halfway through grilling. (For a gas grill, preheat grill. Reduce heat to medium. Place meat slices on grill rack over heat. Cover and grill as above.)

three Serve meat slices on rolls with mayonnaise and, if desired, tomato slices.

NUTRITION FACTS PER SERVING: 440 cal., 17 g total fat (4 g sat. fat), 78 mg chol., 617 mg sodium, 40 g carbo., 1 g fiber, 31 g pro.

Maple-Pecan Pork Chops

START TO FINISH: 15 minutes **MAKES:** 4 servings

- 4 boneless pork loin chops, cut ¾ inch thick
  Salt and black pepper
- 4 tablespoons butter or margarine, softened
- 2 tablespoons maple syrup
- ⅓ cup chopped pecans, toasted (see tip, page 280)

one Trim fat from chops. Sprinkle both sides of chops with salt and pepper.

two In a 12-inch skillet cook chops in 1 tablespoon melted butter over medium-high heat for 8 to 12 minutes or until chops are slightly pink in center and juices run clear (160°F), turning once. Transfer chops to a serving platter.

three Meanwhile, in a small bowl combine the remaining 3 tablespoons butter and the maple syrup. Spread butter mixture evenly over chops. Let stand about 1 minute or until butter mixture melts. Sprinkle with pecans.

NUTRITION FACTS PER SERVING: 333 cal., 23 g total fat (10 g sat. fat), 98 mg chol., 310 mg sodium, 8 g carbo., 1 g fiber, 23 g pro.

GRILLING

Cranberry-Chipotle Pork Chops *See photo on page 119.*

PREP: 10 minutes **GRILL:** 35 minutes **MAKES:** 4 servings

- 4 pork loin chops, cut 1¼ inches thick
- 1 8-ounce can jellied cranberry sauce
- ⅓ cup apricot or peach preserves or apricot or peach spreadable fruit
- ¼ cup chopped onion (optional)
- 1 tablespoon lemon juice or cider vinegar
- 1 canned chipotle pepper in adobo sauce or 1 fresh jalapeño chile pepper, seeded and chopped (see tip, page 59)

one Trim fat from chops. For a charcoal grill, arrange medium-hot coals around a drip pan. Test for medium heat above pan. Place chops on grill rack over pan. Cover and grill for 35 to 40 minutes or until chops are slightly pink in center and juices run clear (160°F), turning once halfway through grilling. (For a gas grill, preheat grill. Reduce heat to medium. Adjust for indirect cooking. Grill as above.)

two Meanwhile, for sauce, in a small saucepan combine cranberry sauce, preserves, onion (if desired), lemon juice, and chipotle pepper. Bring to boiling, stirring constantly; reduce heat. Simmer, uncovered, for 5 minutes, stirring occasionally.

three To serve, brush chops with some of the sauce. Pass the remaining sauce.

NUTRITION FACTS PER SERVING: 445 cal., 10 g total fat (4 g sat. fat), 105 mg chol., 113 mg sodium, 39 g carbo., 1 g fiber, 43 g pro.

Lemon-and-Herb-Rubbed Pork Chops

PREP: 15 minutes **GRILL:** 35 minutes **MAKES:** 4 servings

8	cloves garlic, minced
1½	teaspoons finely shredded lemon peel
1	teaspoon dried rosemary, crushed
½	teaspoon salt
½	teaspoon dried sage, crushed
½	teaspoon black pepper
4	pork loin chops, cut 1¼ inches thick

one For rub, in a small bowl combine garlic, lemon peel, rosemary, salt, sage, and pepper. Trim fat from chops. Sprinkle rub evenly over both sides of chops; rub in with your fingers.

two For a charcoal grill, arrange medium-hot coals around a drip pan. Test for medium heat above pan. Place chops on grill rack over pan. Cover and grill for 35 to 40 minutes or until chops are slightly pink in center and juices run clear (160°F), turning once halfway through grilling. (For a gas grill, preheat grill. Reduce heat to medium. Adjust for indirect cooking. Grill as above.)

NUTRITION FACTS PER SERVING: 292 cal., 10 g total fat (4 g sat. fat), 105 mg chol., 371 mg sodium, 3 g carbo., 1 g fiber, 43 g pro.

Country Chops and Peppers

START TO FINISH: 20 minutes **MAKES:** 4 servings

4	pork loin chops, cut ¾ inch thick
	Seasoned salt and black pepper
	Nonstick cooking spray
1	medium sweet pepper, cut into strips
1	tablespoon butter or margarine
⅓	cup Worcestershire sauce for chicken or 2 tablespoons Worcestershire sauce and ¼ cup water

one Trim fat from chops. Sprinkle both sides of chops with seasoned salt and pepper. Coat a large skillet with cooking spray; heat over medium-high heat. Cook chops in hot skillet for 5 minutes. Turn and top with pepper strips. Cook, covered, for 5 to 7 minutes or until chops are slightly pink in center and juices run clear (160°F). Remove chops and pepper strips from skillet; cover and keep warm.

two For sauce, in the same skillet melt butter, scraping up crusty browned bits. Add Worcestershire sauce. Cook and stir over medium heat until mixture is slightly thickened. Remove from heat.

three Place chops and pepper strips on 4 dinner plates. Spoon sauce over chops and pepper strips.

NUTRITION FACTS PER SERVING: 282 cal., 11 g total fat (5 g sat. fat), 101 mg chol., 282 mg sodium, 6 g carbo., 1 g fiber, 38 g pro.

Pork Chops with Orange-Dijon Sauce

PREP: 15 minutes **COOK:** Low 6 hours, High 3 hours
MAKES: 6 servings

- 6 boneless pork sirloin chops, cut 1 inch thick
  Salt and black pepper
- ½ teaspoon dried thyme, crushed
- 1 cup orange marmalade
- ⅓ cup Dijon-style mustard
- ¼ cup water

one Trim fat from chops. Lightly sprinkle both sides of chops with salt and pepper. Sprinkle chops with thyme. Place chops in a 3½- or 4-quart slow cooker.

two In a small bowl combine orange marmalade and mustard. Remove 2 tablespoons of the mixture; cover and chill until ready to serve. Stir the water into the remaining marmalade mixture; pour over chops.

three Cover and cook on low-heat setting for 6 to 7 hours or on high-heat setting for 3 to 3½ hours. Transfer chops to a serving platter. Discard cooking liquid. Spread the reserved marmalade mixture over chops.

NUTRITION FACTS PER SERVING: 409 cal., 15 g total fat (5 g sat. fat), 166 mg chol., 212 mg sodium, 9 g carbo., 1 g fiber, 56 g pro.

Beer-Glazed Pork Chops

PREP: 15 minutes **MARINATE:** 6 to 24 hours
GRILL: 30 minutes **MAKES:** 4 servings

- 4 boneless pork loin chops, cut 1¼ inches thick
- 1 12-ounce bottle stout (dark beer)
- ¼ cup honey mustard
- 3 cloves garlic, minced
- 1 teaspoon caraway seeds

one Trim fat from chops. Place chops in a resealable plastic bag set in a shallow dish. For marinade, in a medium bowl combine stout, honey mustard, garlic, and caraway seeds. Pour marinade over chops; seal bag. Marinate in the refrigerator for 6 to 24 hours, turning bag occasionally.

two Drain chops, reserving marinade. In a small saucepan bring marinade to boiling; reduce heat. Simmer, uncovered, about 15 minutes or until marinade is reduced by half.

three For a charcoal grill, arrange medium-hot coals around a drip pan. Test for medium heat above pan. Place chops on grill rack over drip pan. Cover and grill for 30 to 35 minutes or until chops are slightly pink in center and juices run clear (160°F), brushing chops frequently with marinade during the last 10 minutes of grilling. Discard any remaining marinade.

NUTRITION FACTS PER SERVING: 327 cal., 11 g total fat (4 g sat. fat), 108 mg chol., 90 mg sodium, 5 g carbo., 0 g fiber, 44 g pro.

Asian Apricot-Glazed Chops

PREP: 15 minutes **GRILL:** 7 minutes **MAKES:** 4 servings

- ⅓   cup apricot preserves
- 1   tablespoon Asian chili sauce
- 2   teaspoons soy sauce
- ¼   teaspoon ground ginger
- 4   boneless pork sirloin chops, cut ¾ inch thick
  Salt and black pepper

one For glaze, place apricot preserves in a small bowl; snip any large pieces of fruit. Stir in chili sauce, soy sauce, and ginger. Set glaze aside.

two Trim fat from chops. Sprinkle both sides of chops with salt and pepper.

three For a charcoal grill, grill chops on the rack of an uncovered grill directly over medium coals for 7 to 9 minutes or until chops are slightly pink in center and juices run clear (160°F), turning once halfway through grilling and brushing with glaze during the last 2 to 3 minutes of grilling. (For a gas grill, preheat grill. Reduce heat to medium. Place chops on grill rack over heat. Cover and grill as above.)

NUTRITION FACTS PER SERVING: 317 cal., 9 g total fat (3 g sat. fat), 106 mg chol., 515 mg sodium, 20 g carbo., 0 g fiber, 36 g pro.

Barbecued Pork Chop Sandwiches *See photo on page 121.*

PREP: 15 minutes **GRILL:** 7 minutes **MAKES:** 6 servings

- 1   cup bottled chili sauce
- 1   teaspoon curry powder
- 1   teaspoon ground cumin
- 6   boneless pork loin chops, cut ¾ inch thick
  Salt and black pepper (optional)
- 6   kaiser rolls, split and toasted
  Tomato slices (optional)
  Leaf lettuce leaves (optional)

one For sauce, in a small bowl stir together chili sauce, curry powder, and cumin. Divide mixture in half.

two Trim fat from chops. If desired, lightly sprinkle both sides of chops with salt and pepper.

three For a charcoal grill, grill chops on the rack of an uncovered grill directly over medium coals for 7 to 9 minutes or until chops are slightly pink in center and juices run clear (160°F), turning and brushing once with one portion of the sauce halfway through grilling. (For a gas grill, preheat grill. Reduce heat to medium. Place chops on grill rack over heat. Cover and grill as above.)

four If desired, thinly slice chops. Serve chops on rolls with, if desired, tomato and lettuce. Pass the remaining sauce.

NUTRITION FACTS PER SERVING: 358 cal., 7 g total fat (2 g sat. fat), 71 mg chol., 901 mg sodium, 41 g carbo., 4 g fiber, 31 g pro.

Ginger-Lemon Pork Chops

PREP: 20 minutes **MARINATE:** 4 to 24 hours **GRILL:** 7 minutes
MAKES: 4 servings

- 4 boneless pork loin chops, cut 1 inch thick
- ½ cup soy sauce
- ¼ cup water
- 1 tablespoon grated fresh ginger
- 1 teaspoon finely shredded lemon peel
- 1 tablespoon lemon juice

one Trim fat from chops. Place chops in a resealable plastic bag set in a shallow dish. For marinade, in a small bowl combine soy sauce, water, ginger, lemon peel, and lemon juice. Pour over chops; seal bag. Marinate in the refrigerator for 4 to 24 hours, turning bag occasionally.

two Drain chops, discarding marinade. For a charcoal grill, grill chops on the rack of an uncovered grill directly over medium coals for 7 to 9 minutes or until chops are slightly pink in center and juices run clear (160°F), turning once halfway through grilling. (For a gas grill, preheat grill. Reduce heat to medium. Place chops on grill rack over heat. Cover and grill as above.)

NUTRITION FACTS PER SERVING: 257 cal., 9 g total fat (3 g sat. fat), 92 mg chol., 989 mg sodium, 0 g carbo., 0 g fiber, 40 g pro.

Margarita-Glazed Pork Chops

PREP: 10 minutes **GRILL:** 7 minutes **MAKES:** 4 servings

- 4 boneless pork loin chops, cut 1 inch thick
- ⅓ cup orange marmalade
- 2 tablespoons tequila or lime juice
- 1 fresh jalapeño chile pepper, seeded and finely chopped (see tip, page 59)
- 1 teaspoon grated fresh ginger or ½ teaspoon ground ginger

one Trim fat from chops. For glaze, in a small bowl combine orange marmalade, tequila, jalapeño pepper, and ginger. Set glaze aside.

two For a charcoal grill, grill chops on the rack of an uncovered grill directly over medium coals for 7 to 9 minutes or until chops are slightly pink in center and juices run clear (160°F), turning once halfway through grilling and brushing frequently with glaze during the last half of grilling. (For a gas grill, preheat grill. Reduce heat to medium. Place chops on grill rack over heat. Cover and grill as above.)

NUTRITION FACTS PER SERVING: 314 cal., 8 g total fat (3 g sat. fat), 106 mg chol., 117 mg sodium, 18 g carbo., 0 g fiber, 38 g pro.

Choucroute Garni

PREP: 10 minutes **COOK:** Low 8 hours, High 4 hours
MAKES: 8 servings

- 1   14- to 15-ounce can Bavarian-style sauerkraut (with caraway seeds),* rinsed and drained
- 1   pound Yukon gold potatoes, quartered
- 1   pound cooked smoked boneless pork chops, halved crosswise
- 1   pound cooked bratwurst, halved crosswise, or cooked smoked Polish sausage, cut into 3-inch lengths
- 1   12-ounce can beer

one In a 4½- to 6-quart slow cooker place sauerkraut and potatoes. Top with smoked chops and bratwurst. Pour beer over mixture in cooker.

one Cover and cook on low-heat setting for 8 to 9 hours or on high-heat setting for 4 to 4½ hours.

*Note: *If Bavarian-style sauerkraut is not available, substitute one 14½-ounce can sauerkraut, rinsed and drained, plus 2 tablespoons packed brown sugar and ½ teaspoon caraway seeds.*

NUTRITION FACTS PER SERVING: 311 cal., 17 g total fat (6 g sat. fat), 64 mg chol., 2,158 mg sodium, 16 g carbo., 1 g fiber, 19 g pro.

Easy Pork Chops Supreme

PREP: 10 minutes **BAKE:** 1 hour **MAKES:** 6 servings

- 6   pork loin chops, cut ¾ inch thick
- 1   cup ketchup
- ⅓   cup honey
- 1   teaspoon bottled hot pepper sauce
- 6   lemon slices

one Trim fat from chops. Arrange chops in a 12×7½×2-inch baking dish. In a small bowl stir together ketchup, honey, and hot pepper sauce. Pour ketchup mixture over chops. Top each chop with a slice of lemon.

two Bake, uncovered, in a 350°F oven about 1 hour or until chops are slightly pink in center and juices run clear (160°F).

NUTRITION FACTS PER SERVING: 230 cal., 5 g total fat (2 g sat. fat), 48 mg chol., 512 mg sodium, 26 g carbo., 1 g fiber, 20 g pro.

Pork Chops Dijon

START TO FINISH: 30 minutes **MAKES:** 4 servings

3   tablespoons Dijon-style mustard

2   tablespoons bottled reduced-calorie Italian salad dressing

¼   teaspoon black pepper

4   pork loin chops, cut ½ inch thick

    Nonstick cooking spray

1   medium onion, halved lengthwise and sliced

one In a small bowl combine mustard, salad dressing, and pepper; set aside. Trim fat from chops. Coat a 10-inch skillet with cooking spray; heat over medium-high heat. Cook chops in hot skillet until brown on both sides. Remove from skillet.

two Add onion to skillet. Cook and stir over medium heat for 3 minutes. Push onion aside; return chops to skillet. Spread mustard mixture over chops.

three Cook, covered, over medium-low heat about 15 minutes or until chops are slightly pink in center and juices run clear (160°F). Serve onion over chops.

NUTRITION FACTS PER SERVING: 153 cal., 5 g total fat (2 g sat. fat), 58 mg chol., 218 mg sodium, 4 g carbo., 1 g fiber, 21 g pro.

SLOW COOKER

Pork Chops and Corn Bread Stuffing

PREP: 20 minutes **COOK:** Low 5 hours, High 2½ hours
MAKES: 4 servings

    Nonstick cooking spray

4   pork rib chops, cut ¾ inch thick

1   10¾-ounce can condensed golden mushroom or cream of mushroom soup

¼   cup butter or margarine, melted

1   16-ounce package frozen broccoli, cauliflower, and carrots

½   of a 16-ounce package (about 3 cups) corn bread stuffing mix

one Lightly coat a 5½- or 6-quart slow cooker with cooking spray; set aside. Trim fat from chops. Lightly coat a 10-inch skillet with cooking spray; heat over medium-high heat. Cook chops in the hot skillet, half at a time, until brown on both sides. Remove chops from skillet; set aside.

two In a very large bowl combine soup and melted butter. Stir in frozen vegetables and stuffing mix. Transfer mixture to the prepared cooker. Place chops on top of stuffing mixture.

three Cover and cook on low-heat setting for 5 to 6 hours or on high-heat setting for 2½ to 3 hours.

NUTRITION FACTS PER SERVING: 558 cal., 22 g total fat (10 g sat. fat), 89 mg chol., 1,533 mg sodium, 56 g carbo., 7 g fiber, 30 g pro.

Smoked Chops and Potatoes

START TO FINISH: 20 minutes **MAKES:** 4 servings

- 3 medium potatoes (about 1 pound), sliced
- 1 cup frozen broccoli, cauliflower, and carrots
- 4 cooked smoked pork chops, cut ½ to ¾ inch thick
- 1 12-ounce jar brown gravy

one In a covered large skillet cook potatoes and frozen vegetables in a small amount of boiling water for 6 to 8 minutes or until tender. Drain in a colander.

two In the same skillet arrange smoked chops. Place drained vegetables on top of chops. Spoon gravy over chops and vegetables. Cook, covered, over medium-low heat for 7 to 8 minutes or until heated through.

NUTRITION FACTS PER SERVING: 349 cal., 19 g total fat (7 g sat. fat), 60 mg chol., 1,452 mg sodium, 24 g carbo., 3 g fiber, 23 g pro.

SLOW COOKER

Apple Butter-Sauced Pork Chops

PREP: 10 minutes **COOK:** Low 6 hours, High 3 hours
MAKES: 6 servings

- 6 cooked smoked boneless pork chops
- 1 cup apple butter
- 1 teaspoon quick-cooking tapioca
- ½ teaspoon dried sage, crushed
- 2 large red cooking apples
- 3 cups hot cooked couscous (optional)

one Place smoked chops in a 3½- or 4-quart slow cooker. For sauce, in a small bowl combine apple butter, tapioca, and sage. Pour sauce over chops. If desired, peel apples. Core and quarter apples; place on top of chops.

two Cover and cook on low-heat setting for 6 to 7 hours or on high-heat setting for 3 to 3½ hours. If desired, serve chops with sauce over hot cooked couscous.

NUTRITION FACTS PER SERVING: 517 cal., 12 g total fat (4 g sat. fat), 40 mg chol., 641 mg sodium, 87 g carbo., 5 g fiber, 16 g pro.

Smoked Pork Chop Skillet

4   cooked smoked pork chops, cut ¾ inch thick

1   16-ounce package frozen French-style green beans

¼   cup water

1½   teaspoons snipped fresh sage or
     ½ teaspoon dried sage, crushed

½   cup balsamic vinegar

one In a large nonstick skillet cook smoked chops over medium heat until lightly browned on both sides. Remove chops from skillet.

two Add green beans, water, and sage to skillet; return chops to skillet. Cook, covered, over medium heat for 5 minutes.

three Meanwhile, in a small saucepan boil vinegar gently about 5 minutes or until reduced to ¼ cup. Brush chops with some of the vinegar; drizzle the remaining vinegar over beans.

NUTRITION FACTS PER SERVING: 257 cal., 14 g total fat (5 g sat. fat), 47 mg chol., 749 mg sodium, 18 g carbo., 3 g fiber, 17 g pro.

Mu Shu-Style Pork Roll-Ups

12   ounces lean boneless pork

1   teaspoon toasted sesame oil

2   cups frozen desired stir-fry vegetables

4   10-inch flour tortillas, warmed (see tip, page 16)

¼   cup bottled plum or hoisin sauce

one Trim fat from meat. Cut meat into bite-size strips. In a large skillet cook and stir meat strips in hot sesame oil over medium-high heat for 2 to 3 minutes or until meat is no longer pink. Add frozen vegetables. Cook and stir for 3 to 4 minutes more or until vegetables are crisp-tender.

two Spread one side of each warmed tortilla with plum sauce. Place one-fourth of the meat mixture just below the center of each tortilla. Fold the bottom edge of each tortilla up and over filling. Fold in the sides until they meet; roll up over the filling.

NUTRITION FACTS PER SERVING: 302 cal., 8 g total fat (2 g sat. fat), 53 mg chol., 311 mg sodium, 34 g carbo., 2 g fiber, 22 g pro.

HEARTY BEEF, PORK & LAMB

Cajun Pork

PREP: 20 minutes **COOK:** Low 6 hours, High 3 hours; plus 30 minutes on High **MAKES:** 6 to 8 servings

1   2½- to 3-pound boneless pork shoulder roast
    Nonstick cooking spray
2   medium yellow sweet peppers, cut into 1-inch pieces
1   tablespoon Cajun seasoning
1   14½-ounce can diced tomatoes with green pepper
    and onion, undrained
1   16-ounce package frozen cut okra
    Bottled hot pepper sauce (optional)

Go Low-Fat: Good news: Very little fat is needed to flavor slow-cooker dishes. So skip it, opting for lean meat and poultry cuts such as pork loin chops and shoulder or sirloin roasts; beef round, sirloin, or flank steaks; round or chuck roasts; and brisket; and chicken or turkey breasts, drumsticks, and thighs.

Trim all visible fat from meats or poultry and remove the skin from poultry before adding it to the cooker. When cooking is complete, move the solid cooked food to a serving dish and let the liquid stand for a minute or two, then use a metal spoon to skim off fat.

one Trim fat from meat. Cut meat into 1-inch pieces. Lightly coat a large skillet with cooking spray; heat over medium-high heat. Cook and stir meat, half at a time, in hot skillet until brown.

two In a 3½- or 4-quart slow cooker place meat and sweet peppers. Sprinkle with Cajun seasoning. Pour undrained tomatoes over meat and peppers.

three Cover and cook on low-heat setting for 6 to 7 hours or on high-heat setting for 3 to 3½ hours.

four If using low-heat setting, turn to high-heat setting. Stir in frozen okra. Cover and cook for 30 minutes more. If desired, pass hot pepper sauce.

NUTRITION FACTS PER SERVING: 233 cal., 8 g total fat (3 g sat. fat), 77 mg chol., 444 mg sodium, 15 g carbo., 4 g fiber, 25 g pro.

Slow-Cooked Asian-Style Pork

PREP: 20 minutes COOK: Low 7 hours, High 3½ hours;
plus 30 minutes on High MAKES: 6 to 8 servings

1 3-pound boneless pork shoulder roast
   Nonstick cooking spray
2 tablespoons quick-cooking tapioca
1 10-ounce jar sweet-and-sour sauce
1 16-ounce package frozen broccoli stir-fry vegetables
   (broccoli, carrots, red peppers, celery, water
   chestnuts, and mushrooms)
3 to 4 cups hot cooked rice or rice noodles

one Trim fat from meat. Cut meat into 1-inch pieces. Lightly coat a large skillet with cooking spray; heat over medium-high heat. Cook and stir meat, half at a time, in hot skillet until brown.

two Place meat in a 3½- or 4-quart slow cooker. Sprinkle with tapioca. Pour sweet-and-sour sauce over meat.

three Cover and cook on low-heat setting for 7 to 8 hours or on high-heat setting for 3½ to 4 hours.

four If using low-heat setting, turn to high-heat setting. Stir in frozen vegetables. Cover and cook for 30 to 60 minutes more or until vegetables are tender. Serve over hot cooked rice.

NUTRITION FACTS PER SERVING: 484 cal., 19 g total fat (6 g sat. fat), 153 mg chol., 342 mg sodium, 40 g carbo., 2 g fiber, 48 g pro.

Honey-Mustard Barbecue Pork Ribs

PREP: 15 minutes COOK: Low 8 hours, High 4 hours
MAKES: 6 to 8 servings

3½ pounds boneless pork country-style ribs
1   cup bottled barbecue sauce
1   8-ounce jar honey mustard
2   teaspoons spicy grilling seasoning blend

one Trim fat from ribs. Place ribs in a 3½- or 4-quart slow cooker. For sauce, in a medium bowl combine barbecue sauce, honey mustard, and seasoning blend. Pour over ribs; stir to coat ribs with sauce.

two Cover and cook on low-heat setting for 8 to 10 hours or on high-heat setting for 4 to 5 hours.

three Using a slotted spoon, transfer ribs to a serving platter. Strain sauce and skim off fat. Drizzle some of the sauce over ribs. Pass the remaining sauce.

NUTRITION FACTS PER SERVING: 322 cal., 12 g total fat (4 g sat. fat), 94 mg chol., 497 mg sodium, 18 g carbo., 1 g fiber, 29 g pro.

Orange Sesame Ribs

PREP: 15 minutes **COOK:** Low 8 hours, High 4 hours
MAKES: 4 servings

2½   to 3 pounds boneless pork country-style ribs
       Nonstick cooking spray
1   10-ounce jar orange marmalade
1   7¼-ounce jar hoisin sauce
3   cloves garlic, minced
1   teaspoon toasted sesame oil
2   cups hot cooked rice (optional)

one Trim fat from ribs. Lightly coat a large skillet with cooking spray; heat over medium heat. Cook ribs in hot skillet until brown on all sides. Drain off fat.

two Place ribs in a 3½- or 4-quart slow cooker. For sauce, in a medium bowl stir together orange marmalade, hoisin sauce, garlic, and sesame oil. Pour over ribs in cooker; stir to coat ribs with sauce.

three Cover and cook on low-heat setting for 8 to 10 hours or on high-heat setting for 4 to 5 hours. Transfer ribs to a serving platter. Skim fat from sauce. Spoon some of the sauce over ribs. Pass the remaining sauce. If desired, serve with hot cooked rice.

NUTRITION FACTS PER SERVING: 532 cal., 16 g total fat (5 g sat. fat), 101 mg chol., 696 mg sodium, 66 g carbo., 0 g fiber, 33 g pro.

Pineapple-Mustard Country-Style Ribs

PREP: 10 minutes **GRILL:** 1½ hours **MAKES:** 4 servings

½   of a 6-ounce can (⅓ cup) frozen pineapple juice
       concentrate, thawed
3   tablespoons Dijon-style mustard
2½   to 3 pounds pork country-style ribs

one For sauce, in a small bowl combine juice concentrate and mustard. Set sauce aside.

two Trim fat from ribs. For a charcoal grill, arrange medium-hot coals around a drip pan. Test for medium heat above pan. Place ribs, bone sides down, on grill rack over pan. (Or place ribs in a rib rack; place on grill rack.)

three Cover and grill for 1½ to 2 hours or until ribs are tender, brushing with sauce during the last 10 minutes of grilling. (For a gas grill, preheat grill. Reduce heat to medium. Adjust for indirect cooking. Grill as above.)

NUTRITION FACTS PER SERVING: 296 cal., 12 g total fat (4 g sat. fat), 101 mg chol., 356 mg sodium, 13 g carbo., 0 g fiber, 33 g pro.

Stout-Glazed Ribs *See photo on page 119.*

PREP: 15 minutes **MARINATE:** 6 to 24 hours **COOK:** 10 minutes
GRILL: 1½ hours **MAKES:** 4 servings

- 4 pounds pork loin back ribs or meaty pork spareribs
- 1 12-ounce bottle stout (dark beer)
- ½ cup chopped onion
- ¼ cup honey mustard
- 3 cloves garlic, minced
- 1 teaspoon caraway seeds (optional)
- Salt and black pepper
- Fresh sage leaves (optional)

Pork Rib Rundown When you're selecting pork ribs to grill, you can choose from three types. Spareribs, cut from the hog's rib cage, are the least meaty. Loin back ribs are cut from the back of the animal and are meatier than spareribs. Country-style ribs, cut from the shoulder, are the meatiest of all.

Although there are numerous grilling gadgets available, one of the most useful is the rib rack. This metal frame allows you to stand slabs of ribs vertically for grilling. By using a rib rack, you can grill more ribs at one time and the fat drains away.

one Trim fat from ribs. Place ribs in a resealable plastic bag set in a shallow dish. For marinade, in a medium bowl combine stout, onion, honey mustard, garlic, and, if desired, caraway seeds. Pour marinade over ribs; seal bag. Marinate in the refrigerator for 6 to 24 hours, turning bag occasionally.

two Drain ribs, reserving marinade. Sprinkle ribs with salt and pepper. Pour marinade into a small saucepan. Bring to boiling; reduce heat. Simmer, uncovered, for 10 minutes.

three For a charcoal grill, arrange medium-hot coals around a drip pan. Test for medium heat above pan. Place ribs, bone sides down, on grill rack over drip pan. (Or place ribs in a rib rack; place on grill rack.)

four Cover and grill for 1½ to 1¾ hours or until ribs are tender, brushing frequently with marinade during the last 10 minutes of grilling. (For a gas grill, preheat grill. Adjust for indirect cooking. Grill as above.) Discard any remaining marinade.

five If desired, garnish ribs with fresh sage leaves.

NUTRITION FACTS PER SERVING: 482 cal., 20 g total fat (7 g sat. fat), 135 mg chol., 296 mg sodium, 5 g carbo., 0 g fiber, 63 g pro.

HEARTY BEEF, PORK & LAMB

Cranberry-Glazed Pork Ribs

PREP: 10 minutes **GRILL:** 1½ hours **MAKES:** 6 servings

1	8-ounce can whole cranberry sauce
3	inches stick cinnamon
1	tablespoon Dijon-style mustard
1	teaspoon finely shredded orange peel
1½	pounds boneless pork country-style ribs

one For glaze, in a small saucepan combine cranberry sauce, stick cinnamon, mustard, and orange peel. Cook and stir over medium heat about 5 minutes or until bubbly. Set glaze aside.

two Trim fat from ribs. For a charcoal grill, arrange medium-hot coals around a drip pan. Test for medium heat above pan. Place ribs on grill rack over pan. (Or place ribs in a rib rack; place on grill rack.)

three Cover and grill for 1½ to 2 hours or until ribs are tender, brushing occasionally with glaze during the last 20 minutes of grilling. (For a gas grill, preheat grill. Reduce heat to medium. Adjust for indirect cooking. Grill as above.)

four To serve, reheat any remaining glaze until bubbly. Remove and discard stick cinnamon. Serve ribs with glaze.

NUTRITION FACTS PER SERVING: 255 cal., 14 g total fat (5 g sat. fat), 65 mg chol., 124 mg sodium, 15 g carbo., 0 g fiber, 16 g pro.

Ribs and Sauerkraut

PREP: 20 minutes **COOK:** Low 6 hours, High 3 hours
MAKES: 6 to 8 servings

2	pounds boneless pork country-style ribs
2	medium tart cooking apples, peeled, cored, and sliced
1	14-ounce can sauerkraut, drained
1	large sweet onion, sliced
1	cup apple juice

one Trim fat from ribs. In a 4- or 4½-quart slow cooker combine apples, sauerkraut, and onion. Place ribs on top of sauerkraut mixture. Pour apple juice over all.

two Cover and cook on low-heat setting for 6 to 7 hours or on high-heat setting for 3 to 3½ hours. Use a slotted spoon to serve ribs and sauerkraut mixture.

NUTRITION FACTS PER SERVING: 312 cal., 12 g total fat (4 g sat. fat), 96 mg chol., 541 mg sodium, 19 g carbo., 4 g fiber, 30 g pro.

Pork Patties with Honey Barbecue Sauce

PREP: 10 minutes **GRILL:** 14 minutes **MAKES:** 4 servings

- ½   cup bottled chili sauce
- 2   tablespoons honey
- 1   pound lean ground pork
- 1   teaspoon sausage seasoning
- 8   slices Texas toast, toasted, or 4 hamburger buns, split and toasted
    Lettuce leaves (optional)
    Tomato slices (optional)

one For sauce, in a small bowl combine chili sauce and honey. Set aside half of the sauce to use for basting. Reserve the remaining sauce until ready to serve.

two In a medum bowl combine ground pork and sausage seasoning; mix well. Shape into four ¾-inch-thick patties.

three For a charcoal grill, grill burgers on the rack of an uncovered grill directly over medium coals for 14 to 18 minutes or until meat is done (160°F), turning once halfway through grilling and brushing frequently with basting sauce during the last half of grilling. (For a gas grill, preheat grill. Reduce heat to medium. Place burgers on grill rack over heat. Cover and grill as above.)

four Serve burgers between slices of Texas toast. If desired, top burgers with lettuce and tomato. Pass the reserved sauce.

NUTRITION FACTS PER SERVING: 437 cal., 14 g total fat (4 g sat. fat), 153 mg chol., 999 mg sodium, 55 g carbo., 2 g fiber, 27 g pro.

Sweet and Spicy Pork Burgers

PREP: 10 minutes **GRILL:** 14 minutes **MAKES:** 4 servings

- ¼   cup fine dry bread crumbs
- ¼   cup bottled barbecue sauce
- 1   teaspoon seasoned pepper blend
- 1   pound lean ground pork
- 4   hamburger buns or kaiser rolls, split and toasted
    Leaf lettuce (optional)
    Onion slices (optional)

one In a large bowl combine bread crumbs, barbecue sauce, and seasoned pepper blend. Add ground pork; mix well. Shape meat mixture into four ¾-inch-thick patties.

two For a charcoal grill, grill burgers on the rack of an uncovered grill directly over medium coals for 14 to 18 minutes or until meat is done (160°F), turning once halfway through grilling. (For a gas grill, preheat grill. Reduce heat to medium. Place burgers on grill rack over heat. Cover and grill as above.)

three Serve burgers on buns. If desired, top burgers with lettuce and onion.

NUTRITION FACTS PER SERVING: 290 cal., 11 g total fat (4 g sat. fat), 53 mg chol., 555 mg sodium, 29 g carbo., 1 g fiber, 19 g pro.

Bow Ties with Sausage and Sweet Peppers

START TO FINISH: 25 minutes **MAKES:** 4 servings

8	ounces dried bow tie pasta
12	ounces uncooked Italian sausage links
2	medium sweet peppers, cut into bite-size pieces
½	cup vegetable broth or beef broth
¼	teaspoon coarsely ground black pepper

one Cook pasta according to package directions; drain. Meanwhile, cut sausage into bite-size pieces. In a large skillet cook sausage and sweet peppers over medium-high heat until sausage is brown. Drain off fat.

two Add broth and black pepper to skillet. Bring to boiling; reduce heat. Simmer, uncovered, for 5 minutes. Remove from heat. Toss sausage mixture with pasta.

NUTRITION FACTS PER SERVING: 479 cal., 22 g total fat (8 g sat. fat), 111 mg chol., 713 mg sodium, 45 g carbo., 3 g fiber, 21 g pro.

Smoked Sausage Pasta Bake

PREP: 25 minutes **BAKE:** 15 minutes **MAKES:** 4 servings

12	ounces dried cavatelli or rotini pasta
1	26- to 28-ounce jar spicy tomato pasta sauce
6	ounces cooked smoked sausage, halved lengthwise and sliced
¾	cup bottled roasted red sweet peppers, drained and coarsely chopped
1	cup shredded provolone or mozzarella cheese (4 ounces)

one Cook pasta according to package directions; drain. Return pasta to pan. Add pasta sauce, sausage, and roasted peppers to cooked pasta; toss gently to coat.

two Spoon pasta mixture into four greased 14- to 16-ounce casseroles. Sprinkle with cheese. Bake, uncovered, in a 375°F oven for 15 to 20 minutes or until pasta mixture is heated through and cheese melts.

NUTRITION FACTS PER SERVING: 654 cal., 25 g total fat (12 g sat. fat), 38 mg chol., 995 mg sodium, 77 g carbo., 6 g fiber, 26 g pro.

Italian-Stuffed Sausage Burgers

PREP: 25 minutes **GRILL:** 20 minutes **MAKES:** 4 servings

¾ cup shredded provolone or mozzarella cheese
   (3 ounces)
3 tablespoons tomato paste
2 tablespoons snipped fresh basil or oregano or
   2 teaspoons dried basil or oregano, crushed
1 clove garlic, minced
1½ pounds bulk pork sausage
2 tablespoons finely shredded Parmesan cheese
   (optional)

one In a small bowl combine provolone cheese, tomato paste, basil, and garlic; shape into 4 slightly flattened mounds. Shape sausage into eight ¼-inch-thick patties. Place a cheese mound in the center of 4 of the patties. Top with the remaining patties; press gently to seal edges.

two For a charcoal grill, arrange medium-hot coals around a drip pan. Test for medium heat above pan. Place burgers on grill rack over drip pan. Cover and grill for 20 to 24 minutes or until meat is done (160°F), turning once halfway through grilling. If desired, sprinkle with Parmesan cheese during the last 1 minute of grilling. (For a gas grill, preheat grill. Reduce heat to medium. Adjust for indirect cooking. Grill as above.)

NUTRITION FACTS PER SERVING: 522 cal., 38 g total fat (15 g sat. fat), 125 mg chol., 1,005 mg sodium, 3 g carbo., 0 g fiber, 32 g pro.

One-Pot Pesto Pasta

PREP: 15 minutes **COOK:** 25 minutes **MAKES:** 4 servings

1 pound mild bulk Italian sausage or lean ground beef
3 cups reduced-sodium chicken broth
8 ounces dried spaghetti, broken
3 tablespoons purchased basil pesto
¼ cup finely shredded Parmesan cheese (1 ounce)

one In a large saucepan cook sausage over medium-heat until brown. Drain off fat. Add broth; bring to boiling. Gradually add spaghetti. Reduce heat.

two Simmer, covered, about 25 minutes or until spaghetti is tender and most of the liquid is absorbed, stirring occasionally. Remove from heat. Stir in pesto. Transfer to a serving dish. Sprinkle with Parmesan cheese.

NUTRITION FACTS PER SERVING: 659 cal., 35 g total fat (12 g sat. fat), 84 mg chol., 1,253 mg sodium, 46 g carbo., 1 g fiber, 29 g pro.

Sausage-Sauced Polenta

START TO FINISH: 20 minutes **MAKES:** 6 servings

2   16-ounce tubes refrigerated cooked polenta with wild mushrooms or dried tomatoes

1   pound bulk pork sausage or Italian sausage

1   26- to 28-ounce jar chunky garden-style pasta sauce

¼   cup finely shredded or grated Parmesan cheese

    Snipped fresh parsley or cilantro

one Cut each tube of polenta into 9 slices; set aside. In a 12-inch skillet cook sausage over medium-high heat until brown. Drain off fat.

two Stir in pasta sauce; bring to boiling. Place polenta slices on top of sausage mixture. Reduce heat. Simmer, covered, about 5 minutes or until heated through. Sprinkle with Parmesan cheese and parsley.

NUTRITION FACTS PER SERVING: 490 cal., 26 g total fat (10 g sat. fat), 47 mg chol., 1,194 mg sodium, 41 g carbo., 5 g fiber, 15 g pro.

`SLOW COOKER`

Mexican Lasagna

PREP: 25 minutes **COOK:** Low 3 hours **STAND:** 15 minutes
MAKES: 8 servings

      Nonstick cooking spray

1½   pounds bulk pork sausage

9   6-inch corn tortillas

1   11-ounce can whole kernel corn with sweet peppers, drained

2   cups shredded taco cheese blend (8 ounces)

2   10-ounce cans enchilada sauce

one Lightly coat a 3½- or 4-quart slow cooker with cooking spray; set aside. In a large skillet cook sausage over medium-heat until brown. Drain off fat.

two Place 3 of the tortillas in the bottom of the prepared cooker, overlapping as necessary. Top with half of the corn and half of the sausage. Sprinkle with ½ cup of the cheese. Pour about ¾ cup of the enchilada sauce over layers in cooker. Repeat with 3 more tortillas, remaining corn, and remaining sausage. Sprinkle with ½ cup of the cheese. Pour ¾ cup enchilada sauce over cheese. Top with remaining tortillas, remaining cheese, and remaining enchilada sauce.

three Cover and cook on low-heat setting for 3 to 4 hours. Remove liner from cooker or turn off cooker. Let stand, covered, for 15 minutes before serving.

NUTRITION FACTS PER SERVING: 512 cal., 34 g total fat (15 g sat. fat), 71 mg chol., 1,082 mg sodium, 27 g carbo., 3 g fiber, 18 g pro.

Pizza by the Yard

PREP: 25 minutes **COOK:** Low 5 hours, High 2½ hours
MAKES: 8 servings

2   pounds bulk Italian sausage

1   26-ounce jar garlic and mushroom pasta sauce

2   large green and/or red sweet peppers, chopped

1   1-pound loaf Italian bread, split lengthwise and
    toasted*

2   cups shredded pizza cheese blend (8 ounces)

one In a large skillet cook sausage over medium-high heat until brown. Drain off fat. In a 3½- or 4-quart slow cooker combine sausage, pasta sauce, and sweet peppers.

two Cover and cook on low-heat setting for 5 to 6 hours or on high-heat setting for 2½ to 3 hours. Spoon sausage mixture over toasted bread. Sprinkle with cheese.

__Note:__ To toast bread, place bread, cut sides up, on a baking sheet. Broil 3 to 4 inches from the heat for 3 to 4 minutes or until toasted.

NUTRITION FACTS PER SERVING: 699 cal., 46 g total fat (17 g sat. fat), 106 mg chol., 1,935 mg sodium, 38 g carbo., 4 g fiber, 30 g pro.

Pasta-Salami Salad

PREP: 20 minutes **CHILL:** 4 to 24 hours **MAKES:** 6 servings

12 ounces dried rotini, cavatelli, or bow tie pasta

1   16-ounce package frozen pepper stir-fry vegetables
    (green, red, and yellow peppers and onions)

4   ounces salami or cooked smoked sausage links

1   2¼-ounce can sliced pitted ripe olives, drained

1   cup bottled Italian salad dressing

one Cook pasta according to package directions. Meanwhile, place frozen vegetables in a colander. Pour pasta and cooking water over vegetables; drain.

two Cut salami into bite-size pieces. In a large bowl combine pasta mixture, salami, and olives. Pour salad dressing over salami mixture; toss gently to coat. Cover and chill for 4 to 24 hours. If necessary, stir in additional Italian dressing before serving.

NUTRITION FACTS PER SERVING: 498 cal., 27 g total fat (5 g sat. fat), 18 mg chol., 765 mg sodium, 52 g carbo., 3 g fiber, 13 g pro.

HEARTY BEEF, PORK & LAMB

Bratwurst with Kickin' Cranberry Ketchup

PREP: 20 minutes **GRILL:** 3 minutes **MAKES:** 6 servings

- ¼ cup dried cranberries, coarsely chopped
- ⅓ cup ketchup
- 2 teaspoons prepared horseradish
  Several dashes bottled hot pepper sauce (optional)
- 6 cooked smoked bratwurst
- 6 hoagie buns, split and toasted
- 1 cup deli vinaigrette-style coleslaw (optional)

one For cranberry ketchup, in a small bowl combine dried cranberries and enough boiling water to cover. Let stand for 5 minutes; drain. Stir ketchup, horseradish, and, if desired, hot pepper sauce into cranberries. Set aside.

two For a charcoal grill, grill bratwurst on the rack of an uncovered grill directly over medium coals for 3 to 7 minutes or until bratwurst are browned and heated through, turning once halfway through grilling. (For a gas grill, preheat grill. Reduce heat to medium. Place bratwurst on grill rack over heat. Cover and grill as above.)

three Serve bratwurst on buns; top with cranberry ketchup and, if desired, coleslaw.

NUTRITION FACTS PER SERVING: 689 cal., 32 g total fat (10 g sat. fat), 50 mg chol., 1,536 mg sodium, 81 g carbo., 4 g fiber, 21 g pro.

Firecracker Foot-Longs *See photo on page 121.*

PREP: 10 minutes **MARINATE:** 2 to 24 hours **GRILL:** 3 minutes
MAKES: 4 servings

- 4 foot-long or bun-length hot dogs
- 1 5-ounce bottle hot pepper sauce
- ⅓ cup finely chopped red onion
- 1 teaspoon dried oregano, crushed
- 4 hot dot buns, split and toasted
  Pickle relish (optional)

one Place hot dogs in a resealable plastic bag set in a shallow dish. For marinade, in a small bowl combine hot pepper sauce, onion, and oregano. Pour over hot dogs; seal bag. Marinate in the refrigerator for 2 to 24 hours, turning bag occasionally.

two Drain hot dogs, reserving marinade. For a charcoal grill, grill hot dogs on the rack of an uncovered grill directly over medium coals for 3 to 7 minutes or until heated through, turning once halfway through grilling. (For a gas grill, preheat grill. Reduce heat to medium. Place hot dogs on grill rack over heat. Cover and grill as above.)

three Meanwhile, heat the reserved marinade until bubbly. Serve hot dogs on buns with some of the marinade. If desired, top with pickle relish.

NUTRITION FACTS PER SERVING: 477 cal., 34 g total fat (13 g sat. fat), 57 mg chol., 2,420 mg sodium, 25 g carbo., 4 g fiber, 18 g pro.

Blackberry-Glazed Ham

PREP: 10 minutes **GRILL:** 2¼ hours **MAKES:** 20 to 28 servings

1	6- to 8-pound cooked ham, shank half
1½	cups seedless blackberry jam or other seedless berry jam
¼	cup coarse-grain brown mustard
2	tablespoons balsamic vinegar

one Score ham in a diamond pattern by making shallow diagonal cuts at 1-inch intervals. Place ham on a rack in a shallow roasting pan.

two For sauce, in a medium saucepan combine jam, mustard, and balsamic vinegar. Bring just to boiling; reduce heat. Simmer, uncovered, for 5 minutes. Set sauce aside.

three For a charcoal grill, arrange medium coals around edge of grill. Test for medium-low heat in center of grill. Place roasting pan with ham on grill rack in center of grill. Cover and grill for 2¼ to 2½ hours or until heated through (140°F), brushing once or twice with sauce during the last 15 minutes of grilling. (For a gas grill, preheat grill. Reduce heat to medium-low. Adjust for indirect cooking. Grill as above.)

four To serve, slice ham. Reheat any remaining sauce and pass with ham.

NUTRITION FACTS PER SERVING: 238 cal., 9 g total fat (3 g sat. fat), 58 mg chol., 1,380 mg sodium, 21 g carbo., 2 g fiber, 17 g pro.

Fruited Baked Ham

PREP: 10 minutes **BAKE:** 1½ hours **MAKES:** 12 to 16 servings

1	3- to 4-pound cooked boneless ham
½	cup apricot preserves
1	cup cherry preserves
¼	cup orange juice

one Place ham in a shallow roasting pan. If desired, score ham in a diamond pattern by making shallow diagonal cuts at 1-inch intervals. Bake, uncovered, in a 325°F oven for 1½ to 2¼ hours or until heated through (140°F).

two Meanwhile, for sauce, snip the large pieces of fruit in the apricot preserves. In a small saucepan combine apricot preserves, cherry preserves, and orange juice. Cook and stir until heated through. Serve ham with sauce.

NUTRITION FACTS PER SERVING: 292 cal., 6 g total fat (2 g sat. fat), 62 mg chol., 1,518 mg sodium, 28 g carbo., 0 g fiber, 29 g pro.

Ham Slice with Basil-Cherry Sauce

START TO FINISH: 20 minutes **MAKES:** 4 servings

1   1- to 1¼-pound cooked center-cut ham slice, cut ½ inch thick

2   tablespoons butter or margarine

1   15- to 17-ounce can pitted dark sweet cherries, undrained

2   teaspoons cornstarch

2   teaspoons fresh snipped basil or ½ teaspoon dried basil, crushed

one In a 12-inch skillet cook ham in 1 tablespoon melted butter over medium heat for 8 to 10 minutes or until heated through, turning once. Transfer ham to a serving platter; cover and keep warm.

two Meanwhile, drain cherries, reserving juice. Set cherries aside. For sauce, in a small saucepan stir the reserved cherry juice into cornstarch. Cook and stir over medium heat until thickened and bubbly. Cook and stir for 2 minutes more. Stir in cherries, basil, and the remaining 1 tablespoon butter; heat through. Serve ham with sauce.

NUTRITION FACTS PER SERVING: 338 cal., 18 g total fat (8 g sat. fat), 74 mg chol., 1,285 mg sodium, 20 g carbo., 2 g fiber, 23 g pro.

GRILLING

Maple-and-Mustard-Glazed Ham Steak

PREP: 10 minutes **GRILL:** 14 minutes **MAKES:** 6 servings

1   1½- to 2-pound cooked center-cut ham slice, cut 1 inch thick

2   tablespoons butter or margarine

¼   cup maple syrup

2   tablespoons brown mustard

one For a charcoal grill, grill ham on the rack of an uncovered grill directly over medium coals for 14 to 18 minutes or until heated through (140°F). (For a gas grill, preheat grill. Reduce heat to medium. Place ham on grill rack over heat. Cover and grill as above.)

two Meanwhile, for glaze, in a small saucepan melt butter. Remove saucepan from heat. Whisk in maple syrup and mustard until smooth. Bring to boiling; reduce heat. Simmer, uncovered, for 1 to 2 minutes or until slightly thickened.

three Brush ham with some of the glaze; pass remaining glaze.

NUTRITION FACTS PER SERVING: 258 cal., 14 g total fat (6 g sat. fat), 75 mg chol., 1,575 mg sodium, 14 g carbo., 2 g fiber, 19 g pro.

Ham and Asparagus Pasta

START TO FINISH: 20 minutes **MAKES:** 4 servings

4 cups dried bow tie, rotini, or other medium pasta

1 10-ounce package frozen cut asparagus or broccoli

8 ounces cooked ham slices, cut into thin strips

1 8-ounce tub cream cheese spread with chive and onion

⅓ cup milk

one Cook pasta according to package directions, adding asparagus during the last 5 minutes and ham during the last 1 minute of cooking; drain. Return pasta mixture to pan.

two In a 2-cup glass measuring cup stir cream cheese into milk. Pour over pasta mixture in pan. Cook and stir gently over medium heat until heated through.

NUTRITION FACTS PER SERVING: 505 cal., 24 g total fat (12 g sat. fat), 140 mg chol., 905 mg sodium, 45 g carbo., 1 g fiber, 25 g pro.

SLOW COOKER

Ham and Potatoes au Gratin *See photo on page 120.*

PREP: 15 minutes **COOK:** Low 7 hours, High 3½ hours
MAKES: 6 servings

Nonstick cooking spray

2 cups diced cooked ham

2 4.9-ounce packages dry au gratin potato mix

¼ cup bottled roasted red sweet peppers, drained and chopped

3 cups water

1 10¾-ounce can condensed cheddar cheese soup

Snipped fresh chives (optional)

one Lightly coat a 3½- or 4-quart slow cooker with cooking spray. Place ham, au gratin potato mixes with seasoning packets, and roasted peppers in the prepared cooker. In a medium bowl gradually stir water into soup; pour over ham mixture.

two Cover and cook on low-heat setting for 7 to 8 hours or on high-heat setting for 3½ to 4 hours. If desired, sprinkle each serving with snipped fresh chives.

NUTRITION FACTS PER SERVING: 255 cal., 7 g total fat (3 g sat. fat), 29 mg chol., 2,087 mg sodium, 45 g carbo., 3 g fiber, 15 g pro.

Ham and Cheese Calzones

PREP: 20 minutes **BAKE:** 15 minutes **STAND:** 5 minutes
MAKES: 4 servings

1	13.8-ounce package refrigerated pizza dough
¼	cup coarse-grain mustard
6	ounces sliced Swiss or provolone cheese
1½	cups cubed cooked ham
½	teaspoon caraway seeds

one Line a baking sheet with foil; lightly grease foil. Unroll pizza dough. On a lightly floured surface, roll or pat dough into a 15×10-inch rectangle. Cut into four 7½×5-inch rectangles.

two Spread mustard over rectangles. Divide half of the cheese among rectangles, placing cheese on half of each and cutting or tearing to fit as necessary. Top with ham and sprinkle with caraway seeds. Top with the remaining cheese. Moisten edges of dough with water. Fold dough over filling to opposite edge, stretching slightly if necessary. Press edges with a fork to seal.

three Place calzones on the prepared baking sheet. Prick tops to allow steam to escape. Bake, uncovered, in a 400°F oven about 15 minutes or until golden brown. Let stand for 5 minutes before serving.

NUTRITION FACTS PER SERVING: 421 cal., 21 g total fat (10 g sat. fat), 72 mg chol., 1,390 mg sodium, 28 g carbo., 1 g fiber, 30 g pro.

Ham, Melon, and Spinach Salad

START TO FINISH: 30 minutes **MAKES:** 4 servings

½	of a small cantaloupe
7	cups torn fresh spinach
1	cup cubed cooked ham
½	cup pecan halves, toasted (see tip, page 280)
⅓	cup bottled poppy seed salad dressing

one Using a melon baller, scoop cantaloupe flesh into balls.

two In a large bowl combine cantaloupe balls, spinach, ham, and pecans. Pour salad dressing over ham mixture; toss gently to coat.

NUTRITION FACTS PER SERVING: 286 cal., 20 g total fat (3 g sat. fat), 19 mg chol., 507 mg sodium, 19 g carbo., 4 g fiber, 12 g pro.

BLT Salad

START TO FINISH: 20 minutes MAKES: 4 servings

 5   cups torn mixed salad greens or spinach

 2   cups grape or cherry tomatoes, halved

 8   ounces bacon (about 10 slices), crisp-cooked
       and crumbled

 2   hard-cooked eggs, chopped

 ⅓   cup bottled poppy seed salad dressing

one Place salad greens in a large bowl. Top with tomatoes, crumbled bacon, and chopped hard-cooked eggs.

two Drizzle with salad dressing; toss gently to coat.

NUTRITION FACTS PER SERVING: 251 cal., 20 g total fat (5 g sat. fat), 123 mg chol., 461 mg sodium, 8 g carbo., 2 g fiber, 10 g pro.

> **Bacon in a Hurry** For recipes that don't require drippings from just-cooked bacon, save a little time and mess by using precooked bacon that's available in your supermarket. It only needs a brief crisping in the oven or on top of the stove.

Canadian Bacon Pizza

PREP: 15 minutes BAKE: 15 minutes MAKES: 4 to 6 servings

 1   12-inch Italian bread shell (such as Boboli brand)

 1   6-ounce jar marinated artichoke hearts, undrained

 1   5.2-ounce container semisoft cheese with garlic
       and herbs

 1   3.5-ounce package pizza-style Canadian-style bacon
       (1½ inches in diameter)

 1   medium sweet pepper, cut into bite-size strips

one Place bread shell on a large baking sheet. Drain artichoke hearts, reserving 1 tablespoon of the marinade. Coarsely chop artichokes; set aside.

two In a small bowl combine cheese and the 1 tablespoon marinade. Spread half of the cheese mixture over bread shell. Top with Canadian-style bacon, sweet pepper, and chopped artichokes. Spoon the remaining cheese mixture by teaspoonfuls over toppings.

three Bake, uncovered, in a 350°F oven about 15 minutes or until heated through.

NUTRITION FACTS PER SERVING: 529 cal., 24 g total fat (9 g sat. fat), 54 mg chol., 1,136 mg sodium, 58 g carbo., 2 g fiber, 23 g pro.

Lemon-Pepper Lamb

PREP: 10 minutes **GRILL:** 1½ hours **STAND:** 15 minutes
MAKES: 8 servings

1   2- to 3-pound boneless lamb shoulder roast
1   teaspoon lemon-pepper seasoning
1   teaspoon dried marjoram, crushed
2   cloves garlic, minced

one Trim fat from meat. For rub, in a small bowl combine lemon-pepper seasoning, marjoram, and garlic. Sprinkle rub evenly over meat; rub in with your fingers.

two For a charcoal grill, arrange medium coals around a drip pan. Test for medium-low heat above the pan. Place meat on grill rack over drip pan. Cover and grill for 1½ to 2 hours for medium-rare (135°F) or 2¼ to 2½ hours for medium (150°F) (For a gas grill, preheat grill. Reduce heat to medium-low. Adjust for indirect cooking. Grill as above.)

three Remove meat from grill. Cover with foil and let stand for 15 minutes before slicing. (The meat's temperature will rise 10°F during standing.)

NUTRITION FACTS PER SERVING: 148 cal., 6 g total fat (2 g sat. fat), 72 mg chol., 195 mg sodium, 0 g carbo., 0 g fiber, 23 g pro.

Honey-Mustard Lamb Chops

PREP: 10 minutes **BROIL:** 10 minutes **MAKES:** 2 servings

4   lamb loin or rib chops, cut 1 inch thick
2   small zucchini, halved lengthwise
1   tablespoon Dijon-style mustard
1   tablespoon honey
1½   teaspoons snipped fresh rosemary or
     ½ teaspoon dried rosemary, crushed

one Trim fat from chops. Arrange chops and zucchini, cut sides up, on the unheated rack of a broiler pan. In a small bowl combine mustard, honey, and rosemary. Spread some of the mustard mixture on top of the chops.

two Broil chops and zucchini 3 to 4 inches from the heat for 5 minutes. Turn chops and zucchini; spread some of the mustard mixture on top of chops.

three Broil for 5 to 10 minutes more or until chops are medium (160°F) and zucchini is tender, spreading the remaining mustard mixture on zucchini during the last 3 minutes of broiling.

NUTRITION FACTS PER SERVING: 182 cal., 6 g total fat (2 g sat. fat), 60 mg chol., 99 mg sodium, 12 g carbo., 1 g fiber, 21 g pro.

Lamb Chops with Mint Marinade

PREP: 10 minutes **MARINATE:** 30 minutes to 24 hours
GRILL: 16 minutes **MAKES:** 4 servings

8	lamb loin chops, cut 1 inch thick
¼	cup snipped fresh mint
2	tablespoons lemon juice
2	tablespoons olive oil
3	cloves garlic, minced
¼	teaspoon black pepper
¼	teaspoon salt

one Trim fat from chops. Place chops in a resealable plastic bag set in a shallow dish. For marinade, in a small bowl combine 3 tablespoons of the mint, the lemon juice, olive oil, garlic, and pepper. Pour marinade over chops; seal bag. Marinate in the refrigerator for 30 minutes to 24 hours, turning bag occasionally.

two Drain chops, discarding marinade. Sprinkle chops with salt. For a charcoal grill, grill chops on the rack of an uncovered grill directly over medium coals for 16 to 18 minutes for medium-rare (145°F) or 18 to 20 minutes for medium (160°F), turning once halfway through grilling. (For a gas grill, preheat grill. Reduce heat to medium. Place chops on grill rack over heat. Cover and grill as above.)

three Sprinkle chops with the remaining 1 tablespoon mint.

NUTRITION FACTS PER SERVING: 236 cal., 13 g total fat (3 g sat. fat), 80 mg chol., 217 mg sodium, 2 g carbo., 0 g fiber, 26 g pro.

Balsamic-Glazed Lamb and Greens

START TO FINISH: 25 minutes **MAKES:** 4 servings

1	cup balsamic vinegar
8	lamb loin or rib chops, cut 1 inch thick
3	cups sugar snap peas, strings and tips removed
6	cups torn mixed salad greens
¼	cup hazelnuts or coarsely chopped walnuts, toasted (see tip, page 280)

one For glaze, in a small saucepan bring vinegar just to boiling. Boil gently, uncovered, about 10 minutes or until vinegar is reduced to ⅓ cup. Set aside.

two Meanwhile, trim fat from chops. Broil chops on the unheated rack of a broiler pan 3 to 4 inches from the heat for 10 to 15 minutes for medium (160°F), turning once.

three In a covered small saucepan cook sugar snap peas in a small amount of boiling salted water for 2 to 4 minutes or until crisp-tender; drain. Divide salad greens among 4 dinner plates. Top with chops and sugar snap peas. Drizzle with glaze; sprinkle with nuts.

NUTRITION FACTS PER SERVING: 293 cal., 10 g total fat (2 g sat. fat), 60 mg chol., 68 mg sodium, 24 g carbo., 3 g fiber, 23 g pro.

Herbed Lamb Chops

PREP: 15 minutes **MARINATE:** 4 to 24 hours **GRILL:** 12 minutes
MAKES: 4 servings

8	lamb rib chops, cut 1 inch thick
½	cup dry white wine
2	tablespoons snipped fresh oregano, basil, and/or thyme
2	tablespoons olive oil
2	cloves garlic, minced
½	teaspoon salt
¼	teaspoon black pepper

one Trim fat from chops. Place chops in a resealable plastic bag set in a shallow dish. For marinade, in a small bowl combine wine, herb, oil, garlic, salt, and pepper. Pour marinade over chops; seal bag. Marinate in the refrigerator for 4 to 24 hours, turning bag occasionally.

two Drain chops, discarding marinade. For a charcoal grill, grill chops on the rack of an uncovered grill directly over medium coals for 12 to 14 minutes for medium-rare (145°F) or 15 to 17 minutes for medium (160°F), turning once halfway through grilling. (For a gas grill, preheat grill. Reduce heat to medium. Place chops on grill rack over heat. Cover and grill as above.)

NUTRITION FACTS PER SERVING: 309 cal., 17 g total fat (6 g sat. fat), 112 mg chol., 195 mg sodium, 0 g carbo., 0 g fiber, 34 g pro.

Lamb Shanks with Basil Pesto

PREP: 10 minutes **COOK:** Low 7 hours, High 3½ hours
MAKES: 6 servings

1	16-ounce package frozen Italian-blend vegetables (cauliflower, broccoli, zucchini, and Italian green beans)
1	14½-ounce can diced tomatoes with basil, garlic, and oregano, undrained
1	14-ounce can chicken broth
3	to 3½ pounds meaty lamb shanks
½	cup purchased basil pesto

one In a 5- to 6-quart slow cooker combine the frozen vegetables, undrained tomatoes, and broth. Top with meat. Spoon pesto over meat.

two Cover and cook on low-heat setting for 7 to 9 hours or on high-heat setting for 3½ to 4½ hours. Using a slotted spoon, transfer meat and vegetables to a serving platter.

NUTRITION FACTS PER SERVING: 314 cal., 16 g total fat (1 g sat. fat), 66 mg chol., 884 mg sodium, 14 g carbo., 2 g fiber, 25 g pro.

Lamb Curry

PREP: 10 minutes **COOK:** Low 7 hours, High 3½ hours
MAKES: 10 servings

- 2 pounds lamb stew meat
- 1 16-ounce package frozen broccoli, cauliflower, and carrots
- 2 10¾-ounce cans condensed cream of onion soup
- ½ cup water
- 2 to 3 teaspoons curry powder
- 5 cups hot cooked rice

one In a 3½- or 4-quart slow cooker combine meat, frozen vegetables, soup, water, and curry powder.

two Cover and cook on low-heat setting for 7 to 8 hours or on high-heat setting for 3½ to 4 hours. Serve over hot cooked rice.

NUTRITION FACTS PER SERVING: 295 cal., 7 g total fat (2 g sat. fat), 68 mg chol., 727 mg sodium, 33 g carbo., 2 g fiber, 23 g pro.

Mediterranean Lamb Burgers *See photo on page 118.*

PREP: 15 minutes **GRILL:** 14 minutes **MAKES:** 4 servings

- 1 pound ground lamb or lean ground beef
- ½ to 1 teaspoon coarsely ground black pepper
- 2 pita bread rounds, halved crosswise, or 4 kaiser rolls, split and toasted
- 4 lettuce leaves
- ½ cup crumbled feta cheese (2 ounces)
- 1 tablespoon snipped fresh mint
   Chopped tomato (optional)

one Shape ground lamb into four ¾-inch-thick patties. Sprinkle pepper over both sides of patties; press into patties with your fingers.

two For a charcoal grill, grill burgers on the rack of an uncovered grill directly over medium coals for 14 to 18 minutes or until meat is done (160°F), turning once halfway through grilling. (For a gas grill, preheat grill. Reduce heat to medium. Place burgers on grill rack over heat. Cover and grill as above.)

three Serve burgers in pita halves with lettuce, feta cheese, mint, and, if desired, tomato.

NUTRITION FACTS PER SERVING: 428 cal., 21 g total fat (9 g sat. fat), 88 mg chol., 533 mg sodium, 31 g carbo., 1 g fiber, 27 g pro.

Greek Cabbage Rolls

PREP: 30 minutes **COOK:** Low 6 hours, High 3 hours
MAKES: 5 servings

1 large head green cabbage

1 pound ground lamb or lean ground beef

2 teaspoons Greek seasoning

1 26-ounce jar mushroom and ripe olive tomato
    pasta sauce

1 cup cooked rice

    Crumbled feta cheese (optional)

one Remove 10 large outer leaves from the cabbage.* In a Dutch oven cook cabbage leaves in boiling water for 3 to 4 minutes or just until leaves are limp. Drain cabbage leaves. Trim the thick rib from the center of each leaf. Set leaves aside. Shred 2 cups of the remaining cabbage; set aside. (Wrap and chill remaining cabbage for another use.)

two In a large skillet cook ground meat and Greek seasoning over medium-high heat until meat is brown. Drain off fat. Add the shredded cabbage, ½ cup of the pasta sauce, and the cooked rice; stir to combine. Evenly divide the lamb mixture among the 10 cabbage leaves. Fold sides of leaves over filling and roll up. Place cabbage rolls in a 3½- or 4-quart slow cooker. Top with the remaining pasta sauce.

three Cover and cook on low-heat setting for 6 to 7 hours or on high-heat setting for 3 to 3½ hours. Carefully remove the cooked cabbage rolls and serve with the pasta sauce. If desired, sprinkle with feta cheese.

__Note:__ To easily remove the cabbage leaves, place the cabbage head in boiling water for 2 to 3 minutes to loosen the outer leaves.

NUTRITION FACTS PER SERVING: 323 cal., 14 g total fat (6 g sat. fat), 61 mg chol., 707 mg sodium, 28 g carbo., 8 g fiber, 22 g pro.

Sweet Ginger Stir-Fry,
page 15

Tangy Lemon Chicken, page 11

Chicken Kabobs with Thai Brushing Sauce, page 14

Cranberry Chicken, page 19

Quick Chicken Fajitas, page 27

Mandarin Chicken Salad, page 26

Turkey with Dried Tomato Pesto, page 29

Barbecued Turkey Tenderloin Sandwiches, page 32

Sesame-Ginger Turkey Wraps, page 33

Bunless Burgers,
page 63

Saucy Meatball Sandwiches, page 69

Bloody Mary Steak, page 54

Pepper Steak, page 55

Flat-Iron Steaks, page 52

Steak with Tuscan Tomato Sauce,
page 53

Veal Rolls Stuffed with Herb Cheese,
page 70

Mediterranean Lamb Burgers, page 109

Cranberry-Chipotle Pork Chops,
   page 81

Stout-Glazed Ribs, page 93

Ham and Potatoes au Gratin, page 103

Barbecued Pork Chop Sandwiches, page 84

Shredded Pork Barbecue Rolls, page 80

Firecracker Foot-Longs, page 100

Grilled Salmon with Mustard Glaze,
page 130

No-Bake Tuna Noodle Casserole, page 129

Stuffed Tuna Steaks, page 128

Pasta with Basil-Shrimp for Two,
page 140

Shrimp with Fruit Salsa, page 138

Polenta and Black Beans, page 151

Mock Cheese Soufflé, page 146

Beef Burgundy,
page 173

Meatball-Vegetable Stew, page 170

Simply Ramen Chicken Soup, page 166

Chicken Tortilla Soup, page 166

Hearty Ham Stew, page 178

fast-fixin'
fish, shellfish & meatless

Stuffed Tuna Steaks *See photo on page 123.*

PREP: 25 minutes **GRILL:** 8 minutes **MAKES:** 6 servings

- 6 6-ounce fresh or frozen tuna steaks, cut 1 inch thick
- ¼ cup finely chopped onion
- ¼ cup finely chopped red sweet pepper
- ¼ cup pimiento-stuffed green olives, finely chopped
- 1 tablespoon hot chile oil

one Thaw fish, if frozen. Rinse fish; pat dry with paper towels. For stuffing, in a small bowl combine onion, sweet pepper, and olives.

two Cut a horizontal pocket in each tuna steak by cutting from one side to, but not through, the other side. Spoon about 2 tablespoons of the stuffing into each pocket. If necessary, secure with short metal skewers or wooden toothpicks. Brush half of the chile oil over both sides of fish.

three For a charcoal grill, grill fish on the greased rack of an uncovered grill directly over medium coals for 8 to 12 minutes or until fish flakes easily when tested with a fork, gently turning and brushing once with the remaining chile oil halfway through grilling. (For a gas grill, preheat grill. Reduce heat to medium. Place fish on greased grill rack over heat. Cover and grill as above.)

NUTRITION FACTS PER SERVING: 279 cal., 12 g total fat (2 g sat. fat), 64 mg chol., 149 mg sodium, 1 g carbo., 0 g fiber, 40 g pro.

Sesame-Seared Tuna

PREP: 10 minutes **COOK:** 8 minutes **MAKES:** 4 servings

- 4 6-ounce fresh or frozen tuna fillets, about ¾ inch thick
- 1 tablespoon olive oil
- ⅓ cup bottled hoisin sauce
- 3 tablespoons orange juice
- 1 tablespoon sesame seeds, toasted (see tip, page 280)

one Thaw fish, if frozen. Rinse fish; pat dry with paper towels. In a large skillet cook fish in hot oil over medium-high heat about 8 minutes or until fish flakes easily when tested with a fork (tuna can be slightly pink in the center), turning once.

two Meanwhile, for sauce, in a small saucepan stir together hoisin sauce and orange juice; heat through. To serve, drizzle sauce over fish. Sprinkle with sesame seeds.

NUTRITION FACTS PER SERVING: 271 cal., 7 g total fat (1 g sat. fat), 76 mg chol., 297 mg sodium, 9 g carbo., 0 g fiber, 41 g pro.

No-Bake Tuna Noodle Casserole *See photo on page 122.*

START TO FINISH: 20 minutes **MAKES:** 4 servings

8	ounces dried wagon wheel and/or elbow macaroni
1	6½-ounce container light semisoft cheese with cucumber and dill or garlic and herbs
¼	to ½ cup milk
1	12-ounce can solid white tuna (water-pack), drained and broken into chunks

one Cook macaroni in lightly salted water according to package directions; drain. Return macaroni to saucepan.

two Add cheese and ¼ cup of the milk to cooked macaroni. Cook and stir over medium heat until cheese melts and macaroni is coated, adding additional milk as needed to make mixture creamy. Gently fold in tuna; heat through.

NUTRITION FACTS PER SERVING: 417 cal., 10 g total fat (7 g sat. fat), 66 mg chol., 552 mg sodium, 45 g carbo., 2 g fiber, 33 g pro.

Tuna Salad with a Twist

START TO FINISH: 15 minutes **MAKES:** 4 servings

1	12-ounce can chunk white tuna (water-pack), drained
⅓	cup bottled creamy Italian salad dressing
⅓	cup finely chopped fresh or drained, canned pineapple
4	Boston lettuce leaves
2	sourdough, sesame, or plain bagels, split and toasted

one In a medium bowl combine tuna, creamy Italian salad dressing, and pineapple.

two Place lettuce leaves on toasted bagel halves. Spoon tuna mixture over the lettuce leaves.

NUTRITION FACTS PER SERVING: 276 cal., 10 g total fat (2 g sat. fat), 38 mg chol., 902 mg sodium, 22 g carbo., 1 g fiber, 24 g pro.

Grilled Salmon with Mustard Glaze *See photo on page 122.*

PREP: 10 minutes **GRILL:** 6 minutes **MAKES:** 4 servings

4   5-ounce fresh or frozen salmon steaks,
      cut ¾ inch thick

3   tablespoons Dijon-style mustard

1   to 2 tablespoons finely chopped canned jalapeño
      chile peppers, seeded (if desired)

1   tablespoon frozen orange juice concentrate, thawed

1   tablespoon light-color corn syrup

½   teaspoon black pepper

one Thaw fish, if frozen. Rinse fish; pat dry wth paper towels.

two For glaze, in a small bowl stir together mustard, jalapeño peppers, orange juice concentrate, corn syrup, and black pepper. Set aside.

three For a charcoal grill, grill fish on the greased rack of an uncovered grill directly over medium coals for 6 to 9 minutes or until fish flakes easily when tested with a fork, turning once halfway through grilling and brushing occasionally with glaze during the last half of grilling. (For a gas grill, preheat grill. Reduce heat to medium. Place fish on greased grill rack over heat. Cover and grill as above.)

NUTRITION FACTS PER SERVING: 192 cal., 5 g total fat (1 g sat. fat), 73 mg chol., 556 mg sodium, 4 g carbo., 0 g fiber, 28 g pro.

Orange-Marinated Salmon Steaks

PREP: 10 minutes **MARINATE:** 1 to 2 hours **GRILL:** 8 minutes
MAKES: 4 servings

4   6-ounce fresh or frozen salmon steaks,
      cut 1 inch thick

½   cup orange juice

3   tablespoons olive oil

¼   teaspoon lemon-pepper seasoning

one Thaw fish, if frozen. Rinse fish; pat dry with paper towels. Place fish in a resealable plastic bag set in a shallow dish.

two For marinade, in a small bowl combine orange juice and olive oil. Pour over fish; seal bag. Marinate in the refrigerator for 1 to 2 hours, turning bag occasionally.

three Drain fish, discarding marinade. Sprinkle fish with lemon-pepper seasoning. For a charcoal grill, grill fish on the greased rack of an uncovered grill directly over medium coals for 8 to 12 minutes or until fish flakes easily when tested with a fork, gently turning once halfway through grilling. (For a gas grill, preheat grill. Reduce heat to medium. Place fish on greased grill rack over heat. Cover and grill as above.)

NUTRITION FACTS PER SERVING: 284 cal., 18 g total fat (3 g sat. fat), 83 mg chol., 152 mg sodium, 1 g carbo., 0 g fiber, 28 g pro.

Salmon with Roasted Pepper Cream

PREP: 15 minutes **BAKE:** 20 minutes **MAKES:** 4 servings

4	6-ounce fresh or frozen boneless salmon fillets
3	tablespoons honey-Dijon mustard
3	tablespoons seasoned fine dry bread crumbs
1	cup whipping cream
½	cup bottled roasted red sweet peppers, drained and chopped

one Thaw fish, if frozen. Rinse fish; pat dry with paper towels. Brush one side of fish with 2 tablespoons of the mustard. Sprinkle with bread crumbs. Place fish, crumb sides up, in a greased 3-quart rectangular baking dish.

two Bake, uncovered, in a 400°F oven for 20 to 25 minutes or until crumbs are golden and fish flakes easily with a fork.

three Meanwhile, for sauce, in a medium saucepan combine the remaining 1 tablespoon mustard, the cream, and roasted peppers. Bring to boiling; reduce heat. Boil gently, uncovered, about 15 minutes or until reduced to 1 cup. Serve with fish.

NUTRITION FACTS PER SERVING: 576 cal., 32 g total fat (15 g sat. fat), 227 mg chol., 359 mg sodium, 11 g carbo., 0 g fiber, 57 g pro.

GRILLING

Foil-Wrapped Salmon Dinner

PREP: 20 minutes **GRILL:** 12 minutes **MAKES:** 4 servings

4	6-ounce fresh or frozen skinless salmon fillets, ½ to ¾ inch thick
	Nonstick cooking spray
1	20-ounce package refrigerated sliced potatoes
6	tablespoons butter or margarine, cut into 12 equal pieces
2	teaspoons herb-pepper seasoning
1	pound fresh asparagus spears, trimmed

one Thaw fish, if frozen. Rinse fish; pat dry with paper towels.

two Tear off four 18-inch squares of heavy foil; lightly coat with cooking spray. Place one-fourth of the potatoes in two 6-inch strips, side by side in the center of each piece of foil. Top each with 2 pieces of the butter and sprinkle with ¼ teaspoon of the herb-pepper seasoning. Top each with a salmon steak, one-fourth of the asparagus, another piece of butter, and ¼ teaspoon of the herb-pepper seasoning.

three Bring up two opposite edges of foil and seal with a double fold. Fold remaining edges together to completely enclose fish and vegetables, leaving space for steam to build.

four For a charcoal grill, grill foil packets, potato sides down, on the rack of an uncovered grill directly over medium coals for 12 to 14 minutes or until fish flakes easily when tested with a fork and potatoes are heated through (carefully open one packet to check doneness). (For a gas grill, preheat grill. Reduce heat to medium. Place foil packets on grill rack over heat. Cover and grill as above.)

NUTRITION FACTS PER SERVING: 506 cal., 25 g total fat (12 g sat. fat), 137 mg chol., 804 mg sodium, 30 g carbo., 2 g fiber, 39 g pro.

Salmon Caesar Salad

START TO FINISH: 15 minutes **MAKES:** 3 servings

1   10-ounce package Caesar salad kit (includes lettuce, dressing, croutons, and cheese)

1   small sweet pepper, cut into thin strips

1   small cucumber, quartered lengthwise and sliced

6   ounces smoked, poached, or canned salmon, skinned, boned, and broken into chunks (1 cup)

½   of a lemon, cut into 3 wedges

one In a large bowl combine lettuce and dressing from packaged salad, the sweet pepper, and cucumber; toss gently to coat. Add croutons and cheese from packaged salad and the salmon; toss gently to combine.

two Divide lettuce mixture among 3 dinner plates. Before serving, squeeze juice from a lemon wedge over each salad.

NUTRITION FACTS PER SERVING: 251 cal., 18 g total fat (3 g sat. fat), 23 mg chol., 826 mg sodium, 11 g carbo., 3 g fiber, 14 g pro.

Smoked Salmon Pasta

START TO FINISH: 25 minutes **MAKES:** 4 to 6 servings

8   ounces dried bow tie or mini lasagna pasta

1   cup whipping cream

½   teaspoon seafood seasoning

8   ounces smoked salmon, flaked, with skin and bones removed, if present

½   cup bottled roasted red sweet peppers, drained and cut into bite-size strips

one In a large saucepan cook pasta according to package directions; drain. Return to saucepan; cover and keep warm.

two Meanwhile, in a medium saucepan combine whipping cream and seafood seasoning. Cook over medium heat until bubbly. Cook, uncovered, about 5 minutes more or until thickened, stirring occasionally. Stir in salmon and roasted peppers; heat through.

three Add salmon mixture to pasta; toss gently to coat.

NUTRITION FACTS PER SERVING: 489 cal., 26 g total fat (14 g sat. fat), 95 mg chol., 552 mg sodium, 45 g carbo., 2 g fiber, 19 g pro.

Almond Walleye

START TO FINISH: 25 minutes **MAKES:** 4 servings

4   8- to 10-ounce fresh or frozen walleye pike fillets or other fish fillets

½   cup all-purpose flour

¼   cup ground almonds (1 ounce)

¼   teaspoon salt

¼   teaspoon black pepper

¼   cup olive oil

one Thaw fish, if frozen. Rinse fish; pat dry with paper towels. In a shallow dish stir together flour, almonds, salt, and pepper. Dip fish into flour mixture, turning to coat.

two In a large skillet cook 2 of the fish fillets in 2 tablespoons of the oil over medium heat for 8 to 12 minutes or until coating is golden and fish flakes easily when tested with a fork, gently turning once. Remove from skillet; cover and keep warm. Repeat with the remaining fish fillets and oil.

NUTRITION FACTS PER SERVING: 423 cal., 20 g total fat (3 g sat. fat), 194 mg chol., 261 mg sodium, 12 g carbo., 1 g fiber, 46 g pro.

Lime-Poached Mahi Mahi

START TO FINISH: 20 minutes **MAKES:** 4 servings

4   6-ounce fresh or frozen mahi mahi or catfish fillets, ½ to ¾ inch thick

2   teaspoons seasoned pepper

1   tablespoon olive oil

⅓   cup frozen margarita mix concentrate, thawed

2   cups hot cooked basmati or long grain rice

one Thaw fish, if frozen. Skin fish, if necessary. Rinse fish; pat dry with paper towels. Rub both sides of fish with seasoned pepper.

two In a large nonstick skillet cook fish in hot oil over medium-high heat for 2 to 4 minutes or until lightly browned, gently turning once. Reduce heat to medium-low.

three Carefully add margarita concentrate to skillet. Cook, covered, for 6 to 8 minutes or until fish flakes easily when tested with a fork. Serve fish and sauce with rice.

NUTRITION FACTS PER SERVING: 336 cal., 5 g total fat (1 g sat. fat), 124 mg chol., 150 mg sodium, 41 g carbo., 0 g fiber, 34 g pro.

Basmati Rice Among the rainbow of rices is a family known as the aromatics. Jasmine (from Thailand), basmati (India), Texmati (Texas), and wild rice pecan (Louisiana) are all long grain, aromatic rices prized for their nutty flavor and sweet aroma. Aromatic rices go nicely with Asian-, Indian-, and Caribbean-style foods.

Steamed Fish with Veggies

PREP: 15 minutes **COOK:** 6 minutes **MAKES:** 2 servings

2   6-ounce fresh or frozen orange roughy or other
    fish fillets

    Whole fresh basil leaves

2   teaspoons shredded fresh ginger

1   cup thinly sliced sweet peppers

8   ounces fresh asparagus spears, trimmed

one Thaw fish, if frozen. Rinse fish; pat dry with paper towels. Using a sharp knife, make diagonal cuts about ¾ inch apart in the fish fillets. (Do not cut completely through fish.) Tuck basil leaves into cuts. Rub fish with ginger.

two Place peppers and asparagus in a steamer basket. Place fish on top of vegetables. Place basket in a saucepan over 1 inch of boiling water. Steam, covered, for 6 to 8 minutes or until fish flakes easily when tested with a fork.

NUTRITION FACTS PER SERVING: 254 cal., 2 g total fat (0 g sat. fat), 37 mg chol., 61 mg sodium, 36 g carbo., 3 g fiber, 21 g pro.

Snapper Veracruz

PREP: 15 minutes **BAKE:** 30 minutes **MAKES:** 4 servings

1¼   to 1½ pounds fresh or frozen skinless red snapper
     fillets or firm-textured white fish fillets (such as
     catfish), ½ to ¾ inch thick

1   14½-ounce can Mexican-style stewed tomatoes,
    undrained

1   cup pitted ripe olives

2   tablespoons olive oil

1   10-ounce package saffron-flavor yellow rice mix

one Thaw fish, if frozen. Rinse fish; pat dry with paper towels. Cut fish into 4 serving-size pieces.

two In a large ovenproof skillet combine undrained tomatoes and olives. Top with fish fillets; drizzle with oil. Bake, uncovered, in a 300°F oven for 15 minutes. Spoon some of the tomato mixture over fish. Bake, uncovered, about 15 minutes more or until fish flakes easily when tested with a fork.

three Meanwhile, prepare rice mix according to package directions. Serve fish and sauce with rice.

NUTRITION FACTS PER SERVING: 566 cal., 19 g total fat (3 g sat. fat), 52 mg chol., 1,466 mg sodium, 63 g carbo., 3 g fiber, 36 g pro.

Crunchy Catfish and Zucchini

PREP: 15 minutes **BAKE:** 12 minutes **MAKES:** 4 servings

1	pound fresh or frozen catfish fillets
1	medium zucchini or yellow summer squash
1	cup bottled ranch salad dressing
2	teaspoons bottled hot pepper sauce
4	cups cornflakes, slightly crushed

one Thaw fish, if frozen. Rinse fish; pat dry with paper towels. Cut fish into 1-inch strips. Cut zucchini in half crosswise. Cut each half lengthwise into 6 wedges.

two In a large bowl combine salad dressing and hot pepper sauce. Set aside half of the dressing to use for dipping. Add fish and zucchini strips to the remaining dressing; stir gently to coat.

three Place crushed cornflakes in a plastic bag. Add fish and zucchini strips, one-third at a time, shaking to coat. Place coated fish and zucchini in a single layer in a greased 15×10×1-inch baking pan.

four Bake, uncovered, in a 425°F oven for 12 to 15 minutes or until crumbs are golden and fish flakes easily when tested with a fork. Serve with the reserved dressing for dipping.

NUTRITION FACTS PER SERVING: 545 cal., 40 g total fat (7 g sat. fat), 58 mg chol., 779 mg sodium, 24 g carbo., 0 g fiber, 20 g pro.

GRILLING

Rocky Mountain Trout

PREP: 15 minutes **GRILL:** 8 minutes **MAKES:** 4 servings

4	8- to 10-ounce fresh or frozen pan-dressed rainbow trout
	Cooking oil
½	to ¾ cup finely chopped red onion and/or green sweet pepper
2	tablespoons snipped fresh cilantro
½	teaspoon ground cumin
¼	teaspoon salt
¼	teaspoon black pepper
	Grilled lemon wedges (optional)

one Thaw fish, if frozen. Rinse fish; pat dry with paper towels. Lightly brush the outside of each fish with oil. In a small bowl combine onion, cilantro, cumin, salt, and pepper. Spoon the onion mixture into fish cavities.

two Place fish in a well-greased grill basket. For a charcoal grill, place basket on the rack of an uncovered grill directly over medium coals. Grill for 8 to 12 minutes or until fish flakes easily when tested with a fork, turning basket once halfway through grilling. (For a gas grill, preheat grill. Reduce heat to medium. Place fish in basket on grill rack over heat. Cover and grill as above.)

three If desired, serve fish with grilled lemon wedges.

NUTRITION FACTS PER SERVING: 340 cal., 15 g total fat (4 g sat. fat), 133 mg chol., 228 mg sodium, 2 g carbo., 0 g fiber, 48 g pro.

Mustard-Glazed Halibut Steaks

PREP: 10 minutes **GRILL:** 8 minutes **MAKES:** 4 servings

- 4 6-ounce fresh or frozen halibut steaks, cut 1 inch thick
- 2 tablespoons butter or margarine
- 2 tablespoons lemon juice
- 1 tablespoon Dijon-style mustard
- 2 teaspoons snipped fresh basil or ½ teaspoon dried basil, crushed

one Thaw fish, if frozen. Rinse fish; pat dry with paper towels. In a small saucepan combine butter, lemon juice, mustard, and basil. Cook and stir over low heat until butter melts. Brush both sides of fish with mustard mixture.

two For a charcoal grill, grill fish on the greased rack of an uncovered grill directly over medium coals for 8 to 12 minutes or until fish flakes easily when tested with a fork, turning once halfway through grilling and brushing occasionally with mustard mixture during the last half of grilling. (For a gas grill, preheat grill. Reduce heat to medium. Place fish on greased grill rack over heat. Cover and grill as above.)

NUTRITION FACTS PER SERVING: 243 cal., 10 g total fat (4 g sat. fat), 70 mg chol., 254 mg sodium, 1 g carbo., 0 g fiber, 36 g pro.

Lemon-Dill Fish Fillets

PREP: 15 minutes **GRILL:** 12 minutes **MAKES:** 4 servings

- 1 pound fresh or frozen fish fillets, ½ to ¾ inch thick
- 1 lemon, thinly sliced
- 2 tablespoons snipped fresh dill or 1 teaspoon dried dill
- 1 tablespoon drained capers
- ½ teaspoon lemon-pepper seasoning

one Thaw fish, if frozen. Rinse fish; pat dry with paper towels. Cut fish into 4 serving-size pieces.

two Tear off four 24×18-inch pieces of heavy foil; fold each in half to make an 18×12-inch rectangle. Place lemon slices in the center of each foil rectangle. Top each with a fish fillet, tucking under any thin edges. Sprinkle fish with dill, capers, and lemon-pepper seasoning. Bring up two opposite edges of foil and seal with a double fold. Fold the remaining edges together to completely enclose fish and seasonings, leaving space for steam to build.

three For a charcoal grill, grill foil packets on the rack of an uncovered grill directly over medium coals for 12 to 14 minutes or until fish flakes easily when tested with a fork (carefully open one packet to check doneness), turning packet once halfway through grilling. (For a gas grill, preheat grill. Reduce heat to medium. Place foil packets on grill rack over heat. Cover and grill as above.)

NUTRITION FACTS PER SERVING: 97 cal., 1 g total fat (0 g sat. fat), 48 mg chol., 261 mg sodium, 2 g carbo., 0 g fiber, 20 g pro.

Glazed Prosciutto-Wrapped Shrimp

PREP: 30 minutes **GRILL:** 5 minutes **MAKES:** 4 servings

24   fresh or frozen large shrimp in shells

½   cup bourbon grilling sauce (such as
      Jack Daniel's brand)

½   teaspoon chili powder

8   thin slices prosciutto

2   cups hot cooked couscous (optional)

> **Peeling and Deveining Shrimp** To peel a shrimp, open the shell lengthwise down the body. Starting at the head end, peel back the shell. Gently pull on the tail to remove it, or leave it intact, if you prefer.
>
> To devein a shrimp, use a sharp knife to make a shallow slit along the back from the head to the tail end. Locate the black vein. If the vein is visible, hold the shrimp under cold running water to rinse it away. Or use the tip of a knife to remove the vein, then rinse the shrimp.

one Thaw shrimp, if frozen. Peel and devein shrimp. Rinse shrimp; pat dry with paper towels. Set shrimp aside.

two In a small bowl combine grilling sauce and chili powder. Cut each prosciutto slice lengthwise into 3 strips. Wrap a prosciutto strip around each shrimp. Thread shrimp onto 4 long metal skewers, leaving ¼ inch between each shrimp. Brush shrimp with grilling sauce mixture.

three For a charcoal grill, grill shrimp on the rack of an uncovered grill directly over medium coals for 5 to 8 minutes or until shrimp are opaque, turning once halfway through grilling and brushing occasionally with sauce during the last half of grilling. (For a gas grill, preheat grill. Reduce heat to medium. Place shrimp skewers on grill rack over heat. Cover and grill as above.)

four If desired, serve shrimp with hot cooked couscous.

NUTRITION FACTS PER SERVING: 195 cal., 4 g total fat (1 g sat. fat), 207 mg chol., 932 mg sodium, 5 g carbo., 0 g fiber, 32 g pro.

Shrimp with Fruit Salsa *See photo on page 123.*

PREP: 25 minutes **GRILL:** 4 minutes **MAKES:** 6 servings

1½	pounds fresh or frozen large shrimp in shells (about 36 shrimp)
1	tablespoon butter or margarine, melted
¼	teaspoon salt
¼	teaspoon ground cumin
¼	teaspoon black pepper
⅛	teaspoon cayenne pepper
2	cups bottled fruit salsa or 1 recipe Papaya Salsa (see recipe, page 255)
	Grilled pineapple wedges (optional)

one Thaw shrimp, if frozen. Peel and devein shrimp, leaving tails intact. Rinse shrimp; pat dry with paper towels.

two In a small bowl combine melted butter, salt, cumin, black pepper, and cayenne pepper. Drizzle butter mixture over shrimp; toss gently to coat.

three Place shrimp in a lightly greased grill basket. For a charcoal grill, place basket on the rack of an uncovered grill directly over medium coals. Grill for 4 to 6 minutes or until shrimp are opaque, turning basket once halfway through grilling. (For a gas grill, preheat grill. Reduce heat to medium. Place shrimp in basket on grill rack over heat. Cover and grill as above.)

four Serve shrimp with fruit salsa and, if desired, grilled pineapple wedges.

NUTRITION FACTS PER SERVING: 204 cal., 4 g total fat (2 g sat. fat), 177 mg chol., 493 mg sodium, 17 g carbo., 3 g fiber, 23 g pro.

> **Gas Grill Features** There's no denying it: Gas grills are extraordinarily convenient. For most models, all you have to do is turn a valve, push a button, and within minutes you're off and grilling.
>
> When purchasing a gas grill, look for multiple burners with an individual control for each burner. This feature enables indirect grilling or barbecuing in addition to direct grilling over the flames. And when purchasing any type of grill, remember that solid construction is a virtue all its own.

Cilantro Shrimp

PREP: 20 minutes GRILL: 5 minutes MAKES: 4 servings

- 1 pound fresh or frozen jumbo shrimp in shells (20 to 24 shrimp)
- 2 tablespoons snipped fresh cilantro
- 1 tablespoon lemon juice
- 1 tablespoon butter, melted
- 3 or 4 cloves garlic, minced
- 1 fresh red serrano chile pepper, seeded and finely chopped (see tip, page 59) (optional)

one Thaw shrimp, if frozen. Using a sharp knife, butterfly each shrimp by cutting a deep slit along its back through the shell (do not cut all the way through shrimp), leaving tail intact. Devein shrimp; flatten with your hand. Rinse shrimp; pat dry.

two In a small bowl combine cilantro, lemon juice, melted butter, garlic, and, if desired, serrano pepper. Brush shrimp with lemon mixture. Place shrimp, split sides down, in a lightly greased grill basket.

three For a charcoal grill, place basket on the rack of an uncovered grill directly over medium coals. Grill for 5 to 8 minutes or until shrimp are opaque, turning basket once halfway through grilling. (For a gas grill, preheat grill. Reduce heat to medium. Place shrimp in basket on grill rack over heat. Cover and grill as above.)

NUTRITION FACTS PER SERVING: 120 cal., 4 g total fat (2 g sat. fat), 137 mg chol., 148 mg sodium, 2 g carbo., 0 g fiber, 18 g pro.

Garlic-Buttered Shrimp Kabobs

PREP: 25 minutes GRILL: 5 minutes MAKES: 4 servings

- 1 pound fresh or frozen jumbo shrimp in shells (20 to 24 shrimp)
- 2 tablespoons butter
- 1 tablespoon snipped fresh parsley (optional)
- 2 cloves garlic, minced
   Dash cayenne pepper
- 3 tablespoons dry white wine

one Thaw shrimp, if frozen. Peel and devein shrimp, leaving tails intact. Rinse shrimp; pat dry. Thread shrimp onto 4 long or 8 short metal skewers, leaving ¼ inch between each shrimp.

two For sauce, in a small saucepan melt butter over medium heat. Stir in parsley (if desired), garlic, and cayenne pepper. Cook for 1 minute. Stir in wine; heat through. Set aside.

three For a charcoal grill, grill shrimp on the greased rack of an uncovered grill directly over medium coals for 5 to 8 minutes or until shrimp are opaque, turning once halfway through grilling and brushing frequently with sauce during the last half of grilling. (For a gas grill, preheat grill. Reduce heat to medium. Place shrimp skewers on grill rack over heat. Cover and grill as above.)

NUTRITION FACTS PER SERVING: 152 cal., 7 g total fat (4 g sat. fat), 145 mg chol., 167 mg sodium, 2 g carbo., 0 g fiber, 17 g pro.

Pasta with Basil-Shrimp for Two *See photo on page 123.*

START TO FINISH: 20 minutes   **MAKES:** 2 servings

- 8   ounces fresh or frozen large shrimp in shells (about 12 shrimp)
- 3   ounces dried spinach linguine and/or plain fusilli pasta
- 1   teaspoon snipped fresh basil or tarragon or ½ teaspoon dried basil or tarragon, crushed
- 1   tablespoon butter or margarine
    Thinly sliced fresh basil or tarragon (optional)

one Thaw shrimp, if frozen. Peel and devein shrimp, leaving tails intact. Rinse shrimp; pat dry with paper towels. Cook pasta according to package directions; drain. Return pasta to saucepan.

two Meanwhile, in a large skillet cook shrimp and the snipped basil in melted butter over medium-high heat for 3 to 4 minutes or until shrimp are opaque, stirring frequently.

three Add shrimp mixture to cooked pasta; toss gently to combine. If desired, sprinkle each serving with the thinly sliced fresh basil.

NUTRITION FACTS PER SERVING: 329 cal., 8 g total fat (4 g sat. fat), 188 mg chol., 227 mg sodium, 33 g carbo., 2 g fiber, 28 g pro.

Capellini with Shrimp and Pesto

START TO FINISH: 20 minutes   **MAKES:** 4 servings

- 12   ounces fresh or frozen peeled and deveined shrimp
- 8   ounces dried plain and/or tomato angel hair pasta (capellini), fettuccine, or linguine
    Nonstick cooking spray
- 2   medium yellow summer squash and/or zucchini, cut into ½-inch chunks (about 2 cups)
- ⅓   cup purchased basil pesto
- 1   medium roma tomato, chopped

one Thaw shrimp, if frozen. Rinse shrimp; pat dry with paper towels. Cook pasta according to package directions; drain. Return pasta to saucepan.

two Meanwhile, coat a large nonstick skillet with cooking spray; heat over medium-high heat. Add shrimp to hot skillet; cook and stir for 2 minutes. Add squash; cook and stir about 2 minutes more or until shrimp are opaque and squash is crisp-tender. Remove from heat.

three Add pesto to shrimp mixture; toss gently to coat. Serve shrimp mixture over cooked pasta and sprinkle with chopped tomato.

NUTRITION FACTS PER SERVING: 246 cal., 12 g total fat (3 g sat. fat), 135 mg chol., 305 mg sodium, 14 g carbo., 2 g fiber, 23 g pro.

Curried Coconut Shrimp

START TO FINISH: 30 minutes **MAKES:** 4 servings

1   pound fresh or frozen jumbo shrimp in shells
    (20 to 24 shrimp)
1   cup uncooked jasmine rice
1   15¼-ounce can tropical fruit salad or pineapple
    chunks, undrained
1   teaspoon red curry paste
1   cup unsweetened coconut milk

one Thaw shrimp, if frozen. Cook rice according to package directions. Meanwhile, peel and devein shrimp. Rinse shrimp; pat dry with paper towels. Drain fruit, reserving ½ cup liquid. Set fruit and liquid aside.

two In a large nonstick skillet cook and stir shrimp and curry paste over medium-high heat for 3 to 4 minutes or until shrimp are opaque. Remove shrimp from skillet.

three For sauce, add the ½ cup liquid from fruit and the coconut milk to skillet. Bring to boiling; reduce heat. Simmer, uncovered, for 5 to 7 minutes or until mixture is slightly thickened and reduced to about 1 cup.

four Divide the cooked rice among 4 shallow bowls. Arrange shrimp on top of rice and spoon sauce over shrimp. Top each serving with fruit.

NUTRITION FACTS PER SERVING: 463 cal., 17 g total fat (13 g sat. fat), 151 mg chol., 263 mg sodium, 55 g carbo., 2 g fiber, 24 g pro.

Mediterranean Shrimp and Couscous

START TO FINISH: 15 minutes **MAKES:** 4 servings

12 ounces fresh or frozen peeled and deveined
    shrimp
1   14½-ounce can diced tomatoes with onion and
    garlic, undrained
1   5.6-ounce package toasted pine nut-flavor
    couscous mix
¾   cup water
½   cup golden raisins

one Thaw shrimp, if frozen. Rinse shrimp; pat dry with paper towels. In a large skillet combine undrained tomatoes, seasoning packet from couscous mix, and water. Bring to boiling. Stir in shrimp. Cook over high heat for 2 to 3 minutes or until shrimp are opaque.

two Stir in couscous and raisins. Remove from heat. Cover and let stand about 5 minutes or until liquid is absorbed.

NUTRITION FACTS PER SERVING: 338 cal., 4 g total fat (1 g sat. fat), 129 mg chol., 967 mg sodium, 53 g carbo., 6 g fiber, 25 g pro.

Shrimp and Scallop Skewers

PREP: 20 minutes **MARINATE:** 30 minutes to 2 hours
GRILL: 5 minutes **MAKES:** 4 servings

12	fresh or frozen extra large shrimp in shells
12	fresh or frozen large sea scallops
⅔	cup bottled Italian salad dressing
2	medium sweet peppers, cut into 1½-inch pieces

one Thaw shrimp and scallops, if frozen. Peel and devein shrimp. Rinse shrimp and scallops; pat dry with paper towels. Place shrimp and scallops in a resealable plastic bag set in a shallow dish. Add ½ cup of the dressing; seal bag. Marinate in the refrigerator for 30 minutes to 2 hours, turning bag once.

two Drain shrimp and scallops, discarding marinade. In a small saucepan cook peppers in a small amount of boiling water for 2 minutes; drain. Alternately thread shrimp, scallops, and peppers onto sixteen 10-inch metal skewers, using 2 skewers side by side for each kabob.

three For a charcoal grill, grill shrimp and scallop skewers on the greased rack of an uncovered grill directly over medium coals for 5 to 8 minutes or until shrimp and scallops are opaque, turning once halfway through grilling. (For a gas grill, preheat grill. Reduce heat to medium. Place shrimp and scallop skewers on greased grill rack over heat. Cover and grill as above.)

four To serve, brush kabobs with the remaining dressing.

NUTRITION FACTS PER SERVING: 174 cal., 8 g total fat (1 g sat. fat), 76 mg chol., 264 mg sodium, 7 g carbo., 1 g fiber, 18 g pro.

Sweet-and-Sour Shrimp

START TO FINISH: 15 minutes **MAKES:** 4 servings

12	ounces fresh or frozen peeled and deveined shrimp
⅓	cup bottled stir-fry sauce
¼	cup pineapple-orange juice
	Nonstick cooking spray
3	cups fresh cut stir-fry vegetables (such as broccoli, pea pods, carrots, sweet peppers, and celery)

one Thaw shrimp, if frozen. Rinse shrimp; pat dry with paper towels. In a small bowl combine stir-fry sauce and juice.

two Coat a large nonstick skillet with cooking spray; heat over medium-high heat. Add vegetables to hot skillet; cook and stir for 3 to 5 minutes or until crisp-tender. Remove from skillet. (Add cooking oil, if necessary.) Add shrimp; cook and stir for 2 to 3 minutes or until shrimp are opaque. Push shrimp from center of skillet.

three Add sauce mixture to skillet. Return vegetables; stir to coat ingredients with sauce. Cook and stir until heated through.

NUTRITION FACTS PER SERVING: 119 cal., 1 g total fat (0 g sat. fat), 131 mg chol., 666 mg sodium, 11 g carbo., 2 g fiber, 17 g pro.

Peppy Asparagus-Shrimp Toss

START TO FINISH: 20 minutes **MAKES:** 4 servings

- 8 ounces fresh asparagus spears, trimmed and cut into bite-size pieces
- 3 cups cooked brown rice, chilled
- 8 ounces fresh or frozen peeled and deveined cooked shrimp
- 3 tablespoons oil-packed dried tomatoes, drained and chopped
- 2 tablespoons sweet-hot mustard

one In a covered small saucepan cook asparagus in a small amount of boiling water for 3 to 5 minutes or until crisp-tender; drain. Rinse under cold water; drain again.

two In a large bowl combine asparagus, chilled brown rice, shrimp, dried tomatoes, and mustard; toss gently to combine.

NUTRITION FACTS PER SERVING: 306 cal., 7 g total fat (1 g sat. fat), 111 mg chol., 205 mg sodium, 42 g carbo., 5 g fiber, 20 g pro.

Shrimp with Honey-Ginger Sauce

PREP: 20 minutes **BROIL:** 4 minutes **MAKES:** 4 servings

- 1½ pounds fresh or frozen jumbo shrimp in shells (20 to 24 shrimp)
- 3 tablespoons honey
- ¼ teaspoon ground ginger
- ½ cup dairy sour cream or plain low-fat yogurt
  Salt and black pepper

one Thaw shrimp, if frozen. Peel and devein shrimp. Rinse shrimp; pat dry with paper towels. Set aside. In a small bowl stir together honey and ginger. Set aside 2 tablespoons of the honey mixture to use for basting. Stir sour cream into the remaining 1 tablespoon honey mixture; set aside until ready to serve.

two Thread shrimp onto 4 long metal skewers, leaving ¼ inch between each shrimp. Place shrimp skewers on the greased unheated rack of a broiler pan. Brush shrimp with the 2 tablespoons honey mixture. Sprinkle with salt and pepper.

three Broil about 4 inches from the heat for 4 to 6 minutes or until shrimp are opaque, turning skewers once. Serve shrimp with the reserved sour cream-honey mixture.

NUTRITION FACTS PER SERVING: 250 cal., 7 g total fat (4 g sat. fat), 226 mg chol., 293 mg sodium, 15 g carbo., 0 g fiber, 30 g pro.

Buttery Bay Scallops

START TO FINISH: 10 minutes **MAKES:** 3 or 4 servings

12   ounces fresh or frozen bay scallops

1   clove garlic, minced

⅛   teaspoon dried tarragon, crushed

2   tablespoons butter or margarine

      Salt and black pepper

one Thaw scallops, if frozen. Rinse scallops; pat dry with paper towels. In a large skillet cook garlic and tarragon in melted butter over medium heat for 1 minute, stirring frequently. Remove from heat.

two Add scallops to hot skillet. Sprinkle lightly with salt and pepper. Cook over medium heat for 2 to 3 minutes or until scallops are opaque, turning occasionally.

NUTRITION FACTS PER SERVING: 173 cal., 9 g total fat (5 g sat. fat), 59 mg chol., 362 mg sodium, 3 g carbo., 0 g fiber, 19 g pro.

Scallop Fried Rice

PREP: 15 minutes **MARINATE:** 30 minutes **MAKES:** 2 servings

8   ounces fresh or frozen bay scallops

¼   cup bottled teriyaki or sesame-ginger stir-fry sauce

      Nonstick cooking spray

1   egg

2   green onions, thinly bias-sliced

1   10-ounce package frozen rice with peas and
      mushrooms, thawed

one Thaw scallops, if frozen. Rinse scallops; pat dry with paper towels. In a small bowl stir together scallops and stir-fry sauce. Cover and marinate in the refrigerator for 30 minutes.

two Coat a wok or large skillet with cooking spray; heat over medium-high heat. Crack egg into hot wok. Cook and stir about 1 minute or until egg is cooked through (should look like scrambled egg). Remove egg from wok.

three Add scallop mixture and green onion to wok. Cook and stir about 2 minutes or until scallops are opaque. Add thawed rice mixture and cooked egg to wok; stir ingredients together to coat with sauce. Cook and stir about 2 minutes more or until heated through.

NUTRITION FACTS PER SERVING: 362 cal., 5 g total fat (1 g sat. fat), 144 mg chol., 1,502 mg sodium, 48 g carbo., 2 g fiber, 26 g pro.

Thai-Spiced Scallop Kabobs

PREP: 10 minutes **GRILL:** 5 minutes **MAKES:** 4 servings

- 1 pound fresh or frozen sea scallops
- ⅔ cup bottled sweet-and-sour sauce
- 2 tablespoons snipped fresh basil
- 1 teaspoon Thai seasoning or five-spice powder
- 1 clove garlic, minced

one Thaw scallops, if frozen. Rinse scallops; pat dry with paper towels. For sauce, in a small bowl combine sweet-and-sour sauce, basil, Thai seasoning, and garlic. Set aside ¼ cup of the sauce to use for basting. Reserve the remaining sauce until ready to serve.

two Thread scallops onto four 8- to 10-inch metal skewers, leaving ¼ inch between each scallop.

three For a charcoal grill, grill scallops on the greased rack of an uncovered grill directly over medium coals for 5 to 8 minutes or until scallops are opaque, turning and brushing once with the ¼ cup sauce halfway through grilling. (For a gas grill, preheat grill. Reduce heat to medium. Place scallop skewers on greased grill rack over heat. Cover and grill as above.) Serve scallops with the reserved sauce.

NUTRITION FACTS PER SERVING: 148 cal., 1 g total fat (0 g sat. fat), 37 mg chol., 517 mg sodium, 15 g carbo., 0 g fiber, 19 g pro.

Lobster Tails with Chive Butter

PREP: 15 minutes **GRILL:** 11 minutes **MAKES:** 4 servings

- 4 6-ounce fresh or frozen rock lobster tails
- ⅓ cup butter
- 2 tablespoons snipped fresh chives
- 1 teaspoon finely shredded lemon peel
   Lemon wedges (optional)

one Thaw lobster tails, if frozen. Rinse lobster; pat dry with paper towels. Using kitchen shears or a large sharp knife, butterfly each lobster tail by cutting through center of hard top shell and meat (do not cut all the way through bottom shell). Open split sides.

two For sauce, in a small saucepan melt butter. Remove from heat. Stir in chives and lemon peel. Set aside 2 tablespoons of the sauce to use for basting. Reserve the remaining sauce until ready to serve.

three Brush lobster meat with some of the 2 tablespoons sauce. For a charcoal grill, grill lobster tails, split sides down, on the rack of an uncovered grill directly over medium coals for 11 to 14 minutes or until meat is opaque in center, turning and brushing once with the rest of the 2 tablespoons sauce halfway through grilling. Do not overcook. (For a gas grill, preheat grill. Reduce heat to medium. Place lobster tails on grill rack over heat. Cover and grill as above.)

four Meanwhile, heat the reserved sauce, stirring occasionally. Transfer sauce to 4 small bowls; serve with lobster for dipping. If desired, serve with lemon wedges.

NUTRITION FACTS PER SERVING: 214 cal., 17 g total fat (10 g sat. fat), 118 mg chol., 395 mg sodium, 1 g carbo., 0 g fiber, 15 g pro.

Mock Cheese Soufflé *See photo on page 124.*

PREP: 15 minutes **CHILL:** 2 to 24 hours
BAKE: 45 minutes **MAKES:** 6 servings

    8   slices white bread, cubed (6 cups)
 1½   cups shredded sharp cheddar cheese or Monterey
        Jack cheese with jalapeño peppers (6 ounces)
    4   eggs, slightly beaten
 1½   cups milk
    2   teaspoons Worcestershire sauce
    ½   teaspoon salt

one Place half of the bread cubes in an ungreased 1½-quart soufflé dish. Top with half of the cheese. Repeat with the remaining bread cubes and the remaining cheese; press lightly.

two In a medium bowl combine eggs, milk, Worcestershire sauce, and salt. Pour egg mixture over layers in dish. Cover and chill for 2 to 24 hours.

three Bake, uncovered, in a 350°F oven for 45 to 50 minutes or until a knife inserted near the center comes out clean. Serve immediately.

NUTRITION FACTS PER SERVING: 284 cal., 15 g total fat (8 g sat. fat), 176 mg chol., 639 mg sodium, 21 g carbo., 1 g fiber, 16 g pro.

Chiles Rellenos

PREP: 45 minutes **COOK:** 3 minutes per batch
MAKES: 6 servings

    6   fresh poblano chile peppers
    2   cups shredded cheddar cheese (8 ounces)
    1   cup all-purpose flour
    4   eggs
 1½   cups cooking oil

one Place whole poblano peppers on a foil-lined baking sheet. Roast in a 425°F oven for 20 to 25 minutes or until skins are bubbly and brown. Bring foil up around peppers to enclose. Let stand about 15 minutes or until cool. Make a slit in each pepper from top to bottom. Remove seeds.

two Fill peppers with cheese. Secure peppers with wooden toothpicks, if necessary. Place flour in a bowl. Whisk eggs in another bowl. Dip peppers into flour, then into beaten eggs to coat. Dip again into flour to coat evenly.

three In a heavy skillet heat the oil to 365°F. Cook peppers, a few at a time, in hot oil for 3 to 4 minutes or until golden, turning once. Drain on paper towels; serve warm.

NUTRITION FACTS PER SERVING: 359 cal., 21 g total fat (10 g sat. fat), 181 mg chol., 282 mg sodium, 24 g carbo., 1 g fiber, 18 g pro.

Spinach and Feta Omelet

START TO FINISH: 25 minutes **MAKES:** 2 servings

- 4   cups chopped fresh spinach
- 6   eggs, slightly beaten
- 1   tablespoon butter or margarine
- ½   cup crumbled feta cheese (2 ounces)

one In a covered medium saucepan cook spinach in a small amount of boiling salted water for 3 to 4 minutes or until tender; drain well. In a medium bowl combine eggs and drained spinach.

two In a 7- or 8- inch omelet pan or skillet that has flared sides melt half of the butter over medium-high heat. Pour half of the egg mixture into pan. As eggs set, run a spatula around the edge of the skillet, lifting eggs so uncooked portion flows underneath. Cook until top of omelet is set but still shiny. Turn omelet; sprinkle with half of the cheese. Cook about 2 minutes more until cheese melts.

three Transfer omelet to a warm dinner plate; roll up omelet. Cover and keep warm in a 300°F oven while using remaining ingredients to make a second omelet.

NUTRITION FACTS PER SERVING: 357 cal., 27 g total fat (13 g sat. fat), 679 mg chol., 639 mg sodium, 3 g carbo., 6 g fiber, 25 g pro.

Oven Omelets with Pesto

START TO FINISH: 35 minutes **MAKES:** 6 servings

- 2   cups frozen mixed vegetables
- 3   tablespoons purchased basil pesto
      Nonstick cooking spray
- 3   cups refrigerated or frozen egg product, thawed, or 12 eggs
- ¼   cup water
- ⅛   teaspoon salt
- ⅛   teaspoon black pepper

one Cook vegetables according to package directions; drain. Cut up any large pieces. Stir in pesto. Meanwhile, coat a 15×10×1-inch baking pan with cooking spray; set aside.

two In a medium bowl combine egg product, water, salt, and pepper. Using a fork or rotary beater, beat until combined but not frothy. Place the prepared pan on center oven rack. Pour egg mixture into pan. Bake, uncovered, in a 400°F oven about 8 minutes or until top of omelet is set but still shiny.

three Cut omelet into six 5-inch squares. Invert omelet squares onto 6 warm dinner plates. Spoon cooked vegetables onto half of each omelet; fold other half of omelet over the vegetables, forming a triangle.

NUTRITION FACTS PER SERVING: 142 cal., 7 g total fat (2 g sat. fat), 4 mg chol., 290 mg sodium, 5 g carbo., 1 g fiber, 15 g pro.

Brie Sandwiches with Greens

PREP: 10 minutes **COOK:** 7 minutes per batch
MAKES: 4 servings

- 2 tablespoons butter or margarine
- 2 cloves garlic, minced
- 6 cups fresh spinach leaves
- 8 ounces cold Brie cheese, cut into ⅛-inch slices
- 8 slices firm-texture whole-grain bread

one In a large skillet melt 1 tablespoon of the butter over medium heat. Add garlic; cook and stir for 30 seconds. Add spinach. Cook until spinach starts to wilt, tossing constantly. Remove from heat.

two Divide cheese among 4 of the bread slices. Top with spinach mixture. Cover with remaining bread slices. Lightly spread outsides of sandwiches with the remaining 1 tablespoon butter.

three In a large skillet cook 2 of the sandwiches over medium-low heat for 7 to 9 minutes or until golden brown, turning once. Repeat with the remaining sandwiches.

NUTRITION FACTS PER SERVING: 405 cal., 27 g total fat (12 g sat. fat), 57 mg chol., 771 mg sodium, 25 g carbo., 7 g fiber, 18 g pro.

Pesto and Cheese Tomato Melts

START TO FINISH: 15 minutes **MAKES:** 2 servings

- ¼ cup purchased basil pesto
- 2 tablespoons chopped nuts
- 4 1-inch slices sourdough French bread, toasted
- ¼ cup oil-packed dried tomatoes, drained and chopped
- 1 cup shredded mozzarella cheese (4 ounces)

one In a small bowl stir together pesto and nuts. Spread pesto mixture over toasted bread slices. Top with dried tomatoes; sprinkle with cheese.

two Place sandwiches on a baking sheet. Broil about 4 inches from the heat for 2 to 3 minutes or until cheese melts.

NUTRITION FACTS PER SERVING: 587 cal., 34 g total fat (6 g sat. fat), 36 mg chol., 918 mg sodium, 44 g carbo., 2 g fiber, 25 g pro.

Pizza Margherita

START TO FINISH: 25 minutes **MAKES:** 4 servings

4	6- to 7-inch Italian bread shells (such as Boboli brand)
1½	cups shredded pizza cheese blend (6 ounces)
4	roma tomatoes or 2 medium tomatoes, thinly sliced
2	to 3 teaspoons olive oil or cooking oil
¼	cup pine nuts (optional)
½	cup finely shredded fresh basil

one Place bread shells on a very large baking sheet. Bake, uncovered, in a 425°F oven for 5 minutes. Remove from oven; sprinkle with cheese. Top with tomato slices; drizzle with oil. If desired, sprinkle with pine nuts. Sprinkle with basil.

two Bake, uncovered, about 10 minutes more or until heated through and cheese melts.

NUTRITION FACTS PER SERVING: 572 cal., 21 g total fat (10 g sat. fat), 30 mg chol., 1,110 mg sodium, 69 g carbo., 3 g fiber, 25 g pro.

Fresh Tomato Pizza with Pesto

START TO FINISH: 20 minutes **MAKES:** 4 servings

½	cup purchased pesto
1	12-inch Italian bread shell (such as Boboli brand)
3	medium ripe tomatoes, thinly sliced
1	2¼-ounce can sliced pitted ripe olives, drained
2	cups shredded Monterey Jack or mozzarella cheese (8 ounces)

one Spread pesto over bread shell. Place in a large pizza pan or on a baking sheet. Top with tomato slices and olives. Sprinkle with cheese.

two Bake, uncovered, in a 425°F oven for 10 to 15 minutes or until heated through and cheese melts. Cut into wedges.

NUTRITION FACTS PER SERVING: 776 cal., 48 g total fat (11 g sat. fat), 60 mg chol., 1,265 mg sodium, 60 g carbo., 4 g fiber, 32 g pro.

Foil-Grilled Cheese Sandwiches

PREP: 20 minutes **GRILL:** 6 minutes **MAKES:** 6 servings

12	slices firm-texture white or whole wheat bread
¼	cup butter or margarine, softened
½	of an 8-ounce container whipped cream cheese
2	to 4 tablespoons bottled salsa
2	cups shredded cheddar cheese (8 ounces)
¼	cup finely chopped green sweet pepper (optional)

one Spread one side of each bread slice with butter. Spread the unbuttered side of 6 of the bread slices with cream cheese. Spoon salsa over cream cheese; sprinkle with cheddar cheese and, if desired, sweet pepper. Top with the remaining bread slices, buttered sides up. Press gently. Place sandwiches on a large piece of foil.

two For a charcoal grill, place sandwiches on foil on the rack of an uncovered grill directly over medium coals. Grill about 6 minutes or until golden brown and cheese melts, turning once halfway through grilling. (For a gas grill, preheat grill. Reduce heat to medium. Place sandwiches on foil on grill rack over heat. Cover and grill as above.)

NUTRITION FACTS PER SERVING: 427 cal., 30 g total fat (17 g sat. fat), 81 mg chol., 631 mg sodium, 27 g carbo., 0 g fiber, 15 g pro.

Black Bean and Corn Quesadillas

START TO FINISH: 20 minutes **MAKES:** 4 servings

2	cups shredded Mexican cheese blend (8 ounces)
8	8-inch flour tortillas
1½	cups bottled black bean and corn salsa
1	medium avocado, seeded, peeled, and chopped
	Dairy sour cream

one Sprinkle ¼ cup of the cheese over half of each tortilla. Top each with 1 tablespoon of the salsa. Divide avocado among tortillas. Fold tortillas in half, pressing gently.

two Heat a large skillet over medium-high heat for 2 minutes; reduce heat to medium. Cook 2 of the quesadillas in hot skillet for 2 to 3 minutes or until lightly browned and cheese melts, turning once.

three Transfer quesadillas to a baking sheet. Keep warm in a 300°F oven. Repeat with the remaining quesadillas. Cut into wedges. Serve with the remaining 1 cup salsa and the sour cream.

NUTRITION FACTS PER SERVING: 512 cal., 33 g total fat (14 g sat. fat), 55 mg chol., 940 mg sodium, 38 g carbo., 4 g fiber, 18 g pro.

Polenta and Black Beans *See photo on page 124.*

START TO FINISH: 25 minutes **MAKES:** 4 servings

- 3 cups water
- 1 cup yellow cornmeal
- 1 cup water
- ½ teaspoon salt
- 1 15-ounce can black beans, rinsed and drained
- 1 14½-ounce can diced tomatoes, undrained
- 1 cup bottled salsa with cilantro or other salsa
- ¾ cup shredded Mexican cheese blend (3 ounces)

Keeping Tabs on Salt If you're watching the sodium in the foods you eat, here's how to minimize the salt in recipes that use canned beans. Place the beans in a colander and rinse them under cold running water to remove as much of the salty canning liquid as possible. Drain well.

one For polenta: In a large saucepan bring the 3 cups water to boiling. In a medium bowl combine cornmeal, the 1 cup water, and the salt. Gradually stir cornmeal mixture into the boiling water. Cook and stir until mixture comes to boiling; reduce heat to low. Cook for 5 to 10 minutes or until mixture is thick, stirring occasionally. (If mixture is too thick, stir in additional water.)

two Meanwhile, in a large skillet combine black beans, undrained tomatoes, and salsa. Bring to boiling; reduce heat. Simmer, uncovered, for 10 minutes, stirring frequently. Stir in ½ cup of the cheese.

three Divide polenta among 4 shallow bowls. Top with the bean mixture and sprinkle with the remaining ¼ cup cheese.

NUTRITION FACTS PER SERVING: 311 cal., 8 g total fat (4 g sat. fat), 19 mg chol., 751 mg sodium, 49 g carbo., 8 g fiber, 15 g pro.

Chipotle-Bean Enchiladas

PREP: 25 minutes **BAKE:** 30 minutes **MAKES:** 5 servings

- 10 6-inch corn tortillas
- 1 15-ounce can pinto beans or black beans, rinsed and drained
- 2 10-ounce cans enchilada sauce
- 2 cups shredded Mexican cheese blend (8 ounces)
- 1 tablespoon chopped canned chipotle pepper in adobo sauce

Chipotle Peppers A chipotle chile pepper is a dried, smoked jalapeño that's milder than a fresh jalapeño and has a smoky, almost chocolatey flavor. In addition to the dried form, they also come canned in adobo sauce—a mixture of ground chiles, herbs, and vinegar. They're available at local supermarkets or Hispanic food markets.

one Stack tortillas; wrap tightly in foil. Bake in a 350°F oven about 10 minutes or until warm.

two Meanwhile, for filling, in a medium bowl combine beans, ½ cup of the enchilada sauce, 1 cup of the cheese, and the chipotle pepper. Spoon about ¼ cup of the filling onto one edge of each tortilla; roll up tortilla.

three Arrange tortilla rolls, seam sides down, in a greased 2-quart rectangular baking dish. Top with the remaining enchilada sauce.

four Bake, covered, in a 350°F oven about 25 minutes or until heated through. Sprinkle with remaining 1 cup cheese. Bake, uncovered, about 5 minutes more or until cheese melts.

NUTRITION FACTS PER SERVING: 487 cal., 19 g total fat (8 g sat. fat), 40 mg chol., 1,091 mg sodium, 63 g carbo., 14 g fiber, 23 g pro.

SLOW COOKER

Bean-and-Rice-Stuffed Peppers

PREP: 15 minutes **COOK:** Low 6 hours, High 3 hours
MAKES: 4 servings

- 4 small to medium green, red, and/or yellow sweet peppers
- 1 15-ounce can chili beans in chili gravy, undrained
- 1 cup cooked converted rice
- 1 cup shredded Monterey Jack cheese (4 ounces)
- 1 15-ounce can tomato sauce with garlic and onion

one Remove tops of sweet peppers; scoop out membranes and seeds. Set aside. For filling, in a medium bowl stir together undrained beans in chili gravy, cooked rice, and ½ cup of the cheese. Spoon filling into peppers.

two Pour tomato sauce into a 5- to 6-quart slow cooker. Arrange stuffed peppers, filling sides up, in cooker.

three Cover and cook on low-heat setting for 6 to 6½ hours or on high-heat setting for 3 to 3½ hours.

four Transfer peppers to 4 dinner plates. Spoon the tomato sauce over peppers; sprinkle with remaining ½ cup cheese.

NUTRITION FACTS PER SERVING: 323 cal., 11 g total fat (5 g sat. fat), 25 mg chol., 918 mg sodium, 41 g carbo., 9 g fiber, 16 g pro.

Red Beans over Spanish Rice

PREP: 25 minutes **STAND:** 1 hour **COOK:** Low 10 hours, High 5 hours **MAKES:** 6 to 8 servings

 2   cups dry red beans or red kidney beans
     Nonstick cooking spray
 4   cups water
2½   cups chopped onion
 1   tablespoon ground cumin
 6   cloves garlic, minced
 1   6¾-ounce package Spanish rice mix
     Lime wedges (optional)

Slow-Cooking Dry Beans Dry beans cook more slowly in a slow cooker than in a saucepan. Therefore, the beans must be precooked for 10 minutes. Soaking dry beans overnight doesn't work for slow-cooker recipes—the beans never get tender.

one Rinse beans. In a large saucepan combine dry beans and enough water to cover beans by 2 inches. Bring to boiling; reduce heat. Simmer, uncovered, for 10 minutes. Remove from heat. Cover and let stand for 1 hour. Drain and rinse beans.

two Lightly coat a 3½- or 4-quart slow cooker with cooking spray. Transfer beans to the prepared cooker. Stir in the 4 cups water, the onion, cumin, and garlic.

three Cover and cook on low-heat setting for 10 to 11 hours or on high-heat setting for 5 to 5½ hours.

four Prepare the rice mix according to package directions. Using a slotted spoon, remove beans from cooker. Serve beans over cooked rice. If desired, spoon some of the cooking liquid over beans and rice and serve with lime wedges.

NUTRITION FACTS PER SERVING: 344 cal., 1 g total fat (0 g sat. fat), 0 mg chol., 450 mg sodium, 68 g carbo., 17 g fiber, 19 g pro.

Taco-Style Black Beans and Hominy

PREP: 15 minutes **COOK:** Low 7 hours, High 3½ hours
MAKES: 9 servings

	Nonstick cooking spray
2	15½-ounce cans golden hominy, drained
2	15-ounce cans black beans, rinsed and drained
1	10¾-ounce can condensed cream of mushroom soup
1¼	cups water
½	of a 1¼-ounce envelope (1½ tablespoons) taco seasoning mix
18	taco shells
	Sliced green onion, chopped tomato, and/or shredded lettuce (optional)

one Coat a 3½- or 4-quart slow cooker with cooking spray. In the prepared cooker stir together hominy, beans, soup, water, and taco seasoning mix.

two Cover and cook on low-heat setting for 7 to 8 hours or on high-heat setting for 3½ to 4 hours.

three To serve, spoon bean mixture into taco shells. If desired, top with green onion, tomato, and/or lettuce.

NUTRITION FACTS PER SERVING: 317 cal., 10 g total fat (2 g sat. fat), 0 mg chol., 1,001 mg sodium, 52 g carbo., 11 g fiber, 12 g pro.

Spicy Simmered Beans and Vegetables

PREP: 10 minutes **COOK:** 15 minutes **MAKES:** 4 servings

1	16-ounce package frozen Brussels sprouts, cauliflower, and carrots
1	15-ounce can garbanzo beans (chickpeas), rinsed and drained
1	15-ounce can tomato sauce with garlic and onion
1	teaspoon curry powder
¼	teaspoon black pepper
2	cups hot cooked rice
1	tablespoon snipped fresh cilantro (optional)

one In a large skillet combine frozen vegetables, garbanzo beans, tomato sauce, curry powder, and pepper. Bring to boiling; reduce heat. Simmer, covered, about 15 minutes or until vegetables are crisp-tender, stirring occasionally.

two Serve bean mixture over hot cooked rice and, if desired, sprinkle with cilantro.

NUTRITION FACTS PER SERVING: 360 cal., 6 g total fat (0 g sat. fat), 0 mg chol., 831 mg sodium, 63 g carbo., 10 g fiber, 12 g pro.

White Beans with Dried Tomatoes

PREP: 15 minutes **COOK:** Low 6 hours, High 3½ hours; plus 15 minutes on High **MAKES:** 6 servings

3   15-ounce cans cannellini beans (white kidney beans), rinsed and drained

1   14-ounce can vegetable broth

3   cloves garlic, minced

1   7-ounce jar oil-packed dried tomatoes, drained and chopped

4   ounces shaved Asiago or Parmesan cheese (1 cup)

⅓ cup pine nuts, toasted (see tip, page 280) (optional)

one In a 3½- or 4-quart slow cooker combine cannellini beans, broth, and garlic.

two Cover and cook on low-heat setting for 6 to 8 hours or on high-heat setting for 3½ to 4 hours.

three If using low-heat setting, turn to high-heat setting. Stir in dried tomatoes. Cover and cook about 15 minutes more or until dried tomatoes are heated through.

four To serve, top each serving with shaved cheese. If desired, sprinkle with pine nuts.

NUTRITION FACTS PER SERVING: 285 cal., 13 g total fat (5 g sat. fat), 20 mg chol., 901 mg sodium, 38 g carbo., 12 g fiber, 19 g pro.

Lentil-Vegetable Turnovers

PREP: 25 minutes **BAKE:** 25 minutes **MAKES:** 4 servings

1   15-ounce package (2 crusts) rolled refrigerated unbaked piecrust

1   9-ounce jar mango chutney

2   teaspoons curry paste

2   cups frozen baby potatoes, broccoli, carrots, baby corn, and red peppers, thawed and chopped

1   cup cooked lentils

one Let piecrusts stand according to package directions. In a medium bowl stir together chutney and curry paste. Add vegetables and lentils; stir to coat.

two Line a large baking sheet with foil; grease foil. Cut each piecrust in half, forming 4 semicircles. Place one-fourth of the lentil mixture in the center of each portion of pastry. Brush the edges with a little water. Fold pastry in half over filling; press edges together and seal with a fork.

three Place turnovers on the prepared baking sheet. Prick tops to allow steam to escape. Bake, uncovered, in a 375°F oven about 25 minutes or until golden brown. Serve warm.

NUTRITION FACTS PER SERVING: 642 cal., 29 g total fat (12 g sat. fat), 20 mg chol., 623 mg sodium, 88 g carbo., 5 g fiber, 7 g pro.

Portobellos Florentine

PREP: 15 minutes **BAKE:** 20 minutes **MAKES:** 4 servings

4   fresh portobello mushrooms (about 5 inches in diameter)
½   cup purchased basil pesto
1   cup finely chopped fresh spinach leaves or half of a 10-ounce package frozen chopped spinach, thawed and well drained
½   cup ricotta cheese
2   medium roma tomatoes, chopped

one Remove and discard stems from mushrooms, if present. Spread stemmed sides of mushrooms with ¼ cup of the pesto. Place mushrooms, stemmed sides up, in a shallow baking pan.

two In a small bowl combine remaining ¼ cup pesto, spinach, and cheese. Divide spinach mixture among mushrooms.

three Bake, uncovered, in a 350°F oven about 20 minutes or until mushrooms are tender and filling is heated through. Sprinkle with tomatoes.

NUTRITION FACTS PER SERVING: 260 cal., 19 g total fat (5 g sat. fat), 21 mg chol., 269 mg sodium, 11 g carbo., 5 g fiber, 11 g pro.

Gardener's Pie

PREP: 15 minutes **BAKE:** 45 minutes **MAKES:** 4 servings

1   16-ounce package frozen vegetable blend, thawed
1   11-ounce can condensed cheddar cheese soup
½   teaspoon dried thyme, crushed
1   20-ounce package refrigerated mashed potatoes
1   cup shredded smoked cheddar cheese (4 ounces)

one In an ungreased 1½-quart casserole combine vegetables, soup, and thyme. Stir mashed potatoes to soften. Carefully spread potatoes over entire surface of vegetable mixture.

two Bake, covered, in a 350°F oven for 30 minutes. Bake, uncovered, about 15 minutes more or until heated through, topping with cheese during the last 5 minutes of baking.

NUTRITION FACTS PER SERVING: 349 cal., 17 g total fat (8 g sat. fat), 39 mg chol., 1,031 mg sodium, 40 g carbo., 4 g fiber, 15 g pro.

Vegetable and Rice Casserole

PREP: 15 minutes **COOK:** Low 3½ hours **MAKES:** 4 servings

- 1 16-ounce package frozen cauliflower, broccoli, and carrots
- 1 15-ounce can garbanzo beans (chickpeas), rinsed and drained
- 1 10¾-ounce can condensed cream of celery or cream of mushroom soup
- 1 cup uncooked instant white rice
- ½ of a 15-ounce jar (about 1 cup) process cheese dip
- 1 cup water

one In a 3½- or 4-quart slow cooker place frozen vegetables and beans. In a medium bowl combine soup, rice, cheese dip, and water. Pour over vegetables and beans.

two Cover and cook on low-heat setting for 3½ to 4½ hours or until vegetables and rice are tender. Stir well before serving.

NUTRITION FACTS PER SERVING: 436 cal., 17 g total fat (10 g sat. fat), 34 mg chol., 1,923 mg sodium, 52 g carbo., 9 g fiber, 17 g pro.

Cashew-Vegetable Stir-Fry

START TO FINISH: 15 minutes **MAKES:** 4 servings

- 1 tablespoon cooking oil
- 1 16-ounce package desired frozen stir-fry vegetables
- ⅓ cup bottled stir-fry sauce
- 3 cups hot cooked rice
- ¾ cup dry roasted cashews

one Pour oil into a large skillet; heat over medium-high heat. Add frozen vegetables. Cook and stir about 5 minutes or until vegetables are crisp-tender. Add sauce; cook and stir for 1 to 2 minutes more until heated through.

two Serve vegetable mixture over hot cooked rice. Sprinkle with cashews.

NUTRITION FACTS PER SERVING: 393 cal., 16 g total fat (3 g sat. fat), 0 mg chol., 720 mg sodium, 54 g carbo., 4 g fiber, 9 g pro.

Bean-Stuffed Cabbage Rolls

PREP: 25 minutes **COOK:** Low 6 hours, High 3 hours
MAKES: 4 servings

½   cup instant brown rice
1   large head green cabbage
1   26- to 28-ounce jar chunky tomato pasta sauce or
     meatless spaghetti sauce
1   15-ounce can black beans or red kidney beans,
     rinsed and drained
½   cup chopped onion
     Shredded cheddar cheese (optional)

one Prepare brown rice according to package directions. Remove from heat; set aside.

two Meanwhile, remove 8 large outer leaves from the cabbage.* In a Dutch oven cook cabbage leaves in boiling water for 3 to 4 minutes or just until leaves are limp. Drain cabbage leaves. Trim the thick rib from the center of each leaf. Set leaves aside. Shred 4 cups of the remaining cabbage; place shredded cabbage in a 3½- or 4-quart slow cooker. (Wrap and chill remaining cabbage for another use.)

three In a medium bowl combine cooked rice, ½ cup of the pasta sauce, the beans, and onion. Evenly divide the bean mixture among the 8 cabbage leaves. Fold sides of leaves over filling and roll up. Pour about half of the remaining pasta sauce over shredded cabbage in cooker; stir to combine. Place cabbage rolls on the shredded cabbage mixture. Top with the remaining pasta sauce.

four Cover and cook on low-heat setting for 6 to 7 hours or on high-heat setting for 3 to 3½ hours. Carefully remove the cooked cabbage rolls and serve with the shredded cabbage mixture. If desired, sprinkle with cheddar cheese.

*Note: *To easily remove the cabbage leaves, place the cabbage head in boiling water for 2 to 3 minutes to loosen the outer leaves.*

NUTRITION FACTS PER SERVING: 332 cal., 6 g total fat (1 g sat. fat), 0 mg chol., 1,042 mg sodium, 64 g carbo., 15 g fiber, 15 g pro.

Curried Couscous with Vegetables

PREP: 15 minutes **COOK:** Low 4 hours, High 2 hours
STAND: 5 minutes **MAKES:** 8 servings

2 14½-ounce cans diced tomatoes and green chiles, undrained

2 cups coarsely chopped yellow summer squash and/or zucchini

2 cups water

1 large onion, cut into thin wedges

2 5.7-ounce packages curry-flavor couscous mix

1 cup chopped slivered almonds, toasted (see tip, page 280)

½ cup raisins (optional)

one In a 3½- or 4-quart slow cooker combine undrained tomatoes, summer squash, water, onion, and seasoning packets from couscous mixes.

two Cover and cook on low-heat setting for 4 to 6 hours or on high-heat setting for 2 to 3 hours. Stir in couscous. Remove liner from cooker or turn off cooker. Let stand, covered, for 5 minutes. Fluff couscous mixture with a fork.

three To serve, sprinkle each serving with almonds and, if desired, raisins.

NUTRITION FACTS PER SERVING: 280 cal., 9 g total fat (1 g sat. fat), 0 mg chol., 842 mg sodium, 43 g carbo., 6 g fiber, 10 g pro.

Couscous- and Pine Nut-Stuffed Peppers

PREP: 20 minutes **BAKE:** 25 minutes **MAKES:** 4 servings

1 5.6-ounce package toasted pine nut-flavor couscous mix

½ cup shredded carrot

2 large sweet peppers

½ cup shredded Italian cheese blend (2 ounces)

1½ cups bottled olive pasta sauce

one Prepare couscous mix according to package directions, except omit oil and add the shredded carrot with couscous.

two Meanwhile, cut peppers in half lengthwise; remove membranes and seeds. Cook pepper halves in boiling water for 5 minutes; drain on paper towels. Place peppers, cut sides up, in an ungreased 2-quart rectangular baking dish. Spoon cooked couscous mixture into pepper halves.

three Bake, covered, in a 350°F oven for 20 to 25 minutes or until filling is heated through and peppers are tender. Sprinkle with cheese. Bake, uncovered, about 5 minutes more or until cheese melts. Meanwhile, in a small saucepan heat pasta sauce. Serve peppers with sauce.

NUTRITION FACTS PER SERVING: 259 cal., 6 g total fat (3 g sat. fat), 10 mg chol., 801 mg sodium, 42 g carbo., 7 g fiber, 11 g pro.

FAST-FIXIN' FISH, SHELLFISH & MEATLESS

Asian Noodle Bowl

START TO FINISH: 25 minutes **MAKES:** 4 servings

8   ounces dried soba (buckwheat noodles), udon (broad
    white noodles), or rice noodles

2   cups vegetable broth

½   cup bottled peanut stir-fry sauce

2   cups frozen broccoli stir-fry vegetables (broccoli,
    carrots, red peppers, celery, water chestnuts,
    and mushrooms)

½   cup dry roasted peanuts, chopped

one Cook noodles according to package directions; drain
in a colander (do not rinse). Set aside.

two In the same saucepan combine broth and peanut sauce.
Bring to boiling. Stir in frozen vegetables and cooked noodles

three Return to boiling; reduce heat. Simmer, uncovered,
for 2 to 3 minutes or until vegetables are heated through.
Sprinkle each serving with peanuts.

NUTRITION FACTS PER SERVING: 403 cal., 15 g total fat (2 g sat. fat),
0 mg chol., 1,326 mg sodium, 59 g carbo., 4 g fiber, 15 g pro.

Spicy Pasta and Broccoli

START TO FINISH: 25 minutes **MAKES:** 4 servings

12   ounces dried orecchiette or medium shell pasta

2   tablespoons olive oil

3   cups chopped baby broccoli (Broccolini®)
     or broccoli florets

1   cup canned chicken broth with Italian herbs

¼   to ½ teaspoon crushed red pepper

one Cook pasta according to package directions; drain. Return
pasta to pan. Drizzle with 1 tablespoon of the oil; toss gently
to coat. Cover and keep warm.

two Meanwhile, in a large skillet cook and stir broccoli in
the remaining 1 tablespoon oil over medium-high heat for
3 minutes. Add broth and crushed red pepper. Bring to boiling
reduce heat. Simmer, covered, for 2 to 3 minutes or until
broccoli is crisp-tender.

three Add broccoli mixture to the cooked pasta; toss gently
to combine.

NUTRITION FACTS PER SERVING: 404 cal., 9 g total fat (1 g sat. fat), 0 mg chol.
214 mg sodium, 67 g carbo., 4 g fiber, 14 g pro.

Pasta Stir-Fry

START TO FINISH: 25 minutes **MAKES:** 4 servings

1 9-ounce package refrigerated cheese-filled tortellini
1 tablespoon cooking oil
1 16-ounce package fresh cut or frozen
    stir-fry vegetables (such as broccoli, pea pods,
    carrots, sweet peppers, and celery)
¾ cup bottled peanut or garlic stir-fry sauce
¼ cup chopped unsalted cashews or peanuts

one Cook pasta according to package directions; drain.

two Meanwhile, pour oil into a wok or large skillet; heat over medium-high heat. Add vegetables. Cook and stir for 3 to 5 minutes (7 to 8 minutes for frozen vegetables) or until vegetables are crisp-tender.

three Add pasta and peanut sauce to vegetables; toss gently to coat. Heat through. Sprinkle with cashews.

NUTRITION FACTS PER SERVING: 304 cal., 10 g total fat (3 g sat. fat), 10 mg chol., 1,842 mg sodium, 48 g carbo., 5 g fiber, 16 g pro.

Summer Spaghetti

START TO FINISH: 20 minutes **MAKES:** 4 servings

8 ounces dried spaghetti
2 cups assorted fresh vegetables (such as sliced yellow
    summer squash, halved baby sunburst squash,
    chopped carrot, and/or sliced green onion)
2 tablespoons olive oil
¼ cup finely shredded Asiago or Parmesan cheese
    (1 ounce)
⅛ teaspoon freshly ground black pepper

one Cook pasta according to package directions. Meanwhile, place fresh vegetables in a colander. Pour pasta and cooking water over vegetables; drain.

two Transfer pasta mixture to a serving bowl. Drizzle with oil; toss gently to coat. Sprinkle with Asiago cheese and pepper.

NUTRITION FACTS PER SERVING: 320 cal., 10 g total fat (6 g sat. fat), 24 mg chol., 152 mg sodium, 48 g carbo., 3 g fiber, 10 g pro.

FAST-FIXN' FISH, SHELLFISH & MEATLESS

Tortilla Lasagna

PREP: 10 minutes **BAKE:** 35 minutes
STAND: 10 minutes **MAKES:** 8 servings

1   6¾-ounce package Spanish rice mix
1   11-ounce can whole kernel corn with sweet peppers, undrained
2   15-ounce cans black beans, undrained
10 6-inch corn tortillas
2   cups shredded Monterey Jack cheese with jalapeño peppers (8 ounces)

one Prepare rice mix according to package directions, except substitute undrained corn for ½ cup of the liquid. In a medium bowl slightly mash undrained beans.

two Place 5 tortillas in the bottom of a greased 3-quart rectangular baking dish, overlapping and placing slightly up the sides of the dish (cut tortillas as necessary to fit). Spoon beans evenly over tortillas. Sprinkle with 1 cup of the cheese. Top with the remaining tortillas and the cooked rice.

three Bake, covered, in a 400°F oven for 30 minutes. Sprinkle with the remaining 1 cup cheese. Bake, uncovered, about 5 minutes more or until cheese melts. Let lasagna stand for 10 minutes before serving.

NUTRITION FACTS PER SERVING: 406 cal., 12 g total fat (7 g sat. fat), 34 mg chol., 1,101 mg sodium, 60 g carbo., 11 g fiber, 20 g pro.

SLOW COOKER

Cheesy Tortellini Casserole

PREP: 5 minutes **COOK:** Low 7 hours, High 3½ hours; plus 15 minutes on Low **STAND:** 10 minutes **MAKES:** 8 servings

    Nonstick cooking spray
2   15-ounce containers refrigerated marinara sauce
2   14½-ounce cans diced tomatoes with basil, garlic, and oregano, undrained
1   12-ounce package frozen cooked and crumbled ground sausage-style meat or ground meat substitute (soy protein)
1   9-ounce package refrigerated cheese-filled tortellini
1   cup shredded mozzarella cheese (4 ounces)

one Lightly coat a 3½- or 4-quart slow cooker with cooking spray. In the prepared cooker stir together marinara sauce, undrained tomatoes, and meat substitute.

two Cover and cook on low-heat setting for 7 to 8 hours or on high-heat setting for 3½ to 4 hours.

three If using high-heat setting, turn to low-heat setting. Stir in tortellini. Cover and cook for 15 to 20 minutes more or until tortellini are tender.

four Sprinkle with mozzarella cheese. Let stand, covered, about 10 minutes or until cheese melts.

NUTRITION FACTS PER SERVING: 298 cal., 10 g total fat (3 g sat. fat), 23 mg chol., 1,377 mg sodium, 34 g carbo., 2 g fiber, 21 g pro.

Greek-Seasoned Lentils

PREP: 15 minutes **COOK:** Low 6 hours, High 3 hours
MAKES: 6 to 8 servings

Nonstick cooking spray
2   cups lentils
3   14-ounce cans vegetable broth
2   cups purchased shredded carrot
1   cup chopped onion
2   teaspoons Greek seasoning

one Lightly coat a 3½- to 5-quart slow cooker with cooking spray. Rinse and drain lentils. Transfer lentils to the prepared cooker. Stir in vegetable broth, shredded carrot, onion, and Greek seasoning.

two Cover and cook on low-heat setting for 6 to 7 hours or on high-heat setting for 3 to 3½ hours. Use a slotted spoon to serve lentils.

NUTRITION FACTS PER SERVING: 260 cal., 2 g total fat (0 g sat. fat), 0 mg chol., 874 mg sodium, 45 g carbo., 21 g fiber, 20 g pro.

Sweet-and-Sour Tofu

PREP: 15 minutes **COOK:** Low 4 hours, High 2 hours
MAKES: 4 to 6 servings

2   16-ounce packages frozen pepper stir-fry vegetables (green, red, and yellow peppers and onions)
1   9-ounce jar sweet-and-sour sauce
1   8-ounce can sliced water chestnuts, drained
1   8-ounce package baked Oriental-style tofu, drained and cut into ½-inch pieces
2   cups hot cooked rice

one In a 3½- or 4-quart slow cooker combine stir-fry vegetables, sweet-and-sour sauce, and water chestnuts.

two Cover and cook on low-heat setting for 4 to 4½ hours or on high-heat setting for 2 to 2¼ hours. Stir in tofu. Serve over hot cooked rice.

NUTRITION FACTS PER SERVING: 318 cal., 7 g total fat (1 g sat. fat), 0 mg chol., 597 mg sodium, 73 g carbo., 4 g fiber, 13 g pro.

Creamy Tomato-Broccoli Sauce with Pasta

PREP: 15 minutes **COOK:** Low 6 hours, High 3 hours; plus 15 minutes on High **MAKES:** 8 to 10 servings

    Nonstick cooking spray

2   14½-ounce cans diced tomatoes with basil, garlic, and oregano, undrained

2   10¾-ounce cans condensed cream of mushroom soup

1   cup water

1   1.3-ounce envelope pasta rosa sauce mix

1   16-ounce package frozen cut broccoli

16   ounces dried penne or mostaccioli pasta

one Coat a 3½- or 4-quart slow cooker with cooking spray. In a large bowl combine undrained tomatoes, soup, water, and sauce mix. Pour mixture into the prepared cooker.

two Cover and cook on low-heat setting for 6 to 8 hours or on high-heat setting for 3 to 4 hours. If using low-heat setting, turn to high-heat setting. Stir in broccoli. Cover and cook about 15 minutes more or until broccoli is crisp-tender.

three Cook pasta according to package directions; drain. Toss the sauce with hot cooked pasta.

NUTRITION FACTS PER SERVING: 365 cal., 7 g total fat (2 g sat. fat), 1 mg chol., 1,270 mg sodium, 62 g carbo., 4 g fiber, 12 g pro.

Eggplant Sauce with Whole Wheat Pasta

PREP: 15 minutes **COOK:** Low 3 hours **MAKES:** 6 servings

    Nonstick cooking spray

1   medium eggplant, cut into 1-inch pieces (5½ cups)

1   large onion, cut into thin wedges

1   2¼-ounce can sliced pitted ripe olives, drained

1   28-ounce jar roasted garlic pasta sauce

12   ounces dried whole wheat penne or rotini pasta

    Shredded Parmesan cheese (optional)

one Coat a 3½- or 4-quart slow cooker with cooking spray. In the prepared cooker combine eggplant, onion, and olives. Stir in pasta sauce.

two Cover and cook on low-heat setting for 3 to 4 hours.

three Cook pasta according to package directions; drain. Serve sauce over hot cooked pasta. If desired, sprinkle with Parmesan cheese.

NUTRITION FACTS PER SERVING: 316 cal., 4 g total fat (0 g sat. fat), 0 mg chol., 512 mg sodium, 60 g carbo., 8 g fiber, 10 g pro.

warming
soups & stews

Chicken Tortilla Soup *See photo on page 126.*

PREP: 10 minutes **COOK:** Low 6 hours, High 3 hours
MAKES: 4 to 6 servings

- 2   14-ounce cans chicken broth with roasted garlic
- 2   cups frozen pepper stir-fry vegetables (green, red, and yellow peppers and onions)
- 1   14½-ounce can Mexican-style stewed tomatoes, undrained
- 1   9-ounce package frozen chopped cooked chicken breast
- 1   cup corn chips
     Sliced fresh jalapeño chile peppers (see tip, page 59) (optional)

one In a 3 ½- or 4-quart slow cooker combine broth, frozen vegetables, undrained tomatoes, and frozen chicken.

two Cover and cook on low-heat setting for 6 to 7 hours or on high-heat setting for 3 to 3 ½ hours.

three Ladle soup into bowls. Sprinkle with corn chips and, if desired, jalapeño peppers.

NUTRITION FACTS PER SERVING: 189 cal., 5 g total fat (0 g sat. fat), 36 mg chol., 1,395 mg sodium, 19 g carbo., 1 g fiber, 18 g pro.

Simply Ramen Chicken Soup *See photo on page 126.*

START TO FINISH: 15 minutes **MAKES:** 4 servings

- 2   14-ounce cans reduced-sodium chicken broth
- 2   3-ounce packages chicken-flavor ramen noodles
- ½   teaspoon dried oregano or basil, crushed (optional)
- 1   10-ounce package frozen cut broccoli
- 2   cups shredded or cubed cooked chicken or turkey
- ¼   cup sliced almonds, toasted (see tip, page 280)

one In a large saucepan combine broth, the contents of seasoning packets from noodles, and, if desired, oregano. Bring to boiling. Break up noodles. Add noodles and frozen broccoli to broth mixture.

two Return to boiling; reduce heat. Simmer, uncovered, for 3 minutes. Stir in chicken; heat through. Ladle soup into bowls. Sprinkle with almonds.

NUTRITION FACTS PER SERVING: 403 cal., 18 g total fat (2 g sat. fat), 62 mg chol., 1,329 mg sodium, 32 g carbo., 3 g fiber, 32 g pro.

SLOW COOKER

Chicken and Wild Rice Soup

PREP: 15 minutes **COOK:** Low 7 hours, High 3½ hours
MAKES: 6 servings

Nonstick cooking spray

1 pound skinless, boneless chicken breast halves, cut into ¾-inch pieces

1½ cups purchased shredded carrots

1 cup uncooked wild rice, rinsed and drained

3 14-ounce cans reduced-sodium chicken broth

2 10¾-ounce cans condensed cream of chicken with herbs soup

1½ cups water

one Lightly coat a large skillet with cooking spray; heat over medium-high heat. Cook chicken in hot skillet until brown.

two In a 4- to 5-quart slow cooker combine chicken, carrots, and wild rice. Pour broth over all. Stir in soup and water.

three Cover and cook on low-heat setting for 7 to 8 hours or on high-heat setting for 3½ to 4 hours.

NUTRITION FACTS PER SERVING: 274 cal., 5 g total fat (2 g sat. fat), 52 mg chol., 1,321 mg sodium, 31 g carbo., 3 g fiber, 27 g pro.

SLOW COOKER

Chicken Curry Soup

PREP: 15 minutes **COOK:** Low 4 hours, High 2 hours;
plus 15 minutes on Low **MAKES:** 6 servings

1 10¾-ounce can condensed cream of chicken or cream of celery soup

1 cup water

2 teaspoons curry powder

1¼ pounds skinless, boneless chicken thighs or breast halves, cut into ¾-inch pieces

2 cups sliced carrot

1 14-ounce can unsweetened coconut milk

Coconut, toasted (see tip, page 280), and/or chopped peanuts (optional)

one In a 3½- to 4½-quart slow cooker combine soup and water. Stir in curry powder. Add chicken and carrot to cooker; stir to combine.

two Cover and cook on low-heat setting for 4 to 5 hours or on high-heat setting for 2 to 2½ hours.

three If using high-heat setting, turn to low-heat setting. Stir in coconut milk. Cover and cook for 15 minutes more.

four Ladle soup into bowls. If desired, garnish with coconut and/or peanuts.

NUTRITION FACTS PER SERVING: 302 cal., 19 g total fat (12 g sat. fat), 79 mg chol., 496 mg sodium, 11 g carbo., 1 g fiber, 22 g pro.

Oriental-Style Chicken Stew

PREP: 15 minutes **COOK:** Low 7 hours, High 3½ hours
MAKES: 4 servings

- 2 pounds skinless, boneless chicken thighs, cut into 1-inch pieces
- 1 15-ounce can straw mushrooms, drained
- 1½ cups thinly sliced carrot
- 1 cup bottled sesame-ginger stir-fry sauce
- ½ cup water
- 4 teaspoons quick-cooking tapioca

one In a 3½- or 4-quart slow cooker combine chicken, mushrooms, and carrot. In a small bowl stir together stir-fry sauce, water, and tapioca; stir into chicken mixture.

two Cover and cook on low-heat setting for 7 to 8 hours or on high-heat setting for 3½ to 4 hours.

NUTRITION FACTS PER SERVING: 393 cal., 9 g total fat (2 g sat. fat), 188 mg chol., 1,701 mg sodium, 25 g carbo., 4 g fiber, 49 g pro.

Chicken and Corn Chowder

PREP: 15 minutes **COOK:** Low 4 hours, High 2 hours
MAKES: 6 servings

- 1 pound skinless, boneless chicken thighs, cut into ½- to ¾-inch pieces
- 2 10¾-ounce cans condensed cream of potato or cream of chicken soup
- 1 11-ounce can whole kernel corn with sweet peppers, undrained
- 1½ cups sliced celery
- 1 cup water
- 1 cup half-and-half or light cream

one In a 3½- to 4½-quart slow cooker combine chicken, soup, undrained corn, celery, and water.

two Cover and cook on low-heat setting for 4 to 6 hours or on high-heat setting for 2 to 3 hours. Stir in half-and-half.

NUTRITION FACTS PER SERVING: 261 cal., 10 g total fat (5 g sat. fat), 86 mg chol., 1,029 mg sodium, 24 g carbo., 3 g fiber, 19 g pro.

Coq au Vin Stew

PREP: 20 minutes **COOK:** Low 5 hours, High 2 ½ hours
MAKES: 4 servings

3   pounds chicken thighs
     Nonstick cooking spray
1   envelope (half of a 2.2-ounce package) beefy onion
        soup mix
2   cups fresh mushrooms, quartered
1½   cups frozen small whole onions
½   cup dry red wine
2   cups hot cooked mashed potatoes (optional)
     Snipped fresh basil or parsley (optional)

one Skin chicken. Lightly coat a large skillet with cooking spray; heat over medium-high heat. Cook chicken thighs, several at a time, in hot skillet until brown on all sides. Place chicken in a 3 ½- or 4-quart slow cooker.

two Sprinkle chicken with dry soup mix. Add mushrooms and frozen onions. Pour wine over all.

three Cover and cook on low-heat setting for 5 to 6 hours or on high-heat setting for 2 ½ to 3 hours. Using a slotted spoon, remove chicken from cooker.

four When cool enough to handle, remove chicken from bones. Using 2 forks, shred chicken into bite-size pieces. Return chicken to mixture in cooker. If desired, ladle stew into bowls over hot cooked mashed potatoes and sprinkle with basil.

NUTRITION FACTS PER SERVING: 305 cal., 8 g total fat (2 g sat. fat), 161 mg chol., 759 mg sodium, 12 g carbo., 2 g fiber, 41 g pro.

Sausage and Chicken Gumbo

PREP: 10 minutes **COOK:** Low 6 hours, High 3 hours
MAKES: 6 servings

12   ounces cooked smoked sausage, halved lengthwise
        and cut into ½-inch slices
12   ounces skinless, boneless chicken thighs, cut into
        1-inch pieces
1   16-ounce package frozen cut okra
2   10½-ounce cans condensed chicken with rice soup
2   cups water
¼   teaspoon cayenne pepper

one In a 3½- or 4-quart slow cooker place sausage, chicken, and frozen okra. Pour soup and water over mixture in cooker. Stir in cayenne pepper.

two Cover and cook on low-heat setting for 6 to 8 hours or on high-heat setting for 3 to 4 hours.

NUTRITION FACTS PER SERVING: 362 cal., 22 g total fat (7 g sat. fat), 90 mg chol., 1,591 mg sodium, 12 g carbo., 3 g fiber, 28 g pro.

Taco Chili

PREP: 20 minutes **COOK:** Low 4 hours, High 2 hours
MAKES: 4 to 6 servings

- 1   pound lean ground beef
- 2   14½-ounce cans diced tomatoes with green pepper and onion, undrained
- 1   15¼- or 15½-ounce can hominy or whole kernel corn, undrained
- 1   15-ounce can chili beans in chili gravy, undrained
- 1   1¼-ounce envelope taco seasoning mix

one In a large skillet cook ground beef over medium-high heat until brown. Drain off fat.

two In a 3½- or 4-quart slow cooker combine meat, undrained tomatoes, undrained hominy, undrained beans in chili gravy, and taco seasoning mix.

three Cover and cook on low-heat setting for 4 to 6 hours or on high-heat setting for 2 to 3 hours.

NUTRITION FACTS PER SERVING: 477 cal., 18 g total fat (6 g sat. fat), 71 mg chol., 1,998 mg sodium, 49 g carbo., 12 g fiber, 35 g pro.

Meatball-Vegetable Stew *See photo on page 125.*

PREP: 10 minutes **COOK:** Low 6 hours, High 3 hours
MAKES: 8 servings

- 2   14½-ounce cans Mexican-style stewed tomatoes, undrained
- 2   14-ounce cans reduced-sodium chicken broth
- 1   16-ounce package (32 small) frozen cooked Italian-style meatballs, thawed
- 1   16-ounce package frozen whole kernel corn
- 1   15-ounce can black beans, rinsed and drained
    Fresh parsley (optional)

one In a 3½- to 4½-quart slow cooker combine undrained tomatoes, broth, meatballs, frozen corn, and black beans.

two Cover and cook on low-heat setting for 6 to 7 hours or on high-heat setting for 3 to 3½ hours. If desired, garnish each serving with parsley.

NUTRITION FACTS PER SERVING: 287 cal., 13 g total fat (6 g sat. fat), 37 mg chol., 1,134 mg sodium, 30 g carbo., 6 g fiber, 16 g pro.

Beef and Barley Soup

PREP: 15 minutes **COOK:** Low 7 hours, High 3½ hours
MAKES: 4 servings

12	ounces boneless beef chuck roast
	Nonstick cooking spray
4	cups water
1	10½-ounce can condensed French onion soup
1	cup purchased shredded carrot
½	cup regular barley
1	teaspoon dried thyme or oregano, crushed
	Salt and black pepper

one Trim fat from meat. Cut meat into ½-inch pieces. Coat a large skillet with cooking spray; heat over medium-high heat. Cook meat in hot skillet until brown.

two In a 3½- to 4½-quart slow cooker combine meat, water, soup, carrot, barley, and thyme.

three Cover and cook on low-heat setting for 7 to 8 hours or on high-heat setting for 3½ to 4 hours. Season to taste with salt and pepper.

NUTRITION FACTS PER SERVING: 252 cal., 5 g total fat (1 g sat. fat), 52 mg chol., 684 mg sodium, 29 g carbo., 5 g fiber, 22 g pro.

Creamy Beef-and-Potato Stew

PREP: 10 minutes **COOK:** Low 7 hours, High 3½ hours; plus 15 minutes on Low **MAKES:** 4 servings

12	ounces boneless beef chuck roast
1	16-ounce package frozen cut green beans
1	4.9-ounce package dry au gratin potato mix
½	teaspoon dried thyme, crushed
3	cups water
1½	cups half-and-half or light cream
	Finely shredded Parmesan cheese (optional)

one Trim fat from meat. Cut meat into ¾-inch pieces. In a 3½- or 4-quart slow cooker combine meat, frozen green beans, au gratin potato mix, and thyme. Pour water over all.

two Cover and cook on low-heat setting for 7 to 8 hours or on high-heat setting 3½ to 4 hours.

three If using high-heat setting, turn to low-heat setting. Stir in half-and-half. Cover and cook about 15 minutes more or until heated through.

four Ladle stew into bowls. If desired, sprinkle with Parmesan cheese.

NUTRITION FACTS PER SERVING: 373 cal., 15 g total fat (8 g sat. fat), 84 mg chol., 845 mg sodium, 39 g carbo., 5 g fiber, 26 g pro.

Simple Short Rib Stew

PREP: 35 minutes **COOK:** Low 7 hours, High 3½ hours

MAKES: 6 servings

- 2 pounds boneless beef short ribs
  Nonstick cooking spray
- 1 pound tiny new potatoes, halved
- 5 medium carrots, cut into 1-inch pieces
- 1 12-ounce jar beef gravy
- ½ cup bottled plum sauce or hoisin sauce

Avoid Switching Sizes If you don't have the size of slow cooker called for in a recipe, it's important not to substitute a smaller or larger size. To work most efficiently, a slow cooker must be at least half but not more than two-thirds full. That's because the heat comes from the coils around the sides, not on the bottom.

Most of the slow-cooker recipes in this book give a range of cooker sizes (such as a 3½- to 4½-quart). Be sure to use one that's within the range so the food cooks to the right doneness within the time listed.

one Trim fat from meat. Cut meat into 1½-inch pieces. Lightly coat a 12-inch skillet with cooking spray; heat over medium-high heat. Cook meat, half at a time, in hot skillet until brown on all sides. Drain off any fat.

two In a 3½- or 4-quart slow cooker place potatoes and carrots. Place meat on top of vegetables. In a small bowl stir together gravy and plum sauce; pour over meat and vegetables in cooker.

three Cover and cook on low-heat setting for 7 to 8 hours or on high-heat setting for 3½ to 4 hours. Skim off fat.

NUTRITION FACTS PER SERVING: 621 cal., 26 g total fat (11 g sat. fat), 173 mg chol., 670 mg sodium, 30 g carbo., 3 g fiber, 62 g pro.

SLOW COOKER

Beef Burgundy *See photo on page 125.*

PREP: 20 minutes **COOK:** Low 7 hours, High 3½ hours
MAKES: 6 servings

Nonstick cooking spray

2   pounds beef stew meat, cut into 1-inch pieces

1   16-ounce package frozen stew vegetables

1   10¾-ounce can condensed golden mushroom soup

⅔   cup Burgundy

⅓   cup water

1   tablespoon quick-cooking tapioca

3   cups hot cooked wide noodles or garlic mashed
      potatoes (optional)

Snipped fresh parsley (optional)

one Lightly coat a large skillet with cooking spray; heat over medium-high heat. Cook meat, half at a time, in hot skillet until brown.

two Place frozen vegetables in a 3½- or 4-quart slow cooker. Add meat. In a medium bowl combine soup, wine, water, and tapioca; pour over meat and vegetables.

three Cover and cook on low-heat setting for 7 to 9 hours or on high-heat setting for 3 ½ to 4 ½ hours.

four If desired, ladle stew into bowls over hot cooked noodles and sprinkle with parsley.

NUTRITION FACTS PER SERVING: 291 cal., 8 g total fat (3 g sat. fat), 91 mg chol., 535 mg sodium, 14 g carbo., 1 g fiber, 34 g pro.

SLOW COOKER

Fruited Beef Stew

PREP: 10 minutes **COOK:** Low 7 hours, High 3½ hours
MAKES: 6 servings

1   pound beef stew meat, cut into ¾- to 1-inch pieces

1   16-ounce package frozen stew vegetables, thawed

1   7-ounce package mixed dried fruit

2   tablespoons quick-cooking tapioca

2   14-ounce cans beef broth

one Place meat in a 3½- to 4½-quart slow cooker. Cut up large pieces of stew vegetables and dried fruit; add to meat in cooker. Sprinkle with tapioca. Pour broth over all.

two Cover and cook on low-heat setting for 7 to 8 hours or on high-heat setting for 3½ to 4 hours.

NUTRITION FACTS PER SERVING: 231 cal., 3 g total fat (1 g sat. fat), 45 mg chol., 546 mg sodium, 32 g carbo., 3 g fiber, 19 g pro.

Old-Fashioned Beef Stew

PREP: 15 minutes **COOK:** Low 8 hours, High 4 hours
MAKES: 4 servings

1 pound beef stew meat, cut into ¾- to 1-inch pieces

12 ounces small potatoes, peeled and quartered (about 2 cups)

4 medium carrots, cut into ½-inch pieces

1 10¾-ounce can condensed cream of potato soup

½ cup water

1 envelope (half of a 2.2-ounce package) beefy onion soup mix

one In a 3½- or 4-quart slow cooker combine the meat, potatoes, and carrots. In a medium bowl stir together canned soup, water, and soup mix. Pour soup mixture over meat and vegetables in cooker.

two Cover and cook on low-heat setting for 8 to 9 hours or on high-heat setting for 4 to 4½ hours.

NUTRITION FACTS PER SERVING: 298 cal., 7 g total fat (2 g sat. fat), 73 mg chol., 1,262 mg sodium, 31 g carbo., 3 g fiber, 28 g pro.

Sweet-and-Sour Beef Stew

PREP: 10 minutes **COOK:** Low 10 hours, High 5 hours
MAKES: 6 to 8 servings

1½ pounds beef stew meat, cut into ¾- to 1-inch pieces

1 16-ounce package frozen stew vegetables

2 11-ounce cans condensed beefy mushroom soup

½ cup bottled sweet-and-sour sauce

½ cup water

⅛ to ¼ teaspoon cayenne pepper

one In a 3½- or 4-quart slow cooker place meat and frozen vegetables. Stir in soup, sweet-and-sour sauce, water, and cayenne pepper.

two Cover and cook on low-heat setting for 10 to 11 hours or on high-heat setting for 5 to 5½ hours.

NUTRITION FACTS PER SERVING: 291 cal., 9 g total fat (3 g sat. fat), 62 mg chol., 1,019 mg sodium, 19 g carbo., 2 g fiber, 30 g pro.

Pork, Lentil, and Apple Soup

PREP: 20 minutes **COOK:** Low 6 hours, High 3 hours
MAKES: 4 servings

1   pound lean boneless pork
     Nonstick cooking spray
3   medium cooking apples, peeled, cored, and cut up
1   cup lentils, rinsed and drained
1   teaspoon dried marjoram, crushed
2   14-ounce cans beef broth

one Trim fat from meat. Cut meat into ½-inch pieces. Lightly coat a 12-inch skillet with cooking spray; heat over medium-high heat. Cook meat in hot skillet until brown.

two Transfer meat to a 3½-quart slow cooker. Add apples, lentils, and marjoram. Pour broth over mixture in cooker; stir to combine.

three Cover and cook on low-heat setting for 6 to 8 hours or on high-heat setting for 3 to 4 hours.

NUTRITION FACTS PER SERVING: 384 cal., 6 g total fat (2 g sat. fat), 71 mg chol., 741 mg sodium, 44 g carbo., 17 g fiber, 39 g pro.

Pork and Winter Squash Stew

PREP: 20 minutes **COOK:** Low 6 hours, High 3 hours
MAKES: 6 servings

2½   pounds boneless pork shoulder roast
      Nonstick cooking spray
1½   pounds winter squash (such as butternut), peeled, seeded, and cut into 1½- to 2-inch pieces
2   tablespoons quick-cooking tapioca
1   teaspoon ground sage
1   10½-ounce can condensed French onion soup
½   cup water
3   cups hot cooked wide noodles or rice (optional)

one Trim fat from meat. Cut meat into 1-inch pieces. Lightly coat a large skillet with cooking spray; heat over medium-high heat. Cook meat, one-third at a time, in hot skillet until brown.

two Place squash in a 3½- or 4-quart slow cooker. Sprinkle with tapioca and sage. Add meat. Pour soup and water over mixture in cooker.

three Cover and cook on low-heat setting for 6 to 8 hours or on high-heat setting for 3 to 4 hours. If desired, ladle stew into bowls over hot cooked noodles.

NUTRITION FACTS PER SERVING: 346 cal., 12 g total fat (4 g sat. fat), 123 mg chol., 565 mg sodium, 19 g carbo., 0 g fiber, 39 g pro.

Pork and Mushroom Stew

PREP: 25 minutes **COOK:** Low 6 hours, High 3 hours
MAKES: 4 to 6 servings

1½   pounds lean boneless pork
       Nonstick cooking spray
  1   16-ounce package frozen small whole onions, thawed
 12   ounces fresh mushrooms, quartered
  1   10¾-ounce can condensed cream of mushroom with
       roasted garlic soup
  ½   teaspoon ground sage

one Trim fat from meat. Cut meat into ¾-inch pieces. Lightly coat a 12-inch skillet with cooking spray; heat over medium-high heat. Cook meat, half at a time, in hot skillet until brown.

two Place meat in a 3½- or 4-quart slow cooker. Add onions and mushrooms. Add soup and sage to mixture in cooker; stir to combine.

three Cover and cook on low-heat setting for 6 to 7 hours or on high-heat setting for 3 to 3½ hours.

NUTRITION FACTS PER SERVING: 317 cal., 10 g total fat (3 g sat. fat), 103 mg chol., 645 mg sodium, 19 g carbo., 4 g fiber, 38 g pro.

Pork and Black Bean Potage

PREP: 20 minutes **COOK:** Low 8 hours, High 4 hours
MAKES: 4 servings

 12   ounces lean boneless pork
       Nonstick cooking spray
  2   18½-ounce cans ready-to-serve black bean soup
  1   cup packaged shredded carrot
  1   cup water
  ½   cup lentils, rinsed and drained
  2   tablespoons grated Parmesan cheese

one Trim fat from meat. Cut meat into ¾-inch pieces. Lightly coat a 3½- or 4-quart slow cooker with cooking spray. In the prepared cooker combine meat, soup, carrot, water, and lentils.

two Cover and cook on low-heat setting for 8 to 10 hours or on high-heat setting for 4 to 5 hours.

three Ladle soup into bowls. Sprinkle with Parmesan cheese.

NUTRITION FACTS PER SERVING: 418 cal., 8 g total fat (3 g sat. fat), f61 mg chol., 938 mg sodium, 50 g carbo., 19 g fiber, 34 g pro.

SLOW COOKER

German-Style Pork Stew

PREP: 25 minutes **COOK:** Low 7 hours, High 3 ½ hours

MAKES: 4 servings

- 2 to 2¼ pounds boneless pork shoulder roast or boneless beef chuck roast

  Nonstick cooking spray

- 1 18- or 20-ounce package refrigerated diced potatoes
- 2 12-ounce jars mushroom gravy
- 1½ cups apple juice
- 2 teaspoons caraway seeds

one Trim fat from meat. Cut meat into ¾-inch pieces. Lightly coat a 12-inch skillet with cooking spray; heat over medium-high heat. Cook meat, half at a time, in hot skillet until brown.

two In a 3½- or 4-quart slow cooker stir together meat, refrigerated potatoes, gravy, apple juice, and caraway seeds.

three Cover and cook on low-heat setting for 7 to 8 hours or on high-heat setting for 3½ to 4 hours.

NUTRITION FACTS PER SERVING: 462 cal., 16 g total fat (5 g sat. fat), 101 mg chol., 1,150 mg sodium, 44 g carbo., 3 g fiber, 34 g pro.

SLOW COOKER

Easy Burgoo

PREP: 15 minutes **COOK:** Low 4 hours, High 2 hours

MAKES: 6 servings

- 1¼ pounds lean boneless pork

  Nonstick cooking spray

- 2 10¾-ounce cans condensed chicken gumbo soup
- 1 16-ounce package frozen succotash, thawed*
- 2 cups frozen diced hash brown potatoes with onions and peppers
- 2 cups water
- ¼ teaspoon cayenne pepper

one Trim fat from meat. Cut meat into ¾-inch pieces. Lightly coat a large skillet with cooking spray; heat over medium-high heat. Cook meat, half at a time, in hot skillet until brown.

two In a 3½- or 4-quart slow cooker combine meat, soup, succotash, frozen potatoes, water, and cayenne pepper.

three Cover and cook on low-heat setting for 4 to 6 hours or on high-heat setting for 2 to 3 hours.

__Note:__ You can substitute one 10-ounce package frozen lima beans, thawed, and 1 cup frozen whole kernel corn, thawed, for the succotash.

NUTRITION FACTS PER SERVING: 310 cal., 8 g total fat (3 g sat. fat), 57 mg chol., 994 mg sodium, 32 g carbo., 5 g fiber, 28 g pro.

Hearty Ham Stew *See photo on page 126.*

START TO FINISH: 20 minutes **MAKES:** 6 to 8 servings

- 2 16-ounce cans pork and beans in tomato sauce, undrained
- 1 16-ounce package frozen vegetable blend, thawed
- 1 8-ounce cooked ham slice, cut into ½-inch pieces
- 1 tablespoon dried minced onion

   Broken corn chips (optional)

one In a 10-inch skillet stir together undrained pork and beans, vegetables, ham, and dried onion. Cook over medium heat until bubbly, stirring occasionally.

two Ladle stew into bowls. If desired, sprinkle with corn chips.

NUTRITION FACTS PER SERVING: 255 cal., 5 g total fat (2 g sat. fat), 32 mg chol., 1,189 mg sodium, 41 g carbo., 10 g fiber, 17 g pro.,

SLOW COOKER

Spicy Ham-and-Garbanzo Bean Soup

PREP: 15 minutes **COOK:** Low 7 hours, High 3½ hours
MAKES: 6 servings

- 2 cups sliced carrot
- 1 15-ounce can garbanzo beans (chickpeas), rinsed and drained
- 1½ cups cubed cooked ham (8 ounces)
- 1 cup sliced celery
- 4 cups hot-style vegetable juice
- 1 cup water

one In a 3½- to 4½-quart slow cooker combine carrot, beans, ham, and celery. Pour vegetable juice and water over mixture in cooker.

two Cover and cook on low-heat setting for 7 to 9 hours or on high-heat setting for 3½ to 4½ hours.

NUTRITION FACTS PER SERVING: 187 cal., 5 g total fat (1 g sat. fat), 22 mg chol., 1,272 mg sodium, 23 g carbo., 5 g fiber, 12 g pro.

Corn and Sausage Chowder

PREP: 15 minutes **COOK:** Low 8 hours, High 4 hours
MAKES: 6 servings

1	pound cooked smoked turkey sausage, halved lengthwise and cut into ½-inch slices
3	cups frozen diced hash brown potatoes with onions and peppers
1	cup coarsely chopped carrot
1	14¾-ounce can cream-style corn, undrained
1	10¾-ounce can condensed golden mushroom soup
2½	cups water
	Snipped fresh chives or parsley (optional)

one In a 3½- to 5-quart slow cooker place sausage, frozen potatoes, and carrot. In a medium bowl combine undrained corn and soup; gradually stir in water. Pour corn mixture over meat and vegetables in cooker.

two Cover and cook on low-heat setting for 8 to 10 hours or on high-heat setting for 4 to 5 hours.

three Ladle soup into bowls. If desired, sprinkle with chives.

NUTRITION FACTS PER SERVING: 238 cal., 8 g total fat (2 g sat. fat), 53 mg chol., 1,280 mg sodium, 28 g carbo., 2 g fiber, 15 g pro.

Tuscan Bean and Sausage Stew

PREP: 15 minutes **COOK:** Low 6 hours, High 3 hours
MAKES: 6 servings

1	pound cooked smoked sausage, sliced
2	18½-ounce cans ready-to-serve minestrone soup
1	15-ounce can cannellini beans (white kidney beans), rinsed and drained
1	14½-ounce can Italian-style stewed tomatoes, undrained
¼	cup grated Parmesan cheese

one In a 3½- to 4½-quart slow cooker combine sausage, soup, beans, and undrained tomatoes.

two Cover and cook on low-heat setting for 6 to 8 hours or on high-heat setting for 3 to 4 hours.

three Ladle soup into bowls. Sprinkle with Parmesan cheese.

NUTRITION FACTS PER SERVING: 516 cal., 28 g total fat (10 g sat. fat), 58 mg chol., 2,008 mg sodium, 37 g carbo., 8 g fiber, 28 g pro.

Texas Two-Step Stew

PREP: 20 minutes **COOK:** Low 4 hours, High 2 hours; plus 1 hour on Low or 45 minutes on High **MAKES:** 6 servings

8	ounces uncooked chorizo sausage
½	cup chopped onion
1	15½-ounce can hominy or one 11-ounce can whole kernel corn with sweet peppers, drained
1	15-ounce can Mexican-style or regular chili beans in chili gravy, undrained
1	6¾-ounce package Spanish rice mix
6	cups water

one Remove casings from sausage, if present. In a medium skillet cook sausage and onion over medium-high heat until sausage is brown. Drain off fat. Transfer sausage mixture to a 3½- or 4-quart slow cooker. Stir in hominy, undrained beans in chili gravy, and the contents of seasoning packet from rice mix, if present. Pour water over mixture in cooker.

two Cover and cook on low-heat setting for 4 to 6 hours or on high-heat setting for 2 to 3 hours. Stir in rice. Cover and cook on low-heat setting for 1 hour more or on high-heat setting for 45 minutes more.

NUTRITION FACTS PER SERVING: 383 cal., 16 g total fat (6 g sat. fat), 33 mg chol., 1,385 mg sodium, 44 g carbo., 6 g fiber, 16 g pro.

Potato and Bratwurst Stew

PREP: 15 minutes **COOK:** Low 7 hours, High 3½ hours
MAKES: 6 servings

3	cups water
1	10¾-ounce can condensed cream of chicken with herbs soup
1	pound cooked bratwurst, halved lengthwise and cut into ½-inch slices
1	20-ounce package refrigerated diced potatoes with onions
1½	cups sliced celery
¼	teaspoon salt
⅛	teaspoon black pepper

one In a 3½- or 4-quart slow cooker stir together water and soup. Stir in bratwurst, refrigerated potatoes, celery, salt, and pepper.

two Cover and cook on low-heat setting for 7 to 8 hours or on high-heat setting for 3½ to 4 hours.

NUTRITION FACTS PER SERVING: 352 cal., 21 g total fat (8 g sat. fat), 50 mg chol., 1,100 mg sodium, 26 g carbo., 3 g fiber, 14 g pro.

North African Lamb Stew

PREP: 20 minutes **COOK:** Low 8 hours, High 4 hours
MAKES: 4 to 6 servings

2¾   pounds boneless lamb shoulder roast
      Nonstick cooking spray
1½   cups thinly sliced carrot
 1   cup sliced celery
 2   cups water
 1   9-ounce jar mango chutney
 2   tablespoons quick-cooking tapioca
 2   to 3 cups hot cooked couscous (optional)

one Trim fat from meat. Cut meat into ¾- to 1-inch pieces. Lightly coat a 12-inch skillet with cooking spray; heat over medium-high heat. Cook meat, one-third at a time, in hot skillet until brown.

two In a 3½-quart slow cooker place carrot and celery. Add meat. In a medium bowl combine water, chutney, and tapioca; pour over meat and vegetables.

three Cover and cook on low-heat setting for 8 to 10 hours or on high-heat setting for 4 to 5 hours.

four If desired, ladle stew into bowls over hot cooked couscous.

NUTRITION FACTS PER SERVING: 569 cal., 19 g total fat (6 g sat. fat), 204 mg chol., 411 mg sodium, 35 g carbo., 3 g fiber, 62 g pro.

Indian Lamb and Potato Stew

PREP: 15 minutes **COOK:** Low 8 hours, High 4 hours
MAKES: 6 servings

 2   pounds lean boneless lamb
 1   tablespoon garam masala
 3   cups cubed peeled potatoes
 ¼   teaspoon salt
 ¼   teaspoon black pepper
 1   14½-ounce can diced tomatoes with onion and garlic, undrained
 ¼   cup water
 ¾   cup plain yogurt (optional)

one Trim fat from meat. Cut meat into 1-inch pieces. In a medium bowl combine meat and garam masala; toss gently to coat.

two In a 3½- or 4-quart slow cooker place potatoes. Add seasoned meat. Sprinkle with salt and pepper. Pour undrained tomatoes and water over mixture in cooker.

three Cover and cook on low-heat setting for 8 to 10 hours or on high-heat setting for 4 to 5 hours.

four Ladle stew into bowls. If desired, top with yogurt.

NUTRITION FACTS PER SERVING: 282 cal., 8 g total fat (3 g sat. fat), 97 mg chol., 538 mg sodium, 18 g carbo., 1 g fiber, 33 g pro.

Mexican-Style Fish Chowder

PREP: 15 minutes **COOK:** Low 3 hours, High 1½ hours;
plus 1 hour on High **MAKES:** 6 to 8 servings

Nonstick cooking spray

- 1 16-ounce package frozen whole kernel corn
- 2 10¾-ounce cans condensed cream of celery soup
- 1½ cups milk
- 1 pound fresh or frozen cod or other white fish fillets
- 2 14½-ounce cans Mexican-style stewed tomatoes, undrained

one Lightly coat a 3½- or 4-quart slow cooker with cooking spray. In the prepared cooker combine frozen corn, soup, and milk.

two Cover and cook on low-heat setting for 3 to 4 hours or on high-heat setting for 1½ to 2 hours. Meanwhile, thaw fish, if frozen. Cover fish and chill until needed.

three If using low-heat setting, turn to high-heat setting. Stir chowder. Place fish on top of chowder. Cover and cook for 1 hour more. Gently stir in undrained tomatoes.

NUTRITION FACTS PER SERVING: 293 cal., 8 g total fat (3 g sat. fat), 39 mg chol., 1,296 mg sodium, 36 g carbo., 2 g fiber, 21 g pro.

Creamy Clam Chowder

PREP: 10 minutes **COOK:** Low 6 hours, High 3 hours;
plus 1 hour on High **MAKES:** 6 servings

- 3 6½-ounce cans minced clams, undrained
- 3 cups cubed peeled potatoes
- 1 10¾-ounce can condensed cream of onion soup
- ½ teaspoon dried dill
- 2 to 3 cups half-and-half or light cream

one Drain clams, reserving liquid. Cover clams and chill until needed. Measure reserved clam liquid; if necessary, add water to clam liquid to equal 1¾ cups.

two In a 3½- or 4-quart slow cooker combine the 1¾ cups clam liquid and the potatoes. Stir in soup and dill.

three Cover and cook on low-heat setting for 6 to 8 hours or on high-heat setting for 3 to 4 hours.

four If using low-heat setting, turn to high-heat setting. Stir in clams and enough half-and-half to make a chowder of desired consistency. Cover and cook for 1 hour more.

NUTRITION FACTS PER SERVING: 330 cal., 13 g total fat (7 g sat. fat), 97 mg chol., 525 mg sodium, 24 g carbo., 1 g fiber, 28 g pro.

Garden Bounty Tomato Soup

PREP: 25 minutes **COOK:** Low 6 hours, High 3 hours
MAKES: 8 to 10 servings

- 2 pounds roma tomatoes, chopped
- 2 cups finely chopped assorted fresh vegetables
    (such as carrots, celery, sweet peppers, fennel,
    and/or onions)
- 2 14-ounce cans beef broth
- 1 6-ounce can tomato paste
- 1 to 2 teaspoons sugar

one In a 3½- or 4-quart slow cooker place tomatoes, assorted vegetables. Stir in broth, tomato paste, and sugar.

two Cover and cook on low-heat setting for 6 to 8 hours or on high-heat setting for 3 to 4 hours.

NUTRITION FACTS PER SERVING: 61 cal., 1 g total fat (0 g sat. fat), 0 mg chol., 372 mg sodium, 12 g carbo., 3 g fiber, 3 g pro.

Cheesy Potato-Bean Soup

PREP: 10 minutes **COOK:** Low 6 hours, High 3 hours
MAKES: 6 servings

- 3 cups frozen diced hash brown potatoes
- 1 26-ounce can condensed cream of mushroom soup
- 1 15- or 19-ounce can cannellini beans (white kidney
    beans), rinsed and drained
- ½ teaspoon fennel seeds, crushed
- 3 cups water
- 8 ounces process Swiss cheese slices, torn

one In a 3½- or 4-quart slow cooker combine frozen potatoes, soup, beans, and fennel seeds. Stir in water.

two Cover and cook on low-heat setting for 6 to 8 hours or on high-heat setting for 3 to 4 hours. Add cheese; stir until cheese melts.

NUTRITION FACTS PER SERVING: 402 cal., 19 g total fat (9 g sat. fat), 42 mg chol., 1,603 mg sodium, 41 g carbo., 5 g fiber, 17 g pro.

Tortellini Soup Alfredo

PREP: 15 minutes **COOK:** Low 5 hours, High 2½ hours; plus 1 hour on High **MAKES:** 4 servings

- 1   28-ounce jar or two 14-ounce jars Alfredo pasta sauce
- 2   14-ounce cans vegetable broth
- ½   cup chopped onion
- 1   2-ounce jar sliced pimiento, drained and chopped
- 1   7- to 8-ounce package dried cheese-filled tortellini

one In a 3½- or 4-quart slow cooker combine pasta sauce, broth, onion, and pimiento.

two Cover and cook on low-heat setting for 5 to 6 hours or on high-heat setting for 2½ to 3 hours.

three If using low-heat setting, turn to high-heat setting. Stir in tortellini. Cover and cook for 1 hour more.

NUTRITION FACTS PER SERVING: 544 cal., 34 g total fat (16 g sat. fat), 114 mg chol., 2,247 mg sodium, 47 g carbo., 2 g fiber, 14 g pro.

Cheesy Vegetable Chowder

START TO FINISH: 20 minutes **MAKES:** 4 servings

- 1   16-ounce package frozen broccoli, cauliflower, and carrots
- ½   cup water
- 2   cups milk
- ⅓   cup all-purpose flour
- 1   14-ounce can chicken broth
- 1   cup shredded smoked or regular Gouda cheese (4 ounces)

one In a large saucepan combine frozen vegetables and water. Bring to boiling; reduce heat. Simmer, covered, about 4 minutes or just until vegetables are tender. Do not drain.

two Meanwhile, in a screw-top jar combine ⅔ cup of the milk and the flour; cover and shake well. Add to vegetable mixture; add the remaining 1⅓ cups milk and the broth.

three Cook and stir until thickened and bubbly. Cook and stir for 1 minute more. Add cheese; cook and stir over low heat until cheese nearly melts.

NUTRITION FACTS PER SERVING: 370 cal., 20 g total fat (13 g sat. fat), 81 mg chol., 942 mg sodium, 22 g carbo., 3 g fiber, 25 g pro.

Vegetable Chili Medley

PREP: 10 minutes **COOK:** Low 6 hours, High 3 hours
MAKES: 6 servings

2 15-ounce cans kidney, garbanzo, and/or black beans, rinsed and drained

2 14½-ounce cans diced tomatoes or diced tomatoes and green chile peppers, undrained

1 15-ounce can tomato sauce

1 10-ounce package frozen whole kernel corn

1 cup water

1 1¼-ounce envelope chili seasoning mix

Shredded cheddar cheese (optional)

one In a 3½- to 4½-quart slow cooker combine beans, undrained tomatoes, tomato sauce, frozen corn, water, and chili seasoning mix.

two Cover and cook on low-heat setting for 6 to 7 hours or on high-heat setting for 3 to 3½ hours. Ladle chili into bowls. If desired, sprinkle with cheddar cheese.

NUTRITION FACTS PER SERVING: 218 cal., 1 g total fat (0 g sat. fat), 0 mg chol., 1,346 mg sodium, 46 g carbo., 10 g fiber, 13 g pro.

Cajun-Seasoned Vegetarian Gumbo

PREP: 10 minutes **COOK:** Low 6 hours, High 3 hours
MAKES: 6 servings

2 15-ounce cans black beans, rinsed and drained

1 28-ounce can diced tomatoes, undrained

1 16-ounce package frozen pepper stir-fry vegetables (green, red, and yellow peppers and onions)

2 cups frozen cut okra

2 to 3 teaspoons Cajun seasoning

3 cups hot cooked white or brown rice (optional)

one In a 3½- to 4½-quart slow cooker combine beans, undrained tomatoes, frozen stir-fry vegetables, frozen okra, and Cajun seasoning.

two Cover and cook on low-heat setting for 6 to 8 hours or on high-heat setting for 3 to 4 hours. If desired, ladle gumbo into bowls over hot cooked rice.

NUTRITION FACTS PER SERVING: 153 cal., 0 g total fat (0 g sat. fat), 0 mg chol., 639 mg sodium, 31 g carbo., 10 g fiber, 12 g pro.

Mexican Cauliflower and Broccoli Chowder

PREP: 10 minutes **COOK:** Low 4 hours, High 2 hours
MAKES: 6 servings

- 2   10¾-ounce cans condensed fiesta nacho cheese soup
- 1   cup water
- 1   16-ounce package frozen broccoli and cauliflower, thawed
- 1   11-ounce can whole kernel corn with sweet peppers, drained
- 1½ cups half-and-half or light cream
- 1   cup chopped roma tomatoes
- ¼   cup sliced green onion and/or sliced fresh jalapeño chile pepper (see tip, page 59) (optional)

one Place soup in a 3½- or 4-quart slow cooker. Whisk water into soup until smooth. Stir in frozen broccoli and cauliflower and the corn.

two Cover and cook on low-heat setting for 4 to 5 hours or on high-heat setting for 2 to 2½ hours. Stir in half-and-half and chopped tomatoes.

three Ladle soup into bowls. If desired, top with green onion and/or jalapeño pepper.

NUTRITION FACTS PER SERVING: 261 cal., 14 g total fat (8 g sat. fat), 35 mg chol., 913 mg sodium, 26 g carbo., 5 g fiber, 9 g pro.

Easy Vegetable Minestrone

PREP: 10 minutes **COOK:** Low 6 hours, High 3 hours; plus 15 minutes on High **MAKES:** 4 to 6 servings

- 2   9-ounce packages frozen cut green beans
- 2   teaspoons spicy pizza seasoning
- 2   14-ounce cans vegetable broth
- 3   cups vegetable juice
- 1½ cups dried rotini pasta
     Grated Parmesan cheese (optional)

one In a 3½- to 5-quart slow cooker place frozen beans. Sprinkle with pizza seasoning. Pour broth and vegetable juice over mixture in cooker.

two Cover and cook on low-heat setting for 6 to 7 hours or on high-heat setting for 3 to 3½ hours.

three If using low-heat setting, turn to high-heat setting. Stir in pasta. Cover and cook for 15 to 20 minutes more or until pasta is tender.

four Ladle soup into bowls. If desired, sprinkle with Parmesan cheese.

NUTRITION FACTS PER SERVING: 201 cal., 2 g total fat (0 g sat. fat), 0 mg chol., 1,414 mg sodium, 42 g carbo., 6 g fiber, 9 g pro.

serve-along sides

Asparagus in Dill Butter

PREP: 10 minutes **GRILL:** 7 minutes **MAKES:** 4 to 6 servings

- 1   pound fresh asparagus spears
- 2   tablespoons butter or margarine, melted
- 1   tablespoon snipped fresh dill or 1 teaspoon dried dill
- 1   clove garlic, minced
- ¼   teaspoon black pepper
      Finely shredded Parmesan cheese

one Snap off and discard woody bases from asparagus. Place asparagus in a disposable foil pan. Drizzle with melted butter. Sprinkle with dill, garlic, and pepper; toss gently to combine.

two For a charcoal grill, grill asparagus in foil pan on the rack of an uncovered grill directly over medium coals for 7 to 10 minutes or until asparagus is crisp-tender, stirring occasionally. (For a gas grill, preheat grill. Reduce heat to medium. Place asparagus in foil pan on grill rack over heat. Cover and grill as above.)

three To serve, transfer asparagus to a serving dish. Sprinkle with Parmesan cheese.

NUTRITION FACTS PER SERVING: 142 cal., 11 g total fat (7 g sat. fat), 28 mg chol., 355 mg sodium, 2 g carbo., 1 g fiber, 8 g pro.

Asparagus with Cheese and Chives

PREP: 25 minutes **GRILL:** 2 minutes **MAKES:** 6 to 8 servings

- 2   pounds fresh asparagus spears
- 2   tablespoons olive oil
      Salt and black pepper
- 2   ounces Parmesan cheese, shaved
- 1   tablespoon snipped fresh chives

one Snap off and discard woody bases from asparagus. Divide asparagus into 4 equal portions; tie portions into bundles with 100-percent-cotton kitchen string.

two Fill a 4-quart Dutch oven halfway with lightly salted water. Bring to boiling; add asparagus bundles. Return to boiling. Cook, uncovered, for 2 minutes. Immediately plunge asparagus bundles into a bowl of ice water; drain.

three Untie bundles and spread asparagus on a baking sheet. Drizzle 1 tablespoon of the oil over asparagus; sprinkle with salt and pepper.

four For a charcoal grill, grill asparagus on the rack of an uncovered grill directly over medium coals for 2 to 3 minutes or until crisp-tender, turning occasionally. (For a gas grill, preheat grill. Reduce heat to medium. Place asparagus on grill rack over heat. Cover and grill as above.)

five To serve, transfer asparagus to a serving dish. Drizzle with the remaining 1 tablespoon oil; sprinkle with cheese and chives.

NUTRITION FACTS PER SERVING: 95 cal., 7 g total fat (2 g sat. fat), 7 mg chol., 259 mg sodium, 3 g carbo., 2 g fiber, 5 g pro.

Asparagus with Citrus Mayonnaise

START TO FINISH: 25 minutes **MAKES:** 4 servings

- 1 pound fresh asparagus spears or one 10-ounce package frozen asparagus spears
- 2 tablespoons plain fat-free yogurt
- 2 tablespoons light mayonnaise or salad dressing
- ½ teaspoon finely shredded orange peel
- Dash cayenne pepper

one Snap off and discard woody bases from asparagus. In a covered medium saucepan cook fresh asparagus in a small amount of boiling water for 3 to 5 minutes or until crisp-tender. (Or cook frozen asparagus according to package directions.) Drain.

two Meanwhile, in a small bowl stir together yogurt, mayonnaise, orange peel, and pepper. Spoon over hot asparagus.

NUTRITION FACTS PER SERVING: 46 cal., 3 g total fat (1 g sat. fat), 3 mg chol., 60 mg sodium, 3 g carbo., 2 g fiber, 2 g pro.

Lemony Herbed Asparagus

START TO FINISH: 15 minutes **MAKES:** 4 servings

- 1 pound fresh asparagus spears
- 1 tablespoon olive oil
- 1 teaspoon lemon juice
- ½ teaspoon snipped fresh basil
- ½ teaspoon snipped fresh oregano

one Snap off and discard woody bases from asparagus. Place asparagus in a steamer basket. Place basket in a saucepan over 1 inch of boiling water. Steam, covered, for 3 to 5 minutes or until tender.

two Meanwhile, in a small bowl stir together oil, lemon juice, basil, and oregano. Transfer asparagus to a serving platter. Drizzle with lemon mixture.

NUTRITION FACTS PER SERVING: 44 cal., 3 g total fat (0 g sat. fat), 0 mg chol., 1 mg sodium, 3 g carbo., 1 g fiber, 1 g pro.

Grilled Green Beans *See photo on page 263.*

PREP: 20 minutes **GRILL:** 25 minutes **MAKES:** 4 servings

- 12 ounces fresh green beans, trimmed
- 1 or 2 fresh jalapeño chile peppers, cut into thin strips (do not seed) (see tip, page 59)
- 8 unpeeled cloves garlic
- 1 tablespoon water
- 1 teaspoon cooking oil
- 2 teaspoons lemon-flavor olive oil (or 1½ teaspoons olive oil and ½ teaspoon lemon juice)

  Salt

one Tear off a 36×18-inch piece of heavy foil; fold in half to make an 18-inch square. In a large bowl combine beans, jalapeño peppers, garlic, water, and cooking oil. Place mixture in center of foil. Bring up two opposite edges of foil and seal with a double fold. Fold remaining edges together to completely enclose bean mixture, leaving space for steam to build.

two For a charcoal grill, grill foil packet on the rack of an uncovered grill directly over medium coals for 20 minutes, turning once. Remove from grill. Carefully open packet; return open packet to grill. Grill about 5 minutes more or just until beans are browned and crisp-tender, stirring occasionally. (For a gas grill, preheat grill. Reduce heat to medium. Place foil packet on grill rack over heat. Cover and grill as above.)

three To serve, transfer bean mixture to a serving bowl. Peel and mash garlic; stir into bean mixture. Drizzle with lemon-flavor oil. Season to taste with salt.

NUTRITION FACTS PER SERVING: 59 cal., 4 g total fat (0 g sat. fat), 0 mg chol., 78 mg sodium, 7 g carbo., 3 g fiber, 2 g pro.

Farm-Style Green Beans

START TO FINISH: 30 minutes **MAKES:** 8 servings

- 1 pound fresh green beans, trimmed
- 4 slices bacon, cut up
- 2 medium onions, sliced
- 2 cups peeled, seeded, and chopped tomato
- ½ teaspoon salt

one Leave beans whole or cut into 1-inch pieces; set aside.

two In a large skillet cook bacon over medium heat until crisp. Using a slotted spoon, remove bacon and drain on paper towels, reserving 3 tablespoons drippings in skillet. Add onions to the reserved drippings; cook until tender, stirring occasionally. Stir in tomato and salt. Cook, uncovered, about 5 minutes more or until most of the liquid is absorbed.

three Meanwhile, in a medium saucepan cook green beans in a small amount of boiling salted water for 10 to 12 minutes or until crisp-tender; drain. Transfer beans to a serving bowl. Top with tomato mixture and bacon.

NUTRITION FACTS PER SERVING: 99 cal., 7 g total fat (2 g sat. fat), 9 mg chol., 244 mg sodium, 8 g carbo., 3 g fiber, 3 g pro.

Golden Green Bean Crunch

PREP: 15 minutes **BAKE:** 30 minutes **MAKES:** 4 to 6 servings

- 1   16-ounce package frozen French-style green beans
- 1   10¾-ounce can condensed golden mushroom soup
- 1   8-ounce can sliced water chestnuts, drained (optional)
- 1   cup chow mein noodles or half of a 2.8-ounce can (about ¾ cup) french-fried onions

one Cook frozen green beans according to package directions; drain.

two In an ungreased 1½-quart casserole combine green beans, soup, and, if desired, water chestnuts.

three Bake, uncovered, in a 350°F oven about 25 minutes or until bubbly around edge. Sprinkle with chow mein noodles. Bake, uncovered, about 5 minutes more or until heated through.

NUTRITION FACTS PER SERVING: 188 cal., 6 g total fat (1 g sat. fat), 3 mg chol., 719 mg sodium, 27 g carbo., 5 g fiber, 5 g pro.

SERVE-ALONG SIDES

Green Beans with Shallot Sauce

START TO FINISH: 35 minutes **MAKES:** 12 servings

- 2   pounds fresh green beans, trimmed
- 3   tablespoons butter
- 1   cup chopped shallot
- ½   teaspoon salt
- ⅛   teaspoon freshly ground black pepper

one Place green beans in a steamer basket. Place basket in a saucepan over 1 inch of boiling water. Steam, covered, for 18 to 20 minutes or until tender.

two Meanwhile, in a 12-inch skillet melt 2 tablespoons of the butter over medium heat. Cook about 7 minutes or until butter is lightly browned, stirring occasionally. Be careful not to burn the butter. Transfer the browned butter to a small bowl, scraping skillet with a rubber spatula.

three In the same skillet melt the remaining 1 tablespoon butter over medium heat. Add shallot; cook, covered, for 8 to 10 minutes or until lightly browned, stirring occasionally. Stir in cooked green beans, browned butter, salt, and pepper; heat through.

NUTRITION FACTS PER SERVING: 57 cal., 3 g total fat (2 g sat. fat), 8 mg chol., 133 mg sodium, 7 g carbo., 2 g fiber, 2 g pro.

Saucy Green Beans and Potatoes

PREP: 20 minutes **COOK:** Low 6 hours, High 3 hours
MAKES: 12 servings

  2   pounds tiny new potatoes
  1   pound fresh green beans, trimmed and halved
       crosswise
  1   10¾-ounce can condensed cream of celery soup
  ¾   cup water
  ¼   cup Dijon-style mustard
  ¾   teaspoon dried dill

one In a 3½- or 4-quart slow cooker combine potatoes and green beans. In a medium bowl stir together soup, water, mustard, and dill. Pour over vegetables in cooker; stir gently to combine.

two Cover and cook on low-heat setting for 6 to 8 hours or on high-heat setting for 3 to 4 hours. Stir gently before serving.

NUTRITION FACTS PER SERVING: 95 cal., 2 g total fat (1 g sat. fat), 1 mg chol., 313 mg sodium, 17 g carbo., 3 g fiber, 3 g pro.

Curried Beans and Apples

PREP: 15 minutes **COOK:** Low 5 hours, High 2½ hours
MAKES: 12 servings

  2   31-ounce cans pork and beans in tomato sauce,
       undrained
  2   medium cooking apples (such as Granny Smith or
       Rome Beauty), peeled, cored, and cut into
       bite-size pieces
  ½   cup bottled chili sauce
  ¼   cup packed brown sugar or mild-flavor molasses
  1   tablespoon curry powder
  ¼   cup sliced green onion (optional)
       Crumbled, crisp-cooked bacon (optional)

one For a less saucy mixture, drain one of the cans of pork and beans. In a 3½- or 4-quart slow cooker combine pork and beans, apples, chili sauce, brown sugar, and curry powder.

two Cover and cook on low-heat setting for 5 to 6 hours or on high-heat setting for 2½ to 3 hours. If desired, stir in green onion and sprinkle with bacon before serving.

NUTRITION FACTS PER SERVING: 184 cal., 2 g total fat (1 g sat. fat), 10 mg chol., 781 mg sodium, 39 g carbo., 8 g fiber, 8 g pro.

Savory Black Beans

START TO FINISH: 15 minutes **MAKES:** 6 to 8 servings

2   15-ounce cans black beans, undrained

1   teaspoon ground cumin

1   clove garlic, minced

1   medium avocado, seeded, peeled, and cubed

½   cup shredded Monterey Jack cheese (2 ounces)

one Rinse and drain one of the cans of beans. In a medium saucepan combine beans, cumin, and garlic. Cook until heated through, stirring occasionally.

two Transfer beans to a serving bowl. Sprinkle with avocado and Monterey Jack cheese.

NUTRITION FACTS PER SERVING: 184 cal., 8 g total fat (3 g sat. fat), 8 mg chol., 403 mg sodium, 24 g carbo., 9 g fiber, 12 g pro.

Beer-Simmered Beans

PREP: 10 minutes **COOK:** 10 minutes **MAKES:** 7 servings

1   15-ounce can pinto beans, rinsed and drained

1   15-ounce can red kidney beans, rinsed and drained

1   cup light beer

2   small fresh jalapeño chile peppers, finely chopped
    (see tip, page 59) (optional)

1½ teaspoons ground cumin

2   cloves garlic, minced

¼   teaspoon salt

one In a large saucepan combine pinto beans, kidney beans, beer, jalapeño peppers (if desired), cumin, garlic, and salt.

two Bring to boiling; reduce heat. Simmer, covered, about 10 minutes or until desired consistency, stirring frequently.

NUTRITION FACTS PER SERVING: 113 cal., 0 g total fat (0 g sat. fat), 0 mg chol., 380 mg sodium, 21 g carbo., 7 g fiber, 8 g pro.

Western Beans

PREP: 15 minutes **COOK:** Low 4 hours, High 2 hours
MAKES: 12 servings

- 3   28-ounce cans vegetarian baked beans, drained
- ¾   cup bottled hot-style barbecue sauce
- ½   cup chopped onion
- ⅓   cup packed brown sugar
- 1   tablespoon dry mustard

one In a 3½- to 5-quart slow cooker combine beans, barbecue sauce, onion, brown sugar, and dry mustard.

two Cover and cook on low-heat setting for 4 to 5 hours or on high-heat setting for 2 to 2½ hours.

NUTRITION FACTS PER SERVING: 238 cal., 1 g total fat (0 g sat. fat), 0 mg chol., 1,015 mg sodium, 53 g carbo., 10 g fiber, 10 g pro.

Cranberry-Apple Spiced Beets

PREP: 25 minutes **COOK:** Low 6 hours, High 3 hours
MAKES: 8 to 10 servings

- 3   pounds fresh medium beets, peeled and quartered
- 1   tablespoon quick-cooking tapioca
- ½   teaspoon apple pie spice
- 1   cup cranberry-apple drink
- 2   tablespoons butter or margarine (optional)

one Place beets in a 3½- or 4-quart slow cooker. Sprinkle with tapioca and apple pie spice; pour cranberry-apple drink over all. If desired, dot with butter.

two Cover and cook on low-heat setting for 6 to 7 hours or on high-heat setting for 3 to 3½ hours.

three Using a slotted spoon, transfer beets to a serving bowl. Spoon some of the sauce over beets.

NUTRITION FACTS PER SERVING: 75 cal., 0 g total fat (0 g sat. fat), 0 mg chol., 85 mg sodium, 17 g carbo., 3 g fiber, 2 g pro.

Baked Beets in Gingered Syrup

PREP: 20 minutes **BAKE:** 1¾ hours **MAKES:** 8 to 12 servings

- 12 fresh medium beets
- 2 cups cider vinegar
- 1 cup sugar
- 1 3- to 4-inch piece fresh ginger, peeled
- ½ teaspoon salt

one Trim beets, leaving roots and 1 inch of stems intact. Place beets in an ungreased 3-quart casserole. Bake, covered, in a 325°F oven for 1¾ to 2 hours or until tender.

two Meanwhile, for syrup, in a medium saucepan stir together vinegar, sugar, ginger, and salt. Bring to boiling; reduce heat. Simmer, uncovered, for 10 minutes. Remove from heat. Discard ginger. Cool syrup.

three Allow beets to cool slightly. Using paper towels, rub beets while still warm to remove skins. Trim stem and root ends. Halve or quarter beets. Pour syrup over beets; toss gently to coat. Use a slotted spoon to serve beets. Serve warm, cold, or at room temperature.

NUTRITION FACTS PER SERVING: 88 cal., 0 g total fat (0 g sat. fat), 0 mg chol., 126 mg sodium, 23 g carbo., 5 g fiber, 1 g pro.

Broccoli and Peppers

PREP: 15 minutes **COOK:** 8 minutes **MAKES:** 6 servings

- 1 pound broccoli, cut into florets (3⅔ cups)
- 1 medium sweet pepper, cut into bite-size pieces
- 2 tablespoons butter or margarine
- 1 teaspoon finely shredded lemon peel
- 1 tablespoon lemon juice

one Place broccoli and sweet pepper in a steamer basket. Place basket in a saucepan over 1 inch of boiling water. Steam, covered, for 8 to 10 minutes or until vegetables are crisp-tender. Arrange vegetables on a serving platter.

two Meanwhile, in a small saucepan melt butter. Stir in lemon peel and lemon juice. Drizzle mixture over vegetables.

NUTRITION FACTS PER SERVING: 63 cal., 4 g total fat (3 g sat. fat), 11 mg chol., 62 mg sodium, 6 g carbo., 3 g fiber, 2 g pro.

Brussels Sprouts with Prosciutto

START TO FINISH: 25 minutes **MAKES:** 12 servings

1½   pounds fresh Brussels sprouts

3   ounces prosciutto or 3 slices bacon, crisp-cooked
     and crumbled

1   teaspoon finely shredded lemon peel

½   teaspoon salt

¼   teaspoon freshly ground black pepper

one In a covered 4-quart Dutch oven cook Brussels sprouts in enough boiling water to cover for 6 to 8 minutes or just until tender; drain in a colander. Rinse with cold water; drain again. Thinly slice Brussels sprouts.

two Heat a 12-inch nonstick skillet over medium-high heat for 1 minute. Add Brussels sprouts; cook and stir for 2 to 3 minutes or until heated through. Stir in prosciutto, lemon peel, salt, and pepper.

NUTRITION FACTS PER SERVING: 38 cal., 1 g total fat (0 g sat. fat), 5 mg chol., 301 mg sodium, 5 g carbo., 2 g fiber, 4 g pro.

Glazed Brussels Sprouts

PREP: 5 minutes **COOK:** 10 minutes **MAKES:** 3 servings

1   10-ounce package frozen Brussels sprouts

2   tablespoons bottled mango chutney

1   tablespoon butter or margarine

     Salt and freshly ground black pepper

one Cook frozen Brussels sprouts according to package directions; drain in a colander.

two In the same saucepan combine chutney and butter. Cook over medium-low heat until butter melts. Add Brussels sprouts to chutney mixture; stir gently to coat. Season to taste with salt and pepper.

NUTRITION FACTS PER SERVING: 110 cal., 4 g total fat (3 g sat. fat), 11 mg chol., 159 mg sodium, 17 g carbo., 4 g fiber, 4 g pro.

Honey-Glazed Carrots *See photo on page 264.*

START TO FINISH: 20 minutes **MAKES:** 4 servings

1	pound small carrots with tops, peeled and trimmed
8	ounces small parsnips, peeled and cut into ½-inch strips
¼	cup water
1	tablespoon butter or margarine
1	tablespoon honey
2	whole star anise
½	teaspoon salt
⅛	teaspoon black pepper

one Cut any thick carrots in half lengthwise. In a large skillet combine carrots, parsnips, water, butter, honey, star anise, salt, and pepper.

two Bring just to boiling; reduce heat to medium-low. Cook, uncovered, for 7 to 10 minutes or until vegetables are crisp-tender, stirring occasionally.

three Increase heat to medium. Cook, stirring gently, for 3 to 5 minutes or until vegetables are lightly browned. Discard star anise.

NUTRITION FACTS PER SERVING: 121 cal., 3 g total fat (2 g sat. fat), 8 mg chol., 242 mg sodium, 23 g carbo., 5 g fiber, 2 g pro.

Sweet Saucy Carrots and Pecans

START TO FINISH: 20 minutes **MAKES:** 4 servings

1	pound packaged peeled baby carrots
2	tablespoons orange marmalade
1	tablespoon butter or margarine
½	teaspoon salt
2	tablespoons pecan pieces, toasted (see tip, page 280)

one In a covered large saucepan cook carrots in a small amount of boiling water for 8 to 10 minutes or until crisp-tender; drain. Return carrots to saucepan.

two Stir in orange marmalade, butter, and salt until carrots are coated. Transfer to a serving bowl. Top with pecans.

NUTRITION FACTS PER SERVING: 124 cal., 6 g total fat (2 g sat. fat), 8 mg chol., 365 mg sodium, 19 g carbo., 4 g fiber, 2 g pro.

Honey-Ginger Carrots

START TO FINISH: 15 minutes **MAKES:** 4 servings

- 1 pound carrots, peeled and cut into ¼-inch slices (3 cups)
- 2 tablespoons water
- 2 tablespoons honey
- 1 tablespoon butter or margarine
- ⅛ teaspoon ground ginger

one In a microwave-safe baking dish or casserole combine carrots and water. Microwave, covered, on 100 percent power (high) for 6 to 8 minutes or just until carrots are tender, stirring once after 4 minutes; drain.

two Add honey, butter, and ginger to the baking dish. Microwave, covered, for 1 to 2 minutes more or until butter melts. Stir to combine.

NUTRITION FACTS PER SERVING: 98 cal., 3 g total fat (2 g sat. fat), 8 mg chol., 64 mg sodium, 18 g carbo., 3 g fiber, 1 g pro.

SLOW COOKER

Sweet Baby Carrots

PREP: 10 minutes **COOK:** Low 6 hours, High 3 hours
STAND: 2 minutes **MAKES:** 8 to 10 servings

- 2 16-ounce packages peeled baby carrots
- 1 16-ounce package frozen small whole onions
- ½ teaspoon dried dill
- ¾ cup water
- 1 cup apple jelly

one In a 4½- to 5½-quart slow cooker combine carrots and frozen onions. Sprinkle with dill. Pour water over vegetables.

two Cover and cook on low-heat setting for 6 to 7 hours or on high-heat setting for 3 to 3½ hours.

three Using a slotted spoon, remove carrots and onions from cooker. Stir apple jelly into liquid in cooker; let stand for 2 to 3 minutes or until jelly melts. Stir sauce. Return carrots and onions to sauce in cooker; stir gently to coat vegetables. Use a slotted spoon to serve carrots and onions.

NUTRITION FACTS PER SERVING: 178 cal., 0 g total fat (0 g sat. fat), 0 mg chol., 53 mg sodium, 43 g carbo., 5 g fiber, 2 g pro.

Glazed Carrot Coins

START TO FINISH: 20 minutes **MAKES:** 8 servings

1½   pounds medium carrots and/or parsnips, peeled and
      cut into ¼-inch slices (4½ cups)
 ¼   cup packed brown sugar
 2   tablespoons olive oil
 2   tablespoons balsamic vinegar or white wine vinegar
 1   teaspoon cornstarch

one In a covered medium saucepan cook carrots in a small amount of boiling water for 7 to 9 minutes or until crisp-tender. Drain carrots in a colander.

two In the same saucepan stir together brown sugar, oil, vinegar, and cornstarch. Cook and stir over medium heat until slightly thickened. Stir in carrots. Cook, uncovered, about 2 minutes more or until carrots are glazed, stirring frequently.

NUTRITION FACTS PER SERVING: 91 cal., 4 g total fat (0 g sat. fat), 0 mg chol., 71 mg sodium, 15 g carbo., 3 g fiber, 1 g pro.

SLOW COOKER

Cheesy Cauliflower for a Crowd

PREP: 15 minutes **COOK:** Low 6 hours, High 3 hours
MAKES: 10 to 12 servings

 8   cups cauliflower florets
 1   large onion, thinly sliced
 ½   teaspoon fennel seeds, crushed
 1   14- to 16-ounce jar cheddar cheese pasta sauce
     Cracked black pepper

one In a 3½- or 4-quart slow cooker place cauliflower, onion, and fennel seeds. Pour pasta sauce over mixture in cooker.

two Cover and cook on low-heat setting for 6 to 7 hours or on high-heat setting for 3 to 3½ hours. Stir gently. Sprinkle with cracked pepper.

NUTRITION FACTS PER SERVING: 59 cal., 6 g total fat (2 g sat. fat), 16 mg chol., 329 mg sodium, 8 g carbo., 2 g fiber, 3 g pro.

Creamy Crunchy Corn

PREP: 5 minutes **COOK:** 30 minutes **STAND:** 10 minutes
MAKES: 6 servings

¼ cup butter or margarine

2 10-ounce packages frozen whole kernel corn

2 to 4 tablespoons sugar

1 tablespoon cornmeal

   Salt and black pepper

one In a large heavy skillet melt butter. Stir in frozen corn, sugar, and cornmeal. Cook, covered, over medium-low heat for 30 minutes, stirring occasionally.

two Season to taste with salt and pepper. Let stand for 10 minutes before serving.

NUTRITION FACTS PER SERVING: 152 cal., 9 g total fat (4 g sat. fat), 22 mg chol., 254 mg sodium, 19 g carbo., 2 g fiber, 2 g pro.

SLOW COOKER

Creamy Corn and Roasted Red Peppers

PREP: 15 minutes **COOK:** Low 6 hours, High 3 hours
MAKES: 8 servings

3 10-ounce packages frozen whole kernel corn or white whole kernel corn (shoe peg) in light or regular butter sauce

1 12-ounce jar roasted red sweet peppers, drained and chopped (about 1 cup)

2 tablespoons thinly sliced green onion

2 cups milk

2 0.9- to 1¼-ounce envelopes hollandaise sauce mix

one In a 3½-quart slow cooker place frozen corn, roasted peppers, and green onion. In a small bowl whisk together milk and sauce mixes. Add sauce mixture to cooker; stir to combine (frozen chunks of vegetables may remain).

two Cover and cook on low-heat setting for 6 to 8 hours or on high-heat setting for 3 to 4 hours. Stir before serving.

NUTRITION FACTS PER SERVING: 155 cal., 2 g total fat (1 g sat. fat), 5 mg chol., 249 mg sodium, 32 g carbo., 2 g fiber, 5 g pro.

Herbed Sweet Corn

PREP: 20 minutes **GRILL:** 25 minutes **MAKES:** 6 servings

- ⅓ cup butter, softened
- 3 tablespoons snipped fresh chives, parsley, cilantro, or tarragon
- ¼ teaspoon salt
- ¼ teaspoon black pepper
- 6 fresh ears sweet corn with husks

one In a small bowl combine butter, chives, salt, and pepper.

two Carefully peel back corn husks but do not remove. Remove and discard silks. Gently rinse corn; pat dry. Spread about 1 tablespoon of the butter mixture over each ear of corn. Carefully fold husks back around ears. Tie husk tops with 100-percent-cotton kitchen string to secure.

three For a charcoal grill, grill corn on the rack of an uncovered grill directly over medium coals for 25 to 30 minutes or until kernels are tender, turning and rearranging corn 3 times during grilling. (For a gas grill, preheat grill. Reduce heat to medium. Place corn on grill rack over heat. Cover and grill as above.)

four Remove string from corn. Remove husks. If desired, serve corn with any remaining butter mixture.

NUTRITION FACTS PER SERVING: 168 cal., 11 g total fat (7 g sat. fat), 27 mg chol., 182 mg sodium, 17 g carbo., 2 g fiber, 3 g pro.

Smoked Mushrooms

PREP: 10 minutes **SOAK:** 1 hour **GRILL:** 45 minutes
MAKES: 4 to 6 servings

- 2 cups hickory wood chips
- 4 cups halved fresh mushrooms
- ¼ cup butter or margarine, cut up
- 1 teaspoon instant chicken bouillon granules

one At least 1 hour before grilling, soak wood chips in water. Drain before using.

two In a disposable foil pan combine mushrooms, butter, and bouillon granules.

three For a charcoal grill, arrange medium-hot coals around edge of grill. Sprinkle wood chips over coals. Test for medium heat above center of grill. Place foil pan on grill rack over center of grill. Cover and grill for 45 minutes, stirring occasionally. (For a gas grill, preheat grill. Reduce heat to medium. Adjust for indirect cooking. Grill as above.)

NUTRITION FACTS PER SERVING: 130 cal., 13 g total fat (8 g sat. fat), 31 mg chol., 306 mg sodium, 3 g carbo., 1 g fiber, 3 g pro.

Garlicky Grilled Portobellos

PREP: 15 minutes **GRILL:** 6 minutes **MAKES:** 4 servings

1   pound fresh portobello mushrooms
¼   cup butter or margarine, melted
3   cloves garlic, minced
¼   teaspoon salt
⅛   teaspoon black pepper
1   tablespoon snipped fresh chives

one Remove and discard stems and gills from mushrooms. In a small bowl combine melted butter, garlic, salt, and pepper brush over mushrooms.

two For a charcoal grill, grill mushrooms on the rack of an uncovered grill directly over medium coals for 6 to 8 minutes or just until mushrooms are tender, turning once halfway through grilling. (For a gas grill, preheat grill. Reduce heat to medium. Place mushrooms on grill rack over heat. Cover and grill as above.) Sprinkle mushrooms with chives.

NUTRITION FACTS PER SERVING: 146 cal., 12 g total fat (7 g sat. fat), 31 mg chol., 241 mg sodium, 6 g carbo., 4 g fiber, 4 g pro.

Grilled Sweet Onions

PREP: 15 minutes **GRILL:** 35 minutes **MAKES:** 4 servings

4   medium sweet onions (4 to 5 ounces each)
1   tablespoon butter or margarine, melted
1   teaspoon Dijon-style mustard
⅛   teaspoon bottled hot pepper sauce
1   tablespoon packed brown sugar
     Black pepper

one Tear off four 18-inch squares of heavy foil. Cut almost through each onion, forming 8 wedges. Place an onion in the center of each piece of foil.

two In a small bowl combine melted butter, mustard, and hot pepper sauce; drizzle over onions. Sprinkle with brown sugar. Bring up two opposite edges of foil and seal with a double fold. Fold remaining edges together to completely enclose each onion, leaving space for steam to build.

three For a charcoal grill, arrange medium-hot coals around a drip pan. Test for medium heat above pan. Place foil packets on grill rack over drip pan. Cover and grill about 25 minutes or until onions are nearly tender. Cut a 2-inch opening in the top of each foil packet. Cover and grill about 10 minutes more or until onions are lightly browned. (For a gas grill, preheat grill. Reduce heat to medium. Adjust for indirect cooking. Grill as above.) Sprinkle with pepper.

NUTRITION FACTS PER SERVING: 83 cal., 3 g total fat (1 g sat. fat), 0 mg chol., 70 mg sodium, 13 g carbo., 2 g fiber, 1 g pro.

Sweet Onions Few vegetables can match the visual and flavor appeal of grilled sweet onions served alongside a sizzling grilled entrée. With their slightly flattened appearance and light, papery skins, sweet onions are a breed apart from more common yellow, white, and red varieties. Top sweet onion varieties to look for are Vidalia, Maui, Walla Walla, and the South American overachiever Oso Sweet, which sometimes features twice the sweetness of delectable Vidalias.

Sweet-and-Sour Onions

START TO FINISH: 35 minutes **MAKES:** 4 servings

- 3 cups white and/or red pearl onions or one 16-ounce package frozen small whole onions
- 2 teaspoons butter or margarine
- ¼ cup white wine vinegar or balsamic vinegar
- 2 tablespoons packed brown sugar
- 1 ounce prosciutto or thinly sliced cooked ham, cut into short thin strips

one In a covered medium saucepan cook unpeeled pearl onions in a small amount of boiling water for 8 to 10 minutes or just until onions are tender; drain. Cool onions slightly; trim ends and remove skins. (Or cook frozen onions in a medium saucepan according to package directions; drain.)

two In the same saucepan melt butter over medium heat. Stir in the vinegar and brown sugar. Cook and stir about 30 seconds or until combined. Stir in onions and prosciutto. Cook, uncovered, for 7 to 8 minutes more or until onions are golden brown and slightly glazed, stirring occasionally.

NUTRITION FACTS PER SERVING: 114 cal., 4 g total fat (0 g sat. fat), 0 mg chol., 155 mg sodium, 16 g carbo., 2 g fiber, 3 g pro.

Glazed Parsnips and Apples

START TO FINISH: 20 minutes **MAKES:** 4 or 5 servings

- ¾ cup apple cider or apple juice
- 1 pound parsnips, peeled and cut into ¼-inch slices
- 2 tablespoons butter or margarine
- 2 tablespoons packed brown sugar
- 2 medium cooking apples, cored and thinly sliced

one In a large skillet bring apple cider to simmering. Add parsnips. Cook, covered, for 7 to 8 minutes or until crisp-tender. Remove parsnips and any liquid from skillet; set parsnips and liquid aside.

two In the same skillet combine butter and brown sugar. Cook, uncovered, over medium-high heat about 1 minute or until mixture starts to thicken. Stir in undrained parsnips and apples. Cook, uncovered, about 2 minutes or until parsnips and apples are glazed, stirring frequently.

NUTRITION FACTS PER SERVING: 206 cal., 7 g total fat (4 g sat. fat), 16 mg chol., 74 mg sodium, 38 g carbo., 7 g fiber, 1 g pro.

Cooking Apples Some apples are best eaten out of hand; others lend themselves better to cooking and baking. To pick prime apples for cooking, consider one of these varieties: Cortland, Granny Smith, Golden Delicious, Newtown Pippin, Northern Spy, Rome Beauty, Stayman, Winesap, or York Imperial.

Mediterranean Parsnips

START TO FINISH: 30 minutes **MAKES:** 8 servings

3½   pounds small parsnips

3   tablespoons olive oil

¼   teaspoon salt

¼   teaspoon black pepper

1   cup pitted kalamata olives, coarsely chopped

1   3½-ounce jar capers, drained

one Peel and slice parsnips lengthwise into ¼-inch strips. In a covered large saucepan cook parsnips in a small amount of boiling, lightly salted water for 7 to 9 minutes or until tender; drain.

two Add olive oil, salt, and pepper to parsnips; toss gently to coat. Transfer to a serving dish. Top with olives and capers.

NUTRITION FACTS PER SERVING: 234 cal., 8 g total fat (1 g sat. fat), 0 mg chol., 535 mg sodium, 41 g carbo., 9 g fiber, 3 g pro.

Dilled Peas and Walnuts

PREP: 35 minutes **MAKES:** 4 servings

2   cups shelled peas or one 10-ounce package frozen peas

¼   cup chopped onion

1   tablespoon butter or margarine

1½   teaspoons snipped fresh dill or ½ teaspoon dried dill

¼   teaspoon salt

¼   teaspoon black pepper

3   tablespoons broken walnuts or slivered almonds, toasted (see tip, page 280)

one In a covered small saucepan cook fresh peas and onion in a small amount of boiling salted water for 10 to 12 minutes or until crisp-tender. (Or cook frozen peas and onion according to the pea package directions.) Drain.

two Stir in butter, dill, salt, and pepper; heat through. Transfer to a serving dish. Sprinkle with walnuts.

NUTRITION FACTS PER SERVING: 127 cal., 7 g total fat (2 g sat. fat), 8 mg chol., 180 mg sodium, 12 g carbo., 4 g fiber, 5 g pro.

Cheesy Peas and Potatoes

PREP: 15 minutes **GRILL:** 17 minutes **MAKES:** 4 servings

4   ounces mild pasteurized prepared cheese product
    with jalapeño peppers, cut up

½   of a 16-ounce package (2 cups) frozen diced hash
    brown potatoes with onions and peppers

¾   cup frozen peas

¼   cup chopped salami

Foil Packet Grilling One of the slickest ways to cook on the
grill is to use aluminum foil packets. Here's how:

- Start with a large sheet of heavy foil—it's better to have too
  much than too little.
- If you think there's a chance the food might stick, use
  nonstick cooking spray on the inside of your packet.
- Place the food in the center of the sheet.
- Bring together two opposite sides of foil, sealing them with
  a double fold. Leave a little extra space for steam to build.
- Seal the remaining sides with another double fold.

one In a medium saucepan melt cheese product over low
heat. Stir in hash brown potatoes, peas, and salami.

two Tear off a 36×18-inch piece of heavy foil; fold in half to
make an 18-inch square. Place potato mixture in center of
piece of foil. Bring up two opposite edges of foil and seal with
a double fold. Fold remaining edges together to completely
enclose potato mixture, leaving space for steam to build.

three For a charcoal grill, grill foil packet on the rack of
an uncovered grill directly over medium coals for 17 to
25 minutes or until heated through, turning packet once
halfway through grilling. (For a gas grill, preheat grill. Reduce
heat to medium. Place foil packet on grill rack over heat.
Cover and grill as above.)

NUTRITION FACTS PER SERVING: 195 cal., 11 g total fat (6 g sat. fat),
34 mg chol., 841 mg sodium, 15 g carbo., 2 g fiber, 10 g pro.

Cider Peas and Apples

START TO FINISH: 15 minutes **MAKES:** 4 servings

3   cups frozen peas

1   medium apple, cored and thinly sliced

⅓   cup apple cider or apple juice

1   teaspoon cornstarch

one Place peas in a steamer basket. Place basket in a
saucepan over 1 inch of boiling water. Steam, covered,
for 5 minutes. Add apple slices; steam, covered, for 2 to
4 minutes more or just until apple slices are tender.

two Meanwhile, for sauce, in a medium saucepan combine
apple cider and cornstarch. Cook and stir until mixture is
thickened and bubbly. Cook and stir for 2 minutes more. Add
peas and apple slices; toss gently to coat with sauce.

NUTRITION FACTS PER SERVING: 102 cal., 0 g total fat (0 g sat. fat), 0 mg chol.,
82 mg sodium, 21 g carbo., 4 g fiber, 5 g pro.

Ginger Pea Pods and Noodles

PREP: 15 minutes **COOK:** Low 5 hours, High 2½ hours; plus 15 minutes on High **MAKES:** 8 servings

- 2   14-ounce cans chicken broth or vegetable broth
- 1   cup bottled stir-fry sauce
- 1   tablespoon bottled grated ginger
- 4   cups fresh snow pea pods (8 ounces)
- 12   ounces dried angel hair or spaghettini pasta, broken

one In a 3½- or 4-quart slow cooker combine broth, stir-fry sauce, and ginger. Add pea pods; stir gently to combine.

two Cover and cook on low-heat setting for 5 to 6 hours or on high-heat setting for 2½ to 3 hours.

three If using low-heat setting, turn to high-heat setting. Stir in uncooked pasta. Gently press pasta with a spoon to cover with the liquid. Cover and cook for 15 to 20 minutes more or until pasta is tender.

NUTRITION FACTS PER SERVING: 225 cal., 2 g total fat (0 g sat. fat), 0 mg chol., 1,482 mg sodium, 43 g carbo., 2 g fiber, 8 g pro.

Minted Snap Peas and Carrots

START TO FINISH: 25 minutes **MAKES:** 6 servings

- 1   pound fresh sugar snap pea pods
- 1   tablespoon butter or margarine
- 1   pound carrots, cut into thin bite-size strips
- 2   medium yellow sweet peppers, cut into 1-inch pieces
- ¼   cup snipped fresh mint
- ½   teaspoon salt
- ⅛   teaspoon black pepper

one Remove strings and tips from snap pea pods; set aside. In a large skillet melt butter over medium heat. Add carrots and sweet peppers; cook and stir for 8 to 9 minutes or until vegetables are tender.

two Meanwhile, in a large saucepan cook snap pea pods in a small amount of boiling water for 2 to 4 minutes or until crisp-tender; drain.

three Add carrot mixture, mint, salt, and pepper to pea pods; toss gently to combine.

NUTRITION FACTS PER SERVING: 98 cal., 2 g total fat (1 g sat. fat), 5 mg chol., 244 mg sodium, 17 g carbo., 5 g fiber, 3 g pro.

Sweet Peppers Stuffed with Goat Cheese and Herbs

PREP: 15 minutes **GRILL:** 5 minutes **MAKES:** 4 servings

- 2 medium red, yellow, or green sweet peppers
- 1 ounce soft goat cheese (chèvre)
- ¼ cup shredded Monterey Jack cheese (1 ounce)
- 1 tablespoon snipped fresh chives
- 1 tablespoon snipped fresh basil or
     1 teaspoon dried basil, crushed

one Cut sweet peppers in half lengthwise. Remove and discard seeds and membranes. In a covered large saucepan cook peppers in a small amount of boiling water for 2 minutes. Drain peppers, cut sides down, on paper towels.

two Meanwhile, in a small bowl combine goat cheese, Monterey Jack cheese, chives, and basil. Divide cheese mixture evenly among sweet pepper halves.

three Tear off a 24×18-inch piece of heavy foil; fold in half to make an 18×12-inch rectangle. Place filled sweet peppers in center of foil rectangle. Bring up two opposite edges of foil and seal with a double fold. Fold remaining edges together to completely enclose peppers, leaving space for steam to build.

four For a charcoal grill, grill foil packet on the rack of an uncovered grill directly over medium coals for 5 to 6 minutes or until peppers are crisp-tender and cheese melts. (For a gas grill, preheat grill. Reduce heat to medium. Place foil packet on grill rack over heat. Cover and grill as above.)

NUTRITION FACTS PER SERVING: 60 cal., 4 g total fat (2 g sat. fat), 13 mg chol., 80 mg sodium, 3 g carbo., 0 g fiber, 3 g pro.

Garlic-Roasted Red Potatoes

PREP: 15 minutes **BAKE:** 40 minutes **MAKES:** 8 servings

- 2 pounds small red potatoes, quartered
- 1 tablespoon snipped fresh rosemary
- 1 teaspoon steak seasoning or seasoning salt
- 2 tablespoons olive oil
- 12 cloves garlic, peeled

one Place potatoes in a 15×10×1-inch baking pan. Sprinkle potatoes with rosemary and seasoning blend. Drizzle with oil, stirring gently to coat.

two Bake, uncovered, in a 400°F oven for 20 minutes. Stir in garlic cloves. Bake about 20 minutes more or until potatoes are tender and golden, stirring occasionally.

NUTRITION FACTS PER SERVING: 120 cal., 4 g total fat (0 g sat. fat), 0 mg chol., 9 mg sodium, 21 g carbo., 8 g fiber, 3 g pro.

Super Creamy Mashed Potatoes

PREP: 10 minutes **COOK:** Low 3½ hours
MAKES: 12 to 14 servings

Nonstick cooking spray

4 16-ounce packages refrigerated mashed potatoes

1 8-ounce container dairy sour cream onion- or chive-flavor dip

1 8-ounce package cream cheese, cut up

¼ teaspoon garlic powder

one Coat a 4- or 4½-quart slow cooker with cooking spray. Place 2 packages of the mashed potatoes in the prepared cooker. Top with sour cream dip and cream cheese. Sprinkle with garlic powder. Top with the remaining mashed potatoes.

two Cover and cook on low-heat setting for 3½ to 4 hours. Stir before serving.

NUTRITION FACTS PER SERVING: 214 cal., 11 g total fat (6 g sat. fat), 21 mg chol., 409 mg sodium, 22 g carbo., 1 g fiber, 5 g pro.

Creamy Potato Wedges

PREP: 10 minutes **COOK:** Low 3½ hours, High 1¾ hours
MAKES: 8 servings

2 8-ounce containers dairy sour cream chive-flavor dip

1 cup finely shredded Asiago cheese (4 ounces)

1 3-ounce package cream cheese, cut up

½ cup mayonnaise

2 20-ounce packages refrigerated red potato wedges

one In a 3½- or 4-quart slow cooker combine sour cream dip, Asiago cheese, cream cheese, and mayonnaise. Stir in refrigerated potato wedges.

two Cover and cook on low-heat setting for 3½ to 4½ hours or on high-heat setting for 1¾ to 2¼ hours. Stir before serving

NUTRITION FACTS PER SERVING: 415 cal., 31 g total fat (14 g sat. fat), 55 mg chol., 835 mg sodium, 23 g carbo., 4 g fiber, 10 g pro.

Cheesy Garlic Potato Gratin

PREP: 15 minutes   **BAKE:** 1¼ hours   **MAKES:** 6 to 8 servings

1½   pounds Yukon gold or other yellow potatoes,
        thinly sliced (about 5 cups)

⅓   cup sliced green onion

1½   cups shredded Swiss cheese (6 ounces)

4   cloves garlic, minced

1   teaspoon salt

¼   teaspoon black pepper

1   cup whipping cream

one In a greased 2-quart square baking dish layer half of the potatoes and half of the green onion. Sprinkle with half each of the cheese, garlic, salt, and pepper. Repeat layers. Pour whipping cream over layers in dish.

two Bake, covered, in a 350°F oven for 1 hour. Bake, uncovered, for 15 to 20 minutes more or until potatoes are tender and top is golden brown.

NUTRITION FACTS PER SERVING: 365 cal., 23 g total fat (14 g sat. fat), 80 mg chol., 454 mg sodium, 30 g carbo., 1 g fiber, 12 g pro.

GRILLING

Buttered Rosemary New Potatoes

PREP: 10 minutes   **GRILL:** 30 minutes   **MAKES:** 4 servings

1   pound tiny new potatoes, halved

2   tablespoons butter or margarine, melted

1   tablespoon snipped fresh chives

2   teaspoons snipped fresh rosemary or ½ teaspoon
        dried rosemary, crushed

⅛   teaspoon chili powder

       Salt and black pepper

one Place potatoes in a greased disposable foil pan. In a small bowl combine melted butter, chives, rosemary, and chili powder. Pour over potatoes; toss gently to coat.

two For a charcoal grill, arrange hot coals around edge of grill. Test for medium-hot heat above center of grill. Place foil pan on grill rack over center of grill. Cover and grill for 30 to 35 minutes or until potatoes are tender. (For a gas grill, preheat grill. Reduce heat to medium-high. Adjust for indirect cooking. Grill as above.) Season to taste with salt and pepper.

NUTRITION FACTS PER SERVING: 136 cal., 6 g total fat (4 g sat. fat), 15 mg chol., 50 mg sodium, 19 g carbo., 2 g fiber, 3 g pro.

Shredded Hash Browns

START TO FINISH: 25 minutes **MAKES:** 2 or 3 servings

3   or 4 small russet or white potatoes, peeled and
     coarsely shredded (about 2 cups)

¼   cup finely chopped onion

1   small fresh jalapeño, banana, or Anaheim chile pepper,
     seeded and chopped (see tip, page 59) (optional)

¼   teaspoon salt

⅛   teaspoon coarsely ground black pepper

2   tablespoons butter, cooking oil, or margarine

     Fresh sage leaves (optional)

one Rinse shredded potatoes in a colander; drain well and pat dry with paper towels. In a medium bowl combine shredded potatoes, onion, chile pepper (if desired), salt, and black pepper.

two In a large nonstick skillet melt butter over medium heat. Add potato mixture, pressing firmly with a spatula into a 7- to 8-inch round. Cook, covered, about 8 minutes or until golden brown, reducing heat, if necessary, to prevent overbrowning.

three Using 2 spatulas or a spatula and fork, turn potato round. (If you're not sure you can turn in a single flip, cut into quarters and turn by sections.)

four Cook, uncovered, for 5 to 7 minutes more or until golden brown and crisp. Remove from skillet; cut into wedges. If desired, garnish with fresh sage.

NUTRITION FACTS PER SERVING: 168 cal., 9 g total fat (1 g sat. fat), 0 mg chol., 197 mg sodium, 19 g carbo., 2 g fiber, 3 g pro.

Baked Sweet Potato Fries

PREP: 15 minutes **BAKE:** 20 minutes **MAKES:** 4 servings

     Nonstick cooking spray

1   pound medium sweet potatoes

1   tablespoon butter or margarine, melted

¼   teaspoon seasoned salt

     Dash ground nutmeg

one Lightly coat a 15×10×1-inch baking pan with cooking spray. Cut potatoes lengthwise into quarters. Cut each quarter into 2 wedges. Arrange potatoes in a single layer in the prepared pan.

two In a small bowl combine melted butter, seasoned salt, and nutmeg. Brush mixture onto potatoes.

three Bake, uncovered, in a 425°F oven for 20 to 30 minutes or until tender and browned.

NUTRITION FACTS PER SERVING: 117 cal., 3 g total fat (2 g sat. fat), 7 mg chol., 122 mg sodium, 22 g carbo., 3 g fiber, 2 g pro.

Apple-Buttered Sweet Potatoes

PREP: 15 minutes **COOK:** Low 6 hours, High 3 hours
MAKES: 10 servings

- 3 pounds sweet potatoes, peeled and cut into 1-inch pieces
- 2 medium Granny Smith or other tart cooking apples, peeled, cored, and cut into wedges
- ½ cup dried cherries or dried cranberries (optional)
- 1 cup whipping cream
- 1 cup apple butter
- 1½ teaspoons pumpkin pie spice

one In a 3½- or 4-quart slow cooker combine sweet potatoes, apples, and, if desired, dried cherries.

two In a medium bowl combine whipping cream, apple butter, and pumpkin pie spice. Add to sweet potato mixture in cooker; stir gently to combine.

three Cover and cook on low-heat setting for 6 to 7 hours or on high-heat setting for 3 to 3½ hours.

NUTRITION FACTS PER SERVING: 351 cal., 9 g total fat (6 g sat. fat), 33 mg chol., 25 mg sodium, 65 g carbo., 5 g fiber, 2 g pro.

Fire-Roasted Acorn Squash

PREP: 10 minutes **GRILL:** 45 minutes **MAKES:** 4 servings

- 1 tablespoon olive oil
- ½ teaspoon salt
- ¼ teaspoon black pepper
- 2 small acorn squash, cut crosswise into 1-inch rings and seeded
- 2 tablespoons butter or margarine, melted
- 2 teaspoons snipped fresh tarragon or ½ teaspoon dried tarragon, crushed

one In a small bowl combine oil, salt, and pepper; brush over squash rings. In another small bowl combine melted butter and tarragon. Set butter mixture aside.

two For a charcoal grill, arrange medium-hot coals around a drip pan. Test for medium heat above pan. Place squash rings on grill rack over drip pan. Cover and grill about 45 minutes or until squash is tender, turning squash occasionally and brushing with butter mixture during the last 15 minutes of grilling. (For a gas grill, preheat grill. Reduce heat to medium. Adjust for indirect cooking. Grill as above.)

NUTRITION FACTS PER SERVING: 153 cal., 10 g total fat (4 g sat. fat), 16 mg chol., 358 mg sodium, 18 g carbo., 3 g fiber, 1 g pro.

Summer Squash with Peppers

PREP: 15 minutes **ROAST:** 15 minutes **MAKES:** 6 servings

- 2 pounds zucchini and/or yellow summer squash, cut into bite-size chunks
- 1 medium green or red sweet pepper, cut into strips
- 2 tablespoons olive oil
- 1½ teaspoons Greek seasoning or Mediterranean seasoning
- ¼ teaspoon black pepper

one Place squash chunks and sweet pepper strips in a large shallow roasting pan. Drizzle with oil. Sprinkle with Greek seasoning and black pepper; toss gently to coat.

two Roast, uncovered, in a 425°F oven about 15 minutes or just until tender, stirring once.

NUTRITION FACTS PER SERVING: 66 cal., 5 g total fat (1 g sat. fat), 0 mg chol., 25 mg sodium, 6 g carbo., 2 g fiber, 2 g pro.

SLOW COOKER

Cheesy Succotash

PREP: 15 minutes **COOK:** Low 7 hours, High 3½ hours
MAKES: 12 servings

- 2 16-ounce packages frozen whole kernel corn
- 1 16-ounce package frozen lima beans
- 1 cup frozen small whole onions
- 1 10¾-ounce can condensed cream of celery soup
- 1 8-ounce tub cream cheese spread with chive and onion
- ¼ cup water

one In a 4- or 4½-quart slow cooker combine frozen corn, frozen lima beans, and frozen onions. In a medium bowl stir together soup, cream cheese spread, and water. Pour soup mixture over vegetables in cooker; stir to combine.

two Cover and cook on low-heat setting for 7 to 8 hours or on high-heat setting for 3½ to 4 hours. Stir before serving.

NUTRITION FACTS PER SERVING: 211 cal., 8 g total fat (5 g sat. fat), 19 mg chol., 296 mg sodium, 29 g carbo., 4 g fiber, 6 g pro.

Saffron Rice-Baked Tomatoes

PREP: 30 minutes **BAKE:** 30 minutes **MAKES:** 6 servings

1 5-ounce package saffron-flavor yellow rice mix

6 large tomatoes (about 3 pounds)

¼ cup pine nuts

¼ cup dried mixed fruit bits or golden raisins

½ teaspoon dried oregano, crushed

one Prepare rice mix according to package directions, except omit the oil or margarine. Meanwhile, cut a slice off the stem end of each tomato; reserve tops. Using a spoon, carefully scoop out·pulp; chop pulp. Measure 1½ cups of the chopped pulp; set aside. Discard the remaining pulp. Drain tomatoes, cut sides down, on paper towels.

two For filling, in a medium bowl combine cooked rice, the 1½ cups tomato pulp, the pine nuts, dried fruit, and oregano. Spoon into tomatoes. Replace tops.

three Place tomatoes in an ungreased 2-quart rectangular baking dish. Spoon any remaining filling into bottom of dish around tomatoes. Bake, uncovered, in a 350°F oven for 30 to 40 minutes or until heated through.

NUTRITION FACTS PER SERVING: 173 cal., 4 g total fat (1 g sat. fat), 0 mg chol., 330 mg sodium, 33 g carbo., 4 g fiber, 6 g pro.

GRILLING

Herb-Grilled Tomatoes *See photo on page 264.*

PREP: 15 minutes **GRILL:** 10 minutes **MAKES:** 4 servings

4 small tomatoes, cored and halved crosswise

3 tablespoons dairy sour cream or plain yogurt

1 tablespoon fine dry bread crumbs

1 tablespoon finely shredded Parmesan cheese

1 tablespoon snipped fresh basil or 1 teaspoon dried basil, crushed

one Spread cut sides of tomatoes with sour cream. Arrange tomatoes in a disposable foil pan. In a small bowl combine bread crumbs, Parmesan cheese, and basil; sprinkle evenly over tomato halves.

two For a charcoal grill, arrange medium-hot coals around edge of grill. Test for medium heat above center of grill. Place foil pan on grill rack over center of grill. Cover and grill for 10 to 15 minutes or until heated through. (For a gas grill, preheat grill. Reduce heat to medium. Adjust for indirect cooking. Grill as above.)

NUTRITION FACTS PER SERVING: 81 cal., 4 g total fat (3 g sat. fat), 10 mg chol., 197 mg sodium, 6 g carbo., 1 g fiber, 5 g pro.

Veggie Mash

PREP: 15 minutes **COOK:** 15 minutes **MAKES:** 6 servings

6   medium carrots, sliced (3 cups)

4   medium red potatoes (1¼ pounds), cubed

1   cup coarsely chopped broccoli

½   of an 8-ounce container dairy sour cream
    French onion-flavor dip

½   teaspoon seasoned pepper

one In a covered Dutch oven or large saucepan cook carrots and potatoes in enough boiling water to cover about 15 minutes or until tender, adding broccoli during the last 3 minutes of cooking; drain.

two Mash vegetables with a potato masher or beat with an electric mixer on low speed. Add French onion dip and seasoned pepper; beat until fluffy. Transfer to a serving bowl.

NUTRITION FACTS PER SERVING: 146 cal., 3 g total fat (2 g sat. fat), 0 mg chol., 173 mg sodium, 27 g carbo., 5 g fiber, 4 g pro.

Herbed Zucchini

START TO FINISH: 15 minutes **MAKES:** 6 servings

2   teaspoons olive oil

4   cups sliced zucchini (4 to 5 small)

1   tablespoon snipped fresh mint or basil or
    1 teaspoon dried mint or basil, crushed

¼   teaspoon salt
    Dash black pepper

2   tablespoons finely shredded Parmesan or
    Romano cheese

one In a large skillet heat oil over medium heat. Add zucchini, dried herb (if using), salt, and pepper.

two Cook, uncovered, about 5 minutes or until zucchini is crisp-tender, stirring occasionally. To serve, sprinkle with Parmesan cheese and fresh herb (if using).

NUTRITION FACTS PER SERVING: 33 cal., 2 g total fat (1 g sat. fat), 2 mg chol., 125 mg sodium, 2 g carbo., 1 g fiber, 2 g pro.

Marinara-Sauced Pasta *See photo on page 265.*

START TO FINISH: 25 minutes **MAKES:** 4 to 6 servings

1	28-ounce can tomatoes, undrained
3	tablespoons snipped fresh basil
2	cloves garlic, minced
2	tablespoons olive oil
¼	teaspoon salt
¼	teaspoon black pepper
8	to 12 ounces dried pasta
	Snipped fresh basil (optional)
	Grated Parmesan cheese (optional)

Snipping Fresh Herbs If a recipe calls for snipped fresh herbs, start with clean, dry herbs; wet ones may clump together. (To dry wet herbs, either blot them with a paper towel or use a salad spinner to spin off excess water.)

Use kitchen shears to simply cut the herbs into small, uniform pieces using short, quick strokes. If the stalks are tough—as is the case with rosemary—don't use them. Snip herbs just before adding them to a recipe to get their maximum flavor.

one Pour undrained tomatoes into a food processor or blender. Cover and process or blend until smooth. Stir in the 3 tablespoons snipped basil; set aside.

two In a large skillet cook garlic in hot olive oil over medium heat until garlic is lightly browned. Add pureed tomatoes, salt, and pepper. Bring to boiling; reduce heat. Simmer, uncovered, for 10 minutes.

three Meanwhile, cook pasta according to package directions; drain.

four Serve tomato mixture over hot cooked pasta. If desired, sprinkle each serving with additional snipped basil and grated Parmesan cheese.

Note: If desired, add frozen cooked meatballs to the tomato sauce. Heat as directed on the meatball package.

NUTRITION FACTS PER SERVING: 310 cal., 8 g total fat (1 g sat. fat), 0 mg chol., 441 mg sodium, 51 g carbo., 4 g fiber, 9 g pro.

Light and Lemony Fettuccine

START TO FINISH: 15 minutes **MAKES:** 3 servings

1   9-ounce package refrigerated plain or spinach
      fettuccine
2   tablespoons butter or margarine
½   teaspoon finely shredded lemon peel
¼   teaspoon salt
¼   teaspoon black pepper

one Cook pasta according to package directions; drain.
Return pasta to hot saucepan.

two Add butter, lemon peel, salt, and pepper to cooked
pasta; toss gently to coat.

NUTRITION FACTS PER SERVING: 164 cal., 6 g total fat (3 g sat. fat),
54 mg chol., 154 mg sodium, 23 g carbo., 1 g fiber, 5 g pro.

Mixed Pastas with Fresh Herbs

START TO FINISH: 20 minutes **MAKES:** 8 servings

8   ounces assorted dried pastas (with similar
      cooking times)
2   tablespoons olive oil
2   tablespoons snipped assorted fresh herbs
      (such as sage, rosemary, and/or basil)
¼   teaspoon salt
¼   teaspoon coarsely ground black pepper

one In a large saucepan cook pasta according to package
directions; drain. Return pasta to hot saucepan.

two Add olive oil, assorted herbs, salt, and pepper to cooked
pasta; toss gently to coat.

NUTRITION FACTS PER SERVING: 136 cal., 4 g total fat (0 g sat. fat), 0 mg chol.
74 mg sodium, 21 g carbo., 11 g fiber, 4 g pro.

Mixing Pastas When you find yourself with several open
boxes of dried pasta in your cupboard—and each contains just
a few noodles—mix things up. Combine pastas with the same
cooking time together in one box. You'll save a few pennies on
pasta and cupboard space too.

Triple-Cheesy Pasta

PREP: 10 minutes **COOK:** Low 4 hours, High 2 hours
MAKES: 12 servings

- 2   10¾-ounce cans condensed broccoli cheese or cheddar cheese soup
- 1   16-ounce jar Alfredo pasta sauce
- ¼   cup grated Parmesan cheese
- 1   teaspoon garlic-pepper seasoning
- 2   cups water
- 3   9-ounce packages refrigerated cheese-filled tortellini or 1 pound dried pasta (any shape)

one In a 3½- or 4-quart slow cooker combine soup, Alfredo pasta sauce, Parmesan cheese, and garlic-pepper seasoning. Gradually stir in water.

two Cover and cook on low-heat setting for 4 to 5 hours or on high-heat setting for 2 to 2½ hours.

three Cook tortellini according to package directions; drain. Add cooked pasta to soup mixture; toss gently to coat.

NUTRITION FACTS PER SERVING: 317 cal., 14 g total fat (7 g sat. fat), 61 mg chol., 976 mg sodium, 35 g carbo., 3 g fiber, 13 g pro.

Saucy Sweet Pepper Pasta

PREP: 20 minutes **COOK:** Low 6 hours, High 3 hours;
plus 30 minutes on High **MAKES:** 10 to 12 servings

- 4   medium red, green, orange, and/or yellow sweet peppers, cut into bite-size strips (about 4 cups)
- 2   14½-ounce cans diced tomatoes with basil, garlic, and oregano, undrained
- 1   15-ounce can tomato sauce
- ¼   to ½ teaspoon crushed red pepper
- 1   9-ounce package refrigerated cheese-filled tortellini

one In a 3½- or 4-quart slow cooker combine sweet peppers, undrained tomatoes, tomato sauce, and crushed red pepper.

two Cover and cook on low-heat setting for 6 to 8 hours or on high-heat setting for 3 to 4 hours.

three If using low-heat setting, turn to high-heat setting. Stir in tortellini. Cover and cook about 30 minutes more or until tortellini is tender.

NUTRITION FACTS PER SERVING: 134 cal., 2 g total fat (1 g sat. fat), 12 mg chol., 713 mg sodium, 24 g carbo., 2 g fiber, 6 g pro.

Easy Spanish Rice

START TO FINISH: 25 minutes **MAKES:** 4 servings

- 2 tablespoons cooking oil
- 1 cup uncooked long grain rice
- 1 14-ounce can chicken broth
- ¼ cup tomato sauce
- ¼ cup water

one In a medium saucepan heat oil over medium-high heat. Add rice: cook and stir for 3 to 5 minutes or until lightly browned. Stir in broth, tomato sauce, and water.

two Bring to boiling; reduce heat. Simmer, covered, for 18 to 20 minutes or until rice is tender.

NUTRITION FACTS PER SERVING: 247 cal., 8 g total fat (1 g sat. fat), 0 mg chol., 533 mg sodium, 39 g carbo., 1 g fiber, 4 g pro.

SLOW COOKER

Wild Rice Pilaf with Squash

PREP: 20 minutes **COOK:** Low 4 hours, High 2 hours
MAKES: 8 to 10 servings

- 2 large oranges
- 3 cups peeled, seeded winter squash (such as butternut) cut into bite-size pieces
- 2 4- or 4.1-ounce packages long grain and wild rice mix with herbs (not quick-cooking)
- ¼ cup packed brown sugar
- 2 14-ounce cans chicken broth

one Finely shred the peel from one of the oranges. Measure 1 teaspoon orange peel; set aside. Squeeze juice from both oranges. Measure ⅔ cup orange juice; set aside.

two In a 3½- or 4-quart slow cooker combine squash, rice mixes, and brown sugar. Add orange peel and orange juice. Pour broth over mixture in cooker; stir to combine.

three Cover and cook on low-heat setting for 4 to 5 hours or on high-heat setting for 2 to 3 hours. Stir gently before serving.

NUTRITION FACTS PER SERVING: 170 cal., 1 g total fat (0 g sat. fat), 0 mg chol., 931 mg sodium, 37 g carbo., 1 g fiber, 4 g pro.

Vegetable Rice Pilaf

PREP: 15 minutes **COOK:** 45 minutes **MAKES:** 6 servings

1   cup finely chopped celery
⅓   cup chopped onion
¼   cup butter or margarine
1½ cups uncooked regular brown rice
3¾ cups chicken broth or reduced-sodium chicken broth

one In a large saucepan cook celery and onion in melted butter over medium heat until tender. Add rice; cook and stir until lightly browned. Carefully stir in broth.

two Bring to boiling; reduce heat. Simmer, covered, about 45 minutes or until rice is tender and liquid is absorbed.

NUTRITION FACTS PER SERVING: 268 cal., 11 g total fat (6 g sat. fat), 22 mg chol., 729 mg sodium, 38 g carbo., 2 g fiber, 5 g pro.

Easy Oven Risotto

PREP: 10 minutes **BAKE:** 55 minutes
STAND: 10 minutes **MAKES:** 6 servings

1   10¾-ounce can condensed cream of chicken with herbs soup or condensed cream of chicken soup
1¼ cups uncooked arborio or medium grain white rice
⅓   cup shredded carrot
3¼ cups water
½   cup frozen snow pea pods, halved diagonally
½   cup grated Parmesan cheese

one In an ungreased 2-quart casserole stir together soup, uncooked rice, and carrot. Gradually stir in water.

two Bake, covered, in a 375°F oven for 55 to 60 minutes or until rice is tender, stirring twice. Stir in pea pods during the last 5 minutes of baking.

three Remove casserole from oven; gently stir in cheese. Let stand for 10 minutes before serving.

NUTRITION FACTS PER SERVING: 233 cal., 6 g total fat (3 g sat. fat), 11 mg chol., 563 mg sodium, 36 g carbo., 1 g fiber, 8 g pro.

Arborio Rice Although other types of rice will give good results for Easy Oven Risotto, arborio rice is favored. The short, fat, high-starch kernels give this classic Italian dish a delicious creamy texture. Arborio rice is readily available at your local supermarket.

Sausage and Corn Bread Stuffing

PREP: 20 minutes **COOK:** Low 4 hours **MAKES:** 10 to 12 servings

    Nonstick cooking spray
1   pound bulk pork sausage
1   cup chopped onion
1   16-ounce package corn bread stuffing mix
3   cups chicken broth
½   cup butter or margarine, melted

one Lightly coat a 3½- to 4½-quart slow cooker with cooking spray; set aside.

two In a large skillet cook sausage and onion until meat is brown and onion is tender. Drain off fat. In the prepared cooker combine meat mixture, stuffing mix, broth, and melted butter; toss gently to combine.

three Cover and cook on low-heat setting for 4 to 5 hours.

NUTRITION FACTS PER SERVING: 466 cal., 30 g total fat (13 g sat. fat), 57 mg chol., 1,214 mg sodium, 37 g carbo., 0 g fiber, 11 g pro.

Raisin-Herb Seasoned Stuffing

PREP: 20 minutes **COOK:** Low 5 hours, High 2½ hours
MAKES: 8 to 10 servings

    Nonstick cooking spray
1   16-ounce package herb-seasoned stuffing mix
1   cup golden and/or dark raisins
½   cup chopped onion
1   10¾-ounce can condensed golden mushroom soup
1   8-ounce carton dairy sour cream
1½ cups water

one Lightly coat a 3½- or 4-quart slow cooker with cooking spray. In the prepared cooker combine stuffing mix, raisins, and onion.

two In a medium bowl combine soup and sour cream; gradually stir in water. Pour soup mixture over stuffing mixture in cooker; stir gently to combine.

three Cover and cook on low-heat setting for 5 to 6 hours or on high-heat setting for 2½ to 3 hours.

NUTRITION FACTS PER SERVING: 377 cal., 9 g total fat (4 g sat. fat), 14 mg chol., 1,105 mg sodium, 65 g carbo., 6 g fiber, 9 g pro.

Herbed Crouton Sticks

PREP: 15 minutes **BAKE:** 25 minutes **MAKES:** about 24 servings

1   8-ounce loaf baguette-style French bread

½   cup butter or margarine

1   tablespoon snipped fresh basil or
    ½ teaspoon dried basil, crushed

⅛   teaspoon garlic powder

one Cut bread in half horizontally. Cut bread into 3½×1-inch breadsticks; set aside.

two In a 12-inch skillet melt butter. Stir in basil and garlic powder. Add half of the breadsticks, stirring until coated with butter mixture. Arrange breadsticks in a single layer in a shallow baking pan. Repeat with the remaining breadsticks.

three Bake, uncovered, in a 300°F oven for 25 to 30 minutes or until sticks are dry and crisp, turning once. Cool on wire racks. Store, tightly covered, at room temperature for up to 3 days or in the freezer for up to 3 months.

NUTRITION FACTS PER SERVING: 62 cal., 4 g total fat (3 g sat. fat), 11 mg chol., 99 mg sodium, 5 g carbo., 0 g fiber, 1 g pro.

Focaccia Breadsticks *See photo on page 266.*

PREP: 15 minutes **BAKE:** 12 minutes **MAKES:** 16 servings

¼   cup oil-packed dried tomatoes, undrained

¼   cup grated Romano or Parmesan cheese

2   teaspoons water

⅛   teaspoon cracked black pepper

1   13.8-ounce package refrigerated pizza dough

Dried Tomatoes Dried tomatoes are dark red with an intense, slightly sweet flavor. They're sold in both oil-packed and dried forms. Look for them in the produce section or the Italian food aisle of the supermarket.

one Drain dried tomatoes, reserving 2 teaspoons of the oil. Finely snip tomatoes. In a small bowl combine dried tomatoes, the 2 teaspoons oil, the cheese, water, and pepper. Set aside.

two Unroll pizza dough. On a lightly floured surface, roll dough into a 10×8-inch rectangle. Spread the tomato mixture crosswise over half of the dough. Fold other half of dough over filling; press lightly to seal edges. Cut the folded dough crosswise into sixteen ½-inch breadsticks.

three Twist each breadstick 2 or 3 times. Place breadsticks 1 inch apart on a lightly greased baking sheet. Bake, uncovered, in a 350°F oven for 12 to 15 minutes or until golden brown. Cool on a wire rack.

NUTRITION FACTS PER SERVING: 84 cal., 2 g total fat (1 g sat. fat), 2 mg chol., 209 mg sodium, 14 g carbo., 1 g fiber, 3 g pro.

Grilled French Bread

PREP: 10 minutes **GRILL:** 3 minutes **MAKES:** 8 to 10 servings

- ¼ cup butter or margarine
- ¼ cup grated Parmesan cheese
- 2 tablespoons snipped fresh parsley
- 1 clove garlic, minced
- ⅛ teaspoon cayenne pepper (optional)
- 1 16-ounce loaf unsliced French bread

one In a small saucepan melt butter; stir in Parmesan chees parsley, garlic, and, if desired, cayenne pepper. Set butter mixture aside.

two Cut French bread in half lengthwise. For a charcoal grill grill bread, cut sides down, on the rack of an uncovered grill directly over medium coals about 2 minutes or until toasted. Turn cut sides up; brush with butter mixture. Grill for 1 to 2 minutes more or until heated through. (For a gas grill, prehea grill. Reduce heat to medium. Place bread on grill rack over heat. Cover and grill as above.)

three Cut French bread into 2-inch slices. Serve warm.

NUTRITION FACTS PER SERVING: 169 cal., 3 g total fat (1 g sat. fat), 3 mg cho 385 mg sodium, 30 g carbo., 2 g fiber, 6 g pro.

Italian Breadsticks

PREP: 10 minutes **GRILL:** 2 minutes **MAKES:** 8 servings

- ½ cup grated Parmesan cheese
- 1¼ teaspoons dried Italian seasoning, crushed
- ¼ teaspoon crushed red pepper
- 8 purchased soft breadsticks
- 3 tablespoons butter or margarine, melted

one In a shallow dish combine Parmesan cheese, Italian seasoning, and crushed red pepper. Brush each breadstick with melted butter; roll in cheese mixture to coat.

two For a charcoal grill, grill breadsticks on the rack of an uncovered grill directly over medium coals for 2 to 3 minutes or until golden, turning to brown evenly. (For a gas grill, preheat grill. Reduce heat to medium. Place breadsticks on grill rack over heat. Cover and grill as above.) Serve warm.

NUTRITION FACTS PER SERVING: 194 cal., 7 g total fat (4 g sat. fat), 16 mg chol., 430 mg sodium, 25 g carbo., 1 g fiber, 7 g pro.

Toasty-Hot French Bread Slices

PREP: 20 minutes **GRILL:** 2 minutes **MAKES:** 6 servings

- 2 tablespoons creamy Dijon-style mustard blend
- 1 tablespoon butter or margarine, melted
- 1 teaspoon honey
- ½ teaspoon dried sage, crushed
- ⅛ teaspoon black pepper
- 6 1-inch slices French or Italian bread

one In a small bowl combine mustard blend, melted butter, honey, sage, and pepper. Set mustard mixture aside.

two For a charcoal grill, grill bread slices on the rack of an uncovered grill directly over medium coals for 1 to 2 minutes or until bottoms are toasted. Turn bread slices; carefully spread with mustard mixture. Grill for 1 to 2 minutes more or until bottoms are toasted. (For a gas grill, preheat grill. Reduce heat to medium. Place bread slices on grill rack over heat. Cover and grill as above.) Serve warm.

NUTRITION FACTS PER SERVING: 164 cal., 4 g total fat (1 g sat. fat), 5 mg chol., 389 mg sodium, 28 g carbo., 2 g fiber, 4 g pro.

Herbed Baguette

PREP: 10 minutes **GRILL:** 2 minutes **MAKES:** 8 servings

- 1 8-ounce loaf baguette-style French bread
- 2 tablespoons olive oil
- 1 tablespoon snipped fresh parsley and/or chives

one Cut bread into 16 slices. In a small bowl combine oil and parsley; brush over one side of each bread slice.

two For a charcoal grill, grill bread slices on the rack of an uncovered grill directly over medium coals for 2 to 4 minutes or until toasted, turning once. (For a gas grill, preheat grill. Reduce heat to medium. Place bread slices on grill rack over heat. Cover and grill as above.) Serve warm.

NUTRITION FACTS PER SERVING: 108 cal., 4 g total fat (1 g sat. fat), 0 mg chol., 173 mg sodium, 15 g carbo., 1 g fiber, 3 g pro.

SERVE-ALONG SIDES

Have-a-Ball Rolls

PREP: 20 minutes **RISE:** 30 minutes **BAKE:** 13 minutes
MAKES: 30 to 36 servings

1   16-ounce loaf frozen white or whole wheat bread
     dough, thawed
1   egg white
1   tablespoon water
     Fennel seeds, mustard seeds, and/or dill seeds

one Lightly grease a baking sheet or thirty to thirty-six
1¾-inch muffin cups; set aside.

two Divide dough into 30 to 36 pieces. Shape into small
balls. Place rolls on the prepared baking sheet or in the
prepared muffin cups. Cover and let rise in a warm place until
nearly double in size (about 30 minutes).

three In a small bowl combine egg white and water. Brush
mixture over rolls. Sprinkle generously with desired seeds.

four Bake, uncovered, in a 350°F oven for 13 to 15 minutes
or until golden brown. Transfer rolls to wire racks. Serve warm.

NUTRITION FACTS PER SERVING: 37 cal., 0 g total fat (0 g sat. fat), 0 mg chol.,
2 mg sodium, 7 g carbo., 0 g fiber, 1 g pro.

Garlic Croutons

START TO FINISH: 15 minutes **MAKES:** 16 servings

2   cups 1- to 1½-inch French or Italian bread cubes
     (about 2 ounces)
1   tablespoon cooking oil
1   tablespoon butter or margarine
2   large cloves garlic, minced
1   teaspoon dried seasoning, crushed (such as Italian
     herbs, Greek seasoning, herbes de Provence,
     bouquet garni seasoning, or desired herb blend)

one Place bread cubes in a medium bowl; set aside. In a large
skillet heat oil and butter over medium-low heat. Add garlic
and desired seasoning; cook and stir for 30 seconds. Drizzle
mixture over bread cubes; toss gently to coat.

two Transfer seasoned bread cubes to skillet. Cook over
medium-low heat for 6 to 8 minutes or until bread is lightly
browned and crisp, stirring occasionally.

three Remove from skillet and drain on paper towels. Store,
tightly covered, at room temperature for up to 1 week.

NUTRITION FACTS PER SERVING: 24 cal., 2 g total fat (0 g sat. fat), 2 mg chol.,
30 mg sodium, 2 g carbo., 0 g fiber, 0 g pro.

Broccoli Corn Bread

PREP: 10 minutes **BAKE:** 30 minutes **MAKES:** 16 servings

1   8½-ounce package corn muffin mix

3   eggs

2   cups shredded cheddar cheese (8 ounces)

1   10-ounce package frozen chopped broccoli, thawed and well drained

½   cup chopped onion

one In a large bowl combine corn muffin mix and eggs. Stir in cheese, broccoli, and onion. Spread mixture in a greased 9×9×2-inch baking pan.

two Bake, uncovered, in a 350°F oven about 30 minutes or until a toothpick inserted near the center comes out clean. Serve corn bread warm.

NUTRITION FACTS PER SERVING: 138 cal., 7 g total fat (3 g sat. fat), 55 mg chol., 209 mg sodium, 12 g carbo., 1 g fiber, 6 g pro.

Cheddary Corn Bread Rolls *See photo on page 266.*

PREP: 15 minutes **RISE:** 20 minutes **BAKE:** 20 minutes
MAKES: 15 servings

1   16-ounce package hot roll mix

1   cup shredded cheddar cheese (4 ounces)

⅓   cup yellow cornmeal

1¼   cups hot water (120°F to 130°F)

1   egg, slightly beaten

2   tablespoons olive oil

Milk (optional)

Yellow cornmeal (optional)

one In a large bowl combine hot roll mix, cheese, and the ⅓ cup cornmeal. Add hot water, egg, and oil; stir until combined.

two Turn dough out onto a well-floured surface. Knead until dough is smooth and elastic (about 5 minutes). Cover and let rest for 5 minutes.

three Divide dough into 15 pieces. Shape each piece into a ball by pulling and tucking dough underneath. Arrange dough balls in a lightly greased 13x9x2-inch baking pan. Cover and let rise in a warm place until nearly double in size (about 20 minutes).

four If desired, brush dough with milk and sprinkle with additional cornmeal. Bake, uncovered, in a 375°F oven for 20 to 22 minutes or until golden brown. Serve warm.

NUTRITION FACTS PER SERVING: 175 cal., 5 g total fat (2 g sat. fat), 22 mg chol., 229 mg sodium, 26 g carbo., 0 g fiber, 7 g pro.

Rosemary and Swiss Buns

PREP: 25 minutes **RISE:** 30 minutes **BAKE:** 12 minutes
MAKES: 12 servings

- 1   16-ounce package hot roll mix
- ¾   cup shredded Swiss cheese (3 ounces)
- 2   small onions, thinly sliced and separated into rings (⅔ cup)
- 1   tablespoon snipped fresh rosemary or 1 teaspoon dried rosemary, crushed
- 1   tablespoon cooking oil

one Prepare hot roll mix according to package directions, except stir in Swiss cheese with the liquid called for in the directions. Continue as directed through the kneading and resting steps.

two After dough rests, divide into 12 pieces. Shape each piece into a ball by pulling and tucking dough underneath. On a lightly floured surface, roll each ball into a 4-inch round. Place on 2 greased large baking sheets. Cover and set aside.

three In a medium skillet cook onions and rosemary in hot oil until onions are tender. Using your fingertips, make ½-inch-deep indentations on surface of dough rounds. Spoon onion mixture into indentations. Cover and let rise in a warm place until nearly double in size (30 to 40 minutes).

four Bake, uncovered, in a 375°F oven for 12 to 15 minutes or until golden brown. Serve warm.

NUTRITION FACTS PER SERVING: 200 cal., 6 g total fat (1 g sat. fat), 23 mg chol., 265 mg sodium, 30 g carbo., 0 g fiber, 7 g pro.

Garlic and Cheese Focaccia

PREP: 10 minutes **BAKE:** 18 minutes **MAKES:** 8 servings

- 1   16-ounce loaf frozen white or whole wheat bread dough, thawed
- 1   tablespoon olive oil
- 4   cloves garlic, minced
- 1½ teaspoons dried Italian seasoning, crushed
- 1   cup shredded pizza cheese blend (4 ounces)

one On a lightly floured surface, roll bread dough into a 12-inch circle. Transfer dough round to a lightly greased 12-inch pizza pan. Using your fingertips, make ½-inch-deep indentations on surface of dough.

two In a small bowl combine oil, garlic, and Italian seasoning; brush over top of dough. Sprinkle with cheese.

three Bake, uncovered, in a 375°F oven for 18 to 20 minutes or until golden brown. Remove from pan; cool on a wire rack. Cut into wedges.

NUTRITION FACTS PER SERVING: 197 cal., 5 g total fat (2 g sat. fat), 10 mg chol., 95 mg sodium, 25 g carbo., 0 g fiber, 8 g pro.

Flaky Biscuits

PREP: 15 minutes **BAKE:** 10 minutes **MAKES:** 10 to 12 servings

- 2 cups all-purpose flour
- 2 teaspoons baking powder
- 1 teaspoon salt
- ½ teaspoon baking soda
- ¼ cup butter or margarine
- ¾ cup buttermilk

one In a medium bowl stir together flour, baking powder, salt, and baking soda. Using a pastry blender or 2 knives, cut in butter until mixture resembles coarse crumbs. Make a well in the center. Add buttermilk all at once; stir just until moistened.

two Turn dough out onto a lightly floured surface. Knead dough by folding and gently pressing it for 10 to 12 strokes or until nearly smooth. Pat or lightly roll dough until ½ inch thick. Cut dough with a floured 2½-inch biscuit cutter.

three Place biscuits 1 inch apart on a lightly greased baking sheet. Bake, uncovered, in a 425°F oven for 10 to 15 minutes or until golden brown. Serve warm.

NUTRITION FACTS PER SERVING: 140 cal., 5 g total fat (3 g sat. fat), 13 mg chol., 421 mg sodium, 20 g carbo., 1 g fiber, 3 g pro.

Pepper-Cheese Biscuits: **Prepare biscuits as above, except stir ¾ cup shredded Monterey Jack cheese with jalapeño peppers (3 ounces), 2 tablespoons snipped fresh chives, and ⅛ teaspoon cayenne pepper into flour-butter mixture.**

NUTRITION FACTS PER SERVING: 173 cal., 8 g total fat (5 g sat. fat), 22 mg chol., 478 mg sodium, 20 g carbo., 1 g fiber, 5 g pro.

Green Onion Parker House Biscuits
See photo on page 266.

PREP: 10 minutes **BAKE:** 8 minutes **MAKES:** 10 servings

- 1 5.2-ounce container semisoft cheese with garlic and herbs
- ¼ cup sliced green onion
- 1 10-ounce package (10) refrigerated biscuits
- 1 egg yolk
- 1 tablespoon water
- 2 tablespoons grated Parmesan cheese
  Sliced green onion (optional)

one In a small bowl stir together cheese and the ¼ cup green onion; set aside.

two Unwrap biscuits. Using your fingers, gently split the biscuits horizontally. (Some refrigerated doughs will need to be sliced.) Place the biscuit bottoms on a greased baking sheet. Spread each biscuit bottom with about 1 tablespoon of the cheese mixture. Replace biscuit tops.

three In a small bowl combine egg yolk and water; brush over biscuit tops. Sprinkle with Parmesan cheese and, if desired, additional green onion. Bake, uncovered, in a 400°F oven for 8 to 10 minutes or until golden brown. Serve warm.

NUTRITION FACTS PER SERVING: 149 cal., 8 g total fat (5 g sat. fat), 23 mg chol., 394 mg sodium, 16 g carbo., 0 g fiber, 4 g pro.

Cheese and Garlic Crescents

PREP: 15 minutes **BAKE:** 11 minutes **MAKES:** 8 servings

- 1   8-ounce package (8) refrigerated crescent rolls
- ¼   cup semisoft cheese with garlic and herbs
- 2   tablespoons finely chopped walnuts, toasted (see tip, page 280)
  Milk
- 1   tablespoon seasoned fine dry bread crumbs

one Unroll crescent rolls; divide into 8 triangles. In a small bowl combine cheese and walnuts. Place a rounded teaspoon of the cheese mixture near the center of wide end of each crescent roll. Starting at the wide end, roll up dough.

two Place rolls, point sides down, on a greased baking sheet. Brush tops lightly with milk; sprinkle with bread crumbs.

three Bake, uncovered, in a 375°F oven about 11 minutes or until bottoms are browned. Serve warm.

NUTRITION FACTS PER SERVING: 141 cal., 10 g total fat (3 g sat. fat), 6 mg chol., 254 mg sodium, 12 g carbo., 0 g fiber, 3 g pro.

Cinnamon Granola Loaf

PREP: 20 minutes **RISE:** 45 minutes **BAKE:** 25 minutes
MAKES: 12 servings

- 1   16-ounce loaf frozen sweet roll dough or white bread dough, thawed
- 2   tablespoons butter or margarine, softened
- 3   tablespoons cinnamon-sugar*
- ½   cup granola (plain or with raisins), crushed
- ½   cup chopped almonds or pecans, toasted (see tip, page 280)

one On a lightly floured surface, roll dough into a 10×8-inch rectangle. Spread with 1 tablespoon of the softened butter. Sprinkle with 2 tablespoons of the cinnamon-sugar. Sprinkle with granola and nuts to within ½ inch of the edges.

two Starting from a short side, roll up rectangle. Pinch dough to seal seam. Place, seam side down, in a greased 8×4×2-inch loaf pan. Cover and let rise in a warm place until nearly double in size (45 to 60 minutes).

three Bake, uncovered, in a 350°F oven about 25 minutes or until bread sounds hollow when lightly tapped. Remove from pan; place on a wire rack. Spread with the remaining 1 tablespoon butter and sprinkle with the remaining 1 tablespoon cinnamon-sugar.

*Note: Look in the spice section of the supermarket for prepared cinnamon-sugar. Or to make your own cinnamon-sugar, in a small bowl stir together 3 tablespoons sugar and 1 teaspoon ground cinnamon.

NUTRITION FACTS PER SERVING: 172 cal., 6 g total fat (2 g sat. fat), 5 mg chol 208 mg sodium, 25 g carbo., 1 g fiber, 4 g pro.

Beet Greens
with Walnuts and Blue Cheese *See photo on page 270.*

START TO FINISH: 15 minutes **MAKES:** 4 servings

2   teaspoons cooking oil

2   tablespoons chopped walnuts

8   ounces fresh beet greens or spinach leaves,
    cut into 1-inch strips

1   tablespoon crumbled blue cheese or feta cheese

¼   teaspoon black pepper

one In a large skillet heat oil over medium-high heat. Add walnuts; cook and stir for 2 minutes. Add beet greens. Cook and stir about 1 minute or just until greens are wilted.

two Top each serving with blue cheese and pepper.

NUTRITION FACTS PER SERVING: 55 cal., 5 g total fat (1 g sat. fat), 0 mg chol., 109 mg sodium, 3 g carbo., 2 g fiber, 2 g pro.

Strawberry-Spinach Salad

START TO FINISH: 20 minutes **MAKES:** 4 servings

4   cups torn fresh spinach or 2 cups torn fresh spinach
    and 2 cups torn mixed salad greens

1   cup watercress

1   cup sliced strawberries

½   of a small red onion, thinly sliced

½   cup bottled oil-and-vinegar salad dressing or poppy
    seed salad dressing

one In a large bowl combine spinach, watercress, strawberries, and red onion.

two Pour dressing over spinach mixture; toss gently to coat.

NUTRITION FACTS PER SERVING: 168 cal., 16 g total fat (2 g sat. fat), 0 mg chol., 468 mg sodium, 8 g carbo., 2 g fiber, 2 g pro.

Mixed Greens with Pears *See photo on page 267.*

START TO FINISH: 15 minutes **MAKES:** 6 servings

1   10-ounce package spring mixed salad greens

2   medium pears, cored and sliced

2   ounces cubed Gruyère cheese

¼   cup bottled white wine vinaigrette salad dressing

2   teaspoons honey

one In a large bowl combine mixed salad greens, pear slices, and Gruyère cheese.

two For dressing, in a small bowl stir together white wine vinaigrette and honey. Drizzle dressing over greens mixture; toss gently to coat.

NUTRITION FACTS PER SERVING: 148 cal., 10 g total fat (4 g sat. fat), 15 mg chol., 52 mg sodium, 12 g carbo., 2 g fiber, 5 g pro.

Iceberg Lettuce with Cucumber-Mint Dressing

PREP: 15 minutes **CHILL:** 1 hour **MAKES:** 6 to 8 servings

1   cup bottled cucumber ranch salad dressing

1   cup peeled, seeded, and finely chopped cucumber

¼   cup snipped fresh mint

1   teaspoon dill seeds, crushed

¼   teaspoon black pepper

1   head iceberg lettuce

12   to 16 cherry tomatoes, halved (optional)

Dill seeds (optional)

one For dressing, in a small bowl combine bottled salad dressing, cucumber, mint, the 1 teaspoon dill seeds, and the pepper. Cover and chill for at least 1 hour.

two Remove core from iceberg lettuce. Cut lettuce into 6 to 8 wedges.

three Divide lettuce wedges among 6 to 8 salad plates; spoon dressing over wedges. If desired, top each serving with cherry tomatoes and sprinkle with additional dill seeds.

NUTRITION FACTS PER SERVING: 204 cal., 20 g total fat (3 g sat. fat), 0 mg chol., 303 mg sodium, 6 g carbo., 1 g fiber, 1 g pro.

Watermelon Salad
with Watercress *See photo on page 267.*

START TO FINISH: 45 minutes **MAKES:** 12 servings

1	13- to 14-pound oval-shape watermelon
4	cups snipped watercress
1	medium red onion, cut into thin wedges
¼	cup snipped fresh mint
2	tablespoons roasted pepper-flavor olive oil or olive oil
¼	teaspoon salt
¼	teaspoon black pepper

one Cut watermelon in half horizontally. Cover and chill one half for another use.

two Using the remaining half, make a watermelon shell by carefully cutting around the edge between the fruit and the rind. Cut fruit in the melon crosswise into 1-inch slices, leaving the rind intact. Cut underneath each slice and remove from the shell. Cut the slices into wedges; pile back into the shell. If desired, cover and chill for up to 6 hours.

three Before serving, in a large bowl combine watercress, red onion, mint, olive oil, salt, and black pepper; toss gently to coat. Sprinkle watercress mixture over watermelon wedges.

NUTRITION FACTS PER SERVING: 64 cal., 3 g total fat (0 g sat. fat), 0 mg chol., 41 mg sodium, 10 g carbo., 1 g fiber, 1 g pro.

Tangy Melon Salad

START TO FINISH: 25 minutes **MAKES:** 6 servings

3	cups cubed and seeded watermelon, chilled
3	cups cubed and seeded cantaloupe, chilled
⅓	cup balsamic vinegar
1½	to 3 teaspoons sugar
1½	teaspoons freshly ground black pepper (optional)

one Divide watermelon and cantaloupe among 6 salad bowls.

two In a small bowl combine vinegar and sugar, stirring to dissolve sugar. Drizzle vinegar mixture over salads. If desired, sprinkle with pepper.

NUTRITION FACTS PER SERVING: 65 cal., 1 g total fat (0 g sat. fat), 0 mg chol., 9 mg sodium, 15 g carbo., 1 g fiber, 1 g pro.

Creamy Apple Salad

START TO FINISH: 15 minutes **MAKES:** 8 to 10 servings

3   cups chopped apple (about 3 medium)

1   8-ounce can pineapple tidbits (juice pack), drained

½   cup coarsely chopped walnuts

⅓   cup finely chopped celery

1   4-ounce container frozen whipped dessert topping, thawed

one In a large bowl combine apple, pineapple, walnuts, and celery. Fold in whipped dessert topping just until combined.

NUTRITION FACTS PER SERVING: 173 cal., 13 g total fat (6 g sat. fat), 31 mg chol., 13 mg sodium, 14 g carbo., 2 g fiber, 2 g pro.

Winter Fruit Bowl

PREP: 25 minutes **CHILL:** 1 hour **MAKES:** 10 servings

3   medium grapefruits

½   cup sugar

½   cup orange marmalade

2   cups fresh or frozen cranberries

3   medium bananas, sliced

one Holding the grapefruits over a bowl to catch the juice, peel and section grapefruits. Set fruit aside. Add enough water to the reserved grapefruit juice to measure 1 cup.

two In a medium saucepan combine the 1 cup grapefruit juice, the sugar, and orange marmalade. Bring to boiling, stirring to dissolve sugar.

three Add cranberries; cook and stir for 5 to 8 minutes or until skins pop. Cool. Stir in reserved grapefruit. Cover and chill for at least 1 hour.

four Before serving, stir bananas into grapefruit mixture.

NUTRITION FACTS PER SERVING: 142 cal., 0 g total fat (0 g sat. fat), 0 mg chol., 10 mg sodium, 37 g carbo., 3 g fiber, 1 g pro.

Orange Dream Fruit Salad

START TO FINISH: 15 minutes **MAKES:** 4 to 6 servings

- 1 cup seeded, peeled, and chopped mango or papaya
- 1 cup seedless red and/or green grapes, halved
- 1 11-ounce can mandarin orange sections, drained
- ½ cup orange low-fat yogurt
- ¼ teaspoon poppy seeds

one In a medium bowl combine mango, grapes, and mandarin orange sections.

two For dressing, in a small bowl combine yogurt and poppy seeds. Pour dressing over mango mixture; stir gently to coat.

NUTRITION FACTS PER SERVING: 136 cal., 1 g total fat (0 g sat. fat), 2 mg chol., 26 mg sodium, 32 g carbo., 2 g fiber, 2 g pro.

Black Cherry-Cranberry Supreme

PREP: 15 minutes **CHILL:** 4¾ hours **MAKES:** 8 to 10 servings

- 2 3-ounce packages black cherry-flavor gelatin
- 2 cups boiling water
- 1 16-ounce can jellied cranberry sauce
- 1 8-ounce carton dairy sour cream or light dairy sour cream
- 1 cup chopped walnuts or pecans, toasted (see tip, page 280) (optional)

one In a large bowl dissolve gelatin in the boiling water. Using a wire whisk or rotary beater, lightly beat in cranberry sauce until smooth. Add sour cream; beat until combined.

two Chill about 45 minutes or until partially set (the consistency of unbeaten egg whites). If desired, fold in nuts.

three Pour mixture into a 5- to 6-cup mold or an 8×8×2-inch baking dish. Cover and chill for at least 4 hours or until set. Unmold or cut into squares.

NUTRITION FACTS PER SERVING: 231 cal., 6 g total fat (4 g sat. fat), 13 mg chol., 99 mg sodium, 42 g carbo., 1 g fiber, 3 g pro.

Fruit and Broccoli Salad

PREP: 15 minutes **CHILL:** 1 hour **MAKES:** 12 to 16 servings

- 1   16-ounce package shredded broccoli (broccoli slaw mix)
- 2   cups seedless red and/or green grapes, halved
- 2   medium apples, cored and chopped
- ⅔   cup bottled citrus salad dressing
- 1   cup coarsely chopped pecans or walnuts, toasted (see tip, page 280)

one In a very large bowl combine shredded broccoli, grapes, and apples. Pour salad dressing over broccoli mixture; toss gently to coat.

two Cover and chill for 1 hour. If desired, transfer to a serving bowl. Stir in toasted nuts.

NUTRITION FACTS PER SERVING: 219 cal., 15 g total fat (2 g sat. fat), 6 mg chol., 131 mg sodium, 21 g carbo., 2 g fiber, 3 g pro.

Fresh Mozzarella Salad

START TO FINISH: 10 minutes **MAKES:** 8 servings

- 4   medium tomatoes or 6 roma tomatoes
- 4   ounces fresh mozzarella cheese
- 2   tablespoons bottled balsamic vinaigrette salad dressing
- ½   cup loosely packed fresh basil leaves, thinly sliced
-     Salt and cracked black pepper

one Cut tomatoes into ½-inch slices. Cut mozzarella cheese into ¼-inch slices. Arrange tomato and cheese slices on a serving platter.

two Drizzle tomato and cheese slices with vinaigrette dressing. Sprinkle with basil, salt, and pepper.

NUTRITION FACTS PER SERVING: 64 cal., 4 g total fat (2 g sat. fat), 11 mg chol., 174 mg sodium, 4 g carbo., 1 g fiber, 3 g pro.

Asian Pea Pod Salad

START TO FINISH: 20 minutes **MAKES:** 6 servings

6 cups torn romaine lettuce

2 cups fresh snow pea pods, trimmed and halved crosswise

⅓ cup bottled Italian salad dressing

1 tablespoon bottled hoisin sauce

1 tablespoon sesame seeds, toasted (see tip, page 280)

one In a large bowl combine romaine lettuce and pea pods.

two For dressing, in a small bowl combine Italian dressing and hoisin sauce. Pour dressing over romaine mixture; toss gently to coat. Sprinkle with sesame seeds.

NUTRITION FACTS PER SERVING: 98 cal., 7 g total fat (1 g sat. fat), 0 mg chol., 153 mg sodium, 6 g carbo., 2 g fiber, 2 g pro.

Pea and Peanut Salad

START TO FINISH: 10 minutes **MAKES:** 4 to 6 servings

1 10-ounce package frozen peas, thawed and drained

1 cup Spanish or honey-roasted peanuts

¼ cup dairy sour cream

2 tablespoons mayonnaise or salad dressing

½ teaspoon sugar

one In a medium bowl combine peas and peanuts.

two For dressing, in a small bowl combine sour cream, mayonnaise, and sugar. Pour dressing over pea mixture; toss gently to coat.

NUTRITION FACTS PER SERVING: 346 cal., 26 g total fat (5 g sat. fat), 9 mg chol., 131 mg sodium, 17 g carbo., 6 g fiber, 15 g pro.

Fresh Corn and Tomato Salad *See photo on page 270.*

PREP: 20 minutes **GRILL:** 25 minutes **MAKES:** 6 servings

- 6 fresh ears sweet corn with husks
- ½ of an 8-ounce bottle Italian salad dressing
- 3 tablespoons snipped fresh rosemary
- 3 to 6 cups fresh baby spinach or spinach leaves
- 4 medium roma tomatoes, finely chopped

one Carefully peel back corn husks but do not remove. Remove and discard silks. Gently rinse corn; pat dry.

two Brush corn with some of the Italian salad dressing and sprinkle with some of the rosemary. Carefully fold husks back around ears. Tie husk tops with 100-percent-cotton kitchen string to secure.

three For a charcoal grill, grill corn on the rack of an uncovered grill directly over medium coals for 25 to 30 minutes or until kernels are tender, turning and rearranging corn 3 times during grilling. (For a gas grill, preheat grill. Reduce heat to medium. Place corn on grill rack over heat. Cover and grill as above.)

four Remove string from corn. Remove husks. When cool enough to handle, use a sharp knife to cut corn kernels off cobs. For dressing, in a small bowl combine the remaining salad dressing and the remaining rosemary.

five To serve, arrange spinach on 6 salad plates. Top with corn kernels and tomatoes. Serve with dressing.

NUTRITION FACTS PER SERVING: 138 cal., 3 g total fat (0 g sat. fat), 1 mg chol., 414 mg sodium, 28 g carbo., 5 g fiber, 4 g pro.

Using Fresh or Dried Herbs If you don't have the fresh herbs called for in a recipe, you can substitute dried. In general, use one-third less of the dried herb than fresh. For instance, if a recipe calls for 1 tablespoon of fresh herb, use 1 teaspoon of dried. If you don't have a particular herb on hand, try these substitutions:

Sage: use savory, marjoram, or rosemary

Basil: use oregano or thyme

Thyme: use basil, marjoram, oregano, or savory

Cilantro: use parsley

Mint: use basil, marjoram, or rosemary

Tomato and Zucchini Salad

START TO FINISH: 20 minutes **MAKES:** 4 servings

- 1   large tomato, coarsely chopped
- 1   small zucchini, thinly sliced
- 2   tablespoons thinly sliced green onion
- 1   teaspoon snipped fresh basil or ¼ teaspoon dried basil, crushed (optional)
- 2   tablespoons bottled dried tomato vinaigrette salad dressing
- 2   tablespoons crumbled feta cheese or shredded mozzarella cheese

one In a salad bowl combine tomato, zucchini, green onion, and, if desired, basil.

two Drizzle vinaigrette dressing over tomato mixture; toss gently to coat. Sprinkle with cheese.

NUTRITION FACTS PER SERVING: 62 cal., 5 g total fat (1 g sat. fat), 3 mg chol., 105 mg sodium, 5 g carbo., 1 g fiber, 2 g pro.

Baby Greens with Veggies

START TO FINISH: 25 minutes **MAKES:** 4 servings

- 4   ounces fresh asparagus spears
- 1   small yellow summer squash, halved lengthwise and sliced (about 1 cup)
- 4   cups mixed baby salad greens
- 2   tablespoons sunflower kernels
- ⅓   cup bottled honey-mustard salad dressing

one Snap off and discard woody bases from asparagus. Cut asparagus into 1-inch pieces.

two In a covered small saucepan cook asparagus and squash in a small amount of boiling salted water for 3 to 5 minutes or until crisp-tender; drain. Plunge into ice water; drain again.

three In a salad bowl combine asparagus, squash, and salad greens. Sprinkle with sunflower kernels. Drizzle with salad dressing; toss gently to coat.

NUTRITION FACTS PER SERVING: 111 cal., 7 g total fat (1 g sat. fat), 7 mg chol., 155 mg sodium, 9 g carbo., 2 g fiber, 3 g pro.

Mediterranean Salad *See photo on page 269.*

START TO FINISH: 15 minutes **MAKES:** 6 servings

- 1   15-ounce can three-bean salad, drained
- 1   large tomato, seeded and chopped
- 1   6½-ounce jar marinated artichoke hearts, drained and halved lengthwise
- 1   tablespoon snipped fresh basil or ½ teaspoon dried basil, crushed
- ¼   cup bottled Italian salad dressing
      Lettuce leaves (optional)

one In a medium bowl combine three-bean salad, tomato, artichoke hearts, and basil.

two Drizzle Italian dressing over bean mixture; toss gently to coat. If desired, serve on lettuce leaves.

NUTRITION FACTS PER SERVING: 109 cal., 5 g total fat (0 g sat. fat), 0 mg chol., 538 mg sodium, 16 g carbo., 3 g fiber, 3 g pro.

Marinated Bean Salad

PREP: 20 minutes **CHILL:** 4 to 24 hours **MAKES:** 8 servings

- 8   ounces fresh green beans, trimmed and cut into bite-size pieces, or one 9-ounce package frozen cut green beans
- 2   15- to 19-ounce cans navy, red kidney, and/or cannellini beans (white kidney beans), rinsed and drained
- ½   cup thinly sliced red onion
- ½   cup bottled balsamic vinaigrette salad dressing
- 3   tablespoons molasses

one In a medium saucepan cook fresh green beans in a small amount of boiling, lightly salted water for 7 to 10 minutes or just until tender; drain. (Or cook frozen green beans according to package directions; drain.) Rinse beans with cold water; drain again.

two In a large bowl combine green beans, canned beans, and onion. For dressing, in a small bowl combine balsamic vinaigrette dressing and molasses. Pour over bean mixture; toss gently to coat.

three Cover and chill for 4 to 24 hours. Use a slotted spoon to serve bean mixture.

NUTRITION FACTS PER SERVING: 196 cal., 5 g total fat (1 g sat. fat), 0 mg chol. 656 mg sodium, 31 g carbo., 6 g fiber, 9 g pro.

Creamy Cucumbers

PREP: 15 minutes **CHILL:** 4 hours **MAKES:** 6 servings

½   cup dairy sour cream or plain yogurt

1   tablespoon vinegar

½   teaspoon salt

¼   teaspoon dried dill

    Dash black pepper

1   large cucumber, peeled (if desired), halved lengthwise, and thinly sliced (3 cups)

⅓   cup thinly sliced onion

one In a medium nonreactive bowl combine sour cream, vinegar, salt, dill, and pepper. Add cucumber and onion; toss gently to coat.

two Cover and chill for at least 4 hours, stirring occasionally. Stir before serving.

NUTRITION FACTS PER SERVING: 45 cal., 3 g total fat (2 g sat. fat), 7 mg chol., 204 mg sodium, 3 g carbo., 1 g fiber, 1 g pro.

Hot-and-Sweet Pineapple Slaw *See photo on page 269.*

PREP: 20 minutes **CHILL:** 1 to 4 hours **MAKES:** 10 servings

1   16-ounce package shredded broccoli (broccoli slaw mix)

2   cups fresh pineapple chunks or one 20-ounce can pineapple chunks, drained

2   cups broccoli florets

½   cup mayonnaise or salad dressing

1   to 2 tablespoons adobo sauce from canned chipotle peppers in adobo sauce

¼   teaspoon salt

one In a large bowl combine shredded broccoli, pineapple, and broccoli florets.

two For dressing, in a small bowl combine mayonnaise, adobo sauce, and salt. Pour dressing over broccoli mixture; toss gently to coat. Cover and chill for 1 to 4 hours. Toss before serving.

NUTRITION FACTS PER SERVING: 112 cal., 11 g total fat (1 g sat. fat), 6 mg chol., 145 mg sodium, 7 g carbo., 3 g fiber, 2 g pro.

Really Red Coleslaw *See photo on page 268.*

START TO FINISH: 15 minutes **MAKES:** 8 servings

1	10-ounce package shredded red cabbage (about 6 cups)
1	medium red onion, slivered (1 cup)
½	cup dried tart cherries
½	cup bottled raspberry vinaigrette salad dressing
1	tablespoon seedless red raspberry preserves

one In a large bowl combine red cabage, red onion, and dried cherries.

two For dressing, in a small bowl combine vinaigrette dressing and preserves. Pour over cabbage mixture; toss gently to coat. If desired, cover and chill for up to 6 hours.

NUTRITION FACTS PER SERVING: 108 cal., 6 g total fat (1 g sat. fat), 0 mg chol. 5 mg sodium, 12 g carbo., 1 g fiber, 1 g pro.

Napa Cabbage Slaw

PREP: 20 minutes **CHILL:** 2 to 24 hours **MAKES:** 6 servings

3	cups finely shredded napa cabbage
1	cup finely shredded bok choy
2	to 3 tablespoons slivered red sweet pepper
¼	cup seasoned rice vinegar or white vinegar
1	tablespoon toasted sesame oil

one In a medium bowl combine napa cabbage, bok choy, and sweet pepper.

two For dressing, in a small bowl combine vinegar and sesame oil. Pour dressing over cabbage mixture; toss gently to coat. Cover and chill for 2 to 24 hours. Toss before serving.

NUTRITION FACTS PER SERVING: 29 cal., 2 g total fat (0 g sat. fat), 0 mg chol., 5 mg sodium, 2 g carbo., 1 g fiber, 1 g pro.

Ginger-Sesame Slaw

START TO FINISH: 25 minutes **MAKES:** 6 servings

4	cups thinly bias-sliced bok choy
2	cups carrot ribbons*
1	daikon radish (8 ounces), shredded, or 1 cup sliced radishes
1	tablespoon finely chopped pickled ginger or 2 teaspoons grated fresh ginger
¼	to ½ cup bottled oriental salad dressing

one In a large bowl combine bok choy, carrot, radish, and ginger. Toss with enough of the salad dressing to moisten.

two If desired, cover and chill for up to 1 hour.

Note: Carrot ribbons lend a stylish note to this Asian salad. To make the ribbons, peel large carrots. Draw a vegetable peeler down the surface of each carrot, making long, thin strips.

NUTRITION FACTS PER SERVING: 71 cal., 4 g total fat (1 g sat. fat), 0 mg chol., 106 mg sodium, 9 g carbo., 2 g fiber, 2 g pro.

Cranberry Coleslaw

START TO FINISH: 15 minutes **MAKES:** 6 servings

¼	cup mayonnaise or salad dressing
1	to 2 tablespoons honey
1	tablespoon vinegar
¼	cup chopped fresh or frozen cranberries or snipped dried cranberries
5	cups shredded cabbage (1 small head)

one For dressing, in a small bowl combine mayonnaise, honey, and vinegar. Stir in cranberries.

two Place shredded cabbage in a large serving bowl. Pour dressing over cabbage; toss gently to coat. If desired, cover and chill for up to 45 minutes before serving.

NUTRITION FACTS PER SERVING: 94 cal., 7 g total fat (1 g sat. fat), 5 mg chol., 63 mg sodium, 7 g carbo., 2 g fiber, 1 g pro.

Poppy Seed-Dressed Pasta Salad *See photo on page 270.*

PREP: 15 minutes **CHILL:** 4 to 24 hours **MAKES:** 8 servings

8	ounces dried penne and/or rigatoni pasta
1½	cups seedless red and/or green grapes, halved
4	ounces cheddar cheese, cubed (about ¾ cup)
4	ounces cooked ham, cubed (about ⅔ cup)
½	cup bottled poppy seed salad dressing
¼	teaspoon finely shredded orange peel (optional)

one Cook pasta according to package directions; drain. Rinse with cold water; drain again. Place pasta in a large bowl. Add grapes, cheese, and ham.

two In a small bowl stir together salad dressing and, if desired, orange peel. Pour over pasta mixture; toss gently to coat. Cover and chill for 4 to 24 hours. Stir before serving.

NUTRITION FACTS PER SERVING: 253 cal., 11 g total fat (4 g sat. fat), 21 mg chol., 448 mg sodium, 28 g carbo., 1 g fiber, 10 g pro.

Lemon Sunshine Salad

PREP: 30 minutes **CHILL:** 2 hours **MAKES:** 15 servings

½	cup dried acini di pepe pasta (tiny beads)
1	4-serving-size package lemon instant pudding and pie filling mix
1	29-ounce can peach slices in light syrup, undrained
2	11-ounce cans mandarin orange sections, drained
1	8-ounce container frozen whipped dessert topping, thawed

one Cook pasta according to package directions; drain. Stir in pudding mix.

two Drain peaches, reserving ½ cup of the syrup. Stir the ½ cup syrup into pasta mixture. Cut peach slices into bite-size pieces. Stir peaches and mandarin orange sections into pasta mixture. Cover and chill for 2 hours.

three Before serving, fold in whipped dessert topping.

NUTRITION FACTS PER SERVING: 150 cal., 3 g total fat (3 g sat. fat), 0 mg chol., 86 mg sodium, 30 g carbo., 1 g fiber, 1 g pro.

Pesto Macaroni Salad

START TO FINISH: 30 minutes **MAKES:** 14 servings

- 3   cups dried elbow macaroni
- 5   ounces green beans, trimmed and cut into 1-inch pieces (about 1 cup)
- 1   pound small fresh mozzarella cheese balls, drained and sliced
- 1   7-ounce container basil pesto
- ½   cup fresh basil leaves, torn
- ½   teaspoon salt

one Cook macaroni according to package directions; drain. Rinse with cold water; drain again.

two Meanwhile, in a covered small saucepan cook green beans in a small amount of boiling salted water for 10 to 12 minutes or until crisp-tender; drain. Rinse with cold water; drain again.

three In a large bowl combine macaroni, green beans, mozzarella cheese, and pesto. Stir in basil and salt. If desired, cover and chill for up to 2 hours.

NUTRITION FACTS PER SERVING: 249 cal., 14 g total fat (4 g sat. fat), 26 mg chol., 255 mg sodium, 20 g carbo., 1 g fiber, 11 g pro.

Feta-Tomato Pasta Salad

PREP: 25 minutes **CHILL:** 4 to 8 hours **MAKES:** 4 or 5 servings

- 1½   cups dried mostaccioli pasta
- 1   cup halved cherry tomatoes or grape tomatoes
- 1   cup crumbled feta cheese (4 ounces)
- ⅓   cup sliced pitted kalamata or other ripe olives
- ½   cup bottled balsamic vinaigrette salad dressing

one Cook pasta according to package directions; drain. Rinse with cold water; drain again.

two In a large bowl combine cooked pasta, tomatoes, feta cheese, and olives. Pour vinaigrette dressing over pasta mixture; toss gently to coat. Cover and chill for 4 to 8 hours. Stir gently before serving.

NUTRITION FACTS PER SERVING: 335 cal., 17 g total fat (5 g sat. fat), 25 mg chol., 792 mg sodium, 36 g carbo., 2 g fiber, 9 g pro.

Fresh Corn-Rice Salad

START TO FINISH: 25 minutes **MAKES:** 6 servings

4	fresh ears sweet corn
1½	cups cooked rice, cooled
1	10-ounce can diced tomatoes and green chiles, undrained
2	tablespoons shredded radishes

> **Cutting Corn Off the Cob** To cut the kernels off fresh ears of corn, place one ear at a time on a cutting board. Holding the corn at a angle, use a sharp knife to cut off the kernels, working from the top down. Repeat, turning the ear until you've captured every kernel.

one Remove and discard corn husks and silks. Rinse corn; pat dry. Cut corn kernels off cobs (you should have about 2 cups of kernels).

two In a covered medium saucepan cook corn in a small amount of boiling salted water for 4 minutes; drain.

three In a medium bowl combine corn and cooled rice. Stir in undrained tomatoes. Sprinkle with radishes. Serve at room temperature.

NUTRITION FACTS PER SERVING: 123 cal., 1 g total fat (0 g sat. fat), 0 mg chol., 332 mg sodium, 28 g carbo., 2 g fiber, 3 g pro.

Fruity Wild Rice Salad

PREP: 50 minutes **CHILL:** 4 to 24 hours **MAKES:** 6 servings

⅔	cup uncooked wild rice
½	cup dried cranberries
⅓	cup sliced green onion
½	cup bottled raspberry vinaigrette salad dressing or other vinaigrette salad dressing
½	cup coarsely chopped pecans, toasted (see tip, page 280)

one Rinse and drain wild rice. Cook wild rice according to package directions; drain if necessary.

two In a medium bowl stir together cooked wild rice, dried cranberries, and green onion. Pour vinaigrette dressing over rice mixture; toss gently to coat.

three Cover and chill for 4 to 24 hours. Stir in pecans before serving.

NUTRITION FACTS PER SERVING: 186 cal., 7 g total fat (1 g sat. fat), 0 mg chol., 275 mg sodium, 30 g carbo., 3 g fiber, 4 g pro.

Berry-Melon Vinaigrette

START TO FINISH: 15 minutes **MAKES:** about 2 cups

- 1   cup seeded watermelon chunks
- 1   cup halved strawberries
- 2   tablespoons white balsamic vinegar
- 1   tablespoon sugar
- 1   teaspoon finely shredded orange peel

one In a blender or food processor combine watermelon, strawberries, vinegar, sugar, and orange peel. Cover and blend or process until smooth.

two Use at once or cover and store in the refrigerator for up to 3 days. Stir before using.

NUTRITION FACTS PER 2 TABLESPOONS: 11 cal., 0 g total fat (0 g sat. fat), 0 mg chol., 1 mg sodium, 3 g carbo., 0 g fiber, 0 g pro.

Lemon-Nut Vinaigrette

START TO FINISH: 10 minutes **MAKES:** ⅔ cup

- ¼   cup walnut oil, salad oil, or olive oil
- 1   teaspoon finely shredded lemon peel or lime peel
- ¼   cup lemon juice or lime juice
- 2   tablespoons ground walnuts, almonds, or pecans
- 1   tablespoon honey

one In a small bowl combine oil, lemon peel, lemon juice, ground nuts, and honey.

two Use at once or cover and store in the refrigerator for up to 3 days. Stir before using.

NUTRITION FACTS PER TABLESPOON: 66 cal., 6 g total fat (1 g sat. fat), 0 mg chol., 0 mg sodium, 2 g carbo., 0 g fiber, 0 g pro.

Strawberry Vinaigrette

START TO FINISH: 10 minutes **MAKES:** 1 cup

- 1   cup cut-up fresh or frozen strawberries
- 2   tablespoons red wine vinegar
- ½   teaspoon sugar
- ⅛   teaspoon cracked black pepper

one In a blender combine strawberries, vinegar, sugar, and pepper. Cover and blend until smooth.

two Use at once or cover and store in the refrigerator for up to 1 day. Stir before using.

NUTRITION FACTS PER TABLESPOON: 3 cal., 0 g total fat (0 g sat. fat), 0 mg chol., 0 mg sodium, 1 g carbo., 0 g fiber, 0 g pro.

Spicy Citrus Dressing

START TO FINISH: 10 minutes **MAKES:** about ⅓ cup

- ¼   cup lemon juice or lime juice
- 2   tablespoons honey
- 1   tablespoon salad oil
- ¼   teaspoon ground cinnamon, allspice, or cardamom
- ⅛   teaspoon paprika

one In a screw-top jar combine lemon juice, honey, salad oil, cinnamon, and paprika. Cover and shake well.

two Use at once or store in the refrigerator for up to 3 days. Shake before using.

NUTRITION FACTS PER TABLESPOON: 53 cal., 3 g total fat (0 g sat. fat), 0 mg chol., 1 mg sodium, 8 g carbo., 0 g fiber, 0 g pro.

Apricot Nectar Dressing

START TO FINISH: 10 minutes **MAKES:** ¾ to 1 cup

- ½   cup plain low-fat yogurt
- 1   tablespoon packed brown sugar
- ⅛   teaspoon ground cinnamon
      Dash ground nutmeg
- ¼   to ½ cup apricot nectar

one In a small bowl stir together yogurt, brown sugar, cinnamon, and nutmeg. Stir in enough of the apricot nectar to make a dressing of drizzling consistency.

two Use at once or cover and store in the refrigerator for 3 to 5 days. Stir before using.

NUTRITION FACTS PER TABLESPOON: 12 cal., 0 g total fat (0 g sat. fat), 1 mg chol., 8 mg sodium, 2 g carbo., 0 g fiber, 1 g pro.

Orange-Poppy Seed Dressing

START TO FINISH: 10 minutes **MAKES:** ½ cup

- ⅓   cup orange juice
- 3   tablespoons salad oil
- 1   tablespoon Dijon-style mustard
- 1   teaspoon poppy seeds
- 2   or 3 dashes bottled hot pepper sauce

one In a small bowl whisk together orange juice, salad oil, mustard, poppy seeds, and hot pepper sauce.

two Use at once or cover and store in the refrigerator for up to 3 days. Stir before using.

NUTRITION FACTS PER TABLESPOON: 54 cal., 5 g total fat (1 g sat. fat), 0 mg chol., 11 mg sodium, 1 g carbo., 0 g fiber, 0 g pro.

Chutney Salad Dressing

START TO FINISH: 10 minutes **MAKES:** 1¾ cups

¼   cup bottled mango chutney

1   cup mayonnaise or salad dressing

½   cup dairy sour cream

one Cut up any large pieces in chutney. In a small bowl stir together chutney, mayonnaise, and sour cream.

two Use at once or cover and store in the refrigerator for up to 1 week.

NUTRITION FACTS PER TABLESPOON: 71 cal., 7 g total fat (1 g sat. fat), 6 mg chol., 49 mg sodium, 2 g carbo., 0 g fiber, 0 g pro.

Honey-Mustard Dressing

START TO FINISH: 10 minutes **MAKES:** ¾ cup

⅓   cup salad oil

2   tablespoons lemon juice

2   tablespoons honey

2   tablespoons coarse-grain brown mustard or Dijon-style mustard

1   clove garlic, minced

one In a small bowl combine salad oil, lemon juice, honey, mustard, and garlic.

two Use at once or cover and store in the refrigerator for up to 3 days. Stir before using.

NUTRITION FACTS PER TABLESPOON: 67 cal., 6 g total fat (1 g sat. fat), 0 mg chol., 34 mg sodium, 3 g carbo., 0 g fiber, 0 g pro.

Thousand Island Dressing

START TO FINISH: 20 minutes **MAKES:** 2 cups

1½   cups mayonnaise or salad dressing

¼   cup bottled chili sauce

1   hard-cooked egg, chopped

1   tablespoon finely chopped onion

1   tablespoon pickle relish

one In a small bowl stir together mayonnaise, chili sauce, hard-cooked egg, onion, and pickle relish.

two Use at once or cover and store in the refrigerator for up to 3 days.

NUTRITION FACTS PER TABLESPOON: 80 cal., 8 g total fat (1 g sat. fat), 10 mg chol., 87 mg sodium, 1 g carbo., 0 g fiber, 0 g pro.

Herb-Buttermilk Dressing

START TO FINISH: 10 minutes **MAKES:** about 1 cup

⅔ cup light mayonnaise or salad dressing

⅓ cup buttermilk

1 teaspoon snipped fresh tarragon or ¼ teaspoon dried tarragon, crushed

1 to 2 teaspoons milk (optional)

one In a small bowl stir together mayonnaise, buttermilk, and tarragon. If necessary, stir in enough of the milk to make a dressing of drizzling consistency.

two Use at once or cover and store in the refrigerator for up to 3 days.

NUTRITION FACTS PER TABLESPOON: 35 cal., 3 g total fat (1 g sat. fat), 3 mg chol., 65 mg sodium, 2 g carbo., 0 g fiber, 0 g pro.

Creamy Chive Dressing

START TO FINISH: 10 minutes **MAKES:** ½ cup

¼ cup plain low-fat yogurt

2 tablespoons light mayonnaise or salad dressing

2 tablespoons fat-free milk

1 tablespoon snipped fresh chives or parsley

¼ teaspoon dried basil, oregano, or thyme, crushed (optional)

one In a small bowl stir together yogurt, mayonnaise, milk, chives, and, if desired, dried herb.

two Use at once or cover and store in the refrigerator for up to 3 days.

NUTRITION FACTS PER TABLESPOON: 19 cal., 1 g total fat (0 g sat. fat), 2 mg chol., 48 mg sodium, 1 g carbo., 0 g fiber, 1 g pro.

Creamy Garlic Dressing

START TO FINISH: 10 minutes **MAKES:** 1 cup

½ cup plain low-fat yogurt

⅓ cup bottled reduced-calorie Italian salad dressing

1 tablespoon grated Parmesan cheese

1 small garlic clove, minced

one In a small bowl stir together yogurt, Italian dressing, Parmesan cheese, and garlic.

two Use at once or cover and store in the refrigerator for up to 3 days.

NUTRITION FACTS PER TABLESPOON: 12 cal., 1 g total fat (0 g sat. fat), 1 mg chol., 50 mg sodium, 1 g carbo., 0 g fiber, 1 g pro.

Tangy Barbecue Sauce

PREP: 10 minutes **COOK:** 10 minutes **MAKES:** about 1½ cups

1   cup ketchup
⅓   cup balsamic vinegar or cider vinegar
⅓   cup light-color corn syrup
¼   cup finely chopped onion or thinly sliced green onions
¼   teaspoon salt
     Several dashes bottled hot pepper sauce

one In a small saucepan combine ketchup, vinegar, corn syrup, onion, salt, and hot pepper sauce. Bring to boiling; reduce heat. Simmer, uncovered, for 10 to 15 minutes or until desired consistency, stirring occasionally.

two To use, brush beef, pork, or poultry with sauce during the last 5 to 10 minutes of grilling or broiling. If desired, reheat any remaining sauce until bubbly. Pass with meat or poultry.

NUTRITION FACTS PER TABLESPOOON: 28 cal., 0 g total fat (0 g sat. fat), 0 mg chol., 140 mg sodium, 7 g carbo., 0 g fiber, 0 g pro.

Apple Butter Barbecue Sauce

START TO FINISH: 10 minutes **MAKES:** about 1½ cups

1   8-ounce can tomato sauce
½   cup apple butter
2   tablespoons light-color corn syrup (optional)
1   tablespoon Pickapeppa sauce or Worcestershire sauce

one In a small saucepan combine tomato sauce, apple butter, corn syrup (if desired), and Pickapeppa sauce. Bring just to boiling. Remove from heat.

two To use, brush pork or poultry with sauce during the last 5 to 10 minutes of grilling or broiling. If desired, reheat any remaining sauce until bubbly. Pass with pork or poultry.

NUTRITION FACTS PER TABLESPOOON: 34 cal., 0 g total fat (0 g sat. fat), 0 mg chol., 51 mg sodium, 8 g carbo., 0 g fiber, 0 g pro.

Molasses Barbecue Sauce

START TO FINISH: 10 minutes **MAKES:** about 1½ cups

1   cup ketchup
¼   cup full-flavor molasses
¼   cup water
½   teaspoon finely shredded lemon peel
1   tablespoon lemon juice
2   teaspoons Worcestershire sauce
½   teaspoon black pepper
⅛   teaspoon salt

one In a small bowl combine ketchup, molasses, water, lemon peel, lemon juice, Worcestershire sauce, pepper, and salt.

two To use, brush beef, pork, or poultry with sauce during the last 5 to 10 minutes of grilling or broiling. If desired, heat any remaining sauce until bubbly. Pass with meat or poultry.

NUTRITION FACTS PER TABLESPOOON: 40 cal., 0 g total fat (0 g sat. fat), 0 mg chol., 260 mg sodium, 10 g carbo., 0 g fiber, 0 g pro.

Basic Moppin' Sauce

PREP: 15 minutes **COOK:** 30 minutes **MAKES:** about 2 cups

1	cup strong brewed coffee
1	cup ketchup
½	cup Worcestershire sauce
¼	cup butter or margarine
1	tablespoon sugar
1	to 2 teaspoons black pepper
½	teaspoon salt (optional)

one In a medium saucepan combine coffee, ketchup, Worcestershire sauce, butter, sugar, pepper, and, if desired, salt. Bring to boiling, stirring occasionally; reduce heat. Simmer, uncovered, for 30 minutes, stirring frequently.

two To use, brush beef, pork, or poultry with sauce during the last 5 to 10 minutes of grilling or broiling. If desired, reheat any remaining sauce until bubbly. Pass with meat or poultry.

NUTRITION FACTS PER TABLESPOOON: 25 cal., 1 g total fat (1 g sat. fat), 4 mg chol., 143 mg sodium, 3 g carbo., 0 g fiber, 0 g pro.

Cranberry-Chipotle Sauce

START TO FINISH: 20 minutes **MAKES:** 1½ cups

1	8-ounce can jellied cranberry sauce
⅓	cup apricot or peach preserves or apricot or peach spreadable fruit
¼	cup chopped onion
1	tablespoon lemon juice or cider vinegar
1	canned chipotle pepper in adobo sauce or 1 fresh jalapeño chile pepper, seeded and chopped (see tip, page 59)

one In a small saucepan combine cranberry sauce, preserves, onion, lemon juice, and chipotle pepper. Bring to boiling, stirring constantly; reduce heat. Simmer, uncovered, for 5 minutes, stirring occasionally.

two To use, brush pork or poultry with sauce during the last 5 to 10 minutes of grilling or broiling. If desired, reheat any remaining sauce until bubbly. Pass with pork or poultry.

NUTRITION FACTS PER ¼ CUP: 112 cal., 0 g total fat (0 g sat. fat), 0 mg chol., 43 mg sodium, 28 g carbo., 1 g fiber, 0 g pro.

Lemon-Herb Brush-On

START TO FINISH: 10 minutes **MAKES:** about ⅓ cup

2	tablespoons butter or margarine
3	tablespoons lemon juice
3	cloves garlic, minced
1	teaspoon dried thyme, savory, or sage, crushed
¼	teaspoon salt
¼	teaspoon black pepper

one In a small saucepan melt butter. Stir in lemon juice, garlic, thyme, salt, and pepper.

two To use, brush pork, poultry, fish, or shellfish with sauce before grilling or broiling. Brush occasionally with sauce during the first half of grilling or broiling. Discard any remaining sauce.

NUTRITION FACTS PER TABLESPOOON: 49 cal., 5 g total fat (3 g sat. fat), 12 mg chol., 150 mg sodium, 2 g carbo., 0 g fiber, 0 g pro.

Tandoori-Style Brush-On

START TO FINISH: 10 minutes **MAKES:** about ¼ cup

2	tablespoons cooking oil
1	tablespoon garam masala
6	cloves garlic, minced
2	teaspoons grated fresh ginger
½	teaspoon salt

one In a small bowl combine cooking oil, garam masala, garlic, ginger, and salt.

two To use, brush lamb or poultry with sauce before grilling or broiling. Brush occasionally with sauce during the first half of grilling or broiling. Discard any remaining sauce.

NUTRITION FACTS PER TABLESPOOON: 71 cal., 7 g total fat (1 g sat. fat), 0 mg chol., 293 mg sodium, 2 g carbo., 0 g fiber, 0 g pro.

Ginger-Orange Brush-On

START TO FINISH: 10 minutes **MAKES:** about ¾ cup

½	cup bottled barbecue sauce
¼	cup frozen orange juice concentrate, thawed
2	tablespoons soy sauce
1	tablespoon grated fresh ginger

one In a small bowl combine barbecue sauce, orange juice concentrate, soy sauce, and ginger.

two To use, brush beef, lamb, pork, or poultry with sauce during the last 5 to 10 minutes of grilling or broiling. If desired, heat any remaining sauce until bubbly. Pass sauce with meat or poultry.

NUTRITION FACTS PER TABLESPOOON: 19 cal., 0 g total fat (0 g sat. fat), 0 mg chol., 238 mg sodium, 4 g carbo., 0 g fiber, 1 g pro.

Teriyaki Glaze

PREP: 5 minutes **COOK:** 10 minutes **MAKES:** about ¼ cup

3	tablespoons soy sauce
3	tablespoons sweet rice wine (mirin)
2	tablespoons dry white wine
1½	teaspoons sugar
1½	teaspoons honey

one In a small saucepan combine soy sauce, rice wine, white wine, sugar, and honey. Bring to boiling; reduce heat. Simmer, uncovered, about 10 minutes or until glaze is reduced to about ¼ cup.

two To use, brush pork, poultry, or fish with glaze during the last 2 to 3 minutes of grilling or broiling.

NUTRITION FACTS PER TABLESPOOON: 29 cal., 0 g total fat (0 g sat. fat), 0 mg chol., 351 mg sodium, 6 g carbo., 0 g fiber, 1 g pro.

SERVE-ALONG SIDES

Mustard-Jalapeño Glaze

START TO FINISH: 10 minutes **MAKES:** about ½ cup

- 3 tablespoons Dijon-style mustard
- 1 to 2 tablespoons finely chopped canned jalapeño chile peppers, seeded (if desired)
- 1 tablespoon frozen orange juice concentrate, thawed
- 1 tablespoon light-color corn syrup
- ½ teaspoon lemon-pepper seasoning

one In a small bowl combine mustard, jalapeño peppers, juice concentrate, corn syrup, and lemon-pepper seasoning.

two To use, brush beef, pork, or fish with glaze during the last 2 to 3 minutes of grilling or broiling.

NUTRITION FACTS PER TABLESPOON: 29 cal., 0 g total fat (0 g sat. fat), 0 mg chol., 442 mg sodium, 7 g carbo., 0 g fiber, 2 g pro.

Cucumber-Dill Sauce

START TO FINISH: 10 minutes **MAKES:** about ⅔ cup

- ⅓ cup finely chopped seeded cucumber
- 3 tablespoons plain yogurt
- 2 tablespoons mayonnaise or salad dressing
- 2 teaspoons prepared horseradish
- 2 teaspoons snipped fresh dill

one In a small bowl combine cucumber, yogurt, mayonnaise, horseradish, and fresh dill. If desired, cover and chill for up to 4 hours.

two To use, serve with beef, poultry, or fish.

NUTRITION FACTS PER TABLESPOON: 24 cal., 2 g total fat (0 g sat. fat), 1 mg chol., 21 mg sodium, 1 g carbo., 0 g fiber, 0 g pro.

Mustard-Horseradish Sauce

START TO FINISH: 10 minutes **MAKES:** about ½ cup

- ⅓ cup dairy sour cream, mayonnaise, or salad dressing
- 1 green onion, finely chopped
- 1 tablespoon Dijon-style mustard
- 1 to 2 teaspoons prepared horseradish

one In a small bowl combine sour cream, green onion, mustard, and horseradish.

two To use, serve with beef, pork, lamb, or poultry.

NUTRITION FACTS PER TABLESPOON: 20 cal., 2 g total fat (1 g sat. fat), 4 mg chol., 16 mg sodium, 1 g carbo., 0 g fiber, 0 g pro.

Lemon Sauce

START TO FINISH: 10 minutes **MAKES:** about ⅓ cup

- ¼ cup mayonnaise or salad dressing
- 2 tablespoons dairy sour cream
- 1 tablespoon snipped fresh flat-leaf parsley
- 1 teaspoon finely shredded lemon peel
- 1 teaspoon lemon juice

one In a small bowl combine mayonnaise, sour cream, parsley, lemon peel, and lemon juice.

two To use, serve with fish or shellfish.

NUTRITION FACTS PER TABLESPOOON: 90 cal., 10 g total fat (2 g sat. fat), 9 mg chol., 66 mg sodium, 1 g carbo., 0 g fiber, 0 g pro.

Honey-Peach Sauce

START TO FINISH: 25 minutes **MAKES:** about 1¾ cups

- 4 medium peaches, peeled (if desired), or nectarines
- 2 tablespoons lemon juice
- 2 tablespoons honey
- ½ teaspoon cracked black pepper
- 1 to 2 teaspoons snipped fresh thyme or ¼ to ½ teaspoon dried thyme, crushed

one Cut up 3 of the peaches. In a blender or food processor combine cut-up peaches, lemon juice, honey, and pepper. Cover and blend or process until smooth.

two Transfer to a small saucepan. Bring to boiling; reduce heat. Simmer, uncovered, about 15 minutes or until slightly thickened, stirring occasionally. Meanwhile, finely chop the remaining peach; stir into sauce. Stir in thyme.

three To use, serve with pork, ham, poultry, or fish.

NUTRITION FACTS PER ¼ CUP: 70 cal., 0 g total fat (0 g sat. fat), 0 mg chol., 0 mg sodium, 19 g carbo., 1 g fiber, 0 g pro.

Portobello Sauce

START TO FINISH: 10 minutes **MAKES:** about ¾ cup

- 2 large fresh portobello mushrooms, halved and sliced
- 8 green onions, cut into 1-inch pieces
- 1 tablespoon butter or margarine
- ⅓ cup beef broth
- 2 tablespoons Madeira or port

one In a large skillet cook and stir mushrooms and green onions in melted butter over medium heat about 5 minutes or until tender. Stir in broth and Madeira. Bring to boiling.

two To use, serve with beef, ham, lamb, or poultry.

NUTRITION FACTS PER ¼ CUP: 53 cal., 4 g total fat (2 g sat. fat), 7 mg chol., 84 mg sodium, 4 g carbo., 1 g fiber, 2 g pro.

serve-along sides simple sauces, salsas & rubs **253**

Raspberry Piquant Sauce

START TO FINISH: 15 minutes **MAKES:** about ⅓ cup

3   tablespoons bottled chili sauce

2   tablespoons seedless raspberry spreadable fruit

1   tablespoon orange juice or apple juice

1½   teaspoons brown mustard

one In a small saucepan combine chili sauce, spreadable fruit, orange juice, and mustard. Cook and stir over low heat until spreadable fruit melts.

two To use, serve with beef, pork, ham, or poultry.

NUTRITION FACTS PER TABLESPOON: 29 cal., 0 g total fat (0 g sat. fat), 0 mg chol., 141 mg sodium, 7 g carbo., 1 g fiber, 0 g pro.

Currant Sauce

START TO FINISH: 10 minutes **MAKES:** about ½ cup

¼   cup currant jelly

3   tablespoons ketchup

1   tablespoon vinegar

⅛   teaspoon ground cinnamon

      Dash ground cloves

one In a small saucepan combine currant jelly, ketchup, vinegar, cinnamon, and cloves. Cook and stir just until boiling.

two To use, serve with beef, pork, ham, or poultry.

NUTRITION FACTS PER TABLESPOON: 33 cal., 0 g total fat (0 g sat. fat), 0 mg chol., 69 mg sodium, 8 g carbo., 0 g fiber, 0 g pro.

Easy Plum-Mustard Sauce

START TO FINISH: 10 minutes **MAKES:** about 1½ cups

1   18-ounce jar red plum jam

2   tablespoons honey mustard or Dijon-style mustard

⅛   teaspoon black pepper

one In a small saucepan cook and stir red plum jam over medium-low heat until bubbly. Stir in mustard and pepper.

two To use, serve with pork, ham, or poultry.

NUTRITION FACTS PER 2 TABLESPOONS: 123 cal., 0 g total fat (0 g sat. fat), 0 mg chol., 16 mg sodium, 30 g carbo., 0 g fiber, 0 g pro.

Papaya Salsa

PREP: 20 minutes **CHILL:** 2 to 24 hours **MAKES:** about 2 cups

1⅓ cups coarsely chopped papaya or mango

⅔   cup chopped red sweet pepper and/or chopped peeled jicama

2   tablespoons pineapple juice or orange juice

1   tablespoon snipped fresh cilantro or parsley

1   fresh serrano chile pepper, seeded and finely chopped (see tip, page 59)

one In a small bowl combine papaya, red sweet pepper, pineapple juice, cilantro, and serrano pepper. Cover and chill for 2 to 24 hours.

two To use, serve with pork, poultry, fish, or shellfish.

NUTRITION FACTS PER ¼ CUP: 18 cal., 0 g total fat (0 g sat. fat), 0 mg chol., 2 mg sodium, 4 g carbo., 1 g fiber, 0 g pro.

Pineapple Relish

PREP: 15 minutes **CHILL:** 2 to 24 hours **STAND:** 30 minutes
MAKES: 2 cups

1   cup chopped fresh pineapple

½   cup chopped red sweet pepper

¼   cup chopped green onion

3   tablespoons snipped fresh cilantro

½   to 1 fresh jalapeño chile pepper, seeded and finely chopped (see tip, page 59)

one In a small bowl combine pineapple, red sweet pepper, green onion, cilantro, and jalapeño pepper. Cover and chill for 2 to 24 hours.

two To use, let stand at room temperature for 30 minutes. Serve with pork, ham, poultry, or fish.

NUTRITION FACTS PER TABLESPOOON: 4 cal., 0 g total fat (0 g sat. fat), 0 mg chol., 1 mg sodium, 1 g carbo., 0 g fiber, 0 g pro.

Pico de Gallo

PREP: 10 minutes **CHILL:** 2 to 24 hours **MAKES:** 1¼ cups

2   medium ripe tomatoes, peeled and finely chopped

2   tablespoons finely chopped red onion

2   tablespoons snipped fresh cilantro

⅛   teaspoon salt

Dash sugar

one In a small bowl combine tomatoes, red onion, cilantro, salt, and sugar. Cover and chill for 2 to 24 hours.

two To use, serve with beef, pork, poultry, fish, shellfish, or tortilla chips.

NUTRITION FACTS PER TABLESPOON: 3 cal., 0 g total fat (0 g sat. fat), 0 mg chol., 16 mg sodium, 1 g carbo., 0 g fiber, 0 g pro.

Grilled Sweet Pepper Relish

PREP: 10 minutes **GRILL:** 8 minutes **MAKES:** about 1 cup

- 1   red or yellow sweet pepper, cut into strips
- 1   medium onion, thinly sliced
- 1   tablespoon red wine vinegar
- 2   teaspoons olive oil
- 1/8 teaspoon black pepper

one Tear off a 24×18-inch piece of heavy foil; fold in half to make an 18×12-inch rectangle. Place sweet pepper and onion in center of foil. Drizzle with vinegar and olive oil; sprinkle with black pepper.

two Bring up two opposite edges of foil and seal with a double fold. Fold remaining edges together to completely enclose vegetables, leaving space for steam to build.

three For a charcoal grill, grill foil packet on the rack of an uncovered grill directly over medium coals for 8 minutes, turning packet once halfway through grilling. (For a gas grill, preheat grill. Reduce heat to medium. Place foil packet on grill rack over heat. Cover and grill as above.)

four To use, serve with beef, pork, poultry, or fish.

NUTRITION FACTS PER 1/4 CUP: 36 cal., 2 g total fat (0 g sat. fat), 0 mg chol., 1 mg sodium, 4 g carbo., 1 g fiber, 1 g pro.

Pear-Chutney Salsa

START TO FINISH: 10 minutes **MAKES:** 2 cups

- 3   tablespoons bottled chutney
- 1   medium pear, peeled, cored, and chopped
- 1/2 cup peeled, seeded, and chopped cucumber
- 1/2 cup bottled chunky salsa
- 2   tablespoons slivered almonds, toasted (see tip, page 280)

one Cut up any large pieces in chutney. In a small bowl combine chutney, pear, cucumber, and salsa. If desired, cover and chill until ready to serve.

two To use, stir in almonds before serving. Serve with pork, ham, or poultry.

NUTRITION FACTS PER TABLESPOON: 12 cal., 0 g total fat (0 g sat. fat), 0 mg chol., 10 mg sodium, 2 g carbo., 0 g fiber, 0 g pro.

Strawberry Salsa

START TO FINISH: 10 minutes **MAKES:** 2 cups

- 1/4 cup apricot jam or preserves
- 1/4 teaspoon ground cinnamon
- 2   cups chopped strawberries

one In a small bowl combine apricot jam and cinnamon. Stir in strawberries. Let stand for a few minutes to blend flavors.

two To use, serve over waffles, pancakes, French toast, or hot cereal, or stir into yogurt.

NUTRITION FACTS PER 1/2 CUP: 78 cal., 0 g total fat (0 g sat. fat), 0 mg chol., 7 mg sodium, 19 g carbo., 2 g fiber, 1 g pro.

Zucchini-Tomato Relish

START TO FINISH: 10 minutes **MAKES:** about 2 cups

- 1   cup chopped tomato
- 1   cup chopped zucchini
- 2   teaspoons olive oil
- 1   teaspoon balsamic vinegar
- 1   clove garlic, minced

one In a small bowl combine tomato, zucchini, oil, vinegar, and garlic. If desired, cover and chill for up to 24 hours.

two To use, serve with beef, pork, lamb, or poultry.

NUTRITION FACTS PER ½ CUP: 9 cal., 1 g total fat (0 g sat. fat), 0 mg chol., 1 mg sodium, 1 g carbo., 0 g fiber, 0 g pro.

Cranberry-Apple-Orange Relish

PREP: 20 minutes **CHILL:** 8 hours **MAKES:** 5 cups

- 4   medium tart apples, cored and cut up
- 2   cups fresh or frozen cranberries
- 2   small navel oranges, peeled and sectioned
- 1   to 1½ cups sugar

one Place apples, cranberries, and oranges, one-fourth at a time, in a food processor. Cover and process with on/off pulses until fruit is coarsely chopped. In a large bowl combine coarsely chopped fruit and sugar. Cover and chill for at least 8 hours.

two To use, stir before serving. Serve with pork, ham, or poultry.

NUTRITION FACTS PER ¼ CUP: 59 cal., 0 g total fat (0 g sat. fat), 0 mg chol., 3 mg sodium, 16 g carbo., 2 g fiber, 0 g pro.

Mango-Habañero Mojo

START TO FINISH: 15 minutes **MAKES:** about 1⅓ cups

- 2   ripe mangoes, seeded, peeled, and chopped
- ½   cup Chardonnay or other dry white wine
- 2   tablespoons orange juice
- ½   of a fresh habañero or Scotch bonnet chile pepper, seeded and finely chopped (see tip, page 59)

one In a blender or food processor combine mangoes, wine, and orange juice. Cover and blend or process until smooth.

two Strain mixture through a medium-fine mesh sieve to remove fruit pulp. Stir in habañero pepper. Cover and chill until ready to serve.

three To use, serve with pork, ham, poultry, or fish.

NUTRITION FACTS PER ⅓ CUP: 93 cal., 0 g total fat (0 g sat. fat), 0 mg chol., 4 mg sodium, 19 g carbo., 2 g fiber, 1 g pro.

Herb Rub

START TO FINISH: 10 minutes
MAKES: enough for 5 pounds of meat, poultry, fish, or shellfish

- 2 teaspoons dried rosemary
- 2 teaspoons dried thyme
- 2 teaspoons dried minced onion
- 2 teaspoons dried minced garlic
- 1 teaspoon salt
- ¾ teaspoon black pepper

one In a blender combine rosemary, thyme, onion, garlic, salt, and pepper. Cover and blend until coarsely ground.

two To use, sprinkle rub evenly over beef, pork, lamb, poultry, fish, or shellfish; rub in with your fingers.

NUTRITION FACTS PER TEASPOON: 7 cal., 0 g total fat (0 g sat. fat), 0 mg chol., 233 mg sodium, 1 g carbo., 0 g fiber, 0 g pro.

Mustard-Peppercorn Rub

PREP: 10 minutes **MARINATE:** 15 minutes to 4 hours
MAKES: enough for 3 pounds of meat

- 1 tablespoon coarse-grain brown mustard
- 2 teaspoons cracked black pepper
- 2 teaspoons snipped fresh tarragon
- 2 teaspoons olive oil
- 1 teaspoon coarse salt

one In a small bowl combine mustard, pepper, tarragon, olive oil, and salt.

two To use, spoon rub over beef, pork, or lamb; rub in with your fingers. Cover and marinate in the refrigerator for 15 minutes to 4 hours.

NUTRITION FACTS PER TEASPOON: 12 cal., 1 g total fat (0 g sat. fat), 0 mg chol., 237 mg sodium, 0 g carbo., 0 g fiber, 0 g pro.

Ginger-Allspice Rub

START TO FINISH: 10 minutes **MAKES:** enough for 1 pound of fish

- 1 tablespoon lime juice
- 1 tablespoon water
- 1 teaspoon paprika
- ½ teaspoon salt
- ¼ teaspoon ground ginger
- ¼ teaspoon ground allspice
- ¼ teaspoon black pepper

one In a small bowl combine lime juice and water. For rub, in another small bowl combine paprika, salt, ginger, allspice, and pepper.

two To use, brush lime juice mixture onto fish. Sprinkle rub evenly over fish; rub in with your fingers.

NUTRITION FACTS PER TEASPOON: 8 cal., 0 g total fat (0 g sat. fat), 0 mg chol., 583 mg sodium, 2 g carbo., 1 g fiber, 0 g pro.

Spanish Olive Rub

START TO FINISH: 10 minutes **MAKES:** enough for 1 pound of meat

½ cup pimiento-stuffed green olives

1 tablespoon capers, drained

3 cloves garlic, chopped

1½ teaspoons finely shredded orange peel

½ teaspoon black pepper

one In a blender or food processor combine olives, capers, garlic, orange peel, and pepper. Cover and blend or process until chunky.

two To use, spoon rub over beef, pork, or lamb; rub in with your fingers.

NUTRITION FACTS PER TEASPOON: 7 cal., 1 g total fat (0 g sat. fat), 0 mg chol., 78 mg sodium, 0 g carbo., 0 g fiber, 0 g pro.

Barbecue Rub

START TO FINISH: 5 minutes
MAKES: enough for 4 pounds of meat or poultry

2 tablespoons barbecue seasoning

1 tablespoon garlic powder

1 teaspoon onion salt

½ teaspoon celery seeds, ground

¼ teaspoon cayenne pepper

one In a small bowl combine barbecue seasoning, garlic powder, onion salt, ground celery seeds, and cayenne pepper.

two To use, sprinkle rub evenly over beef, pork, lamb, or poultry; rub in with your fingers.

NUTRITION FACTS PER TEASPOON: 4 cal., 0 g total fat (0 g sat. fat), 0 mg chol., 658 mg sodium, 1 g carbo., 0 g fiber, 0 g pro.

Curry Rub

PREP: 5 minutes **MARINATE:** 2 to 6 hours
MAKES: enough for 4 pounds of pork or poultry

⅓ cup sugar

2 teaspoons paprika

1 teaspoon curry powder

1 teaspoon black pepper

½ teaspoon salt

one In a small bowl combine sugar, paprika, curry powder, pepper, and salt.

two To use, sprinkle rub evenly over pork or poultry; rub in with your fingers. Cover and marinate in the refrigerator for 2 to 6 hours.

NUTRITION FACTS PER TEASPOON: 12 cal., 0 g total fat (0 g sat. fat), 0 mg chol., 49 mg sodium, 3 g carbo., 0 g fiber, 0 g pro.

Balsamic-Mustard Marinade

PREP: 5 minutes **MARINATE:** 2 to 4 hours
MAKES: enough for 3 pounds of meat or poultry

- ¼ cup Dijon-style mustard
- ¼ cup balsamic vinegar
- 2 teaspoons cracked black pepper

one In a small bowl combine mustard, vinegar, and pepper.

two To use, pour over beef, pork, or poultry in a resealable plastic bag; seal bag. Marinate in the refrigerator for 2 to 4 hours, turning bag occasionally. Drain meat or poultry, discarding marinade.

NUTRITION FACTS PER TABLESPOOON: 19 cal., 0 g total fat (0 g sat. fat), 0 mg chol., 182 mg sodium, 4 g carbo., 0 g fiber, 2 g pro.

Beer Marinade

PREP: 10 minutes **MARINATE:** 4 to 24 hours
MAKES: enough for 3 pounds of meat

- 1 cup beer or apple cider
- 2 tablespoons packed brown sugar
- 1 tablespoon Worcestershire sauce
- 2 teaspoons chili powder
- 1 clove garlic, minced

one In a small bowl combine beer, brown sugar, Worcestershire sauce, chili powder, and garlic.

two To use, pour over beef or pork in a resealable plastic bag; seal bag. Marinate in the refrigerator for 4 to 24 hours, turning bag occasionally. Drain meat, discarding marinade.

NUTRITION FACTS PER TABLESPOON: 13 cal., 0 g total fat (0 g sat. fat), 0 mg chol., 15 mg sodium, 2 g carbo., 0 g fiber, 0 g pro.

Citrus-Honey Marinade

PREP: 10 minutes **MARINATE:** 1 hour
MAKES: enough for 1 pound of pork, poultry, or fish

- ¼ cup orange juice
- 2 tablespoons lemon juice
- 2 tablespoons Dijon-style mustard
- 2 tablespoons honey
- 1 tablespoon soy sauce

one In a small bowl combine orange juice, lemon juice, mustard, honey, and soy sauce.

two To use, pour over pork, poultry, or fish in a resealable plastic bag; seal bag. Marinate in the refrigerator for 1 hour, turning bag occasionally. Drain pork, poultry, or fish, reserving marinade.

three Grill or broil pork, poultry, or fish, brushing occasionally with marinade during the first half of grilling or broiling. Discard any remaining marinade.

NUTRITION FACTS PER TABLESPOON: 18 cal., 0 g total fat (0 g sat. fat), 0 mg chol., 149 mg sodium, 4 g carbo., 0 g fiber, 0 g pro.

Lemon-Rosemary Marinade

PREP: 10 minutes **MARINATE:** 2 to 24 hours
MAKES: enough for 1 pound of pork, poultry, or fish

⅓ cup bottled oil-and-vinegar salad dressing
1 teaspoon finely shredded lemon peel
1 tablespoon lemon juice
1 teaspoon snipped fresh rosemary or
   ¼ teaspoon dried rosemary, crushed
1 teaspoon snipped fresh thyme or
   ¼ teaspoon dried thyme, crushed

one In a small bowl combine salad dressing, lemon peel, lemon juice, rosemary, and thyme.

two To use, pour over pork, poultry, or fish in a resealable plastic bag; seal bag. Marinate in the refrigerator for 2 hours for fish or 3 to 24 hours for pork or poultry, turning bag occasionally. Drain pork, poultry, or fish, discarding marinade.

NUTRITION FACTS PER TABLESPOON: 68 cal., 7 g total fat (1 g sat. fat), 0 mg chol., 67 mg sodium, 1 g carbo., 0 g fiber, 0 g pro.

Espresso Marinade

PREP: 10 minutes **MARINATE:** 2 to 24 hours
MAKES: enough for 1½ pounds of meat or poultry

½ cup chopped onion
½ cup bottled steak sauce or hickory-flavor barbecue
   sauce
¼ to ⅓ cup strong brewed espresso or coffee
2 tablespoons Worcestershire sauce

one In a small bowl combine onion, steak sauce, espresso, and Worcestershire sauce.

two To use, pour over beef, lamb, or poultry in a resealable plastic bag; seal bag. Marinate in the refrigerator for 2 to 24 hours, turning bag occasionally. Drain meat or poultry, discarding marinade.

NUTRITION FACTS PER TABLESPOON: 7 cal., 0 g total fat (0 g sat. fat), 0 mg chol., 101 mg sodium, 2 g carbo., 0 g fiber, 0 g pro.

Sherry Marinade

PREP: 10 minutes **MARINATE:** 30 minutes
MAKES: enough for 1 pound of pork, fish, or shellfish

2 tablespoons cooking oil
2 tablespoons dry sherry
2 tablespoons stone-ground mustard
1 tablespoon honey
1½ teaspoons soy sauce

one In a small bowl combine oil, sherry, mustard, honey, and soy sauce.

two To use, pour over pork, fish, or shellfish in a resealable plastic bag; seal bag. Marinate in the refrigerator for 30 minutes, turning bag once. Drain pork, fish, or shellfish, discarding marinade.

NUTRITION FACTS PER TABLESPOON: 48 cal., 3 g total fat (0 g sat. fat), 0 mg chol., 148 mg sodium, 2 g carbo., 0 g fiber, 0 g pro.

Tomato-Garlic Butter

START TO FINISH: 15 minutes **MAKES:** ½ cup

½	cup butter, softened
1	tablespoon oil-packed dried tomatoes, drained and finely snipped
1	tablespoon chopped pitted kalamata olives
1	tablespoon finely chopped green onion
1	clove garlic, minced

one In a small bowl combine butter, dried tomatoes, olives, green onion, and garlic. If desired, cover and chill until ready to serve.

two To use, let stand at room temperature for 30 minutes before serving, if chilled. Serve with beef, lamb, or poultry.

NUTRITION FACTS PER TABLESPOOON: 112 cal., 12 g total fat (8 g sat. fat), 33 mg chol., 138 mg sodium, 0 g carbo., 0 g fiber, 0 g pro.

Citrus Butter

START TO FINISH: 10 minutes **MAKES:** ½ cup

½	cup butter, softened
2	tablespoons snipped fresh parsley
1	tablespoon finely shredded lemon peel
1	tablespoon finely shredded orange peel
1	clove garlic, minced

one In a small bowl combine butter, parsley, lemon peel, orange peel, and garlic. If desired, cover and chill until ready to serve.

two To use, let stand at room temperature for 30 minutes before serving, if chilled. Serve with pork, poultry, fish, or shellfish.

NUTRITION FACTS PER TABLESPOOON: 103 cal., 12 g total fat (7 g sat. fat), 31 mg chol., 82 mg sodium, 1 g carbo., 0 g fiber, 0 g pro.

Blue Cheese Butter

START TO FINISH: 10 minutes **MAKES:** ½ cup

¼	cup butter, softened
¼	cup crumbled blue cheese (1 ounce)
1	tablespoon snipped fresh parsley
2	teaspoons snipped fresh basil
1	clove garlic, minced

one In a small bowl combine butter, blue cheese, parsley, basil, and garlic. If desired, cover and chill until ready to serve.

two To use, let stand at room temperature for 30 minutes before serving, if chilled. Serve with beef, lamb, poultry, or fish.

NUTRITION FACTS PER TABLESPOOON: 67 cal., 7 g total fat (4 g sat. fat), 18 mg chol., 100 mg sodium, 0 g carbo., 0 g fiber, 1 g pro.

Grilled Breen Beans, page 190

Honey-Glazed Carrots,
page 197

Herb-Grilled Tomatoes, page 213

Marinara-Sauced Pasta, page 215

Cheddary Corn Bread Rolls,
page 225

Focaccia Breadsticks, page 221

Green Onion Parker House Biscuits, page 227

Mixed Greens with Pears, page 230

Watermelon Salad with Watercress, page 231

Really Red Coleslaw, page 240

Hot-and-Sweet Pineapple Slaw, page 239

Mediterranean Salad, page 238

Fresh Corn and Tomato Salad,
page 236

Poppy Seed-Dressed Pasta Salad,
page 242

Beet Greens with Walnuts and Blue Cheese, page 229

Cookies-and-Cream Cupcakes,
page 312

Strawberry-Chocolate Cake, page 302

Fill-the-Grill Nectarine Toss, page 296

Bittersweet Chocolate Soufflé, page 326

Lemonade Ice Cream, page 298

Pineapple Fries with Raspberry Ketchup, page 288

Crispy Onion Rings, page 365

Tropical Fruit Dip, page 343

Spicy Chicken Fajita Bites,
page 356

Goat Cheese Pastry Rounds, page 361

Polynesian Glazed Wings, page 352

Minted Iced Tea, page 376

Hot and Spicy Cranberry Punch, page 371

All-American Fruit Smoothies, page 398

Arizona Corn Bread Cacti,
page 388

Dive-In Party Mix, page 395

Spare-Me Sugar Cookies, page 390

Something More S'More, page 393

Flip-Flop Cake, page 389

Mixed Berry Cobbler

PREP: 15 minutes **COOK:** Low 3 hours; plus 1 hour on High
STAND: 30 minutes **MAKES:** 8 to 10 servings

Nonstick cooking spray

1 21-ounce can blueberry pie filling

1 12-ounce package frozen mixed berries

¼ cup sugar

1 6½- or 7-ounce package blueberry or
   triple-berry muffin mix

⅓ cup water

2 tablespoons cooking oil

Vanilla ice cream (optional)

Give a Toast For a richer, fuller flavor, toast nuts, coconut, or sesame seeds by placing them in a single layer in a shallow baking pan. Bake in a 350°F oven for 5 to 10 minutes or until golden brown. Watch carefully and stir once or twice to keep them from burning.

one Lightly coat a 3½- or 4-quart slow cooker with cooking spray; set aside.

two In a medium bowl combine blueberry pie filling, frozen mixed berries, and sugar. Place berry mixture in the bottom of the prepared cooker.

three Cover and cook on low-heat setting for 3 hours. Turn to high-heat setting. In a medium bowl combine muffin mix, water, and oil; stir just until combined. Spoon muffin mixture over berry mixture.

four Cover and cook about 1 hour more or until a toothpick inserted into center of muffin mixture comes out clean. Remove liner from cooker, if possible, or turn off cooker. Let stand, uncovered, for 30 to 45 minutes to cool slightly before serving.

five To serve, spoon warm cobbler into 8 to 10 dessert dishes. If desired, top with scoops of vanilla ice cream.

NUTRITION FACTS PER SERVING: 250 cal., 6 g total fat (1 g sat. fat), 0 mg chol., 182 mg sodium, 48 g carbo., 5 g fiber, 1 g pro.

Pineapple-Peach Cobbler

PREP: 15 minutes **COOK:** High 2½ hours **STAND:** 30 minutes
MAKES: 8 servings

Nonstick cooking spray
2 21-ounce cans pineapple pie filling
1 6- or 7-ounce package dried peaches, snipped
½ cup orange juice
1 17½-ounce package (5) refrigerated large
   cinnamon rolls
Vanilla ice cream (optional)

one Lightly coat a 3½- or 4-quart slow cooker with cooking spray. In the prepared cooker combine pineapple pie filling, dried peaches, and orange juice.

two Cover and cook on high-heat setting about 1½ hours or until fruit mixture is hot and bubbly; stir fruit mixture. Place cinnamon rolls on a cutting board, cinnamon sides up (set icing aside). Cut each roll in half to make 2 semicircles. Place rolls, cinnamon sides up, on top of fruit mixture in cooker.

three Cover and cook on high-heat setting about 1 hour more or until rolls are fluffy all the way through. Remove liner from cooker, if possible, or turn off cooker. Let stand, uncovered, for 30 to 45 minutes to cool slightly before serving. Spread icing over rolls.

four To serve, spoon warm cobbler into 8 dessert dishes. If desired, top with scoops of vanilla ice cream.

NUTRITION FACTS PER SERVING: 467 cal., 8 g total fat (2 g sat. fat), 0 mg chol., 493 mg sodium, 96 g carbo., 2 g fiber, 4 g pro.

Granola-Nectarine Gratin

PREP: 15 minutes **BAKE:** 7 minutes **MAKES:** 6 servings

4 medium nectarines, pitted and sliced
½ cup blueberries
2 tablespoons orange liqueur or orange juice
2 tablespoons packed brown sugar
1½ cups granola with raisins and dates

one In a medium bowl combine nectarines, blueberries, and orange liqueur; toss gently to coat. Spoon fruit into 6 ungreased 12- to 16-ounce au gratin dishes or casseroles. Sprinkle with brown sugar.

two Bake, uncovered, in a 450°F oven for 7 to 8 minutes or until fruit is warm and most of the sugar is melted. Sprinkle with granola.

NUTRITION FACTS PER SERVING: 130 cal., 1 g total fat (0 g sat. fat), 0 mg chol., 10 mg sodium, 28 g carbo., 3 g fiber, 3 g pro.

Easy Fruit Cobbler

PREP: 15 minutes **BAKE:** 25 minutes **MAKES:** 2 servings

3   cups desired frozen fruit (such as sliced peaches,
    raspberries, and/or blueberries), thawed
2   tablespoons sugar
1   tablespoon quick-cooking tapioca
1   cup packaged biscuit mix
¼   cup milk
1   tablespoon sugar
1   tablespoon sugar (optional)
½   teaspoon ground cinnamon (optional)

one In medium bowl stir together undrained fruit, the 2 tablespoons sugar, and the tapioca. Divide fruit mixture between 2 ungreased 10-ounce ramekins or custard cups.

two In a small bowl stir together biscuit mix, milk, and 1 tablespoon sugar until combined. Spoon batter over fruit mixture. If desired, in small bowl combine 1 tablespoon sugar and the cinnamon; sprinkle over batter. Place ramekins in a shallow baking pan.

three Bake, uncovered, in a 400°F oven about 25 minutes or until filling is bubbly and topping is golden. Serve warm.

NUTRITION FACTS PER SERVING: 457 cal., 10 g total fat (3 g sat. fat), 2 mg chol., 755 mg sodium, 92 g carbo., 5 g fiber, 7 g pro.

Apricot-Peach Cobbler

PREP: 10 minutes **BAKE:** per package directions
MAKES: 6 servings

1   15-ounce can unpeeled apricot halves
    in light syrup, undrained
1   7¾-ounce packet cinnamon swirl biscuit mix
1   21-ounce can peach pie filling
1   teaspoon vanilla
    Vanilla ice cream (optional)

one Drain apricot halves, reserving syrup. Prepare biscuit mix according to package directions, except use ½ cup of the syrup for the water called for on the package. Bake according to package directions.

two Meanwhile, in a medium saucepan combine pie filling, apricot halves, and any remaining apricot syrup; heat through. Remove saucepan from heat; stir in vanilla. Spoon fruit mixture into 6 dessert dishes. Top with warm biscuits. If desired, serve with scoops of ice cream.

NUTRITION FACTS PER SERVING: 284 cal., 4 g total fat (0 g sat. fat), 0 mg chol. 346 mg sodium, 59 g carbo., 2 g fiber, 3 g pro.

Slow-Cooked Apple Betty

PREP: 25 minutes **COOK:** Low 4 hours **STAND:** 30 minutes
MAKES: 6 to 8 servings

Nonstick cooking spray

5   tart cooking apples, peeled, cored, and sliced (5 cups)

¾   cup packed brown sugar

⅔   cup apple butter

½   cup water

5   cups soft ½-inch cinnamon-raisin bread cubes

⅓   cup butter or margarine, melted

Caramel ice cream topping and/or vanilla ice cream (optional)

one Lightly coat a 3½- or 4-quart slow cooker with cooking spray; set aside.

two In a medium bowl combine apples, brown sugar, apple butter, and water; toss to coat. Place bread cubes in a medium bowl. Drizzle with melted butter; toss gently to combine.

three Place half of the buttered bread cubes in the prepared cooker. Pour all of the apple mixture over bread cubes. Sprinkle with the remaining bread cubes.

four Cover and cook on low-heat setting for 4 hours. Remove liner from cooker, if possible, or turn off cooker. Let stand, uncovered, about 30 minutes to cool slightly before serving.

five To serve, spoon warm dessert into 6 to 8 dessert dishes. If desired, top with caramel ice cream topping and/or scoops of vanilla ice cream.*

NUTRITION FACTS PER SERVING: 492 cal., 12 g total fat (7 g sat. fat), 29 mg chol., 209 mg sodium, 97 g carbo., 5 g fiber, 2 g pro.

Easy Fruit Crisp

PREP: 20 minutes **BAKE:** 30 minutes **MAKES:** 6 servings

5   cups peeled and sliced apples, pears, or peaches or frozen unsweetened peach slices, thawed

¼   cup dried cherries, dried cranberries, or mixed dried fruit bits

2   tablespoons sugar

1½   cups granola

3   tablespoons butter or margarine, melted

one In an ungreased 2-quart square baking dish combine sliced fruit and dried fruit; sprinkle with sugar. In a small bowl combine granola and melted butter; sprinkle over fruit.

two Bake, uncovered, in a 350°F oven for 30 to 35 minutes or until fruit is tender. Serve warm.

NUTRITION FACTS PER SERVING: 306 cal., 13 g total fat (5 g sat. fat), 16 mg chol., 66 mg sodium, 46 g carbo., 5 g fiber, 3 g pro.

Roasted Mango with Coconut

PREP: 15 minutes **BAKE:** 10 minutes **MAKES:** 4 servings

- 2 medium ripe mangoes, seeded, peeled, and cubed
- 2 tablespoons flaked coconut
- 2 teaspoons finely shredded orange peel
- 2 teaspoons finely chopped crystallized ginger

one Place mango cubes in 4 ungreased 6-ounce custard cups. For topping, in a small bowl combine coconut, orange peel, and crystallized ginger. Sprinkle topping over mango cubes.

two Bake, uncovered, in a 350°F oven about 10 minutes or just until topping starts to brown.

NUTRITION FACTS PER SERVING: 89 cal., 2 g total fat (1 g sat. fat), 0 mg chol., 14 mg sodium, 20 g carbo., 2 g fiber, 1 g pro.

Quick Strawberry Shortcakes

PREP: 20 minutes **BAKE:** per package directions
MAKES: 4 servings

- 4 frozen unbaked buttermilk biscuits
- ⅓ cup strawberry jelly
- 2 cups strawberries, sliced
- ⅓ cup lemon curd or strawberry curd
- Sweetened whipped cream

one Bake biscuits according to package directions. Cool on a wire rack.

two In a small saucepan heat jelly just until it melts. Place strawberries in a medium bowl. Drizzle with melted jelly; toss gently to coat. Set aside.

three Split biscuits horizontally. Spread biscuit bottoms with lemon curd; replace tops. Place biscuits on 4 dessert plates. Spoon strawberries over biscuits and top with whipped cream.

NUTRITION FACTS PER SERVING: 472 cal., 22 g total fat (10 g sat. fat), 61 mg chol., 619 mg sodium, 48 g carbo., 5 g fiber, 5 g pro.

Praline Baked Apples

PREP: 20 minutes BAKE: 30 minutes MAKES: 4 servings

½   cup apple juice

¼   teaspoon ground cinnamon

4   small red baking apples

¼   cup pecans or walnuts, coarsely chopped

¼   cup packed brown sugar

one In a small bowl combine apple juice and ⅛ teaspoon of the cinnamon. Divide mixture among 4 ungreased 6-ounce custard cups. Core apples; remove 1 inch of peel from the top of each apple. Place apples in the custard cups.

two Place custard cups in a shallow baking pan. In a small bowl combine nuts, brown sugar, and remaining ⅛ teaspoon cinnamon. Sprinkle over apples. Bake, covered, in a 350°F oven for 30 to 40 minutes or until apples are tender.

NUTRITION FACTS PER SERVING: 195 cal., 5 g total fat (1 g sat. fat), 0 mg chol., 6 mg sodium, 39 g carbo., 4 g fiber, 1 g pro.

GRILLING

Gorgonzola-Walnut-Stuffed Apples

PREP: 20 minutes GRILL: 30 minutes MAKES: 4 servings

4   medium cooking apples (such as Granny Smith or Jonathan)

¼   cup crumbled Gorgonzola, Stilton, or Roquefort cheese (1 ounce)

¼   cup chopped walnuts

2   tablespoons butter or margarine, melted

4   teaspoons honey
     Honey (optional)

one Core apples almost to the bottoms, leaving about ½-inch bases. Remove 1 inch of peel from the top of each apple.

two In a small bowl combine Gorgonzola cheese, walnuts, and melted butter. Spoon three-fourths of the cheese mixture into centers of apples. Drizzle 1 teaspoon honey into each center. Spoon the remaining cheese mixture into centers of apples. Place apples in a disposable foil pan.

three For a charcoal grill, arrange medium-hot coals around edge of grill. Test for medium heat above center of grill. Place foil pan on grill rack over center of grill. Cover and grill for 30 to 40 minutes or until apples are tender. (For a gas grill, preheat grill. Reduce heat to medium. Adjust for indirect cooking. Grill as above.)

four If desired, drizzle with additional honey. Serve warm.

NUTRITION FACTS PER SERVING: 218 cal., 13 g total fat (5 g sat. fat), 21 mg chol., 142 mg sodium, 26 g carbo., 4 g fiber, 3 g pro.

Cream-Topped Pears in Orange Sauce

PREP: 15 minutes **COOK:** Low 4 hours, High 2 hours
STAND: 30 minutes **MAKES:** 8 servings

- ¾ cup orange juice
- 6 tablespoons orange marmalade
- 2 teaspoons quick-cooking tapioca
- 8 small to medium firm ripe pears, peeled, cored, and quartered
- 1 cup whipping cream

one For sauce, in a 3½- or 4-quart slow cooker combine orange juice, 4 tablespoons of the marmalade, and the tapioca. Add pears; toss gently to coat.

two Cover and cook on low-heat setting for 4 to 5 hours or on high-heat setting for 2 to 2½ hours. Remove liner from cooker, if possible, or turn off cooker. Let stand, uncovered, about 30 minutes to cool slightly before serving.

three In a medium bowl combine whipping cream and the remaining 2 tablespoons marmalade. Beat with an electric mixer on medium speed until soft peaks form (tips curl).

four To serve, spoon pears and orange sauce into 8 dessert dishes. Top with whipped cream mixture.

NUTRITION FACTS PER SERVING: 221 cal., 12 g total fat (7 g sat. fat), 41 mg chol., 20 mg sodium, 31 g carbo., 3 g fiber, 1 g pro.

Mocha Pears

PREP: 10 minutes **COOK:** 15 minutes **CHILL:** 4 hours
MAKES: 6 servings

- 2 16-ounce cans or one 29-ounce can pear halves in heavy syrup (12 pear halves), undrained
- 2 teaspoons instant coffee crystals
- 1 teaspoon vanilla
- ¾ cup vanilla low-fat yogurt
   Miniature semisweet chocolate pieces

one Drain pears, reserving syrup. Place pears in a medium bowl; set aside. In a small saucepan combine the syrup and coffee crystals.

two Bring to boiling; reduce heat. Simmer, uncovered, about 15 minutes or until mixture is slightly thickened and reduced to ½ cup. Remove from heat. Stir in vanilla. Pour mixture over pears. Cover and chill for at least 4 hours, turning pears once.

three Using a slotted spoon, remove pear halves from coffee mixture. Divide pear halves among 6 dessert dishes; drizzle with coffee mixture. Top with yogurt and chocolate pieces.

NUTRITION FACTS PER SERVING: 168 cal., 2 g total fat (1 g sat. fat), 2 mg chol., 30 mg sodium, 37 g carbo., 3 g fiber, 2 g pro.

Poached Pears in Cran-Amaretto Sauce

PREP: 25 minutes **COOK:** Low 4 hours, High 2 hours
STAND: 30 minutes **MAKES:** 6 servings

1½   cups fresh or frozen cranberries

⅔   cup water

½   cup sugar

⅓   cup amaretto or hazelnut liqueur

6   medium ripe pears, peeled, cored, and halved

Vanilla ice cream (optional)

Sliced almonds, toasted (see tip, page 280)
(optional)

one For sauce, in a 3½- or 4-quart slow cooker combine cranberries, water, sugar, and amaretto. Add pears, stirring to coat.

two Cover and cook on low-heat setting for 4 to 5 hours or on high-heat setting for 2 to 2½ hours. Remove liner from cooker, if possible, or turn off cooker. Let stand, uncovered, about 30 minutes to cool slightly before serving.

three To serve, divide cranberry sauce among 6 dessert dishes; place 2 pear halves in each dish. If desired, serve with ice cream and sprinkle with toasted almonds.

NUTRITION FACTS PER SERVING: 241 cal., 4 g total fat (0 g sat. fat), 0 mg chol., 1 mg sodium, 49 g carbo., 6 g fiber, 2 g pro.

Dessert Burritos

PREP: 10 minutes **GRILL:** 13 minutes **COOL:** 5 minutes
MAKES: 4 servings

4   9- to 10-inch flour tortillas

¼   cup caramel ice cream topping

1   medium ripe banana, sliced

½   cup crushed chocolate sandwich cookies with
white filling

2   tablespoons butter or margarine, melted

Desired jam and/or whipped cream (optional)

one Wrap tortillas in foil. For a charcoal grill, grill tortilla packet on the rack of an uncovered grill directly over medium coals about 10 minutes or until warm, turning once halfway through grilling. Spread 1 tablespoon caramel topping down center of each tortilla. Top with 3 or 4 banana slices and 2 tablespoons crushed cookies. Fold one-third of the tortilla over filling. Fold in ends and roll up, forming a burrito. Secure with wooden toothpicks. Brush with melted butter.

two Grill burritos directly over medium coals for 3 to 4 minutes more or until tortillas are lightly browned, turning once halfway through grilling. (For a gas grill, preheat grill. Reduce heat to medium. Place tortilla packet and burritos on grill rack over heat. Cover and grill as above.)

three Remove burritos from grill; cool about 5 minutes. If desired, serve with jam and/or whipped cream.

NUTRITION FACTS PER SERVING: 358 cal., 13 g total fat (5 g sat. fat), 16 mg chol., 382 mg sodium, 56 g carbo., 3 g fiber, 4 g pro.

DELECTABLE DESSERTS

Pineapple Fries
with Raspberry Ketchup *See photo on page 273.*

PREP: 25 minutes **GRILL:** 5 minutes **MAKES:** 6 servings

- 1 medium fresh pineapple
- 2 cups frozen raspberries, thawed
- 1 to 2 tablespoons sugar
     Nonstick cooking spray
- 6 giant waffle ice cream cones

one Remove crown and cut off top and base of pineapple. Cut off wide strips of peel. Remove eyes by cutting narrow wedge-shape grooves diagonally around fruit, following pattern of the eyes. Slice pineapple lengthwise into ½-inch slices. Coarsely chop ⅓ cup of the pineapple from an end piece. Set remaining slices aside.

two For ketchup, in a blender combine raspberries and suga Cover and blend until smooth. Press berry mixture through a sieve; discard seeds. Return berry mixture to blender. Add the ⅓ cup chopped pineapple. Cover and blend until smooth. Cover and chill ketchup until ready to serve.

three Lightly coat pineapple slices with nonstick cooking spray. For a charcoal grill, grill pineapple slices on the rack of an uncovered grill directly over hot coals for 5 to 7 minutes or until lightly browned, turning once halfway through grilling (For a gas grill, preheat grill. Place pineapple slices on grill rack over high heat. Cover and grill as above.)

four Remove pineapple slices from grill; cool slightly. Cut grilled pineapple into about ½-inch strips. Divide pineapple fries among waffle cones; top with some of the ketchup. Pass the remaining ketchup.

NUTRITION FACTS PER SERVING: 158 cal., 1 g total fat (0 g sat. fat), 0 mg cho 36 mg sodium, 35 g carbo., 5 g fiber, 2 g pro.

Strawberries with Lime Dip

START TO FINISH: 10 minutes **MAKES:** 8 servings

- 1 8-ounce carton light dairy sour cream
- 2 tablespoons powdered sugar
- 2 teaspoons finely shredded lime peel
- 1 tablespoon lime juice
- 3 cups strawberries

one In a small bowl stir together sour cream, powdered sugar, lime peel, and lime juice.

two Wash strawberries but do not remove stems or caps. Drain strawberries on several layers of paper towels.

three Serve berries with sour cream mixture for dipping.

NUTRITION FACTS PER SERVING: 62 cal., 2 g total fat (1 g sat. fat), 9 mg chol. 19 mg sodium, 8 g carbo., 1 g fiber, 2 g pro.

Banana Split Trifles

START TO FINISH: 15 minutes **MAKES:** 4 servings

2   to 3 cups tin roof sundae, chocolate chunk, or
    vanilla ice cream

4   soft-style oatmeal or chocolate chip cookies,
    crumbled

⅔   cup hot fudge ice cream topping and/or strawberry
    preserves

½   cup whipped cream

2   small bananas, halved lengthwise and cut into
    1- to 2-inch pieces

one In a chilled medium bowl stir ice cream just enough to soften, pressing it against side of bowl with a wooden spoon.

two To assemble, in 4 parfait glasses layer half of the cookie crumbs, half of the ice cream, and half of the fudge topping and/or preserves.

three Add the remaining cookie crumbs, the remaining ice cream, the whipped cream, banana pieces, and the remaining fudge topping and/or preserves. If desired, cover and freeze for up to 1 hour.

NUTRITION FACTS PER SERVING: 524 cal., 23 g total fat (12 g sat. fat), 48 mg chol., 161 mg sodium, 73 g carbo., 3 g fiber, 6 g pro.

Cheesecake-Fruit Parfaits

PREP: 15 minutes **CHILL:** 1 to 24 hours **MAKES:** 4 to 6 servings

1   8-ounce package cream cheese, softened

½   cup dairy sour cream

⅔   cup powdered sugar

½   teaspoon vanilla (optional)

2   to 3 cups raspberries, blueberries, and/or sliced
    strawberries

4   to 6 cookies, crumbled

one For sauce, in a medium bowl combine cream cheese and sour cream. Beat with an electric mixer on low to medum speed until fluffy. Add powdered sugar and, if desired, vanilla; beat until smooth. Cover and chill for 1 to 24 hours.

two To serve, layer berries, sauce, and crumbled cookies in 4 to 6 parfait glasses.

NUTRITION FACTS PER SERVING: 371 cal., 26 g total fat (16 g sat. fat), 79 mg chol., 199 mg sodium, 30 g carbo., 4 g fiber, 6 g pro.

Red, White, and Blue Parfaits

START TO FINISH: 15 minutes **MAKES:** 6 servings

1	cup vanilla low-fat yogurt
¼	teaspoon almond extract or ½ teaspoon vanilla
½	of an 8-ounce container frozen light whipped dessert topping, thawed
3	cups raspberries and/or cut-up strawberries
3	cups blueberries

one In a medium bowl stir together yogurt and almond extract. Fold in whipped topping.

two To assemble, in 6 parfait glasses or dessert dishes alternately layer berries and yogurt mixture. If desired, cover and chill for up to 1 hour.

NUTRITION FACTS PER SERVING: 129 cal., 3 g total fat (2 g sat. fat), 2 mg chol., 26 mg sodium, 21 g carbo., 8 g fiber, 3 g pro.

Strawberry-Lime Fool

START TO FINISH: 20 minutes **MAKES:** 6 servings

4	cups strawberries, quartered (3 cups)
½	cup whipping cream
1	tablespoon sugar
¼	teaspoon finely shredded lime peel
	Lime wedges

one In a shallow dish mash 1 cup of the strawberries with a potato masher. In a medium bowl beat whipping cream, sugar, and lime peel with an electric mixer until stiff peaks form (tips stand straight). Fold in mashed strawberries.

two To assemble, in 6 dessert glasses or dishes layer whipped cream mixture and the remaining strawberries. Top with lime wedges. If desired, cover and chill for up to 2 hours.

NUTRITION FACTS PER SERVING: 114 cal., 8 g total fat (5 g sat. fat), 27 mg chol., 9 mg sodium, 11 g carbo., 3 g fiber, 1 g pro.

Mango-Papaya Fool: Prepare as directed, except substitute 3 cups seeded, peeled, and chopped mangoes and/or papayas for the 3 cups strawberries and ⅛ teaspoon ground nutmeg for the lime peel; omit the lime wedges.

NUTRITION FACTS PER SERVING: 131 cal., 8 g fat (5 g sat. fat), 27 mg chol., 9 mg sodium, 17 g carbo., 1 g fiber, 1 g pro.

Blueberry-Kiwi Fool: Prepare as directed, except substitute 2 cups blueberries for the 3 cups strawberries and ⅛ teaspoon ground cinnamon for the lime peel. Toss 1 cup peeled and cut-up kiwifruit with the whole blueberries. Layer whipped cream mixture and fruit mixture; omit lime wedges.

NUTRITION FACTS PER SERVING: 122 cal., 8 g fat (5 g sat. fat), 27 mg chol., 12 mg sodium, 14 g carbo., 2 g fiber, 1 g pro.

Mango Cream

START TO FINISH: 20 minutes **MAKES:** 6 servings

- 1 26-ounce jar refrigerated mango slices, drained
- 3 tablespoons sugar
- 1 tablespoon lemon juice
- 1 cup whipping cream
- 2 oranges, peeled and sectioned

one Place mango in a blender or food processor; cover and blend or process until smooth. Add 2 tablespoons of the sugar and the lemon juice; cover and blend or process until combined. Transfer mixture to a medium bowl; set aside.

two In a small bowl combine whipping cream and the remaining 1 tablespoon sugar. Beat with an electric mixer on medium speed until soft peaks form (tips curl). Fold whipped cream into mango mixture. Spoon into 6 dessert glasses or dishes; top with oranges. If desired cover and chill for up to 4 hours.

NUTRITION FACTS PER SERVING: 281 cal., 15 g total fat (9 g sat. fat), 55 mg chol., 20 mg sodium, 37 g carbo., 1 g fiber, 1 g pro.

Raspberry Whip

PREP: 10 minutes **CHILL:** 1¼ hours **MAKES:** 6 servings

- 1 cup fresh or frozen raspberries
- 1 cup boiling water
- 1 3-ounce package raspberry-flavor gelatin
- ⅔ cup cold water
- 1 6-ounce carton vanilla low-fat yogurt

one Thaw raspberries, if frozen; drain and set aside. In a medium bowl stir boiling water into gelatin until dissolved. Add cold water. Cover and chill about 45 minutes or until mixture is partially set (the consistency of unbeaten egg whites).

two Add yogurt. Beat with an electric mixer on medium speed for 1 to 2 minutes or until light and foamy. If necessary, chill mixture until it mounds when spooned.

three Meanwhile, divide half of the raspberries among 6 dessert dishes. Spoon gelatin mixture over berries. Top with the remaining raspberries. Chill about 30 minutes or until firm or cover and chill for up to 24 hours.

NUTRITION FACTS PER SERVING: 99 cal., 1 g total fat (0 g sat. fat), 2 mg chol., 65 mg sodium, 21 g carbo., 1 g fiber, 3 g pro.

Apricot-Peach Dessert Soup

PREP: 15 minutes **COOK:** Low 5 hours, High 2½ hours
STAND: 30 minutes **MAKES:** 10 servings

- 4 cups orange-peach-mango juice or orange-tangerine juice
- 1 16-ounce package frozen unsweetened peach slices
- 1 7-ounce package dried apricots, cut into 1-inch pieces
- 1 6-ounce package dried cherries and golden raisins
- 6 inches stick cinnamon

one In a 3½- or 4-quart slow cooker combine orange-peach-mango juice, frozen peaches, dried apricots, dried cherries and raisins, and cinnamon.

two Cover and cook on low-heat setting for 5 to 6 hours or on high-heat setting for 2½ to 3 hours.

three Remove liner from cooker, if possible, or turn off cooker Let stand, uncovered, for 30 to 45 minutes to cool slightly before serving. Remove stick cinnamon.

NUTRITION FACTS PER SERVING: 167 cal., 0 g total fat (0 g sat. fat), 0 mg chol 11 mg sodium, 42 g carbo., 3 g fiber, 2 g pro.

Double Berry Soup

START TO FINISH: 20 minutes **MAKES:** 4 servings

- 2 cups frozen unsweetened blueberries
- 1 10-ounce package frozen strawberries in syrup
- ½ teaspoon finely shredded orange peel (optional)
- ¾ cup orange juice
- 2 cups orange or other fruit sorbet or sherbet

one In a medium saucepan combine frozen blueberries with their syrup, half of the frozen strawberries with their syrup, the orange peel (if desired), and orange juice. Cook over medium heat for 4 to 5 minutes or just until berries are thawed, stirring occasionally. Remove from heat.

two Stir in the remaining frozen strawberries with their syrup; let stand for 5 minutes. Ladle soup into 4 shallow dessert bowls. Top each serving with a scoop of sorbet.

NUTRITION FACTS PER SERVING: 262 cal., 2 g total fat (1 g sat. fat), 5 mg chol. 37 mg sodium, 63 g carbo., 8 g fiber, 2 g pro.

Raspberries and Lemon Cream

START TO FINISH: 20 minutes **MAKES:** 4 servings

2   cups red raspberries

4   teaspoons raspberry liqueur

1   6-ounce carton lemon low-fat yogurt

¼   of an 8-ounce container frozen fat-free whipped
        dessert topping, thawed

3   tablespoons sugar

one Reserve ¼ cup of the raspberries. In a medium bowl drizzle liqueur over remaining raspberries; toss gently to coat.

two In a small bowl stir together yogurt and whipped topping. Spoon berry mixture into 4 dessert dishes. Top with yogurt mixture. If desired, cover and chill for up to 4 hours.

three Before serving, for caramelized sugar, place sugar in a small heavy saucepan. Cook over medium-high heat until sugar starts to melt, shaking pan occasionally to heat sugar evenly. Do not stir. Once sugar starts to melt, reduce heat to low and cook about 5 minutes or until all of the sugar is melted and golden, stirring as needed with a wooden spoon. Remove from heat. Let stand for 1 minute.

four Dip a fork into caramelized sugar and let syrup run off tines for several seconds. Then shake fork over desserts, drizzling thin stands of caramelized sugar over yogurt mixture. If sugar starts to harden in pan, return to heat, stirring until sugar melts. Top with the reserved raspberries.

NUTRITION FACTS PER SERVING: 148 cal., 1 g total fat (0 g sat. fat), 2 mg chol., 41 mg sodium, 32 g carbo., 3 g fiber, 3 g pro.

Honeyed Figs and Yogurt

PREP: 15 minutes **CHILL:** 8 to 24 hours **MAKES:** 2 servings

1   cup plain low-fat yogurt

½   teaspoon vanilla

2   fresh figs or apricots, cut up

1   tablespoon coarsely chopped walnuts, toasted
        (see tip, page 280)

2   teaspoons honey

        Finely shredded lemon peel (optional)

one Line a sieve with a paper coffee filter or 100-percent-cotton cheesecloth; set sieve over a small bowl. Spoon yogurt into sieve. Cover and chill for 8 to 24 hours. (Yogurt will thicken to form a soft cheese.)

two Discard liquid from yogurt. Gently stir vanilla into thickened yogurt.

three To serve, spoon figs into 2 small dessert dishes. Top with yogurt mixture and walnuts. Drizzle with honey. If desired, sprinkle with lemon peel.

NUTRITION FACTS PER SERVING: 157 cal., 4 g total fat (1 g sat. fat), 7 mg chol., 80 mg sodium, 24 g carbo., 2 g fiber, 7 g pro.

Ginger Fruit with Pineapple Sherbet

PREP: 10 minutes FREEZE: 15 minutes MAKES: 4 servings

1   8-ounce can pineapple chunks (juice pack), undrained

⅓   cup orange marmalade or apricot preserves

1   tablespoon finely snipped crystallized ginger or
     ¼ teaspoon ground ginger

¼   teaspoon vanilla (optional)

1   11-ounce can mandarin orange sections, drained

2   cups pineapple, orange, lemon, or lime sherbet

one Drain pineapple, reserving juice. In a medium bowl combine pineapple juice, orange marmalade, ginger, and, if desired, vanilla. Add pineapple and mandarin oranges; toss gently to coat.

two Cover and quick-chill in the freezer for 15 minutes or chill in the refrigerator for 30 minutes, stirring occasionally.

three To serve, scoop sherbet into 4 dessert dishes. Top with fruit mixture.

NUTRITION FACTS PER SERVING: 267 cal., 2 g total fat (1 g sat. fat), 5 mg chol. 64 mg sodium, 65 g carbo., 1 g fiber, 2 g pro.

GRILLING

Peaches with Quick Cherry Sauce

PREP: 15 minutes GRILL: 6 minutes MAKES: 6 servings

3   medium peaches or nectarines, pitted and quartered

3   tablespoons orange juice

1½ cups fresh or frozen unsweetened pitted dark sweet
     cherries, thawed

½   cup cherry jam

3   cups vanilla ice cream

2   tablespoons coconut or almonds, toasted
     (see tip, page 280) (optional)

one Thread peaches onto 2 long metal skewers, leaving 1¼ inches between each piece. Brush peaches with 1 tablespoon of the orange juice. Set aside.

two For sauce, in a small saucepan combine the remaining 2 tablespoons orange juice, the cherries, and cherry jam. Bring to boiling over medium heat, stirring frequently; reduce heat. Simmer, uncovered, for 3 minutes. Set sauce aside.

three For a charcoal grill, grill peaches on the rack of an uncovered grill directly over medium coals for 6 to 8 minutes or until heated through, turning once halfway through grilling. (For a gas grill, preheat grill. Reduce heat to medium. Place peach skewers on grill rack over heat. Cover and grill as above.)

four To serve, scoop ice cream into 6 dessert dishes. Top with grilled peaches and sauce. If desired, sprinkle with coconut.

NUTRITION FACTS PER SERVING: 304 cal., 12 g total fat (7 g sat. fat), 68 mg chol., 54 mg sodium, 46 g carbo., 2 g fiber, 4 g pro.

Caramel Clementines

START TO FINISH: 30 minutes **MAKES:** 6 servings

- 6   clementines or tangerines
- 1   12-ounce can apricot nectar
- ½   cup sugar
       Dash cayenne pepper (optional)
- 2   tablespoons Southern Comfort® orange liqueur, or orange juice

one Peel clementines and remove the fibrous strands of pith from the fruit. In a medium saucepan combine clementines, apricot nectar, sugar, and, if desired, cayenne pepper. Bring to boiling; reduce heat. Simmer, covered, for 5 minutes. Using a slotted spoon, transfer clementines to 6 dessert dishes.

two Continue to gently boil apricot nectar mixture about 15 minutes or until thick and syrupy. Remove from heat. Stir in Southern Comfort. Spoon over clementines. Serve warm.

NUTRITION FACTS PER SERVING: 151 cal., 0 g total fat (0 g sat. fat), 0 mg chol., 3 mg sodium, 36 g carbo., 2 g fiber, 1 g pro.

Dessert Waffles with Raspberry Sauce

START TO FINISH: 10 minutes **MAKES:** 6 servings

- 1   10-ounce package frozen raspberries in syrup, thawed
- ¼   cup powdered sugar
- 2   tablespoons crème de cassis (optional)
- 6   frozen waffles, toasted
- 3   cups vanilla ice cream

one For raspberry sauce, press raspberries and syrup through a fine-mesh sieve into a small bowl; discard seeds. Stir in powdered sugar and, if desired, crème de cassis.

two To serve, cut each waffle in half diagonally. Divide waffle halves among 6 dessert plates. Top with vanilla ice cream and drizzle with raspberry sauce.

NUTRITION FACTS PER SERVING: 300 cal., 11 g total fat (4 g sat. fat), 29 mg chol., 310 mg sodium, 48 g carbo., 3 g fiber, 5 g pro.

Fill-the-Grill Nectarine Toss *See photo on page 272.*

PREP: 15 minutes **GRILL:** 8 minutes **MAKES:** 6 servings

6 medium ripe nectarines, halved and pitted

2 tablespoons olive oil

 Ground cinnamon or nutmeg

3 cups vanilla ice cream

 Coarsely chopped chocolate chunks

one Brush nectarines with oil. Sprinkle with cinnamon.

two For a charcoal grill, place a grill wok or grill basket on the rack of an uncovered grill directly over medium coals; heat for 5 minutes. Place nectarine halves in the wok or basket. Grill for 8 to 10 minutes or until heated through, gently turning once halfway through grilling. (For a gas grill, preheat grill. Reduce heat to medium. Place nectarines in grill wok or basket on grill rack over heat. Cover and grill as above.)

three To serve, divide scoops of ice cream among 6 dessert dishes. Top with the grilled nectarine halves. Sprinkle with chocolate chunks.

NUTRITION FACTS PER SERVING: 312 cal., 19 g total fat (9 g sat. fat), 46 mg chol., 46 mg sodium, 36 g carbo., 2 g fiber, 4 g pro.

Cherry-Bananas Foster

START TO FINISH: 15 minutes **MAKES:** 4 servings

¼ cup butter

⅓ cup packed brown sugar

3 ripe bananas, sliced (about 2 cups)

⅓ cup dried tart cherries

⅓ cup spiced rum or rum (optional)

one In a large skillet melt butter over medium heat. Stir in brown sugar until combined. Add bananas and dried cherries; cook for 1 to 2 minutes or until heated through, stirring gently.

two If desired, pour rum into a small saucepan heat. Bring rum almost to simmering. Ignite rum with a long match. Pour over bananas and dried cherries. To use, serve immediately over ice cream, pound cake, or angel food cake.

NUTRITION FACTS PER SERVING: 290 cal., 13 g total fat (8 g sat. fat), 33 mg chol., 132 mg sodium, 46 g carbo., 3 g fiber, 1 g pro.

Apple-Pear Sauce

START TO FINISH: 20 minutes **MAKES:** 6 servings

2 tablespoons butter or margarine

2 tablespoons sugar

2 cooking apples, peeled and cut into ½-inch chunks

2 pears, peeled and cut into ½-inch chunks

1 tablespoon brandy

one In a large skillet melt butter over medium heat. Add sugar; cook and stir about 2 minutes or just until sugar starts to melt. Stir in apples and pears.

two Cook, covered, over medium-high heat about 10 minutes or until fruit is tender, stirring frequently. Stir in brandy. Cook, uncovered, for 1 minute more. To use, serve warm over ice cream or sherbet.

NUTRITION FACTS PER SERVING: 112 cal., 4 g total fat (2 g sat. fat), 10 mg chol., 28 mg sodium, 19 g carbo., 3 g fiber, 0 g pro.

Easy Blueberry Sauce

START TO FINISH: 15 minutes **MAKES:** 24 servings

3 cups blueberries

¾ cup sugar

1 tablespoon lemon juice

one In a food processor or blender combine blueberries, sugar, and lemon juice. Cover and process or blend for 15 seconds. Stop machine and scrape down side with a spatula. Cover and process or blend for 2½ to 3 minutes more or until nearly smooth.

two To use, serve over pancakes, ice cream, fruit, or cake. If desired, top with whipped cream. Store, tightly covered, in the refrigerator. Bring sauce to room temperature and stir before serving.

NUTRITION FACTS PER SERVING: 32 cal., 0 g total fat (0 g sat. fat), 0 mg chol., 0 mg sodium, 8 g carbo., 1 g fiber, 0 g pro.

DELECTABLE DESSERTS

Lemonade Ice Cream *See photo on page 273.*

PREP: 10 minutes **FREEZE:** per manufacturer's directions
MAKES: 16 servings

   4   cups whipping cream
   1   14-ounce can sweetened condensed milk, chilled
   1   12-ounce can frozen lemonade concentrate, thawed
       Several drops yellow food coloring (optional)

one In a large bowl combine whipping cream, sweetened condensed milk, lemonade concentrate, and, if desired, yellow food coloring.

two Freeze mixture in a 4-quart ice cream freezer according to the manufacturer's directions. If desired, ripen for 4 hours.

NUTRITION FACTS PER SERVING: 325 cal., 24 g total fat (15 g sat. fat), 91 mg chol., 55 mg sodium, 25 g carbo., 0 g fiber, 3 g pro.

Ripening Ice Cream Ripen or harden homemade ice cream to improve the texture and keep it from melting too quickly.

For the optional ripening step, remove the lid and dasher when the ice cream is done. Cover the top of the freezer canister with waxed paper or foil. Plug the hole in the lid with a small piece of cloth; replace the lid. Pack the outer bucket with enough ice and rock salt to cover the freezer canister. Use 4 cups ice to 1 cup salt. Let stand about 4 hours.

If you use a no-ice, no-salt freezer, ripen the ice cream by transferring it to a freezer container. Freeze in your regular freezer about 4 hours.

Frosty Chocolate-Cherry Yogurt

PREP: 25 minutes **FREEZE:** per manufacturer's directions
MAKES: 12 servings

   5   6-ounce cartons vanilla yogurt (no gelatin added)
   2½   cups fresh or frozen pitted dark sweet cherries
   ⅓   cup milk
   ⅓   cup light-color corn syrup
   ½   cup miniature semisweet chocolate pieces

one In a blender or food processor combine yogurt, 1 cup of the cherries, the milk, and corn syrup. Cover and blend or process until nearly smooth. (If using a food processor, process half of the mixture at a time.)

two Freeze mixture in a 2-quart ice cream freezer according to the manufacturer's directions until nearly firm. Add the remaining 1½ cups cherries and the chocolate pieces; continue to freeze until firm.

NUTRITION FACTS PER SERVING: 173 cal., 4 g total fat (2 g sat. fat), 5 mg chol., 63 mg sodium, 30 g carbo., 1 g fiber, 5 g pro.

Frozen Berry Yogurt

PREP: 15 minutes **CHILL:** 6 hours **FREEZE:** per manufacturer's directions **MAKES:** 6 to 8 servings

1¼	cups sugar
1	cup water
3	cups raspberries, blackberries, and/or strawberries
4	6-ounce cartons vanilla yogurt
1	teaspoon vanilla

one For syrup, in a medium saucepan combine sugar and water. Bring just to boiling over medium-high heat, stirring to dissolve sugar. Cool slightly.

two In a blender or food processor combine half of the syrup and half of the berries. Cover and blend or process until nearly smooth. Strain through a fine-mesh sieve into a bowl; discard seeds. Repeat with the remaining syrup and the remaining berries. Transfer berry mixture to a large bowl. Stir in yogurt and vanilla. Cover and chill for at least 6 hours.

three Freeze mixture in a 2-quart ice cream freezer according to the manufacturer's directions. If desired, ripen for 4 hours.

NUTRITION FACTS PER SERVING: 283 cal., 2 g total fat (1 g sat. fat), 6 mg chol., 76 mg sodium, 63 g carbo., 4 g fiber, 6 g pro.

Strawberry Gelato

PREP: 25 minutes **CHILL:** 8 hours **FREEZE:** per manufacturer's directions **MAKES:** 16 servings

4	cups cut-up strawberries
4	cups milk
1⅓	cups sugar
10	egg yolks, slightly beaten
	Several drops red food coloring (optional)

one Place berries in a blender or food processor. Cover and blend or process until nearly smooth.

two In a large saucepan combine 3 cups of the milk, the sugar, and egg yolks. Cook and stir over medium heat just until mixture coats a metal spoon. Remove from heat. Stir in the remaining 1 cup milk, the pureed berries, and, if desired, red food coloring.

three Cover surface of gelato mixture with plastic wrap and chill for at least 8 hours. (Or place saucepan in a sink of ice water to cool quickly; then cover and chill for 2 hours.)

four Freeze mixture in a 4- to 5-quart ice cream freezer according to the manufacturer's directions. If desired, ripen for 4 hours.

NUTRITION FACTS PER SERVING: 137 cal., 4 g total fat (2 g sat. fat), 133 mg chol., 30 mg sodium, 22 g carbo., 1 g fiber, 4 g pro.

Mint-Ginger Fruit Sorbet

PREP: 20 minutes **STAND:** 10 minutes **CHILL:** 1 hour
FREEZE: per manufacturer's directions **MAKES:** 8 servings

2¾   cups water

¼   cup sugar

1   inch fresh ginger, thinly sliced

1   cup lightly packed fresh mint leaves

½   of a 12-ounce can frozen apple-orange-pineapple
    juice concentrate, thawed

one In a small saucepan combine water, sugar, and ginger.
Cook and stir until sugar is dissolved. Remove from heat. Sti
in mint. Cover and let stand for 10 minutes.

two Strain mixture through a sieve into a large bowl; discard
ginger and mint. Stir in juice concentrate. Cover and chill for
at least 1 hour.

three Freeze mixture in a 2-quart ice cream freezer
according to the manufacturer's directions.* If desired, ripen
for 4 hours.

***Note:** If you don't have an ice cream freezer, transfer the
mixture to a nonmetal freezer container. Cover and freeze
for 4 to 6 hours or until nearly firm. Break mixture into small
chunks; transfer to a chilled bowl. Beat with an electric mixer
until smooth but not melted. Return to container. Cover and
freeze for at least 6 hours or until firm.*

NUTRITION FACTS PER SERVING: 73 cal., 0 g total fat (0 g sat. fat), 0 mg chol
3 mg sodium, 19 g carbo., 0 g fiber, 0 g pro.

Daiquiri Sorbet

PREP: 10 minutes **FREEZE:** 4 hours **MAKES:** 6 servings

1   16-ounce package frozen unsweetened peach slices
    or unsweetened whole strawberries

½   cup water

⅓   cup powdered sugar

¼   cup bottled daiquiri drink mix (contains no alcohol)

3   tablespoons rum or orange juice

one In a food processor combine frozen fruit, water,
powdered sugar, daiquiri drink mix, and rum. Cover and
process until smooth and fluffy.

two Transfer mixture to a nonmetal freezer container. Cover
and freeze for at least 4 hours or until firm.

NUTRITION FACTS PER SERVING: 76 cal., 0 g total fat (0 g sat. fat), 0 mg chol.
11 mg sodium, 15 g carbo., 1 g fiber, 1 g pro.

Mango-Raspberry Granita

PREP: 20 minutes **FREEZE:** 7 hours **STAND:** 5 minutes
MAKES: 4 servings

- 1 cup water
- ½ cup sugar
- 1 12-ounce package frozen red raspberries
- 1 medium mango, seeded, peeled, and chopped
  Fresh red raspberries (optional)

one For syrup, in a medium saucepan combine water and sugar. Bring just to boiling over medium-high heat, stirring to dissolve sugar. Cool slightly.

two Stir in frozen raspberries and mango. Pour into a blender or food processor. Cover and blend or process until smooth. Strain through a fine-mesh sieve into a bowl; discard seeds.

three Transfer fruit mixture to a 3-quart rectangular baking dish or nonmetal freezer container. Cover and freeze for 1 to 2 hours or until nearly firm. Stir well, scraping frozen mixture from sides of dish. Spread evenly in dish. Cover and freeze for at least 6 hours or until firm.

four Let stand at room temperature for 5 to 10 minutes before serving. If desired, garnish each serving with fresh red raspberries.

NUTRITION FACTS PER SERVING: 214 cal., 0 g total fat (0 g sat. fat), 0 mg chol., 4 mg sodium, 56 g carbo., 2 g fiber, 0 g pro.

Watermelon-Berry Ice

PREP: 25 minutes **FREEZE:** 2½ hours **MAKES:** 6 to 8 servings

- 1 cup water
- ½ cup sugar
- 2 cups cubed and seeded watermelon
- 2 cups raspberries, strawberries, and/or blueberries
  Raspberries and/or blueberries (optional)

one For syrup, in a medium saucepan combine water and sugar. Bring to boiling, stirring to dissolve sugar. Boil gently, uncovered, for 2 minutes. Cool slightly.

two In a blender or food processor combine melon and the 2 cups berries. Cover and blend or process for 30 seconds. Add syrup; cover and blend or process until nearly smooth.

three Transfer mixture to a 3-quart rectangular baking dish or a 13×9×2-inch baking pan. Cover and freeze about 1½ hours or until nearly firm. Break up frozen mixture with a fork. Cover and freeze for at least 1 hour or until firm.

four If necessary, let frozen mixture stand at room temperature for 20 minutes to soften. To serve, break up mixture with fork. If desired, garnish each serving with additional raspberries and/or blueberries.

NUTRITION FACTS PER SERVING: 98 cal., 0 g total fat (0 g sat. fat), 0 mg chol., 2 mg sodium, 24 g carbo., 3 g fiber, 1 g pro.

Fruit Ribbon Cake

PREP: 20 minutes **BAKE:** per package directions **COOL:** 1 hour
MAKES: 16 servings

1	package 2-layer-size white cake mix
1⅓	cups seedless red raspberry preserves
⅔	cup lemon curd
1	8-ounce container frozen whipped dessert topping, thawed

one Prepare cake mix according to package directions. Divide batter evenly between two greased and lightly floured 8×1½-inch or 9×1½-inch round cake pans. Bake, uncovered, in a 350°F oven according to package directions.

two Cool cake layers in pans on wire racks for 10 minutes. Remove cake layers from pans; cool on wire racks. Using a long-blade serrated knife, cut each layer in half horizontally.

three To assemble, place one split cake layer on a serving plate; spread with half of the raspberry preserves. Top with second cake layer; spread with lemon curd. Top with third cake layer; spread with the remaining preserves. Top with fourth cake layer. If desired, cover and chill cake for up to 24 hours before icing.

four Spread top and side of cake with whipped topping. Serve at once or chill for up to 4 hours before serving.

NUTRITION FACTS PER SERVING: 326 cal., 9 g total fat (4 g sat. fat), 10 mg chol., 231 mg sodium, 57 g carbo., 2 g fiber, 2 g pro.

Strawberry-Chocolate Cake *See photo on page 271.*

PREP: 30 minutes **BAKE:** per package directions **COOL:** 1 hour
MAKES: 12 servings

1	package 2-layer-size strawberry cake mix
1	cup canned chocolate frosting
1	8-ounce container frozen whipped dessert topping, thawed
	Strawberries

one Prepare cake mix according to package directions. Divide batter evenly between two greased and lightly floured 8×1½-inch or 9×1½-inch round cake pans. Bake, uncovered, in a 350°F oven according to package directions.

two Cool cake layers in pans on wire racks for 10 minutes. Remove cake layers from pans; cool on wire racks.

three To assemble, place one cake layer on a serving plate; spread with frosting. Top with the remaining cake layer. Frost top and side of cake with whipped topping. Before serving, decorate top of cake with strawberries.

NUTRITION FACTS PER SERVING: 406 cal., 20 g total fat (8 g sat. fat), 55 mg chol., 353 mg sodium, 52 g carbo., 1 g fiber, 3 g pro.

Chocolate-Raspberry Cake

PREP: 30 minutes **BAKE:** per package directions
COOL: 1 hour **MAKES:** 12 to 16 servings

1 package 2-layer-size devil's food cake mix

2 2.8-ounce packages chocolate or chocolate-
   raspberry mousse mix

⅔ cup milk

⅓ cup raspberry liqueur

1 12-ounce jar fudge ice cream topping

one Prepare cake mix according to package directions. Divide batter evenly between two greased and lightly floured 9×1½-inch round cake pans. Bake, uncovered, in a 350°F oven according to package directions.

two Cool cake layers in pans on wire racks for 10 minutes. Remove cake layers from pans; cool on wire racks. Using a long-blade serrated knife, carefully cut each cake layer in half horizontally.

three Prepare chocolate mousse mixes according to package directions, except use the ⅔ cup milk and the ⅓ cup raspberry liqueur for the liquid called for on the package.

four To assemble, place one split cake layer on a serving plate. Spread with about ⅓ cup of the fudge topping and about ½ cup of the mousse mixture. Repeat layers two more times. Top with the remaining cake layer.

five Frost top and side of cake with the remaining mousse mixture. Store frosted cake in the refrigerator.

NUTRITION FACTS PER SERVING: 371 cal., 11 g total fat (4 g sat. fat), 2 mg chol., 464 mg sodium, 63 g carbo., 1 g fiber, 6 g pro.

Gooey Chocolate-Caramel Cake

PREP: 15 minutes **BAKE:** per package directions
COOL: 1 hour **MAKES:** 30 servings

- 1   package 2-layer-size German chocolate cake mix
- 1   14-ounce can sweetened condensed milk
- 1   12-ounce jar caramel ice cream topping
- 1   8-ounce carton frozen whipped dessert topping, thawed
- 3   1.4-ounce bars chocolate-covered English toffee, chopped

one Prepare cake mix according to package directions. Pour batter into a greased 13×9×2-inch baking pan. Bake, uncovered, in a 350°F oven according to package directions. Cool in pan on a wire rack.

two Using the handle of a wooden spoon, poke holes about 1 inch apart over surface of cake. Pour sweetened condensed milk and caramel topping over cake. Spread dessert topping evenly over top.

three Before serving, sprinkle with toffee bars. Store leftover cake in the refrigerator for up to 24 hours.

NUTRITION FACTS PER SERVING: 220 cal., 7 g total fat (4 g sat. fat), 6 mg cho 174 mg sodium, 33 g carbo., 0 g fiber, 2 g pro.

Shortcut Malted Chocolate Cake

PREP: 15 minutes **BAKE:** 30 minutes **COOL:** 1 hour
MAKES: 20 servings

- 1   package 2-layer-size dark chocolate fudge or devil's food cake mix
- 1/3   cup malted milk powder
- 1   16-ounce can whipped chocolate frosting
- 1/4   cup malted milk powder
- 1½   cups coarsely crushed malted milk balls

one Prepare cake mix according to package directions, except stir the 1/3 cup malted milk powder into batter. Pour batter into a greased 13×9×2-inch baking pan.

two Bake, uncovered, in a 350°F oven for 30 to 35 minutes or until a toothpick inserted near the center comes out clean. Cool in pan on a wire rack.

three In a medium bowl stir together frosting and the 1/4 cup malted milk powder. Spread evenly over cake. Sprinkle with crushed malted milk balls.

NUTRITION FACTS PER SERVING: 231 cal., 7 g total fat (2 g sat. fat), 2 mg cho 281 mg sodium, 41 g carbo., 1 g fiber, 3 g pro.

Easy Crème de Menthe Cake

PREP: 25 minutes **BAKE:** per package directions
COOL: 1 hour **MAKES:** 12 servings

- 1 package 2-layer-size chocolate cake mix
- ¼ cup crème de menthe
- ½ cup fudge ice cream topping
- 1 16-ounce can vanilla frosting
- 1 tablespoon crème de menthe
  Few drops green food coloring (optional)
  Layered chocolate-mint candies, coarsely chopped (optional)

one Prepare cake mix according to package directions, except use the ¼ cup crème de menthe for ¼ cup of the water called for on the package. Divide batter evenly between two greased and lightly floured 8×1½-inch or 9×1½-inch round cake pans. Bake, uncovered, in a 350°F oven according to package directions.

two Cool cake layers in pans on wire racks for 10 minutes. Remove cake layers from pans; cool on wire racks. In a small saucepan heat fudge topping just until spreadable.

three To assemble, place one cake layer on a serving plate; spread with fudge topping. Top with the remaining cake layer.

four For frosting, in a medium bowl combine vanilla frosting and the 1 tablespoon crème de menthe. If desired, stir in green food coloring. Spread frosting over top and side of cake. If desired, garnish with chocolate-mint candies.

NUTRITION FACTS PER SERVING: 435 cal., 19 g total fat (4 g sat. fat), 35 mg chol., 383 mg sodium, 66 g carbo., 1 g fiber, 3 g pro.

Angel Shortcake with Cream

START TO FINISH: 20 minutes **MAKES:** 12 servings

- ½ cup whipping cream
- ¼ cup powdered sugar
- ½ cup lemon low-fat yogurt
- 1 9- or 10-inch round angel food cake
- 4 cups sliced strawberries

one For lemon cream, in a small bowl combine whipping cream and powdered sugar. Beat with an electric mixer on medium speed just until soft peaks form (tips curl). Fold in yogurt. If desired, cover and chill for up to 4 hours.

two Cut angel food cake into 12 slices. Serve cake slices with strawberries. Spoon lemon cream over cake and berries.

NUTRITION FACTS PER SERVING: 140 cal., 4 g total fat (2 g sat. fat), 14 mg chol., 224 mg sodium, 24 g carbo., 1 g fiber, 3 g pro.

Dipped Chocolate Angel Cake

PREP: 35 minutes **BAKE:** 35 minutes **COOL:** 2 hours
FREEZE: 4 minutes **MAKES:** 8 servings

- 1   16-ounce package angel food cake mix
- ¼   cup unsweetened cocoa powder
- 1¼   cups water
- 4   cups strawberries
- 6   ounces semisweet chocolate, coarsely chopped
- 1   tablespoon shortening

one In a large bowl combine cake mix and cocoa powder; add water. Beat with an electric mixer on low speed for 30 seconds. Beat on medium speed for 1 minute. Pour into an ungreased 10-inch tube pan. Gently cut through batter with a knife to remove any large air pockets.

two Bake, uncovered, on the lowest oven rack in a 350°F oven for 35 to 40 minutes or until top springs back when lightly touched. Immediately invert cake; cool in pan. Loosen sides of cake from pan; remove cake.

three Place 2 cups of the strawberries in a blender; cover and blend until smooth. Strain through a fine-mesh sieve into a bowl; discard seeds. Halve the remaining berries; set aside.

four Using a serrated knife, cut half of the cake into 8 slices. Cut slices in half diagonally; set aside. Freeze the remaining cake for another use.

five In a small saucepan combine chocolate and shortening. Cook and stir over low heat until chocolate melts. Remove from heat. Place waxed paper on a tray. Dip one corner of each cake triangle into melted chocolate, allowing excess to drip off. Place dipped cake triangles on waxed paper. Place tray in freezer for 4 to 5 minutes or until chocolate is firm.

six To serve, divide cake triangles among 8 dessert plates. Top each serving with a few halved strawberries and about 1 tablespoon of the pureed strawberries.

NUTRITION FACTS PER SERVING: 245 cal., 9 g total fat (4 g sat. fat), 0 mg chol., 190 mg sodium, 40 g carbo., 3 g fiber, 5 g pro.

Coffee Angel Dessert

PREP: 20 minutes **CHILL:** 4 to 24 hours **MAKES:** 4 servings

- 1   cup whipping cream
- ¼   cup powdered sugar
- ⅓   cup coffee liqueur or strong brewed coffee
- ½   of an 8- to 10-inch angel food cake
- ¼   cup shaved semisweet chocolate (1 ounce)

one In a medium bowl combine whipping cream, powdered sugar, and 1 tablespoon of the liqueur. Beat with an electric mixer on high speed until stiff peaks form (tips stand straight).

two Cut cake into bite-size cubes. Place half of the cake cubes in 4 parfait glasses. Drizzle with half of the remaining liqueur. Spoon half of the whipped cream mixture over cake in glasses; sprinkle with half of the shaved chocolate. Repeat layers. Cover and chill for 4 to 24 hours.

.**NUTRITION FACTS PER SERVING:** 466 cal., 25 g total fat (15 g sat. fat), 82 mg chol., 396 mg sodium, 48 g carbo., 1 g fiber, 5 g pro.

Tropical Angel Cake

START TO FINISH: 25 minutes **MAKES:** 10 servings

1   8- to 9-inch angel food cake

3   cups fruit sherbet

¼   cup frozen fruit juice concentrate, thawed

1   cup whipping cream, whipped

Coconut (optional)

one Slice cake in half horizontally. Hollow out the insides of the top and bottom halves, leaving 1-inch shells. Spoon sherbet into bottom shell. Replace top half, hollow side down.

two Poke holes in top. Drizzle with juice concentrate. Frost top and side with whipped cream. If desired, sprinkle with coconut. If desired, cover loosely with foil and freeze until ready to serve. Let stand for 10 minutes before serving, if frozen.

NUTRITION FACTS PER SERVING: 315 cal., 10 g total fat (6 g sat. fat), 36 mg chol., 123 mg sodium, 52 g carbo., 0 g fiber, 5 g pro.

Little Peppermint Cakes

START TO FINISH: 30 minutes **MAKES:** 15 servings

1   10¾-ounce loaf frozen pound cake, thawed

1   16-ounce can vanilla frosting

2   to 3 drops peppermint extract

1   drop red food coloring

4   ounces white baking chocolate with cocoa butter, chopped

¼   teaspoon peppermint extract

Small peppermint candy pillows (optional)

one Using a serrated knife, cut cake crosswise into 10 slices. Set aside.

two For peppermint filling, in a small bowl combine ¼ cup of the frosting, the 2 to 3 drops peppermint extract, and the red food coloring. Spread half of the cake slices with filling. Top with the remaining cake slices, making sandwiches. Cut each sandwich into 3 triangles, starting from center of one long side and cutting to each opposite corner. Set aside.

three For icing, in a small heavy saucepan cook and stir white chocolate over low heat until chocolate melts. Stir in the remaining frosting; cook and stir until smooth. Remove from heat. Stir in the ¼ teaspoon peppermint extract.

four Insert a fork into the side of a cake piece. Holding cake over saucepan, spoon on enough icing to cover sides and top. Using another fork, gently push cake piece onto a wire rack set over waxed paper. If necessary, spoon icing onto side of cake where fork was inserted. Repeat with the remaining cake pieces and icing, reheating icing if necessary.

five If desired, top cakes with peppermint candies. Let stand until icing is set.

NUTRITION FACTS PER SERVING: 256 cal., 12 g total fat (5 g sat. fat), 24 mg chol., 139 mg sodium, 35 g carbo., 0 g fiber, 2 g pro.

DELECTABLE DESSERTS

Chocolate-Covered Strawberry Cakes

START TO FINISH: 30 minutes **MAKES:** 18 servings

1   10¾-ounce loaf frozen pound cake, thawed
3   tablespoons strawberry jam
½   cup semisweet chocolate pieces
½   of a 16-ounce can (about 1 cup) chocolate frosting
1   tablespoon strawberry liqueur or amaretto
18 medium strawberries (optional)

one Using a serrated knife, cut cake crosswise into 12 slices. Spread half of the cake slices with strawberry jam. Top with the remaining cake slices, making sandwiches. Cut each sandwich into 3 triangles, starting from center of one long side and cutting to each opposite corner.

two For icing, in a small heavy saucepan cook and stir chocolate pieces over low heat until chocolate melts. Stir in frosting and liqueur. Cook and stir for 1 to 2 minutes more or until smooth. Remove from heat.

three Insert a fork into the side of a cake piece. Holding cake over saucepan, spoon on enough icing to cover sides and top. Using another fork, gently push cake piece onto a wire rack set over waxed paper. If necessary, spoon icing onto side of cake where fork was inserted. Repeat with the remaining cake pieces and icing, reheating icing if necessary. Let stand until icing is set.

four If desired, top cakes with strawberries before serving.

NUTRITION FACTS PER SERVING: 167 cal., 7 g total fat (3 g sat. fat), 19 mg chol., 106 mg sodium, 23 g carbo., 1 g fiber, 1 g pro.

Crunchy Pound Cake Slices

START TO FINISH: 20 minutes **MAKES:** 4 servings

4   ½-inch slices purchased pound cake
¼   cup chocolate-hazelnut spread
½   cup roasted mixed nuts, coarsely chopped
1   pint caramel or cinnamon ice cream

one Place pound cake slices on a baking sheet. Broil 3 to 4 inches from the heat about 2 minutes or until lightly browned, turning once. Cool slightly.

two Spread cake slices with chocolate-hazelnut spread. Sprinkle with nuts; pat gently to form an even layer. Serve cake slices with scoops of ice cream.

NUTRITION FACTS PER SERVING: 763 cal., 45 g total fat (22 g sat. fat), 206 mg chol., 421 mg sodium, 82 g carbo., 2 g fiber, 12 g pro.

Upside-Down Caramel Apple Cake

PREP: 15 minutes **BAKE:** 40 minutes **COOL:** 10 minutes
MAKES: 15 servings

- 2 large cooking apples, peeled, cored, and thinly sliced
- ½ cup chopped Brazil nuts or walnuts (optional)
- 3 tablespoons butter
- 3 tablespoons packed brown sugar
- 1 package 2-layer-size spice cake mix
- 3 tablespoons molasses

one In a large skillet cook apples and, if desired, nuts in melted butter over medium heat about 5 minutes or until apples are tender. Remove from heat. Stir in brown sugar. Spread in a greased 13×9×2-inch baking pan.

two Prepare cake mix according to package directions, except reduce water called for on package to 1 cup. Stir molasses into batter. Pour batter evenly over apple mixture.

three Bake, uncovered, in a 350°F oven for 40 to 45 minutes or until a toothpick inserted near the center comes out clean. Cool in pan on a wire rack for 10 minutes. Loosen sides of cake from pan; invert cake onto a serving platter. Serve warm.

NUTRITION FACTS PER SERVING: 252 cal., 11 g total fat (3 g sat. fat), 50 mg chol., 251 mg sodium, 37 g carbo., 0 g fiber, 2 g pro.

SLOW COOKER

Brownie Pudding Cake

PREP: 15 minutes **COOK:** High 2 hours **STAND:** 30 minutes
MAKES: 8 servings

- Nonstick cooking spray
- 1 19.8-ounce package brownie mix
- ½ cup butter or margarine, melted
- 2 eggs
- ¼ cup water
- ¾ cup sugar
- ¾ cup unsweetened cocoa powder
- 3 cups boiling water
- Vanilla ice cream (optional)

one Lightly coat a 3½- or 4-quart slow cooker with cooking spray; set aside. In a medium bowl stir together brownie mix, melted butter, eggs, and the ¼ cup water until nearly smooth. Spread batter evenly in bottom of prepared cooker.

two In another medium bowl combine sugar and cocoa powder. Gradually stir boiling water into sugar mixture. Pour evenly over batter in cooker.

three Cover and cook on high-heat setting for 2 hours (center may appear moist but will set up upon standing). Remove liner from cooker, if possible, or turn off cooker. Let stand, uncovered, for 30 to 45 minutes to cool slightly before serving.

four To serve, spoon warm cake into 8 dessert dishes; spoon the pudding that forms over cake. If desired, top with ice cream.

NUTRITION FACTS PER SERVING: 534 cal., 25 g total fat (10 g sat. fat), 86 mg chol., 355 mg sodium, 76 g carbo., 0 g fiber, 6 g pro.

DELECTABLE DESSERTS

Gingerbread Pudding Cake

PREP: 15 minutes **COOK:** High 2 hours **STAND:** 45 minutes
MAKES: 8 servings

Nonstick cooking spray
1   14½-ounce package gingerbread mix
½   cup milk
½   cup raisins
2¼ cups water
¾   cup packed brown sugar
¾   cup butter or margarine
Vanilla ice cream (optional)

one Lightly coat a 3½- or 4-quart slow cooker with cooking spray; set aside.

two In a medium bowl stir together gingerbread mix and milk until moistened. Stir in raisins (batter will be thick). Spread batter evenly in the bottom of the prepared cooker.

three In a medium saucepan combine water, brown sugar, and butter; bring to boiling. Carefully pour mixture over batter in cooker.

four Cover and cook on high-heat setting for 2 hours (center may appear moist but will set up upon standing). Remove liner from cooker, if possible, or turn off cooker. Let stand, uncovered, about 45 minutes to cool slightly before serving.

five To serve, spoon warm cake into 8 dessert dishes; spoon the pudding that forms over cake. If desired, top with scoops of vanilla ice cream.

NUTRITION FACTS PER SERVING: 501 cal., 24 g total fat (13 g sat. fat), 50 mg chol., 548 mg sodium, 70 g carbo., 1 g fiber, 4 g pro.

Cherry Trifle Cake

START TO FINISH: 20 minutes **MAKES:** 8 servings

1   9½-inch tart-shape sponge cake or 8 individual sponge shortcake cups
½   cup cherry juice blend or orange juice
1   6-ounce carton cherry-vanilla or strawberry yogurt
¼   of an 8-ounce container frozen whipped dessert topping, thawed
2   cups light or dark sweet cherries (such as Rainier or Bing), pitted and halved

one Place cake on a serving plate. Drizzle with juice. Set aside. For topping, in a small bowl stir together yogurt and whipped topping. Spread topping over cake. If desired, cover and chill for up to 2 hours.

two Before serving, arrange halved cherries, cut sides down, on top of cake.

NUTRITION FACTS PER SERVING: 263 cal., 5 g total fat (2 g sat. fat), 109 mg chol., 158 mg sodium, 50 g carbo., 1 g fiber, 6 g pro.

Rosemary Mini Cupcakes

PREP: 20 minutes **BAKE:** 12 minutes **COOL:** 30 minutes
MAKES: 36 servings

- 1   package 1-layer-size white cake mix
- 1   teaspoon snipped fresh rosemary or ¼ teaspoon dried rosemary, crushed
- ½   teaspoon finely shredded orange peel
- ½   cup powdered sugar
- 1   tablespoon orange juice

one Line thirty-six 1¾-inch muffin cups with miniature paper bake cups.* Set aside.

two Prepare cake mix according to package directions, except, stir rosemary and orange peel into batter. Spoon 1 well-rounded teaspoon of the batter into each prepared muffin cup.

three Bake, uncovered, in a 350°F oven about 12 minutes or until tops spring back when lightly touched and cupcakes are golden brown. Cool in muffin pans on wire racks for 5 minutes.

four Meanwhile, for glaze, in a small bowl stir together powdered sugar and juice. Remove cupcakes from muffin pans. Dip tops of cupcakes into glaze. Cool on wire racks.

NUTRITION FACTS PER SERVING: 34 cal., 1 g total fat (0 g sat. fat), 0 mg chol., 46 mg sodium, 7 g carbo., 0 g fiber, 0 g pro.

Note: *If you don't have 1¾-inch muffin cups, line twelve 2½-inch muffin cups with paper bake cups. Prepare batter as directed. Spoon batter into prepared muffin cups, filling each about half full. Bake, uncovered, in a 350°F oven about 15 minutes or until golden brown. Continue as directed.*

Cupcake Mania: Fun to make and fun to eat, cupcakes are a perfect sweet for any occasion.

- Most butter-type cakes can be baked as cupcakes. Grease and flour a muffin pan or line cups with paper bake cups. Fill cups about half full with batter.

- Bake at the same temperature called for in the cake recipe but reduce the baking time by one-third to one-half.

* A two-layer cake usually makes 24 to 36 cupcakes. If all of the cupcakes do not fit in the oven at one time, refrigerate the unbaked extras until the first ones finish baking.

- Cool cupcakes and frost as desired.

Cookies-and-Cream Cupcakes *See photo on page 271.*

PREP: 20 minutes **BAKE:** per package directions
COOL: 1 hour **MAKES:** 24 servings

- 1   package 2-layer-size white cake mix
- 1   cup coarsely crushed chocolate sandwich cookies with white filling
- 1   16-ounce can creamy white frosting
- 24   miniature chocolate sandwich cookies with white filling

one Line twenty-four 2½-inch muffin cups with paper bake cups; set aside. Prepare cake mix according to package directions, except fold the crushed cookies into batter. Spoon batter into prepared cups, filling each about half full.

two Bake, uncovered, in a 350°F oven according to package directions. Cool in muffin pans on wire racks for 5 minutes. Remove cupcakes from pans. Cool on wire racks.

three Pipe or spread frosting onto cupcakes. Top with the miniature cookies.

NUTRITION FACTS PER SERVING: 211 cal., 7 g total fat (2 g sat. fat), 0 mg chol., 229 mg sodium, 35 g carbo., 0 g fiber, 2 g pro.

Brownie Surprise Cupcakes

PREP: 15 minutes **BAKE:** 22 minutes **COOL:** 1 hour
MAKES: 15 servings

- 1   21-ounce package fudge brownie mix
- 25   miniature chocolate-coated caramel-topped nougat bars with peanuts

one Line fifteen 2½-inch muffin cups with paper bake cups. Set aside.

two Prepare brownie mix according to package directions. Spoon 1 tablespoon of the batter into each prepared cup. Place a candy bar in each cup. Divide the remaining batter among cups. Chop the remaining candy bars; sprinkle on top of batter in cups.

three Bake, uncovered, in a 350°F oven for 22 minutes. Cool in muffin pans on wire racks for 5 minutes (tops may dip slightly). Remove cupcakes from pans. Cool on wire racks.

NUTRITION FACTS PER SERVING: 298 cal., 13 g total fat (3 g sat. fat), 29 mg chol., 184 mg sodium, 41 g carbo., 0 g fiber, 4 g pro.

Mint Surprise Cupcakes: Prepare as directed, except place 2 miniature chocolate-covered cream-filled mint patties between batter layers of each cupcake. Bake and cool as directed. Before serving, top cupcakes with canned vanilla forsting and, if desired, additional mint patties.

NUTRITION FACTS PER SERVING: 301 cal., 11 g total fat (2 g sat. fat), 27 mg chol., 179 mg sodium, 50 g carbo., 0 g fiber, 3 g pro.

Icy Orange-Filled Cupcakes

PREP: 20 minutes **FREEZE:** 3 hours **MAKES:** 6 servings

1   pint frozen vanilla yogurt

¼   cup frozen orange juice concentrate

6   purchased frosted white or yellow cupcakes

one Line a 9-inch pie plate with foil; set aside. In a chilled small bowl soften half of the frozen yogurt by pressing it against side of bowl with a wooden spoon. Spread softened yogurt in the prepared pie plate. Cover with plastic wrap; freeze about 1 hour or until firm.

two In another chilled small bowl combine the remaining frozen yogurt and the orange juice concentrate. Stir with wooden spoon until frozen yogurt is softened and mixture is smooth. Spread orange mixture over yogurt layer. Cover with plastic wrap; freeze about 2 hours or until firm.

three If present, remove paper liners from cupcakes. Cut cupcakes in half horizontally. Lift the frozen layered yogurt from pie plate using edge of foil.

four Using a scalloped round 2- to 2½-inch cookie cutter (depending on size of cupcakes), cut 6 rounds from the frozen layered yogurt. Return the remaining frozen yogurt to freezer for another use. Place rounds of frozen yogurt between cupcake halves.

NUTRITION FACTS PER SERVING: 232 cal., 6 g total fat (2 g sat. fat), 6 mg chol., 138 mg sodium, 41 g carbo., 0 g fiber, 3 g pro.

Crunchy Nut-Caramel Cupcakes

START TO FINISH: 15 minutes **MAKES:** 12 servings

¾ cup caramel ice cream topping

12 purchased German chocolate, yellow, or white cupcakes

½ gallon chocolate ice cream

½ to ¾ cup pecan pieces, toasted (see tip, page 280)

⅓ cup semisweet chocolate pieces

⅓ cup coconut, toasted (see tip, page 280) (optional)

one In a small saucepan cook and stir caramel topping over medium heat until warm. Remove from heat.

two If present, remove paper liners from cupcakes. Place cupcakes on 12 dessert plates. Top each cupcake with a generous scoop of ice cream.

three Spoon caramel topping over ice cream. Sprinkle with pecans, chocolate pieces, and, if desired, coconut.

NUTRITION FACTS PER SERVING: 429 cal., 19 g total fat (8 g sat. fat), 30 mg chol., 257 mg sodium, 59 g carbo., 2 g fiber, 6 g pro.

Chocolate Cookie Cheesecakes

PREP: 20 minutes **BAKE:** 20 minutes **CHILL:** 1 to 24 hours
MAKES: 12 servings

12 chocolate sandwich cookies with white filling

2 8-ounce packages cream cheese, softened

½ cup sugar

1 teaspoon vanilla

2 eggs

one Line twelve 2½-inch muffin cups with foil bake cups; set aside. Split each sandwich cookie, keeping the filling intact on one cookie half. Place a cookie half with filling, filling side up, in each prepared cup.

two In a medium bowl combine cream cheese, sugar, and vanilla. Beat with an electric mixer until smooth. Add eggs; beat on low speed just until combined. Spoon mixture into cups. Crush the remaining cookies; sprinkle over filling.

three Bake, uncovered, in a 325°F oven for 20 to 25 minutes or until set (tops may dip slightly). Cool. Cover and chill for 1 to 24 hours. Remove foil bake cups before serving.

NUTRITION FACTS PER SERVING: 223 cal., 16 g total fat (9 g sat. fat), 77 mg chol., 183 mg sodium, 16 g carbo., 0 g fiber, 4 g pro.

Passion Fruit and Strawberry Sorbet Cake

PREP: 30 minutes **FREEZE:** 24 hours **CHILL:** 10 minutes
MAKES: 8 to 10 servings

8	ounces coconut macaroon cookies (about 11 cookies)
2	pints strawberry sorbet
1	pint passion fruit sorbet or mango sorbet
2	cups strawberries, sliced
1	cup raspberries

one Place a 9-inch springform pan in the freezer for 15 minutes. Place macaroon cookies in a food processor; cover and process until crumbly.

two Spread the crumbs in an ungreased 15×10×1-inch baking pan. Bake, uncovered, in a 375°F oven for 7 to 8 minutes or until golden brown. Cool. Sprinkle 1 cup of the crumbs on the bottom of the prepared springform pan. Set the remaining crumbs aside.

three In a chilled small bowl soften 1 pint of the strawberry sorbet by pressing it against side of bowl with a wooden spoon. Spread sorbet over crumbs in the prepared pan. Sprinkle with half of the reserved crumbs. Cover with plastic wrap; freeze about 2 hours or until firm.

four In a chilled small bowl soften the passion fruit sorbet by pressing it against side of bowl; spread over strawberry layer. Sprinkle with the remaining crumbs. Cover and freeze about 2 hours or until firm. In a chilled small bowl soften the remaining strawberry sorbet by pressing it against side of bowl; spread over passion fruit layer. Cover and freeze overnight.

five To serve, run a thin knife along side of pan to loosen edge of cake. Remove side of pan and place cake on a serving plate. Arrange strawberries and raspberries on top of cake. Chill for 10 to 15 minutes to soften cake before serving.

NUTRITION FACTS PER SERVING: 307 cal., 4 g total fat (3 g sat. fat), 0 mg chol., 15 mg sodium, 68 g carbo., 4 g fiber, 2 g pro.

Shimmering Strawberry Pie

PREP: 35 minutes **COOL:** 2 hours **CHILL:** 3 to 4 hours
MAKES: 8 servings

- ½ of a 15-ounce package (1 crust) rolled refrigerated unbaked piecrust
- 6 cups strawberries, halved and/or sliced
- 1 cup water
- ¼ cup sugar
- 2 tablespoons cornstarch
  Few drops red food coloring (optional)
  Frozen whipped dessert topping, thawed (optional)

one Let piecrust stand according to package directions. Unroll piecrust and fit into a 9-inch pie plate. Trim pastry to ½-inch beyond edge of pie plate. Fold under extra pastry; crimp edge. Prick bottom and side of pastry with a fork.

two Bake, uncovered, in a 450°F oven for 9 to 11 minutes or until golden brown. Cool on a wire rack.

three For filling, in a blender or food processor combine 1 cup of the strawberries and the water. Cover and blend or process until smooth.

four In a small saucepan combine sugar and cornstarch; stir in berry mixture. Cook and stir over medium heat until thickened and bubbly. Cook and stir for 2 minutes more. Transfer to a large bowl. If desired, stir in food coloring. Cool for 2 hours.

five Fold the remaining 5 cups strawberries into cooled mixture. Transfer filling to pastry shell. Cover and chill for 3 to 4 hours. If desired, serve with whipped topping.

NUTRITION FACTS PER SERVING: 184 cal., 7 g total fat (3 g sat. fat), 5 mg chol., 110 mg sodium, 29 g carbo., 2 g fiber, 1 g pro.

Strawberry-Chocolate Pie

PREP: 20 minutes **CHILL:** 1 to 2 hours **MAKES:** 8 servings

- 1 cup semisweet chocolate pieces (6 ounces)
- 1 8-ounce package cream cheese
- 3 tablespoons honey
- 1 9-inch baked pastry shell
- 4 cups strawberries, stems and caps removed

one In a small heavy saucepan cook and stir chocolate pieces over low heat until chocolate melts. Cool to room temperature.

two In a medium bowl beat cream cheese with an electric mixer on low speed until softened. Gradually beat in cooled chocolate and honey. Spread chocolate mixture in pastry shell. Cover and chill for 1 to 2 hours. Arrange strawberries on top of pie before serving.

NUTRITION FACTS PER SERVING: 387 cal., 25 g total fat (12 g sat. fat), 31 mg chol., 160 mg sodium, 40 g carbo., 3 g fiber, 5 g pro.

Juicy Raspberry Pie

PREP: 30 minutes **BAKE:** 45 minutes **COOL:** 2 hours
MAKES: 6 to 8 servings

- 1   15-ounce package (2 crusts) rolled refrigerated unbaked piecrust
- 4   cups fresh or frozen raspberries
- ¾   to 1 cup sugar
- 3   tablespoons quick-cooking tapioca
- 2   tablespoons butter, melted
-     Vanilla ice cream (optional)

> **Quick Lattice Top** Here's a fast and easy way to make a lattice top for your fruit pie. Assemble the bottom of the pie as your recipe directs. Roll out the top crust. Using a fluted pastry wheel or a sharp knife, cut the pastry into twelve ½-inch strips. Lay six strips crosswise on the pie and arrange six strips lengthwise across the first six strips. Press the ends of the strips into the rim of the bottom pastry, trimming the ends as necessary. Fold the bottom pastry over the ends of strips; crimp edge.

one Let piecrusts stand according to package directions. For filling, in a large bowl combine raspberries, sugar, tapioca, and melted butter; toss gently to combine. (If using frozen berries, let mixture stand for 15 to 30 minutes or until berries are partially thawed but still icy. Stir well.)

two For bottom crust, unroll one piecrust and fit into a 9-inch pie plate. Trim pastry to ½ inch beyond edge of pie plate. Transfer filling to pastry-lined pie plate.

three For lattice top crust, roll remaining piecrust into a 12-inch circle. Cut pastry into ½-inch strips. Weave strips over filling in a lattice pattern. Or use Quick Lattice Top (see tip, left). Press ends of strips into bottom pastry rim. Fold bottom pastry over ends of strips; crimp edge. Cover edge of pie with foil to prevent overbrowning.

four Place pie on a baking sheet. Bake in a 375°F oven for 25 minutes (50 minutes if using frozen berries). Remove foil. Bake, uncovered, for 20 to 25 minutes more or until filling is bubbly and pastry is golden brown. Cool on a wire rack. If desired, serve with ice cream.

NUTRITION FACTS PER SERVING: 259 cal., 5 g total fat (2 g sat. fat), 8 mg chol., 403 mg sodium, 51 g carbo., 5 g fiber, 6 g pro.

Parfait Pie with Coconut Shell

PREP: 20 minutes **BAKE:** 20 minutes **CHILL:** 4 hours
MAKES: 8 servings

2   cups flaked coconut

3   tablespoons butter or margarine, melted

1   10-ounce package frozen red raspberries in syrup, thawed

1   3-ounce package raspberry-flavor gelatin

1   pint vanilla ice cream

one In a medium bowl combine coconut and melted butter. Press mixture evenly onto the bottom and up the side of a 9-inch pie plate. Bake, uncovered, in a 325°F oven for 20 minutes. Cool on a wire rack.

two Drain raspberries, reserving syrup. Set raspberries aside. Add enough water to the syrup to measure 1¼ cups. In a medium saucepan combine gelatin and the 1¼ cups syrup. Cook and stir until gelatin is dissolved. Remove from heat.

three Add the ice cream by spoonfuls to gelatin mixture, stirring until melted. Cover and chill until mixture mounds when spooned. Fold in raspberries. Pour into coconut crust. Cover and chill for at least 4 hours or until set.

NUTRITION FACTS PER SERVING: 291 cal., 14 g total fat (10 g sat. fat), 27 mg chol., 114 mg sodium, 40 g carbo., 2 g fiber, 3 g pro.

Frozen Cranberry Pie

PREP: 20 minutes **FREEZE:** 4 hours **MAKES:** 8 servings

Nonstick cooking spray

6   chocolate wafer cookies, finely crushed (about ⅓ cup)

1   quart vanilla low-fat or light ice cream

1   cup whole-berry cranberry sauce

1   teaspoon finely shredded orange peel

one Coat a 9-inch pie plate with cooking spray. Cover bottom and side of pie plate evenly with crushed cookies. Set aside.

two In a chilled medium bowl soften ice cream by pressing it against side of bowl with a wooden spoon. Fold in cranberry sauce and orange peel. Spread mixture in the cookie crust. Cover and freeze for at least 4 hours or until firm.

NUTRITION FACTS PER SERVING: 176 cal., 3 g total fat (1 g sat. fat), 10 mg chol., 92 mg sodium, 36 g carbo., 1 g fiber, 2 g pro.

Peanut Butter S'more Tarts

PREP: 15 minutes **CHILL:** 2 to 24 hours **STAND:** 30 minutes
MAKES: 6 servings

    1   cup semisweet chocolate pieces (6 ounces)
    ½   cup peanut butter
    1½   cups tiny marshmallows
    ½   cup chopped peanuts
    1   4-ounce package (6) graham cracker crumb
         tart shells

one In a small heavy saucepan cook and stir chocolate pieces over low heat until chocolate melts. Remove from heat. Stir in peanut butter until smooth. Stir in marshmallows and peanuts. Spoon mixture into tart shells.

two Cover and chill for 2 to 24 hours. Let stand at room temperature for 30 minutes before serving.

NUTRITION FACTS PER SERVING: 505 cal., 31 g total fat (8 g sat. fat), 0 mg chol., 257 mg sodium, 42 g carbo., 7 g fiber, 10 g pro.

GRILLING

Rustic Pear Tart

PREP: 20 minutes **GRILL:** 35 minutes **COOL:** 20 minutes
MAKES: 6 to 8 servings

    ½   of a 15-ounce package (1 crust) rolled refrigerated
         unbaked piecrust
    2   large ripe pears, peeled, cored, and very thinly sliced
         (3½ cups)
    2   tablespoons sugar
    1   tablespoon cornstarch
    ¼   teaspoon ground cardamom
         Whipped cream (optional)

one Let piecrust stand according to package directions. Meanwhile, in a medium bowl combine pear slices, sugar, cornstarch, and cardamom; toss gently to combine.

two Wrap a 10- to 12-inch pizza pan with heavy foil. Unroll piecrust onto the prepared pizza pan. Arrange pear slices in center of piecrust in a single layer, leaving a 2-inch border around the edge. Fold piecrust border up over the pears, pleating as necessary to fit.

three For a charcoal grill, arrange medium-hot coals around edge of grill. Test for medium heat above center of grill. Place pizza pan on grill rack over center of grill. Cover and grill for 35 to 45 minutes or until pears are tender and pastry is golden brown. (For a gas grill, preheat grill. Reduce heat to medium. Adjust for indirect cooking. Grill as above.)

four Cool tart on a wire rack for 20 to 30 minutes before serving. If desired, serve with whipped cream.

NUTRITION FACTS PER SERVING: 234 cal., 9 g total fat (4 g sat. fat), 7 mg chol., 145 mg sodium, 37 g carbo., 3 g fiber, 1 g pro.

Fruit-Topped Phyllo Cups

START TO FINISH: 15 minutes **MAKES:** 15 servings

3   tablespoons apple jelly

½   of an 8-ounce package cream cheese, softened

1   2.1-ounce package (15) baked miniature phyllo
     dough shells

15   red and/or green seedless grape halves and/or
     strawberry halves

one In a small saucepan cook and stir apple jelly over medium-low heat until jelly melts. Stir 2 tablespoons of the melted jelly into cream cheese until smooth. Spoon cream cheese mixture into phyllo shells.

two In a small bowl combine grapes and/or strawberries and the remaining melted jelly; stir gently to coat. Spoon a piece of fruit on top of each tart. If desired, cover and chill for up to 4 hours.

NUTRITION FACTS PER SERVING: 62 cal., 4 g total fat (2 g sat. fat), 8 mg chol., 33 mg sodium, 6 g carbo., 0 g fiber, 1 g pro.

Raspberry and Chocolate Tulips

START TO FINISH: 15 minutes **MAKES:** 15 servings

½   cup frozen raspberries

2   tablespoons sugar

1   2.1-ounce package (15) baked miniature phyllo
     dough shells

4   teaspoons chocolate-flavor syrup

     Pressurized whipped dessert topping

one In a small saucepan combine frozen raspberries and sugar. Cook over medium heat, stirring frequently, for 3 to 5 minutes or just until raspberries are completely thawed. Remove from heat; cool slightly.

two Spoon about ½ teaspoon of the raspberry mixture into the bottom of each phyllo shell. Top each with about ¼ teaspoon of the chocolate-flavor syrup and a small amount of whipped dessert topping.

NUTRITION FACTS PER SERVING: 46 cal., 2 g total fat (0 g sat. fat), 0 mg chol., 11 mg sodium, 6 g carbo., 0 g fiber, 0 g pro.

Cherry-Chocolate Pastries

PREP: 20 minutes **BAKE:** 15 minutes **COOL:** 20 minutes
MAKES: 8 servings

½   of a 17.3-ounce package (1 sheet) frozen
     puff pastry, thawed

¾   cup cherry pie filling

3   tablespoons fudge ice cream topping

2   tablespoons chopped nuts

one On a lightly floured surface, unfold pastry sheet. Using a 3½- to 4-inch desired cookie cutter, cut out 8 pastry shapes, discarding scraps or reserving for another use. Place pastry cutouts on an ungreased large baking sheet.

two Bake, uncovered, in a 375°F oven for 15 to 18 minutes or until pastries are puffed and golden. Cool on wire racks.

three Split pastries in half horizontally. Fill with cherry pie filling. Drizzle with fudge topping and sprinkle with nuts.

NUTRITION FACTS PER SERVING: 193 cal., 11 g total fat (0 g sat. fat), 0 mg chol., 144 mg sodium, 22 g carbo., 0 g fiber, 2 g pro.

Fruit-Filled Napoleons

PREP: 20 minutes **BAKE:** 20 minutes **MAKES:** 8 servings

½   of a 17.3-ounce package (1 sheet) frozen puff pastry,
     thawed

2   cups pudding, fruit yogurt, sweetened whipped
     cream, or softened ice cream

1   cup peeled and sliced kiwifruits, halved seedless red
     grapes, berries, and/or halved orange slices

     Powdered sugar (optional)

one On a lightly floured surface, unfold pastry sheet. Using a sharp knife, cut pastry into 8 rectangles. Place pastry rectangles on an ungreased large baking sheet.

two Bake, uncovered, in a 375°F oven about 20 minutes or until pastries are puffed and golden. Cool on wire racks.

three Split pastries in half horizontally. Fill with pudding and fruit. If desired, sprinkle with powdered sugar.

NUTRITION FACTS PER SERVING: 266 cal., 13 g total fat (0 g sat. fat), 1 mg chol., 184 mg sodium, 35 g carbo., 1 g fiber, 3 g pro.

Semisweet-Chocolate Bread Pudding

PREP: 20 minutes **COOL:** 10 minutes **COOK:** Low 2½ hours
STAND: 30 minutes **MAKES:** 8 servings

   Nonstick cooking spray
3 cups milk
¾ cup semisweet chocolate pieces
¾ cup presweetened cocoa powder
3 eggs, slightly beaten
5 cups dried ½-inch Hawaiian sweet bread or cinnamon
   swirl bread cubes (see tip, below)
   Whipped cream (optional)

> **Drying Bread** To make dried bread cubes for bread puddings and stuffings, cut fresh bread into ½-inch cubes. It takes 8 or 9 slices to make 5 cups of dried cubes. Spread the bread cubes in a single layer in an ungreased 15x10x1-inch baking pan. Bake, uncovered, in a 300°F oven for 10 to 15 minutes or until cubes are dried, stirring twice; cool. The bread will continue to dry and crisp as it cools. Or let bread cubes stand, loosely covered, at room temperature for 8 to 12 hours.

one Lightly coat a 3½- or 4-quart slow cooker with cooking spray; set aside.

two In a medium saucepan bring milk to simmering; remove from heat. Add chocolate pieces and cocoa powder (do not stir); let stand for 5 minutes. Whisk until chocolate melts and mixture is smooth. Cool for 10 minutes.

three In a large bowl whisk together eggs and chocolate mixture. Gently stir in bread cubes. Pour mixture into the prepared cooker.

four Cover and cook on low-heat setting about 2½ hours or until puffed and a knife inserted near center comes out clear. Remove liner from cooker, if possible, or turn off cooker. Let stand, uncovered, for 30 to 45 minutes to cool slightly before serving (pudding will fall as it cools).

five To serve, spoon warm pudding into 8 dessert dishes. If desired, top with spoonfuls of whipped cream.

NUTRITION FACTS PER SERVING: 360 cal., 12 g total fat (6 g sat. fat), 95 mg chol., 214 mg sodium, 62 g carbo., 4 g fiber, 9 g pro.

Pumpkin Custard Bread Pudding

PREP: 15 minutes **COOK:** 3½ hours **STAND:** 30 minutes
MAKES: 8 servings

Nonstick cooking spray

2 eggs

⅔ cup half-and-half or light cream

1 30-ounce can pumpkin pie mix

5 cups dried ½-inch bread cubes (see tip, page 322)

½ cup chopped pecans

Caramel ice cream topping (optional)

one Lightly coat a 3½- or 4-quart slow cooker with cooking spray; set aside.

two In a large bowl whisk together eggs and half-and-half. Stir in pumpkin pie mix until combined. Gently stir in bread cubes. Pour mixture into the prepared cooker.

three Cover and cook on low-heat setting for 3½ to 4 hours or until a knife inserted near center comes out clean (160°F). Remove liner from cooker, if possible, or turn off cooker. Let stand, uncovered, for 30 to 45 minutes to cool slightly before serving.

four To serve, spoon bread pudding into 8 dessert dishes. Sprinkle with pecans and, if desired, drizzle with caramel ice cream topping.

NUTRITION FACTS PER SERVING: 268 cal., 9 g total fat (2 g sat. fat), 61 mg chol., 379 mg sodium, 42 g carbo., 10 g fiber, 6 g pro.

Quick and Creamy Rice Pudding

START TO FINISH: 25 minutes **MAKES:** 4 servings

1 4-serving-size package vanilla instant pudding and pie filling mix

3¼ cups milk

1 cup instant rice

¼ cup dried tart cherries, dried blueberries, or snipped dried apricots

¼ teaspoon ground cardamom or cinnamon

one Prepare pudding and pie filling mix according to package directions using 2 cups of the milk; set aside.

two Meanwhile, in a small saucepan heat remaining 1¼ cups milk over medium heat just to boiling. Stir in rice and dried fruit. Remove from heat; cover and let stand for 5 minutes.

three Stir in prepared pudding and cardamom. Serve warm or cover surface with plastic wrap and chill.

NUTRITION FACTS PER SERVING: 234 cal., 2 g total fat (1 g sat. fat), 6 mg chol., 178 mg sodium, 51 g carbo., 0 g fiber, 5 g pro.

DELECTABLE DESSERTS

Fruity Rice Pudding

PREP: 15 minutes **COOK:** Low 2 hours **STAND:** 30 minutes
MAKES: 8 servings

  Nonstick cooking spray
3 cups whole milk
2 5½-ounce packages rice pudding mix with raisins
  and cinnamon
½ cup snipped dried apricots or dried cherries
2 tablespoons butter or margarine, softened
⅓ cup pecans or almonds, toasted (see tip, page 280)

one Lightly coat a 3½- or 4-quart slow cooker with cooking spray. In the prepared cooker combine milk, rice pudding mixes, dried apricots, and softened butter.

two Cover and cook on low-heat setting about 2 hours or until rice is tender. Remove liner from cooker, if possible, or turn off cooker. Stir mixture. Let stand, uncovered, about 30 minutes to cool slightly before serving.

three To serve, stir well and spoon into 8 dessert dishes. Sprinkle with toasted nuts.

NUTRITION FACTS PER SERVING: 280 cal., 10 g total fat (4 g sat. fat), 21 mg chol., 214 mg sodium, 44 g carbo., 2 g fiber, 6 g pro.

Chocolate Pots de Crème

PREP: 15 minutes **CHILL:** 2 to 24 hours **MAKES:** 4 to 6 servings

1 cup half-and-half or light cream
1 4-ounce package sweet baking chocolate,
  coarsely chopped
2 teaspoons sugar
3 egg yolks, slightly beaten
½ teaspoon vanilla

one In a small heavy saucepan combine half-and-half, chocolate, and sugar. Cook and stir over medium heat about 10 minutes or until mixture reaches a full boil and thickens.

two Gradually stir about half of the hot mixture into egg yolks. Return all of the egg yolk mixture to saucepan. Cook and stir over low heat for 2 minutes. Remove from heat; stir in vanilla.

three Pour chocolate mixture into 4 to 6 small cups or dessert dishes. Cover and chill for 2 to 24 hours.

NUTRITION FACTS PER SERVING: 276 cal., 21 g total fat (11 g sat. fat), 182 mg chol., 31 mg sodium, 22 g carbo., 2 g fiber, 5 g pro.

Coffee Custards

PREP: 20 minutes **BAKE:** 30 minutes **COOL:** 45 minutes
MAKES: 6 servings

½ cup sugar

2 to 3 teaspoons instant coffee crystals

2½ cups light or reduced-fat milk

4 eggs, slightly beaten

1 teaspoon vanilla

Raspberries (optional)

one In a medium saucepan combine sugar and coffee crystals; add milk. Cook and stir until coffee crystals are dissolved and mixture is heated through. In a medium bowl gradually whisk hot milk mixture into eggs. Stir in vanilla.

two Place 6 ungreased 6-ounce custard cups in a 13×9×2-inch baking pan. Divide egg mixture among custard cups. Place baking pan on oven rack. Pour boiling water into baking pan around custard cups to a depth of 1 inch.

three Bake, uncovered, in a 325°F oven for 30 to 40 minutes or until a knife inserted near the centers comes out clean. Remove custard cups from water. Cool on a wire rack for 45 minutes. If desired, cover and chill for up to 24 hours. If desired, serve with raspberries.

NUTRITION FACTS PER SERVING: 157 cal., 4 g total fat (2 g sat. fat), 146 mg chol., 94 mg sodium, 21 g carbo., 0 g fiber, 8 g pro.

Flan

PREP: 20 minutes **BAKE:** 35 minutes **CHILL:** 4 to 24 hours
MAKES: 6 servings

⅔ cup sugar

3 eggs, slightly beaten

1 12-ounce can evaporated milk

1 teaspoon vanilla

one For caramelized sugar, place ⅓ cup of the sugar in a small heavy saucepan. Cook over medium-high heat until sugar starts to melt, shaking pan occasionally to heat sugar evenly. Do not stir. Once sugar starts to melt, reduce heat to low. Cook about 5 minutes or until all of the sugar is melted and golden, stirring as needed with a wooden spoon. Remove from heat.

two Immediately pour caramelized sugar into 6 ungreased 6-ounce custard cups. Working quickly, turn cups so sugar evenly coats bottoms. Place cups in a 13×9×2-inch baking pan.

three In a medium bowl whisk together eggs, evaporated milk, vanilla, and the remaining ⅓ cup sugar. Divide egg mixture among custard cups. Place baking pan on oven rack. Pour hot water into baking pan around custard cups to a depth of 1 inch.

four Bake, uncovered, in a 325°F oven for 35 to 40 minutes or until a knife inserted near the centers comes out clean. Remove cups from water. Cool on a wire rack. Cover and chill for 4 to 24 hours.

five To serve, loosen custards from sides of custard cups. Invert onto 6 desert plates.

NUTRITION FACTS PER SERVING: 198 cal., 7 g total fat (3 g sat. fat), 123 mg chol., 92 mg sodium, 28 g carbo., 0 g fiber, 7 g pro.

Bittersweet Chocolate Soufflé *See photo on page 273.*

PREP: 25 minutes **STAND:** 30 minutes **BAKE:** 18 minutes
MAKES: 9 servings

7	egg whites
10	ounces bittersweet chocolate, coarsely chopped
½	cup butter
¼	cup granulated sugar
	Powdered sugar (optional)

one Place egg whites in a large bowl. Let stand at room temperature for 30 minutes. Meanwhile, in a medium heavy saucepan combine chocolate and the ½ cup butter. Cook and stir over low heat until chocolate melts. Cool about 30 minutes.

two Butter the sides of nine 4-ounce ramekins or 6-ounce custard cups. Sprinkle with granulated sugar. Set prepared ramekins aside.

three Beat egg whites with an electric mixer on medium speed until soft peaks form (tip curl). Gradually add the ¼ cup granulated sugar, about 1 tablespoon at a time, beating until stiff peaks form (tips stand straight).

four Fold about 1 cup of the beaten egg whites into cooled chocolate mixture. Fold chocolate-egg white mixture into the remaining beaten egg whites. Divide mixture evenly among the prepared ramekins.

five Bake, uncovered, in a 375°F oven about 18 minutes or until a knife inserted near the centers comes out clean. If desired, sprinkled with powdered sugar. Serve immediately.

NUTRITION FACTS PER SERVING: 298 cal., 22 g total fat (13 g sat. fat), 32 mg chol., 162 mg sodium, 24 g carbo., 2 g fiber, 5 g pro.

Chocolate-Caramel Fondue

PREP: 10 minutes **COOK:** 2 hours **MAKES:** 12 servings

1   14-ounce can sweetened condensed milk

1   12-ounce jar caramel ice cream topping

9   ounces semisweet chocolate, coarsely chopped, or
    1½ cups semisweet chocolate pieces

    Assorted dippers (such as angel food or pound cake
    cubes, large marshmallows, strawberries, banana
    slices, pineapple chunks, and/or dried apricots)

    Milk, warmed (optional)

one In a 1½-quart slow cooker stir together sweetened condensed milk, caramel topping, and chocolate.

two Cover and cook for 2 hours (use low-heat setting if available). Stir until mixture is smooth. Serve immediately or keep warm, covered, for up to 1 hour (use low-heat setting if available), stirring occasionally. (Chocolate mixture will become grainy if held longer.)

three To serve, spear dippers with fondue forks. Dip into chocolate mixture, swirling as you dip. If the mixture thickens, stir in a little warm milk to make the fondue of desired consistency.

NUTRITION FACTS PER SERVING FONDUE: 295 cal., 10 g total fat (6 g sat. fat), 11 mg chol., 104 mg sodium, 50 g carbo., 2 g fiber, 6 g pro.

Glazed Nut Topping

START TO FINISH: 10 minutes **MAKES:** 4 servings

½   cup chopped walnuts

2   tablespoons butter or margarine

3   tablespoons packed brown sugar

1   tablespoon milk

one In a small saucepan combine walnuts and butter. Cook and stir over medium heat until nuts are lightly browned.

two Stir in brown sugar and milk. Cook and stir until brown sugar is dissolved. To use, serve topping over ice cream.

NUTRITION FACTS PER SERVING: 179 cal., 16 g total fat (5 g sat. fat), 17 mg chol., 67 mg sodium, 9 g carbo., 1 g fiber, 2 g pro.

Hot Fudge Sauce

START TO FINISH: 15 minutes **MAKES:** 16 servings

½ cup unsweetened cocoa powder

⅓ cup granulated sugar

⅓ cup packed dark brown sugar

½ cup whipping cream

3 tablespoons butter or margarine

one In a small bowl stir together cocoa powder, granulated sugar, and brown sugar; set aside.

two In a small heavy saucepan combine cream and butter. Cook and stir over low heat until butter melts. Cook and stir over medium heat about 3 minutes or until mixture bubbles around edge. Stir in sugar mixture. Cook and stir for 1 to 2 minutes more or until sugar is dissolved and mixture is thickened.

three To use, serve immediately over ice cream, cake, or other desserts. Store, tightly covered, in the refrigerator. To reheat sauce, in a small heavy saucepan cook over low heat, stirring frequently, until heated through.

NUTRITION FACTS PER SERVING: 89 cal., 5 g total fat (4 g sat. fat), 73 mg chol., 34 mg sodium, 10 g carbo., 0 g fiber, 1 g pro.

Butterscotch-Caramel Sauce

START TO FINISH: 10 minutes **MAKES:** 18 servings

1½ cups light-color corn syrup

1 cup packed brown sugar

2 tablespoons butter

¼ cup half-and-half or light cream

one In a medium heavy skillet combine corn syrup, brown sugar, and butter. Cook and stir over medium heat until sugar is dissolved and mixture starts to boil. Remove from heat; cool slightly. Stir in half-and-half.

two To use, serve warm over ice cream, cake, or other desserts. Store, tightly covered, in the refrigerator. To reheat sauce, in a small heavy saucepan cook over low heat, stirring frequently, until heated through.

NUTRITION FACTS PER SERVING: 68 cal., 1 g total fat (0 g sat. fat), 2 mg chol., 26 mg sodium, 16 g carbo., 0 g fiber, 0 g pro.

Surprise Chocolate Bites

PREP: 25 minutes **BAKE:** 10 minutes per batch
MAKES: 30 servings

1	18-ounce roll refrigerated sugar cookie dough
⅓	cup unsweetened cocoa powder
⅔	cup powdered sugar
⅔	cup creamy peanut butter
	Granulated sugar

one In a large bowl combine cookie dough and cocoa powder; knead until mixed. In a small bowl combine powdered sugar and peanut butter. Using floured hands, shape peanut butter mixture into thirty 1-inch balls.

two Using 1 tablespoon dough for each cookie, make an indentation in the center. Press a peanut butter ball into indentation and form dough around ball to enclose it; roll gently in your hands until smooth.

three Place balls 2 inches apart on an ungreased cookie sheet. Flatten the balls slightly with the bottom of a glass dipped in granulated sugar.

four Bake, uncovered, in a 350°F oven for 10 to 12 minutes or until set. Transfer cookies to a wire rack; cool.

NUTRITION FACTS PER SERVING: 118 cal., 6 g total fat (1 g sat. fat), 5 mg chol., 87 mg sodium, 15 g carbo., 0 g fiber, 2 g pro.

Pine Nut Cookies

PREP: 20 minutes **BAKE:** 15 minutes per batch
MAKES: about 42 servings

1	12-ounce can almond pastry and dessert filling
½	cup granulated sugar
1	cup powdered sugar
4	egg whites
1½	cups pine nuts (8 ounces)

one Line 2 cookie sheets with foil; lightly grease foil. Set aside. In a food processor combine almond filling and granulated sugar. Cover and process until smooth. Add powdered sugar and 2 of the egg whites; cover and process until smooth.

two Place the remaining egg whites in a small bowl; beat with a fork. Place pine nuts on a shallow plate. Using lightly floured hands, shape almond mixture into 1-inch balls. Roll balls in egg whites, then roll in pine nuts to coat. Place balls on the prepared cookie sheets. Flatten slightly to form 1½-inch rounds.

three Bake, uncovered, in a 325°F oven for 15 to 18 minutes or until lightly browned. Cool on cookie sheet for 1 minute. Transfer cookies to a wire rack; cool.

NUTRITION FACTS PER SERVING: 86 cal., 5 g total fat (1 g sat. fat), 0 mg chol., 6 mg sodium, 9 g carbo., 0 g fiber, 2 g pro.

Chocolate Chip Thumbprints

PREP: 25 minutes **BAKE:** 10 minutes per batch
MAKES: about 30 servings

- 1 18-ounce roll refrigerated chocolate chip cookie dough
- ⅓ cup all-purpose flour
- ¾ cup finely chopped hazelnuts (filberts) or almonds
- ¼ cup milk
- ½ cup chocolate-hazelnut spread
- Candy sprinkles (optional)

one In a large bowl combine refrigerated cookie dough and flour; knead until mixed.

two Place hazelnuts in a shallow dish. Pour milk into another shallow dish. Using 1 tablespoon dough for each cookie, shape into balls. Roll balls in milk, then roll in hazelnuts to coat. Place balls 2 inches apart on an ungreased cookie sheet. Press your thumb into the center of each ball to make an indentation.

three Bake, uncovered, in a 375°F oven for 10 to 12 minutes or until lightly browned. Transfer cookies to a wire rack; cool.

four Place chocolate-hazelnut spread in a resealable plastic bag; snip off one of the corners. Pipe into each indentation. If desired, sprinkle cookies with candy sprinkles.

NUTRITION FACTS PER SERVING: 125 cal., 7 g total fat (1 g sat. fat), 4 mg chol. 40 mg sodium, 15 g carbo., 1 g fiber, 2 g pro.

Sunflower Chip Cookies

PREP: 20 minutes **BAKE:** 9 minutes per batch
MAKES: about 30 servings

- 1 18-ounce roll refrigerated chocolate chip cookie dough
- ½ cup flaked coconut
- ½ cup dry roasted sunflower kernels

one In a large bowl combine cookie dough and coconut; knead until mixed. Using 1 rounded teaspoon dough for each cookie, shape into balls. Roll balls in sunflower seeds to coat. Place balls 2 inches apart on an ungreased cookie sheet.

two Bake, uncovered, in a 375°F oven for 9 to 11 minutes or until golden brown. Cool on cookie sheet for 1 minute. Transfer cookies to a wire rack; cool.

NUTRITION FACTS PER SERVING: 101 cal., 5 g total fat (2 g sat. fat), 2 mg chol., 66 mg sodium, 12 g carbo., 1 g fiber, 1 g pro.

Easy Peanut Butter Cookies

PREP: 20 minutes **BAKE:** 10 minutes per batch
MAKES: about 32 servings

1 cup sugar

1 cup peanut butter

1 egg

   Sugar

one In a medium bowl combine the 1 cup sugar, the peanut butter, and egg; mix well. Place additional sugar in a shallow dish. Shape dough into 1-inch balls. Roll balls in the additional sugar to coat.

two Place balls 2 inches apart on a greased cookie sheet. Flatten the balls slightly with the bottom of a glass. If desired, lightly press a 1½-inch cookie cutter into the center of each cookie to make a design (do not cut through cookie).

three Bake, uncovered, in a 375°F oven about 10 minutes or until edges of cookies are lightly browned. Transfer cookies to a wire rack; cool.

NUTRITION FACTS PER SERVING: 75 cal., 4 g total fat (1 g sat. fat), 7 mg chol., 39 mg sodium, 8 g carbo., 0 g fiber, 2 g pro.

Peanut Butter and Chocolate Pinwheels

PREP: 25 minutes **CHILL:** 1 hour **BAKE:** 8 minutes per batch
MAKES: about 72 servings

1 18-ounce roll refrigerated peanut butter cookie dough

¼ cup all-purpose flour

1 18-ounce roll refrigerated sugar cookie dough

¼ cup unsweetened cocoa powder

½ cup finely chopped peanuts (optional)

one Place peanut butter cookie dough in a large bowl; knead in flour. Divide dough in half. Place sugar cookie dough in another large bowl; knead in cocoa powder. Divide in half.

two Roll one portion of the peanut butter dough between pieces of waxed paper into a 12×6-inch rectangle. Repeat with one portion of the sugar cookie dough. Remove top pieces of waxed paper. Invert one rectangle on top of the other; press down gently to seal. Remove top piece of waxed paper.

three Starting from a long side, roll up dough; press edge to seal. If desired, roll in peanuts. Repeat with the remaining dough and, if desired, peanuts. Wrap in waxed paper or plastic wrap; chill about 1 hour or until firm enough to slice.

four Cut rolls into ¼-inch slices. Place slices 2 inches apart on an ungreased cookie sheet. Bake, uncovered, in a 375°F oven for 8 to 10 minutes or until edges are firm. Transfer cookies to a wire rack; cool.

NUTRITION FACTS PER SERVING: 79 cal., 4 g total fat (1 g sat. fat), 5 mg chol., 70 mg sodium, 10 g carbo., 0 g fiber, 1 g pro.

Five-Layer Bars

PREP: 10 minutes **BAKE:** 37 minutes **MAKES:** 30 servings

2	13-ounce packages (32 cookies) soft coconut macaroon cookies
¾	cup sweetened condensed milk
1	cup coarsely chopped peanuts
¾	cup semisweet chocolate pieces
¾	cup raisins, dried cranberries, or dried cherries and golden raisins

one Arrange cookies in the bottom of a greased 13×9×2-inch baking pan. Press cookies together to form a crust. Bake, uncovered, in a 350°F oven for 12 minutes. Remove from oven

two Drizzle crust evenly with sweetened condensed milk. Sprinkle with peanuts, chocolate pieces, and dried fruit.

three Bake, uncovered, about 25 minutes more or until edges are lightly browned. Cool in pan on a wire rack. Cut into bars.

NUTRITION FACTS PER SERVING: 198 cal., 10 g total fat (6 g sat. fat), 3 mg chol., 109 mg sodium, 26 g carbo., 2 g fiber, 3 g pro.

Praline Crunch Bars

PREP: 15 minutes **BAKE:** 12 minutes **STAND:** 5 minutes
MAKES: 28 servings

1	18-ounce roll refrigerated sugar cookie dough
½	cup toffee pieces
½	cup finely chopped pecans
1	12-ounce package miniature semisweet chocolate pieces
⅓	cup toffee pieces

one In a large bowl combine cookie dough, the ½ cup toffee pieces, and the pecans; knead until mixed. Press dough evenly onto bottom of an ungreased 13×9×2-inch baking pan.

two Bake, uncovered, in a 350°F oven for 12 to 15 minutes or until golden brown. Immediately sprinkle with chocolate pieces; let stand for 5 to 10 minutes or until softened. Spread chocolate evenly over uncut cookies.

three Sprinkle with the ⅓ cup toffee pieces. Chill until chocolate is set. Cut into bars.

NUTRITION FACTS PER SERVING: 191 cal., 11 g total fat (4 g sat. fat), 8 mg chol., 105 mg sodium, 19 g carbo., 2 g fiber, 1 g pro.

All-American Apple Pie Bars

REP: 15 minutes **BAKE:** 45 minutes **STAND:** 15 minutes
AKES: 16 servings

1   15-ounce package (2 crusts) rolled refrigerated
    unbaked piecrust
1   21-ounce can apple pie filling
½   teaspoon ground cinnamon
    Milk
½   cup powdered sugar
1   tablespoon milk

one Let piecrusts stand according to package directions.
Unroll piecrusts. Cut each piecrust into a 9-inch square;
discard trimmings. Place one pastry square in an ungreased
8×8×2-inch baking pan; press edges of pastry up sides of pan.

two In a medium bowl combine pie filling and cinnamon.
Spoon into pastry-lined pan. Top with the remaining pastry
square, folding edges under and pressing into edges of
bottom pastry. Prick top pastry all over with a fork. Brush
lightly with milk.

three Bake, uncovered, in a 375°F oven about 45 minutes or
until crust is golden brown. Place pan on a wire rack.

four For glaze, in a small bowl combine powdered sugar and
the 1 tablespoon milk. Brush glaze over uncut cookies. Cool
on wire rack. Cut into bars.

NUTRITION FACTS PER SERVING: 171 cal., 7 g total fat (2 g sat. fat), 3 mg chol.,
127 mg sodium, 26 g carbo., 0 g fiber, 1 g pro.

S'mores Bars

REP: 10 minutes **BAKE:** 8 minutes **MAKES:** 24 servings

24   graham crackers (2½-inch squares)
 2   cups tiny marshmallows
 1   11½-ounce package (2 cups) milk chocolate pieces
 ¾   cup butter
 ¾   cup packed brown sugar

one Arrange graham crackers in a single layer in a foil-lined
15×10×1-inch baking pan (cut crackers to fit if necessary).
Sprinkle with marshmallows and chocolate pieces.

two In a medium microwave-safe bowl combine butter and
brown sugar. Microwave, uncovered, on 100 percent power
(high) for 1 to 2 minutes or until butter melts. Stir to combine.
Pour mixture evenly over marshmallows and chocolate pieces.

three Bake, uncovered, in a 350°F oven for 8 to 10 minutes
or just until golden. Cool in pan on a wire rack. Cut into bars.

NUTRITION FACTS PER SERVING: 199 cal., 11 g total fat (6 g sat. fat),
20 mg chol., 119 mg sodium, 24 g carbo., 1 g fiber, 2 g pro.

DELECTABLE DESSERTS

Macadamia Nut Shortbread

PREP: 25 minutes **BAKE:** 10 minutes per batch
MAKES: 32 servings

1¼   cups all-purpose flour

3   tablespoons packed brown sugar

½   cup butter

2   tablespoons finely chopped macadamia nuts

Powdered sugar

one In a medium bowl stir together flour and brown sugar. Using a pastry blender, cut in butter until mixture resembles fine crumbs and starts to cling. Stir in nuts. Shape mixture into a ball and knead until smooth.

two On a lightly floured surface, pat or roll dough into an 12×6-inch rectangle. Using a fluted pastry wheel or table knife, cut into 3×¾-inch strips. Place strips 1 inch apart on an ungreased cookie sheet.

three Bake, uncovered, in a 325°F oven about 10 minutes just until bottoms start to brown. Transfer to wire racks; coo Lightly sprinkle cookies with powdered sugar.

NUTRITION FACTS PER SERVING: 55 cal., 4 g total fat (2 g sat. fat), 9 mg chol 34 mg sodium, 5 g carbo., 0 g fiber, 1 g pro.

Cashew-Toffee Cookies

PREP: 25 minutes **BAKE:** 10 minutes per batch
MAKES: about 60 servings

1   18-ounce roll refrigerated sugar cookie dough

1½   cups chopped cashews or peanuts

¾   cup toffee pieces

one Lightly grease 2 cookie sheets; set aside. Cut cookie dough in half. Roll one portion of the dough between pieces of waxed paper into a 10×6-inch rectangle. Remove top piec of waxed paper. Invert dough onto a prepared cookie sheet. Remove remaining waxed paper.

two Sprinkle dough evenly with half of the nuts and half of the toffee pieces. Repeat with the remaining dough, nuts, ar toffee pieces.

three Bake one sheet at a time, uncovered, in a 375°F over for 10 to 12 minutes or until golden brown. Cool on cookie sheet on a wire rack. Using a sharp knife, cut cooled cookies into irregular (about 2-inch) shapes.

NUTRITION FACTS PER SERVING: 71 cal., 4 g total fat (1 g sat. fat), 4 mg chol 48 mg sodium, 8 g carbo., 0 g fiber, 1 g pro.

Fudgy Peanut Butter Bites

PREP: 20 minutes **BAKE:** 11 minutes **COOL:** 15 minutes
MAKES: 24 servings

Nonstick cooking spray

½   of an 18-ounce roll refrigerated peanut butter cookie dough

½   cup semisweet chocolate pieces

¼   cup sweetened condensed milk

2   tablespoons finely chopped peanuts (optional)

one Coat twenty-four 1¾-inch muffin cups with cooking spray; set aside. Cut dough into 6 pieces. Cut each piece into 4 slices. Place each slice in a prepared cup. Bake, uncovered, in a 350°F oven about 9 minutes or until edges are lightly browned and dough is slightly firm.

two Press an indentation into each cookie shell with the back of a ½-teaspoon measuring spoon. Bake about 2 minutes more or until edges are firm. Cool in muffin pan on a wire rack for 15 minutes. Remove from pan. Cool on wire rack.

three For filling, in a small heavy saucepan combine chocolate pieces and sweetened condensed milk. Cook and stir over medium heat until chocolate melts. Spoon filling into cookie shells. If desired, sprinkle with peanuts. Cool.

NUTRITION FACTS PER SERVING: 76 cal., 4 g total fat (1 g sat. fat), 4 mg chol., 46 mg sodium, 8 g carbo., 1 g fiber, 1 g pro.

Gingersnap Dips

START TO FINISH: 25 minutes **MAKES:** 30 servings

¼   cup lemon curd or orange curd

2   tablespoons butter, softened

¾   cup powdered sugar

30   gingersnap cookies

Coconut or nuts, toasted (see tip, page 280)

one In a medium bowl combine lemon curd and butter. Beat with an electric mixer on medium to high speed for 30 seconds. Add powdered sugar. Beat until smooth and fluffy, scraping side of bowl occasionally.

two Spread lemon mixture over tops of gingersnap cookies. Sprinkle with toasted coconut.

NUTRITION FACTS PER SERVING: 62 cal., 2 g total fat (1 g sat. fat), 4 mg chol., 57 mg sodium, 11 g carbo., 1 g fiber, 0 g pro.

White Citrus Fudge

PREP: 15 minutes **CHILL:** 2 hours **MAKES:** 64 servings

3	cups white baking pieces
1	14-ounce can sweetened condensed milk
2	teaspoons finely shredded lime peel
2	tablespoons bottled Key lime juice or regular lime juice
1	cup chopped macadamia nuts, toasted (see tip, page 280)

one Line an 8×8×2-inch or 9×9×2-inch baking pan with foil, extending foil over edges of pan. Butter foil; set aside.

two In a large heavy saucepan combine baking pieces and sweetened condensed milk. Cook and stir over low heat until baking pieces melt. Remove from heat. Stir in lime peel and lime juice. Stir in nuts. Spread mixture evenly into the prepared pan. If desired, sprinkle a few additional coarsely chopped nuts over top. Cover and chill about 2 hours or until firm.

three Lift fudge from pan using edges of foil; peel off foil. Using a sharp knife, cut into pieces. Store, tightly covered, at room temperature or in the freezer.

NUTRITION FACTS PER SERVING: 80 cal., 4 g total fat (2 g sat. fat), 5 mg cho 16 mg sodium, 8 g carbo., 0 g fiber, 1 g pro.

Almond-Butter Crunch

PREP: 15 minutes **COOL:** 1 hour **MAKES:** about 12 servings

½	cup butter, cut up
1	cup slivered almonds
½	cup sugar
1	tablespoon light-color corn syrup

one Line a 9×1½-inch round baking pan with foil; butter foil. Set aside.

two In a large skillet combine the ½ cup butter, the almonds sugar, and corn syrup. Cook and stir over medium heat until mixture comes to boiling. Cook and stir for 5 to 6 minutes more or until mixture is a medium-brown color and almonds are toasted.

three Quickly pour mixture into the prepared pan. Cool in pan on a wire rack. Lift candy from pan using edge of foil; peel off foil. Break candy into pieces.

NUTRITION FACTS PER SERVING: 172 cal., 14 g total fat (5 g sat. fat), 22 mg chol., 85 mg sodium, 11 g carbo., 1 g fiber, 2 g pro.

Chocolaty Candy Cane Cups

PREP: 45 minutes **CHILL:** 30 minutes **MAKES:** 40 servings

6   ounces chocolate-flavor candy coating, cut up

1   cup semisweet chocolate pieces

1   tablespoon shortening

¾   cup finely crushed candy canes or peppermint sticks

40   tiny chocolate sandwich cookies with white filling

one Place 40 foil or paper candy cups on a baking sheet; set aside. In a medium saucepan combine candy coating, chocolate pieces, and shortening. Cook and stir over low heat until chocolate melts. Remove from heat. Stir in ½ cup of the crushed candy.

two Drop chocolate mixture by teaspoons into candy cups. Press sandwich cookies, one edge down, into cups. Sprinkle with the remaining ¼ cup crushed candy. Cover and chill about 30 minutes or until firm.

NUTRITION FACTS PER SERVING: 111 cal., 5 g total fat (3 g sat. fat), 0 mg chol., 65 mg sodium, 16 g carbo., 1 g fiber, 1 g pro.

Peanut Butter Cups

PREP: 30 minutes **CHILL:** 20 minutes **MAKES:** 8 servings

1   cup semisweet chocolate pieces

½   cup milk chocolate pieces

½   cup chunk-style peanut butter

2   tablespoons chopped peanuts

one Line eight 2½-inch muffin cups with paper bake cups; set aside. In a small saucepan combine semisweet chocolate and milk chocolate pieces. Cook and stir over low heat until chocolate melts. Remove from heat. In another small saucepan cook and stir peanut butter over low heat until it melts. Remove from heat.

two Pour about 1 tablespoon of the melted chocolate into each muffin cup; chill about 5 minutes or until chocolate is firm. Pour about 1 tablespoon of the melted peanut butter over chocolate in each cup; chill about 5 minutes more or until peanut butter is firm.

three If necessary, reheat the remaining melted chocolate over low heat. Pour melted chocolate over peanut butter in each cup, spreading to cover peanut butter. Sprinkle with peanuts. Chill about 10 minutes or until firm.

NUTRITION FACTS PER SERVING: 252 cal., 18 g total fat (7 g sat. fat), 1 mg chol., 89 mg sodium, 24 g carbo., 4 g fiber, 6 g pro.

Double-Dipped Caramels

PREP: 30 minutes **STAND:** 30 minutes
MAKES: about 48 servings

- 12 ounces chocolate-flavor candy coating, cut up
- 1 10-ounce package toffee pieces, crushed, or 2 cups finely chopped pistachio nuts
- 1 14-ounce package vanilla caramels (about 48), unwrapped

one In a medium heavy saucepan cook and stir candy coating over low heat just until coating melts. Remove from heat.

two Place toffee pieces in a bowl. Using a fork, dip caramels, one at a time, into coating, allowing excess to drip off. Then dip caramels into toffee pieces, turning to coat.

three Place caramels on a baking sheet lined with waxed paper. Let stand about 30 minutes or until coating is set.

NUTRITION FACTS PER SERVING: 103 cal., 6 g total fat (3 g sat. fat), 0 mg chol., 22 mg sodium, 12 g carbo., 0 g fiber, 2 g pro.

Peanut Butter Balls

PREP: 35 minutes **STAND:** 10 minutes
MAKES: about 25 servings

- ½ cup peanut butter
- 3 tablespoons butter, softened
- 1 cup powdered sugar
- ¼ cup crisp rice cereal (optional)
- 6 ounces chocolate-flavor candy coating, cut up

one In a medium bowl stir together peanut butter and butter. Gradually add powdered sugar and, if desired, cereal, stirring until combined. If necessary, knead with hands until smooth. Shape mixture into 1-inch balls; place on a baking sheet lined with waxed paper. Set aside.

two In a small heavy saucepan cook and stir candy coating over low heat until coating melts. Cool slightly. Using a fork, dip balls, one at a time, into coating, allowing excess to drip off. Return to waxed paper; let stand about 10 minutes or until coating is set.

NUTRITION FACTS PER SERVING: 98 cal., 7 g total fat (3 g sat. fat), 4 mg chol., 36 mg sodium, 9 g carbo., 0 g fiber, 1 g pro.

Milk Chocolate-Caramel Clusters

PREP: 20 minutes **STAND:** 30 minutes
MAKES: about 28 servings

12	vanilla caramels, unwrapped
½	cup milk chocolate pieces
2	tablespoons water
2	cups honey graham cereal, slightly crushed (about 1½ cups)
¾	cup peanuts

one In a heavy medium saucepan combine caramels, milk chocolate pieces, and water. Cook and stir over low heat until caramels melt. Remove from heat. Stir in cereal and peanuts.

two Quickly drop cereal mixture by rounded teaspoons onto a large baking sheet lined with waxed paper. Let stand about 30 minutes or until firm.

NUTRITION FACTS PER SERVING: 67 cal., 4 g total fat (1 g sat. fat), 1 mg chol., 59 mg sodium, 8 g carbo., 0 g fiber, 1 g pro.

Haystacks

PREP: 30 minutes **STAND:** 30 minutes
MAKES: about 30 servings

1	3-ounce can chow mein noodles
½	cup peanuts
⅔	cup sweetened condensed milk
½	cup semisweet chocolate pieces
½	cup butterscotch- or peanut butter-flavor pieces

one In a large bowl combine chow mein noodles and peanuts; set aside. In a medium saucepan combine sweetened condensed milk, chocolate pieces, and butterscotch pieces. Cook and stir over low heat until pieces melt.

two Pour chocolate mixture over noodle mixture; stir gently to coat. Drop by rounded teaspoons onto a baking sheet lined with waxed paper. Let stand about 30 minutes or until firm.

NUTRITION FACTS PER SERVING: 86 cal., 5 g total fat (2 g sat. fat), 2 mg chol., 53 mg sodium, 10 g carbo., 0 g fiber, 2 g pro.

White Chocolate-Cereal Drops

PREP: 35 minutes **STAND:** 30 minutes
MAKES: about 40 servings

1½   cups tiny marshmallows
1½   cups peanut butter cereal or puffed corn cereal
1½   cups crisp rice cereal
1½   cups mixed nuts
1¼   pounds vanilla-flavor candy coating, cut up

one In a large bowl combine marshmallows, peanut butter cereal, rice cereal, and nuts.

two In a medium saucepan cook and stir candy coating over low heat until coating melts. Pour melted coating over cereal mixture; toss gently to coat.

three Drop mixture by rounded teaspoons onto baking sheets lined with waxed paper. Let stand about 30 minutes or until firm.

NUTRITION FACTS PER SERVING: 129 cal., 8 g total fat (4 g sat. fat), 0 mg chol. 22 mg sodium, 14 g carbo., 1 g fiber, 1 g pro.

Macadamia-Vanilla Bark

PREP: 15 minutes **STAND:** 30 minutes
MAKES: about 16 servings

1   pound vanilla-flavor candy coating, cut up
¾   cup chopped macadamia nuts

one In a large microwave-safe bowl microwave candy coating, uncovered, on 100 percent power (high) for 4 to 6 minutes or until coating melts, stirring every minute. (Or in a large saucepan cook and stir candy coating over low heat until coating melts.) Stir in ½ cup of the nuts.

two Pour mixture onto a baking sheet lined with waxed paper. Spread until about ⅜ inch thick. Sprinkle with the remaining ¼ cup nuts. Let stand about 30 minutes or until firm. Break candy into pieces.

NUTRITION FACTS PER SERVING: 205 cal., 14 g total fat (9 g sat. fat), 0 mg chol., 17 mg sodium, 20 g carbo., 1 g fiber, 0 g pro.

Molded Peppermint Bark: Melt candy coating as directed; substitute ¾ cup crushed candy canes or peppermint candies for the nuts. Coat about 16 candy molds with nonstick cooking spray. Divide the crushed candy among molds. Spoon the melted coating over crushed candy. Let stand about 30 minutes or until firm. Unmold candies.

NUTRITION FACTS PER SERVING: 185 cal., 9 g total fat (8 g sat. fat), 0 mg chol. 3 mg sodium, 25 g carbo., 0 g fiber, 0 g pro.

take five
for fun

Fruit and Peanut Snack Mix

START TO FINISH: 10 minutes **MAKES:** 12 servings

1   7-ounce package dried apricots, snipped

1   6-ounce package bite-size, assorted-shape
    cheese, pretzel, and/or plain crackers

1   6-ounce package dried cranberries

1   cup peanuts

one In a medium bowl combine dried apricots, bite-size
crackers, dried cranberries, and peanuts. Store, tightly
covered, at room temperature.

NUTRITION FACTS PER SERVING: 213 cal., 7 g total fat (1 g sat. fat),
0 mg chol., 206 mg sodium, 35 g carbo., 3 g fiber, 5 g pro.

Crunchy Trail Mix

START TO FINISH: 5 minutes **MAKES:** 7 servings

1½   cups puffed corn cereal, round toasted oat cereal,
     or crispy corn and rice cereal

1   cup honey-roasted peanuts

½   cup chewy fruit snacks or candy-coated milk
     chocolate pieces

½   cup raisins

one In a medium bowl combine cereal, peanuts, fruit snacks,
and raisins. Store, tightly covered, at room temperature.

NUTRITION FACTS PER SERVING: 191 cal., 9 g total fat (2 g sat. fat),
0 mg chol., 108 mg sodium, 28 g carbo., 1 g fiber, 4 g pro.

Sweet Spiced Popcorn

PREP: 10 minutes **BAKE:** 30 minutes **MAKES:** 16 servings

- 8 cups popped popcorn
- ¾ cup dry roasted peanuts
- ¼ cup honey
- ¼ cup butter or margarine
- ½ teaspoon curry powder or five-spice powder

one In an ungreased large roasting pan combine popcorn and peanuts. In a small saucepan combine honey, butter, and curry powder. Cook and stir until butter melts. Pour honey mixture over popcorn mixture; toss gently to coat.

two Bake, uncovered, in a 300°F oven for 30 minutes, stirring every 10 minutes. Transfer mixture to a large piece of foil to cool. Store, tightly covered, at room temperature.

NUTRITION FACTS PER SERVING: 98 cal., 7 g total fat (2 g sat. fat), 8 mg chol., 32 mg sodium, 9 g carbo., 1 g fiber, 2 g pro.

Tropical Fruit Dip *See photo on page 274.*

START TO FINISH: 25 minutes **MAKES:** 6 to 8 servings

- 1 large banana
- 1 tablespoon honey
- 1 6-ounce carton vanilla low-fat yogurt
- 1 small fresh pineapple
- 1 tablespoon coconut, toasted (see tip, page 280) (optional)

  Assorted fruit dippers

one For dip, in a blender or food processor combine banana and honey. Cover and blend or process until smooth. Transfer mixture to a medium bowl. Stir in yogurt. If desired, cover and chill for up to 24 hours.

two Cut pineapple in half lengthwise, with leaves intact. Reserve one pineapple half for another use. Using a grapefruit knife or a small knife, hollow out the center of the remaining pineapple half, leaving a ½- to ¾-inch shell. If desired, cut decorative notches along outer edge of pineapple.

three Spoon dip into pineapple shell. If desired, sprinkle with toasted coconut. Serve with assorted fruit dippers.

NUTRITION FACTS PER SERVING DIP: 84 cal., 0 g total fat (0 g sat. fat), 1 mg chol., 20 mg sodium, 20 g carbo., 1 g fiber, 2 g pro.

Spiced Yogurt Dip

START TO FINISH: 15 minutes **MAKES:** 6 servings

1   cup vanilla low-fat yogurt

¼   cup unsweetened applesauce

⅛   teaspoon ground cinnamon, nutmeg, or ginger

     Assorted fruit dippers

one In a small bowl combine yogurt, applesauce, and cinnamon. Serve with assorted fruit dippers.

NUTRITION FACTS PER SERVING DIP: 27 cal., 0 g total fat (0 g sat. fat), 1 mg chol., 9 mg sodium, 6 g carbo., 0 g fiber, 1 g pro.

SLOW COOKER

Creamy Avocado-Lime Dip

PREP: 15 minutes **COOK:** 2½ hours **STAND:** 15 minutes
MAKES: 16 servings

2   limes

2   8-ounce tubs cream cheese spread with chive and
     onion

2   8-ounce cartons refrigerated guacamole dip

½   cup chopped onion

     Several dashes bottled hot pepper sauce (optional)

     Lime-flavor and/or plain tortilla chips

one Finely shred the peel from limes. Measure 1 teaspoon peel; set aside. Squeeze the juice from limes. Measure 3 tablespoons juice; set aside.

two In a 1½-quart slow cooker combine cream cheese spread, guacamole dip, onion, hot pepper sauce (if desired), the 1 teaspoon lime peel, and the 3 tablespoons lime juice.

three Cover and cook for 2½ to 3 hours (use low-heat setting if available). Remove liner from cooker, if possible, or turn off cooker. Let stand, uncovered, for 15 minutes to cool slightly before serving. Stir just before serving. Serve with tortilla chips.

NUTRITION FACTS PER SERVING DIP: 156 cal., 13 g total fat (6 g sat. fat), 27 mg chol., 336 mg sodium, 5 g carbo., 0 g fiber, 2 g pro.

Chipotle Con Queso Dip

PREP: 10 minutes **COOK:** Low 3 hours, High 1½ hours
MAKES: 16 servings

- 2 pounds pasteurized prepared cheese product, cubed
- 1 10-ounce can diced tomatoes and green chiles, undrained
- 1 to 3 canned chipotle peppers in adobo sauce, chopped
- 1 tablespoon Worcestershire sauce
  Tortilla chips

one In a 3½- or 4-quart slow cooker combine cubed cheese product, undrained tomatoes, chipotle peppers in adobo sauce, and Worcestershire sauce.

two Cover and cook on low-heat setting for 3 to 3½ hours or on high-heat setting for 1½ to 1¾ hours.

three Serve immediately or keep warm, covered, on low-heat setting for up to 2 hours, stirring occasionally. Stir just before serving. Serve with tortilla chips.

NUTRITION FACTS PER SERVING DIP: 210 cal., 14 g total fat (9 g sat. fat), 47 mg chol., 880 mg sodium, 6 g carbo., 0 g fiber, 13 g pro.

Layered Black Bean Dip

PREP: 10 minutes **BAKE:** 20 minutes **MAKES:** 8 to 10 servings

- 1 15-ounce can black beans, rinsed and drained
- 2 cups shredded Monterey Jack cheese with jalapeño peppers or Monterey Jack cheese (8 ounces)
- ¾ cup bottled salsa
- 1 medium avocado, seeded, peeled, and chopped
  Tortilla chips

one In a large bowl mash beans with a fork. Stir in 1 cup of the cheese and the salsa. Spread bean mixture in an ungreased 9-inch pie plate. Top with avocado and sprinkle with the remaining 1 cup cheese.

two Bake, uncovered, in a 350°F oven about 20 minutes or until mixture is heated through and cheese melts. Serve warm with tortilla chips.

NUTRITION FACTS PER SERVING DIP: 291 cal., 18 g total fat (7 g sat. fat), 25 mg chol., 448 mg sodium, 25 g carbo., 6 g fiber, 12 g pro.

Sausage-Cheese Dip

PREP: 15 minutes **COOK:** Low 2 hours **MAKES:** 24 servings

1   pound bulk pork sausage

2   pounds pasteurized prepared cheese product with jalapeño peppers, cubed

1   14½-ounce can diced tomatoes with onion and garlic, undrained

Toasted baguette slices or toasted pita wedges

one In a large skillet cook sausage over medium-high heat until brown. Drain off fat. Transfer sausage to a 3½- or 4-qua[rt] slow cooker. Stir in cubed cheese and undrained tomatoes.

two Cover and cook on low-heat setting for 2 to 3 hours, stirring after 1 hour to mix in the cheese.

three Serve immediately or keep warm, covered, on low-he[at] setting for up to 2 hours, stirring occasionally. Serve with baguette slices.

NUTRITION FACTS PE SERVING DIP: 190 cal., 15 g total fat (9 g sat. fat), 37 mg chol., 671 mg sodium, 4 g carbo., 0 g fiber, 9 g pro.

Cheesy Beer-Salsa Dip

PREP: 15 minutes **COOK:** Low 2 hours **MAKES:** 22 servings

6   cups shredded American cheese (1½ pounds)

1   16-ounce jar salsa

1   8-ounce package cream cheese, cut up

⅔   cup beer or milk

Tortilla chips

one In a 3½- or 4-quart slow cooker combine American cheese, salsa, cream cheese, and beer.

two Cover and cook on low-heat setting for 2 to 3 hours. Serve immediately or keep warm, covered, on low-heat setting for up to 2 hours, stirring occasionally. Stir just before serving. Serve with tortilla chips.

NUTRITION FACTS PER SERVING DIP: 150 cal., 11 g total fat (7 g sat. fat), 31 mg chol., 543 mg sodium, 5 g carbo., 1 g fiber, 7 g pro.

Artichoke Dip with Pretzels

START TO FINISH: 10 minutes **MAKES:** 20 servings

1   14-ounce can artichoke hearts, drained and
    finely chopped

1   8-ounce carton dairy sour cream

½   cup bottled blue cheese salad dressing

¼   cup snipped fresh chives or finely chopped
    green onion tops

    Large pretzel rods, small pretzel knots, and/or
    melba toast rounds

one In a medium bowl stir together artichoke hearts, sour
cream, salad dressing, and chives. Transfer to a serving bowl.

two Serve with pretzels and/or melba toast rounds.

NUTRITION FACTS PER SERVING DIP: 62 cal., 6 g total fat (2 g sat. fat),
8 mg chol., 112 mg sodium, 2 g carbo., 1 g fiber, 2 g pro.

`SLOW COOKER`

Tomato Sauce with Garlic Cheese Bread

PREP: 10 minutes **COOK:** 3 hours **MAKES:** 14 servings

1   14½-ounce can diced tomatoes with basil, garlic,
    and oregano, undrained

1   14-ounce jar tomato pasta sauce

1   4½-ounce jar (drained weight) sliced mushrooms,
    drained

¼   cup finely shredded Parmesan cheese (1 ounce)

1   11¾-ounce package frozen garlic cheese bread or
    garlic bread

one In a 1½-quart slow cooker combine undrained tomatoes,
pasta sauce, and mushrooms.

two Cover and cook for 3 to 4 hours (use low-heat setting if
available). Stir in Parmesan cheese.

three Prepare garlic cheese bread according to package
directions. Cut crosswise into slices. Serve cheese bread with
warm tomato mixture for dipping.

NUTRITION FACTS PER SERVING: 90 cal., 3 g total fat (1 g sat. fat), 1 mg chol.,
352 mg sodium, 10 g carbo., 1 g fiber, 4 g pro.

Baked Cheese Fondue

PREP: 10 minutes **BAKE:** 5 minutes **MAKES:** 8 servings

1   8-ounce wedge or round Cambozola, Camembert, or
    Brie cheese

2   tablespoons chopped walnuts or pecans

    Coarsely ground mixed peppercorns

    Toasted baguette-style French bread slices or
    assorted crackers

one If using a cheese round, peel rind from top of cheese.
Place cheese in an ungreased quiche dish or shallow baking
dish. Sprinkle with nuts and peppercorns.

two Bake, uncovered, in a 450°F oven for 5 to 8 minutes or
until cheese is softened and just starts to melt. Serve warm
with toasted bread slices.

NUTRITION FACTS PER SERVING FONDUE: 175 cal., 9 g total fat (5 g sat. fat)
20 mg chol., 411 mg sodium, 15 g carbo., 1 g fiber, 8 g pro.

Herbed Feta Spread

START TO FINISH: 10 minutes **MAKES:** 15 to 20 servings

1   8-ounce package reduced-fat cream cheese
    (Neufchâtel)

1   4-ounce package crumbled feta cheese with garlic
    and herb

1   tablespoon milk

    Several dashes freshly ground black pepper

    Sweet pepper wedges or assorted crackers

one In a small bowl stir together cream cheese, feta cheese
milk, and black pepper. Beat with an electric mixer on
medium speed until mixture is of spreading consistency.

two Serve on sweet pepper wedges.

NUTRITION FACTS PER SERVING SPREAD: 119 cal., 8 g total fat (8 g sat. fat)
18 mg chol., 245 mg sodium, 8 g carbo., 0 g fiber, 3 g pro.

Eggplant-Garlic Spread

PREP: 10 minutes **BAKE:** 45 minutes **COOL:** 1½ hours
MAKES: 16 servings

- 1   medium eggplant
- ⅓   cup olive oil
- 2   whole garlic bulbs, separated into cloves, peeled, and thinly sliced
- 2   tablespoons snipped fresh flat-leaf parsley
  Assorted crackers, toasted pita wedges, or assorted vegetables

one Cut eggplant in half lengthwise; brush all over with some of the oil. Grease a shallow baking pan with the remaining oil. Place sliced garlic on the cut sides of the eggplant halves. Carefully invert eggplant halves into the prepared pan, tucking garlic slices under eggplant.

two Bake, uncovered, in a 350°F oven for 45 to 60 minutes or until skin begins to wrinkle. Turn off oven; cool eggplant in the oven for 1½ hours.

three Using a large spatula, carefully transfer eggplant halves, cut sides up, and garlic to a serving platter. Garnish with parsley. Serve on assorted crackers.

NUTRITION FACTS PER SERVING SPREAD: 53 cal., 5 g total fat (1 g sat. fat), 0 mg chol., 2 mg sodium, 3 g carbo., 1 g fiber, 1 g pro.

Sweet Onion Spread

PREP: 15 minutes **BAKE:** 30 minutes **MAKES:** 4 servings

- 2   teaspoons olive oil
- 2   teaspoons honey
- 2   medium sweet onions (such as Vidalia, Maui, Walla Walla, or Oso Sweet), quartered
- 4   large cloves garlic, peeled
  Toasted baguette-style French bread slices

one In a large bowl stir together oil and honey. Add onions and garlic; toss well to coat. Transfer mixture to a lightly greased 2-quart baking dish.

two Bake, uncovered, in a 350°F oven for 30 to 40 minutes or until onions are golden brown, stirring occasionally. Remove from oven; cool slightly.

three Transfer mixture to a food processor or blender. Cover and process or blend until smooth. Serve on toasted bread slices.

NUTRITION FACTS PER SERVING SPREAD: 50 cal., 2 g total fat (0 g sat. fat), 0 mg chol., 75 mg sodium, 7 g carbo., 1 g fiber, 1 g pro.

Creamy Cheese Spread

PREP: 10 minutes **STAND:** 30 minutes **MAKES:** 24 servings

2   cups shredded brick cheese (8 ounces)

1   8-ounce tub cream cheese spread with chive
      and onion

½   teaspoon bottled hot pepper sauce

      Party rye or pumpernickel bread, assorted crackers,
      or bagel chips

one Place brick cheese and cream cheese in a medium bowl; let stand at room temperature for 30 minutes. Add hot pepper sauce. Beat with an electric mixer on medium speed until mixture is nearly smooth.

two Serve on rye or pumpernickel bread.

NUTRITION FACTS PER SERVING SPREAD: 94 cal., 6 g total fat (4 g sat. fat), 18 mg chol., 154 mg sodium, 5 g carbo., 1 g fiber, 3 g pro.

Almond-Brie Spread

PREP: 10 minutes **STAND:** 1 hour **MAKES:** 20 servings

2   4½-ounce rounds Brie cheese

2   tablespoons cream sherry or milk

3   tablespoons sliced almonds, toasted
      (see tip, page 280)

      Assorted crackers

one Using a small paring knife or vegetable peeler, cut the thin white covering from cheese rounds. Place cheese in a medum bowl; let stand at room temperature about 1 hour or until softened.

two Beat with an electric mixer on medium speed for 1 minute. Add sherry; beat until light and smooth. Chop 2 tablespoons of the almonds; stir into cheese mixture.

three If desired, cover and chill until ready to serve. Let stand at room temperature for 30 to 45 minutes before serving if chilled. Sprinkle with the remaining 1 tablespoon toasted almonds. Serve on assorted crackers.

NUTRITION FACTS PER SERVING SPREAD: 51 cal., 4 g total fat (2 g sat. fat), 13 mg chol., 79 mg sodium, 0 g carbo., 0 g fiber, 3 g pro.

Warm Brie

PREP: 10 minutes BAKE: 10 minutes MAKES: 8 servings

1   8-ounce round Brie cheese
¼   cup butter or margarine
¼   cup packed brown sugar
¼   cup chopped nuts
1   tablespoon honey

one Place cheese in an ungreased shallow baking dish or pie plate. Bake, uncovered, in a 350°F oven for 10 minutes.

two Meanwhile, in a small saucepan combine butter, brown sugar, nuts, and honey. Bring to boiling over medium heat, stirring constantly. Pour honey mixture over cheese. Cut into wedges. Serve warm.

NUTRITION FACTS PER SERVING: 206 cal., 16 g total fat (9 g sat. fat), 44 mg chol., 241 mg sodium, 9 g carbo., 0 g fiber, 6 g pro.

Baked Cheese

PREP: 5 minutes BAKE: 20 minutes MAKES: 16 servings

1   8-ounce package cream cheese
⅓   cup bottled fruit salsa
⅓   cup honey-roasted cashews, finely chopped
    Toasted pita wedges, assorted crackers, and/or apple or pear slices

one Place cream cheese in an ungreased pie plate. Spoon salsa over cream cheese. Sprinkle with cashews.

two Bake, uncovered, in a 350°F oven about 20 minutes or until cheese is softened and heated through. Serve warm with pita wedges, crackers, and/or apple slices.

NUTRITION FACTS PER SERVING SPREAD: 136 cal., 7 g total fat (3 g sat. fat), 16 mg chol., 136 mg sodium, 17 g carbo., 2 g fiber, 3 g pro.

Polynesian Glazed Wings *See photo on page 275.*

PREP: 20 minutes **BROIL:** 15 minutes **COOK:** Low 3 hours, High 1½ hours **MAKES:** 32 servings

- 16 chicken wings (about 2½ pounds)
- 1 10-ounce bottle sweet-and-sour sauce
- 2 tablespoons soy sauce
- 2 teaspoons grated fresh ginger
- ¼ to ½ teaspoon crushed red pepper

  Thinly sliced green onion (optional)

one Cut off and discard tips of chicken wings. Cut wings at joints to make 32 pieces. Place wing pieces on the unheated rack of a broiler pan. Broil 4 to 5 inches from the heat for 15 to 20 minutes or until chicken is browned, turning once.

two For sauce, in a 3½- or 4-quart slow cooker combine sweet-and-sour sauce, soy sauce, ginger, and crushed red pepper. Add chicken wings, stirring to coat with sauce.

three Cover and cook on low-heat setting for 3 to 4 hours or on high-heat setting for 1½ to 2 hours. If desired, transfer to a serving plate and sprinkle with green onion.

NUTRITION FACTS PER SERVING: 61 cal., 5 g total fat (1 g sat. fat), 29 mg chol., 112 mg sodium, 2 g carbo., 0 g fiber, 5 g pro.

Five-Spice Drummies

PREP: 20 minutes **MARINATE:** 4 to 24 hours **BAKE:** 30 minutes **MAKES:** 24 servings

- 12 chicken wings (about 2 pounds)
- ¼ cup soy sauce
- ¼ cup orange juice
- 1 tablespoon honey
- 2 teaspoons five-spice powder

one Cut off and discard tips of chicken wings. Cut wings at joints to make 24 pieces. Place wing pieces in a resealable plastic bag set in a shallow dish.

two For marinade, in a small bowl combine soy sauce, orange juice, honey, and five-spice powder. Pour over chicken; seal bag. Marinate in the refrigerator for 4 to 24 hours, turning bag occasionally. Drain chicken, discarding marinade.

three Arrange chicken wings in an ungreased 15×10×1-inch baking pan. Bake, uncovered, in a 400°F oven for 30 to 35 minutes or until chicken is tender and no longer pink.

NUTRITION FACTS PER SERVING: 68 cal., 5 g total fat (2 g sat. fat), 24 mg chol., 57 mg sodium, 0 g carbo., 0 g fiber, 6 g pro.

Buffalo Wings

PREP: 20 minutes MARINATE: 30 minutes
BROIL: 20 minutes MAKES: 24 servings

12 chicken wings (about 2 pounds)

2 tablespoons butter or margarine, melted

2 to 3 tablespoons bottled hot pepper sauce

1 teaspoon paprika

Bottled blue cheese salad dressing

one Cut off and discard tips of chicken wings. Cut wings at joints to make 24 pieces. Place wing pieces in a resealable plastic bag set in a shallow dish.

two For marinade, in a small bowl combine melted butter, hot pepper sauce, and paprika. Pour over chicken; seal bag. Marinate in the refrigerator for 30 minutes, turning once.

three Place chicken wings on the unheated rack of a broiler pan. Broil 4 to 5 inches from the heat for 20 to 25 minutes or until chicken is tender and no longer pink, turning once. Serve with blue cheese dressing.

NUTRITION FACTS PER SERVING: 131 cal., 12 g total fat (3 g sat. fat), 21 mg chol., 198 mg sodium, 1 g carbo., 0 g fiber, 5 g pro.

SLOW COOKER

Chicken Wings with Barbecue Sauce

PREP: 20 minutes BROIL: 15 minutes COOK: Low 3 hours,
High 1½ hours MAKES: 32 servings

16 chicken wings (about 2½ pounds)

1½ cups bottled barbecue sauce

¼ cup honey

2 teaspoons yellow mustard

1½ teaspoons Worcestershire sauce

one Cut off and discard tips of chicken wings. Cut wings at joints to make 32 pieces. Place wing pieces on the unheated rack of a broiler pan. Broil 4 to 5 inches from the heat for 15 to 20 minutes or until chicken is browned, turning once.

two For sauce, in a 3½- or 4-quart slow cooker combine barbecue sauce, honey, mustard, and Worcestershire sauce. Add chicken wings, stirring to coat with sauce.

three Cover and cook on low-heat setting for 3 to 4 hours or on high-heat setting for 1½ to 2 hours.

NUTRITION FACTS PER SERVING: 83 cal., 4 g total fat (1 g sat. fat), 20 mg chol., 197 mg sodium, 6 g carbo., 0 g fiber, 5 g pro.

Plum Good Sausage and Meatballs

PREP: 10 minutes **COOK:** Low 5 hours, High 2½ hours
MAKES: 16 servings

- 1 18-ounce bottle barbecue sauce
- 1 10- or 12-ounce jar plum jam or preserves
- 1 pound hot or mild cooked smoked sausage, sliced into bite-size pieces
- 1 16-ounce package (16 large) Italian-style or plain frozen cooked meatballs, thawed

one For sauce, in a 3½- or 4-quart slow cooker combine barbecue sauce and jam. Add sausage and meatballs, stirring to coat with sauce.

two Cover and cook on low-heat setting for 5 to 6 hours or on high-heat setting for 2½ to 3 hours. Serve immediately or keep warm, covered, on low-heat setting for up to 2 hours, stirring occasionally. Serve with decorative picks.

NUTRITION FACTS PER SERVING: 267 cal., 16 g total fat (6 g sat. fat), 38 mg chol., 898 mg sodium, 19 g carbo., 2 g fiber, 12 g pro.

Tangy Cranberry Meatballs

PREP: 15 minutes **COOK:** 20 minutes **MAKES:** 16 to 20 servings

- 1 16-ounce can jellied cranberry sauce
- ⅓ cup bottled barbecue sauce or steak sauce
- 1 tablespoon packed brown sugar
- 2 teaspoons Dijon-style mustard
- 1 16-ounce package (32 small) plain frozen cooked meatballs, one 16-ounce package cocktail wieners, or 1 pound cooked smoked sausage, sliced into 1-inch pieces

one In a large saucepan combine cranberry sauce, barbecue sauce, brown sugar, and mustard. Cook and stir over medium heat until cranberry sauce melts. Stir in meatballs.

two Reduce heat to medium-low. Cook, covered, about 20 minutes or until meatballs are heated through, stirring occasionally. Serve with decorative picks.

NUTRITION FACTS PER SERVING: 149 cal., 8 g total fat (3 g sat. fat), 11 mg chol., 311 mg sodium, 14 g carbo., 1 g fiber, 4 g pro.

Cranberry-Sauced Franks

PREP: 10 minutes **COOK:** Low 4 hours, High 2 hours
MAKES: 32 servings

- 1   16-ounce can jellied cranberry sauce
- 1   cup bottled barbecue sauce
- 2   16-ounce packages cocktail wieners and/or small cooked smoked sausage links

one For sauce, in a 3½- or 4-quart slow cooker combine cranberry sauce and barbecue sauce. Add wieners and/or sausage links, stirring to coat with sauce.

two Cover and cook on low-heat setting for 4 to 5 hours or on high-heat setting for 2 to 2½ hours.

three Serve immediately or keep warm, covered, on low-heat setting for up to 2 hours, stirring occasionally. Serve with decorative picks.

NUTRITION FACTS PER SERVING: 118 cal., 8 g total fat (4 g sat. fat), 15 mg chol., 275 mg sodium, 8 g carbo., 0 g fiber, 3 g pro.

Hot Honeyed Spareribs

PREP: 20 minutes **BROIL:** 10 minutes **COOK:** Low 6 hours, High 3 hours **MAKES:** 10 to 12 servings

- 3½   to 4 pounds pork loin back ribs, cut into 1-rib portions
- 2   cups bottled picante sauce or salsa
- ½   cup honey
- 1   tablespoon quick-cooking tapioca
- 1   teaspoon ground ginger

one Trim fat from ribs. Place ribs on the unheated rack of a broiler pan. Broil about 6 inches from the heat about 10 minutes or until browned, turning once. Transfer ribs to a 3½- to 6-quart slow cooker.

two For sauce, in a medium bowl combine picante sauce, honey, tapioca, and ginger. Pour sauce over ribs.

three Cover and cook on low-heat setting for 6 to 7 hours or on high-heat setting for 3 to 3½ hours. Skim fat from sauce. Serve ribs with sauce.

NUTRITION FACTS PER SERVING: 215 cal., 6 g total fat (2 g sat. fat), 43 mg chol., 246 mg sodium, 18 g carbo., 0 g fiber, 20 g pro.

Cheesy Pecan Quesadillas

START TO FINISH: 15 minutes **MAKES:** 4 servings

- 2 8- to 9-inch flour tortillas
- 3 ounces Brie or Muenster cheese, chopped (about ¾ cup)
- 2 tablespoons chopped pecans or walnuts, toasted (see tip, page 280)
- 2 tablespoons snipped fresh flat-leaf parsley

   Dairy sour cream

one Sprinkle half of each tortilla with cheese. Top with nuts and parsley. Fold tortillas in half; press gently.

two In a medium skillet or griddle cook quesadillas over medium heat for 2 to 3 minutes or until lightly browned, turning once. Cut quesadillas into wedges. Serve with sour cream.

NUTRITION FACTS PER SERVING: 170 cal., 12 g total fat (6 g sat. fat), 27 mg chol., 202 mg sodium, 9 g carbo., 0 g fiber, 6 g pro.

SLOW COOKER

Spicy Chicken Fajita Bites *See photo on page 275.*

PREP: 25 minutes **COOK:** 6 hours **MAKES:** about 25 servings

   Nonstick cooking spray
- 1 pound packaged chicken or beef stir-fry strips
- ½ cup spicy brown mustard
- ½ cup water
- 4 teaspoons fajita seasoning
- 5 7- to 8-inch flour tortillas, warmed (see tip, page 16)
- 1 cup red, green, and/or yellow sweet pepper strips
   Snipped fresh cilantro and/or sliced green onion (optional)

one Lightly coat a large skillet with cooking spray; heat over medium-high heat. Cook and stir chicken in hot skillet until browned. Remove from heat.

two In a 1½-quart slow cooker combine mustard, water, and fajita seasoning. Add chicken; stir to coat with mustard mixture

three Cover and cook for 6 to 7 hours (use low-heat setting if available). Using a slotted spoon, remove chicken from cooker. Discard mustard mixture in cooker.

four Divide chicken evenly among warmed tortillas. Top with sweet pepper strips and, if desired, cilantro and/or green onion. Roll up tortillas.

five Using a serrated knife, cut filled tortillas crosswise into bite-size slices. Serve with decorative picks.

NUTRITION FACTS PER SERVING: 47 cal., 1 g total fat (0 g sat. fat), 13 mg chol 131 mg sodium, 4 g carbo., 0 g fiber, 5 g pro.

Tortellini in Ratatouille Sauce

Nonstick cooking spray

2 cups peeled and cubed eggplant

1 medium zucchini, cut into bite-size pieces

1 26-ounce jar marinara sauce

1 cup water

2 9-ounce packages refrigerated cheese-filled tortellini

one Lightly coat a 4-quart Dutch oven with cooking spray; heat over medium-high heat. Add eggplant and zucchini; cook and stir for 5 minutes. Stir in marinara sauce and water.

two Bring to boiling. Stir in tortellini. Return to boiling; reduce heat to medium-low. Cook, covered, about 8 minutes or until tortellini is tender. Serve with decorative picks.

NUTRITION FACTS PER SERVING: 86 cal., 2 g total fat (1 g sat. fat), 11 mg chol., 210 mg sodium, 13 g carbo., 2 g fiber, 4 g pro.

Toasted Ravioli

PREP: 25 minutes **BAKE:** 15 minutes **MAKES:** 10 to 12 servings

1 9-ounce package refrigerated cheese-filled ravioli

½ cup seasoned fine dry bread crumbs

1 egg

¼ cup milk

1½ cups bottled pasta sauce

one In a large saucepan cook ravioli in boiling water for 3 minutes; drain. Cool slightly.

two Place bread crumbs in a shallow dish. In another shallow dish combine egg and milk. Dip cooked ravioli into egg mixture, then roll in bread crumbs to coat. Place ravioli on a greased baking sheet.

three Bake, uncovered, in a 425°F oven about 15 minutes or until crisp and golden. Meanwhile, in a small saucepan heat pasta sauce until bubbly. Serve warm ravioli with sauce.

NUTRITION FACTS PER SERVING: 141 cal., 3 g total fat (1 g sat. fat), 32 mg chol., 391 mg sodium, 22 g carbo., 1 g fiber, 6 g pro.

Chicken and Rice Spring Rolls

PREP: 25 minutes **CHILL:** 1 to 2 hours **MAKES:** 24 servings

8	8-inch round rice papers
16	thin fresh asparagus spears
1	cup finely chopped cooked chicken
1	cup cooked long grain rice
¾	cup bottled sweet-and-sour sauce

one Place some warm water in a shallow dish. Dip each rice paper into warm water and place between damp towels for 5 minutes.

two Meanwhile, snap off and discard woody bases from asparagus. Cook asparagus spears in a small amount of boiling water for 3 minutes; drain. Rinse with cold water; drain again.

three In a medium bowl combine chicken, cooked rice, and ¼ cup of the sweet-and-sour sauce. For each spring roll, place 2 asparagus spears about 1 inch from the bottom edge of a rice paper. Top with ¼ cup chicken mixture. Fold up bottom edge of rice paper over filling. Fold in sides; roll up.

four Cover and chill for 1 to 2 hours. Cut each spring roll into thirds. Serve with the remaining ½ cup sweet-and-sour sauce.

NUTRITION FACTS PER SERVING: 56 cal., 1 g total fat (0 g sat. fat), 5 mg chol., 35 mg sodium, 12 g carbo., 1 g fiber, 3 g pro.

B.L.T. Bruschetta

START TO FINISH: 15 minutes **MAKES:** 16 servings

16	½-inch slices baguette-style French bread, toasted
½	cup semisoft cheese with garlic and herb
½	cup thinly sliced fresh basil leaves or shredded leaf lettuce
½	cup chopped tomato
4	slices bacon, crisp-cooked and crumbled

one Spread one side of each toasted bread slice with cheese. Top with basil, tomato, and crumbled bacon.

NUTRITION FACTS PER SERVING: 75 cal., 4 g total fat (2 g sat. fat), 8 mg chol., 112 mg sodium, 8 g carbo., 0 g fiber, 2 g pro.

Tomato-Pesto Toast

PREP: 15 minutes   **BROIL:** 3 minutes   **MAKES:** 12 to 16 servings

2   French-style rolls (about 6 inches long),
      cut into ½-inch slices

¾   cup purchased pesto

2   to 3 roma tomatoes, cut lengthwise into
      thin slices

⅓   cup crumbled feta cheese
      Coarsely cracked black pepper

one Arrange bread slices on the unheated rack of a broiler pan. Broil 4 to 5 inches from the heat about 2 minutes or until lightly browned, turning once.

two Spread a scant 1 tablespoon of the pesto on each toasted bread slice; top each with a tomato slice. Sprinkle with cheese and pepper. Broil for 1 to 2 minutes more or until heated through.

NUTRITION FACTS PER SERVING: 160 cal., 9 g total fat (2 g sat. fat), 8 mg chol., 289 mg sodium, 15 g carbo., 1 g fiber, 6 g pro.

Strawberry and Cheese Bites

START TO FINISH: 25 minutes   **MAKES:** about 24 servings

1   8-ounce loaf baguette-style French bread,
      cut into ¼-inch slices

1   8-ounce tub cream cheese spread

1   tablespoon honey

2   cups strawberries, sliced

¼   cup strawberry jelly

one Place bread slices in a single layer on an ungreased baking sheet. Bake, uncovered, in a 375°F oven about 10 minutes or until lightly browned, turning once.

two In a small bowl combine cream cheese and honey; spread on one side of each bread slice. Top with strawberry slices.

three In a custard cup microwave jelly, uncovered, on 100 percent power (high) about 30 seconds or until jelly melts. Stir until smooth. (Or in a small saucepan cook and stir jelly over low heat until jelly melts). Brush melted jelly over strawberries.

NUTRITION FACTS PER SERVING: 73 cal., 3 g total fat (2 g sat. fat), 9 mg chol., 90 mg sodium, 9 g carbo., 1 g fiber, 2 g pro.

Bread and Cheddar Wedges

PREP: 10 minutes **BAKE:** 15 minutes **MAKES:** 12 servings

1   small round loaf of bread (about 8 inches in diameter)
1   tablespoon Dijon-style mustard
½   of a 5-ounce jar (¼ cup) process cheese spread
1   teaspoon grated Parmesan cheese
    Apple slices

one Cut bread in half horizontally. Reserve one half for another use. Hollow out the remaining half, leaving a ½-inch shell. Spread mustard over inside of bread shell. Spread cheese spread over mustard. Sprinkle with Parmesan cheese Place bread shell on an ungreased baking sheet.

two Bake, uncovered, in a 400°F oven about 15 minutes or until cheese starts to bubble. Cut hot bread into 12 wedges; transfer to a serving plate. Serve with apple slices.

NUTRITION FACTS PER SERVING: 89 cal., 2 g total fat (1 g sat. fat), 4 mg chol. 233 mg sodium, 14 g carbo., 1 g fiber, 3 g pro.

Puff Pastry Cheese Straws

PREP: 20 minutes **BAKE:** 12 minutes **MAKES:** about 36 servings

1   17.3-ounce package (2 sheets) frozen puff pastry sheets, thawed
1   egg white, slightly beaten
    Paprika
    Cayenne pepper (optional)
1   cup finely shredded sharp cheddar, Asiago, or Parmesan cheese (4 ounces)

one On a cutting board, unfold one pastry sheet at a time. Brush each sheet with half of the beaten egg white. Sprinkle lightly with paprika and, if desired, cayenne pepper. Sprinkle each with half of the cheese. Using a floured rolling pin, gent press cheese into pastry.

two Cut pastry lengthwise into ½-inch strips. Gently twist each strip several times. Place strips 1 inch apart on a bakin sheet lined with parchment paper.

three Bake, uncovered, in a 375°F oven for 12 to 14 minut or until golden. Cool on a wire rack. Serve the same day.

NUTRITION FACTS PER SERVING: 73 cal., 5 g total fat (1 g sat. fat), 3 mg chol 72 mg sodium, 5 g carbo., 0 g fiber, 1 g pro.

Goat Cheese Pastry Rounds *See photo on page 275.*

See photo on page 275.

REP: 20 minutes **BAKE:** 20 minutes **STAND:** 15 minutes
MAKES: 12 servings

½ of a 17.3-ounce package (1 sheet) frozen puff pastry sheets, thawed

3 tablespoons tomato preserves or favorite fruit preserves

3 3- to 4-ounce rounds goat cheese (chèvre)*

1 egg, sightly beaten

Fresh figs (optional)

one Line a baking sheet with foil; grease foil. Set aside. On a lightly floured surface, unfold pastry sheet. Roll into a 12-inch square. Cut pastry into four 6-inch squares.

two Divide preserves among 3 of the pastry squares. Place goat cheese on top of preserves. Bring edges of pastry up and over cheese, pleating to fit as necessary. Pinch edges to seal. Trim any excess pastry.

three Place bundles, smooth sides up, on the prepared baking sheet. Brush pastry with some of the beaten egg. Cut small slits in pastry to allow steam to escape. Cut the remaining pastry square into decorative leaves; place on top of bundles and brush with additional egg.

four Bake, uncovered, in a 400°F oven for 20 to 22 minutes or until pastry is golden brown. Let stand for 15 to 20 minutes before serving. If desired, serve with fresh figs.

NUTRITION FACTS PER SERVING: 166 cal., 11 g total fat (3 g sat. fat), 27 mg chol., 162 mg sodium, 11 g carbo., 0 g fiber, 5 g pro.

*Note: *If the goat cheese comes in logs, use damp hands to shape each cheese log into a round.*

Olive-Tomato Tarts

REP: 15 minutes **BAKE:** 12 minutes **MAKES:** 16 servings

½ of a 17.3-ounce package (1 sheet) frozen puff pastry sheets, thawed

⅓ cup purchased tapenade or finely chopped pitted ripe olives

8 cherry tomatoes, quartered

1 4-ounce package crumbled feta cheese

one On a cutting board, unfold pastry sheet. Cut pastry into sixteen 2½-inch squares. Place each square in an ungreased 2½-inch muffin cup. Place about 1 teaspoon of the tapenade on each square; top each with 2 tomato quarters. Sprinkle pastry squares with cheese.

two Bake, uncovered, in a 425°F oven for 12 to 15 minutes or until pastry is puffed and golden brown. Remove tarts from muffin cups. Serve warm.

NUTRITION FACTS PER SERVING: 92 cal., 7 g total fat (1 g sat. fat), 6 mg chol., 174 mg sodium, 6 g carbo., 0 g fiber, 2 g pro.

Prosciutto-Arugula Roll-Ups

START TO FINISH: 30 minutes **MAKES:** about 48 servings

- 1 5-ounce container semisoft cheese with garlic and herb
- 2 ounces soft goat cheese (chèvre)
- ⅓ cup pine nuts or chopped almonds, toasted (see tip, page 280)
- 4 ounces thinly sliced prosciutto (8 slices)
- 1½ cups arugula or fresh spinach leaves

one In a small bowl stir together semisoft cheese, goat cheese, and pine nuts. Spread about 2 tablespoons of the cheese mixture on each prosciutto slice. Top with arugula.

two Starting from a short side, roll up each prosciutto slice. Cut prosciutto rolls into ½-inch slices. If desired, cover and chill for up to 6 hours.

NUTRITION FACTS PER SERVING: 33 cal., 3 g total fat (1 g sat. fat), 4 mg chol 55 mg sodium, 0 g carbo., 0 g fiber, 2 g pro.

Easy Artichoke Roll

PREP: 25 minutes **BAKE:** 30 minutes **MAKES:** 16 servings

- 1 8-ounce package (8) refrigerated crescent rolls
- ½ cup finely shredded Parmesan cheese (2 ounces)
- ¼ cup mayonnaise or salad dressing
- 1 6- or 6½-ounce jar marinated artichoke hearts, drained and finely chopped
- ½ cup chopped sweet pepper

one On a lightly floured surface, unroll crescent roll dough; seal perforations between rolls. Using a lightly floured rolling pin, roll dough into a 15×8-inch rectangle.

two In a medium bowl stir together cheese and mayonnaise Stir in artichoke hearts. Spread mixture over dough, leaving ½-inch border on each side. Sprinkle with sweet pepper.

three Starting from a long side, roll up dough. Moisten and pinch edges to seal. Place roll, seam side down, on a lightly greased baking sheet.

four Bake, uncovered, in a 350°F oven about 30 minutes o until golden brown. Cool slightly on a wire rack.

NUTRITION FACTS PER SERVING: 103 cal., 7 g total fat (2 g sat. fat), 5 mg chol., 200 mg sodium, 7 g carbo., 0 g fiber, 2 g pro.

Spinach Pizza Bread

PREP: 20 minutes **RISE:** 45 minutes **BAKE:** 30 minutes
MAKES: 16 servings

½ of a 10-ounce package frozen chopped spinach

1 16-ounce loaf frozen bread dough, thawed

½ of a 2-ounce can anchovies, drained and cut up
    (optional)

1 tablespoon olive oil

4 or 5 cloves garlic, minced

one Cook frozen spinach according to package directions; drain spinach in a colander. Press and squeeze to remove excess liquid. Set aside.

two On a lightly floured surface, roll bread dough into a 12×9-inch rectangle. In a medium bowl combine anchovies (if desired), oil, and garlic. Stir in spinach. Spread spinach mixture over dough, leaving a ½-inch border on each side.

three Starting from a short side, roll up dough. Moisten and pinch edges to seal. Place loaf, seam side down, in a greased 9×5×3-inch or 8×4×2-inch loaf pan. Cover and let rise in a warm place until nearly double in size (about 45 minutes).

four Bake, uncovered, in a 375°F oven for 30 to 40 minutes or until bread sounds hollow when lightly tapped. If necessary, cover loosely with foil during the last 10 minutes to prevent overbrowning. Remove from pan. Cool slightly on a wire rack.

NUTRITION FACTS PER SERVING: 77 cal., 1 g total fat (0 g sat. fat), 0 mg chol., 7 mg sodium, 13 g carbo., 0 g fiber, 2 g pro.

Zucchini Bites

START TO FINISH: 20 minutes **MAKES:** about 36 servings

1 medium to large zucchini, cut into ¼-inch slices

½ of an 8-ounce tub cream cheese spread with salmon
    or ⅓ cup semisoft cheese with garlic and herb

1 tablespoon sliced or chopped pitted ripe olives

1 tablespoon snipped fresh chives

one Pat zucchini slices dry with paper towels. Spread cream cheese over zucchini slices. Sprinkle with olives and chives.

NUTRITION FACTS PER SERVING: 12 cal., 1 g total fat (1 g sat. fat), 3 mg chol., 27 mg sodium, 1 g carbo., 0 g fiber, 0 g pro.

Hoisin-Garlic Mushroom Appetizers

PREP: 15 minutes **COOK:** Low 5 hours, High 2½ hours
MAKES: 10 servings

½	cup bottled hoisin sauce
¼	cup water
2	tablespoons bottled minced garlic
¼	to ½ teaspoon crushed red pepper
24	ounces whole fresh button mushrooms, trimmed

one In a 3½- or 4-quart slow cooker combine hoisin sauce, water, garlic, and crushed red pepper. Add mushrooms, stirring to coat with hoisin mixture.

two Cover and cook on low-heat setting for 5 to 6 hours or on high-heat setting for 2½ to 3 hours.

three Using a slotted spoon, remove mushrooms from cooker. Discard cooking liquid. Serve mushrooms with decorative picks.

NUTRITION FACTS PER SERVING: 39 cal., 1 g total fat (0 g sat. fat), 0 mg chol, 107 mg sodium, 6 g carbo., 1 g fiber, 3 g pro.

Feta-Stuffed Mushrooms

PREP: 20 minutes **BAKE:** 10 minutes **MAKES:** 16 servings

4	fresh portobello mushrooms (5 to 6 ounces each)
1	tablespoon olive oil
1	4-ounce package crumbled feta cheese with garlic and herb or crumbled feta cheese
¼	cup chopped pitted ripe olives
2	tablespoons oil-packed dried tomatoes, drained and snipped

one Remove and discard mushroom stems. Place mushroom caps, stemmed sides up, on an ungreased baking sheet. Brush with olive oil (or use the oil from the tomatoes); set aside.

two In a small bowl combine cheese, olives, and dried tomatoes. Divide mixture among mushrooms.

three Bake, uncovered, in a 425°F oven about 10 minutes until heated through. To serve, cut each mushroom cap into 4 wedges.

NUTRITION FACTS PER SERVING: 40 cal., 3 g total fat (1 g sat. fat), 6 mg chol, 102 mg sodium, 2 g carbo., 1 g fiber, 2 g pro.

Cheesy Potato Wedges

PREP: 10 minutes **BAKE:** 25 minutes **MAKES:** 12 servings

- 1   24-ounce package frozen oven-fried potato wedges
- 1   16-ounce jar cheddar cheese pasta sauce
- 1   2-ounce jar cooked bacon pieces
- 1   medium tomato, chopped
- ½   cup sliced green onion

one Arrange frozen potato wedges in an even layer in an ungreased 15×10×1-inch baking pan. Bake, uncovered, in a 400°F oven for 15 minutes. Remove from oven.

two Pour pasta sauce over potato wedges; sprinkle with bacon pieces. Bake, uncovered, about 10 minutes more or until potatoes are tender and sauce is heated through. Sprinkle with tomato and green onion.

NUTRITION FACTS PER SERVING: 146 cal., 8 g total fat (3 g sat. fat), 18 mg chol., 456 mg sodium, 15 g carbo., 1 g fiber, 5 g pro.

Crispy Onion Rings   *See photo on page 274.*

PREP: 25 minutes **BAKE:** 12 minutes **MAKES:** 6 servings

- ¾   cup fine dry bread crumbs
- 3   tablespoons butter or margarine, melted
- ¼   teaspoon salt
- 2   medium sweet yellow or white onions, cut into ¼-inch slices and separated into rings
- 2   egg whites, slightly beaten
      Bottled ranch salad dressing

one In a small bowl stir together bread crumbs, melted butter, and salt. Spread about one-fourth of the crumb mixture on a sheet of waxed paper.

two Dip onion rings into beaten egg whites, then roll in bread crumb mixture on waxed paper to coat. Replace waxed paper and add more crumb mixture as needed. Place coated onion rings in a single layer on a greased large baking sheet.

three Bake, uncovered, in a 450°F oven for 12 to 15 minutes or until onions are tender and coating is crisp and golden brown. Serve onion rings with ranch dressing.

NUTRITION FACTS PER SERVING: 128 cal., 7 g total fat (4 g sat. fat), 16 mg chol., 283 mg sodium, 13 g carbo., 1 g fiber, 4 g pro.

Soft Pretzels

PREP: 15 minutes **BAKE:** 12 minutes **MAKES:** 8 servings

1   11-ounce package (8) refrigerated breadsticks
1   egg white
1   tablespoon water
    Poppy seeds, sesame seeds, or coarse salt

one Unroll breadsticks. Gently pull each breadstick into a 16-inch rope. For each pretzel, cross one end of a rope over the other, overlapping about 4 inches from each end. Holding an end in each hand, twist once at the crossover point. Fold pretzel in the middle and lay ends over bottom edge of the circle. Moisten ends, tuck them under the circle, and press to seal. Place on a greased baking sheet.

two In a small bowl combine egg white and water; brush over pretzels. Sprinkle with poppy seeds. Bake, uncovered, in a 375°F oven for 12 to 15 minutes or until golden brown. Cool on a wire rack.

NUTRITION FACTS PER SERVING: 114 cal., 3 g total fat (1 g sat. fat), 0 mg chol., 297 mg sodium, 18 g carbo., 1 g fiber, 4 g pro.

Olive Bread

PREP: 20 minutes **BAKE:** 18 minutes **MAKES:** 12 servings

½   cup grated Parmesan cheese
1   2¼-ounce can sliced pitted ripe olives, drained
4   to 5 cloves garlic, minced
1   13.8-ounce package refrigerated pizza dough
    Bottled pizza sauce, heated

one Set aside 1 tablespoon of the cheese. In a small bowl combine the remaining cheese, the olives, and garlic.

two On a lightly floured surface, roll pizza dough into a 14×10-inch rectangle. Sprinkle ⅓ cup of the olive mixture crosswise in a 2-inch-wide band on half of the dough. Fold other half of dough over filling, allowing about two-thirds of the dough to extend beyond the filling.

three Add another ⅓ cup of the olive mixture on top of the filled layer; press filling gently. Fold dough back over filling, making about a 3-inch pleat. Repeat filling and folding dough one more time. Gently pat sides to form a 10½×3-inch loaf; press ends to seal.

four Place on a lightly greased baking sheet. Brush with a little water and sprinkle with the reserved cheese. Bake, uncovered, in a 400°F oven for 18 to 20 minutes or until golden browm. Cut into slices. Serve warm with pizza sauce.

NUTRITION FACTS PER SERVING: 83 cal., 3 g total fat (1 g sat. fat), 3 mg chol., 285 mg sodium, 11 g carbo., 1 g fiber, 3 g pro.

Toasted Cheese Pita Chips

PREP: 15 minutes **BAKE:** 10 minutes **MAKES:** 12 servings

3   pita bread rounds

3   tablespoons butter or margarine, melted

3   tablespoons grated Parmesan or Romano cheese

one Split pita bread rounds in half horizontally. Lightly brush cut sides of pita halves with melted butter. Cut each half into 6 wedges. Spread wedges in a single layer on an ungreased baking sheet. Sprinkle with cheese.

two Bake, uncovered, in a 350°F oven about 10 minutes or until chips are crisp and edges are lightly browned.

NUTRITION FACTS PER SERVING: 74 cal., 4 g total fat (2 g sat. fat), 9 mg chol., 135 mg sodium, 8 g carbo., 0 g fiber, 2 g pro.

Italian-Style Chips

PREP: 15 minutes **BAKE:** 8 minutes **MAKES:** 8 servings

⅔   cup finely chopped onion

2   tablespoons butter or margarine, melted

1   teaspoon dried Italian seasoning, crushed

4   8-inch flour tortillas

    Bottled salsa (optional)

one In a small skillet cook onion in melted butter for 3 to 5 minutes or until tender. Stir in Italian seasoning. Brush onion mixture evenly over one side of each tortilla. Cut each tortilla into 8 wedges. Spread wedges in a single layer in an ungreased 15×10×1-inch baking pan.

two Bake, uncovered, in a 350°F oven for 8 to 10 minutes or until chips are crisp and edges are lightly browned. If desired, serve with salsa.

NUTRITION FACTS PER SERVING: 105 cal., 7 g total fat (2 g sat. fat), 8 mg chol., 127 mg sodium, 9 g carbo., 0 g fiber, 1 g pro.

Cheese-Stuffed Pecans

PREP: 20 minutes **STAND:** 30 minutes **CHILL:** 30 minutes
MAKES: 10 servings

 1 cup finely shredded Gouda cheese (4 ounces)
 3 tablespoons dairy sour cream
40 large pecan halves

one Place cheese in a medium bowl; let stand at room temperature for 30 minutes. Add sour cream. Beat with an electric mixer on low to medium speed until creamy.

two Mound a scant 1 teaspoon of the cheese mixture onto the flat side of half of the pecan halves. Top with the remainir pecan halves, flat sides down. Cover and chill for 30 minutes

NUTRITION FACTS PER SERVING: 102 cal., 10 g total fat (3 g sat. fat), 14 mg chol., 94 mg sodium, 1 g carbo., 1 g fiber, 4 g pro.

Toasted Almonds with Rosemary

START TO FINISH: 15 minutes **MAKES:** 16 servings

 8 ounces unblanched almonds or pecan halves
    (about 2 cups)
1½ teaspoons butter or margarine
 1 tablespoon finely snipped fresh rosemary
1½ teaspoons packed brown sugar
 ¼ to ½ teaspoon salt

one Spread almonds in a single layer on an ungreased bakin sheet. Bake, uncovered, in a 350°F oven about 10 minutes until nuts are lightly toasted and fragrant.

two Meanwhile, in a medium saucepan heat butter over mediu heat until sizzling. Remove from heat. Stir in the rosemary, brown sugar, and salt. Add almonds to butter mixture; toss gently to coat. Cool slightly before serving.

NUTRITION FACTS PER SERVING: 80 cal., 7 g total fat (1 g sat. fat), 1 mg chol 37 mg sodium, 3 g carbo., 1 g fiber, 4 g pro.

Peach Nectar Punch

4   cups peach nectar, chilled

1   6-ounce can frozen orange juice concentrate, thawed

1   1-liter bottle ginger ale, chilled

2   16-ounce packages frozen unsweetened peach slices

    Ice cubes

one In a large punch bowl stir together peach nectar and orange juice concentrate. Slowly pour in ginger ale; stir gently.

two Stir frozen peach slices into punch. Serve over ice cubes.

NUTRITION FACTS PER SERVING: 86 cal., 0 g total fat (0 g sat. fat), 0 mg chol., 8 mg sodium, 22 g carbo., 1 g fiber, 1 g pro.

Apple-Cranberry Punch

1   32-ounce bottle apple juice or apple cider, chilled

1   32-ounce bottle cranberry juice, chilled

2   cups carbonated water, chilled

    Ice cubes

    Orange slices (optional)

one In a large punch bowl stir together apple juice and cranberry juice. Slowly pour in carbonated water; stir gently.

two Serve punch over ice cubes. If desired, garnish each serving with an orange slice.

NUTRITION FACTS PER SERVING: 86 cal., 0 g total fat (0 g sat. fat), 0 mg chol., 14 mg sodium, 22 g carbo., 0 g fiber, 0 g pro.

Orange Cream Punch

START TO FINISH: 15 minutes **MAKES:** 16 servings

- 1   14-ounce can sweetened condensed milk
- 1   12-ounce can frozen orange juice concentrate, thawed

    Orange food coloring (optional)
- 2   1-liter bottles carbonated water or ginger ale, chilled

    Orange sherbet

one In a large punch bowl stir together sweetened condensed milk and orange juice concentrate. If desired, stir in orange food coloring.

two Slowly pour in carbonated water; stir gently. Top with scoops of orange sherbet. Serve immediately.

NUTRITION FACTS PER SERVING: 164 cal., 3 g total fat (2 g sat. fat), 11 mg chol., 75 mg sodium, 33 g carbo., 0 g fiber, 3 g pro.

Champagne Fruit Punch

START TO FINISH: 20 minutes **MAKES:** 12 servings

- 1   16-ounce package frozen unsweetened whole strawberries or sliced peaches, thawed
- ¼   cup sugar
- 2½   cups orange juice
- 2   tablespoons lemon juice or lime juice
- 1   750-milliliter bottle champagne or sparkling wine or 4 cups unsweetened pineapple juice, chilled

one In a blender or food processor combine fruit and any juice from the fruit. Add sugar. Cover and blend or process until smooth. Pour fruit mixture through a sieve lined with a double thickness of 100-percent-cotton cheesecloth. Discard seeds or pulp.

two Transfer fruit mixture to a 2-quart pitcher. Stir in orange juice and lemon juice. Slowly pour in champagne; stir gently.

NUTRITION FACTS PER SERVING: 95 cal., 0 g total fat (0 g sat. fat), 0 mg chol. 2 mg sodium, 14 g carbo., 1 g fiber, 1 g pro.

Hot and Spicy Cranberry Punch *See photo on page 276.*

PREP: 10 minutes **COOK:** Low 4 hours, High 2 hours
MAKES: 18 servings

8	whole cardamom pods
16	inches stick cinnamon, broken
12	whole cloves (optional)
4	cups dry red wine
3	cups water
1	11½- or 12-ounce can frozen cranberry juice concentrate
⅓	cup honey
	Fresh cranberries (optional)

one For spice bag, cut a double thickness of 100-percent-cotton cheesecloth into a 6-inch square. Pinch cardamom pods to break open. Place cardamom, cinnamon, and, if desired, cloves in center of cloth. Tie closed with clean kitchen string.

two In a 3½- to 6-quart slow cooker combine spice bag, wine, water, frozen juice concentrate, and honey. Cover and cook on low-heat setting for 4 to 6 hours or on high-heat setting for 2 to 2½ hours. Discard spice bag.

three Ladle punch into cups. If desired, garnish each serving with cranberries threaded onto a small skewer.

NUTRITION FACTS PER SERVING: 91 cal., 0 g total fat (0 g sat. fat), 0 mg chol., 5 mg sodium, 15 g carbo., 0 g fiber, 0 g pro.

Tomato Sipper

PREP: 10 minutes **COOK:** Low 4 hours, High 2 hours
MAKES: 8 servings

1	46-ounce can vegetable juice
1	stalk celery, halved crosswise
2	tablespoons packed brown sugar
2	tablespoons lemon juice
2	teaspoons Worcestershire sauce

one In a 3½- or 4-quart slow cooker combine vegetable juice, celery, brown sugar, lemon juice, and Worcestershire sauce.

two Cover and cook on low-heat setting for 4 to 5 hours or on high-heat setting for 2 to 2½ hours. Discard celery halves.

NUTRITION FACTS PER SERVING: 50 cal., 0 g total fat (0 g sat. fat), 0 mg chol., 443 mg sodium, 11 g carbo., 1 g fiber, 1 g pro.

TAKE FIVE FOR FUN

Fancy Fruit Float

START TO FINISH: 10 minutes **MAKES:** 4 servings

- 2 cups cut-up fruit (such as strawberries, grapes, bananas, oranges, and/or apples)
- 1 1-liter bottle diet lemon-lime carbonated beverage or diet ginger ale
- 2 cups favorite fruit sherbet

one Divide fruit pieces among 4 tall glasses. Slowly pour carbonated beverage into glasses, filling each glass about three-fourths full. Top each with a scoop of sherbet.

NUTRITION FACTS PER SERVING: 172 cal., 2 g total fat (1 g sat. fat), 5 mg chol., 83 mg sodium, 39 g carbo., 2 g fiber, 2 g pro.

Fizzy Mint-Chocolate Soda

START TO FINISH: 10 minutes   **MAKES:** 4 servings

- ¼ cup chocolate-flavor syrup
- 1 pint mint-chocolate chip ice cream
- 2 cups carbonated water or cream soda, chilled

one Divide half of the chocolate syrup among 4 tall glasses. Add a scoop of ice cream to each glass.

two Divide the remaining chocolate syrup among glasses. Top each with another scoop of ice cream. Slowly pour the carbonated water into glasses.

NUTRITION FACTS PER SERVING: 245 cal., 11 g total fat (6 g sat. fat), 26 mg chol., 84 mg sodium, 33 g carbo., 0 g fiber, 4 g pro.

Quick Ice Cream Shake

START TO FINISH: 10 minutes **MAKES:** 3 servings

- 1 pint vanilla ice cream
- ¼ cup amaretto, Irish cream, or hazelnut liquid creamer, or strawberry-flavor syrup

   Milk

one In a blender combine ice cream and liquid creamer. Cover and blend until smooth. If necessary, add a little milk to reach desired consistency.

NUTRITION FACTS PER SERVING: 250 cal., 10 g total fat (6 g sat. fat), 39 mg chol., 74 mg sodium, 30 g carbo., 0 g fiber, 3 g pro.

Berry-Banana Smoothies

START TO FINISH: 10 minutes **MAKES:** 2 servings

1 cup orange juice

1 small banana, peeled, cut up, and frozen

¼ cup fresh or frozen berries (such as raspberries, blackberries, and/or strawberries)

3 tablespoons vanilla low-fat yogurt

Fresh berries (optional)

one In a blender combine orange juice, frozen banana, the ¼ cup berries, and the yogurt. Cover and blend until smooth.

two Pour into 2 glasses. If desired, top with additional berries.

NUTRITION FACTS PER SERVING: 121 cal., 1 g total fat (0 g sat. fat), 2 mg chol., 18 mg sodium, 28 g carbo., 2 g fiber, 2 g pro.

Strawberry Smoothies

START TO FINISH: 10 minutes **MAKES:** 4 servings

2 cups strawberries

⅓ cup powdered sugar

½ of a 6-ounce can (⅓ cup) frozen lemonade or limeade concentrate

2½ to 3 cups ice cubes

one In a blender combine strawberries, powdered sugar, and frozen lemonade concentrate.

two With the blender running, add ice cubes, one at a time, through the opening in the lid until mixture is slushy.

NUTRITION FACTS PER SERVING: 104 cal., 0 g total fat (0 g sat. fat), 0 mg chol., 5 mg sodium, 26 g carbo., 2 g fiber, 1 g pro.

Watermelon Lemonade

PREP: 10 minutes **MAKES:** 2 or 3 servings

- 2 cups cubed and seeded watermelon
- ½ cup apple juice or unsweetened white grape juice
- ⅓ cup lemon juice or lime juice
- 1 to 2 tablespoons honey
- Ice cubes

one In a blender combine watermelon, apple juice, lemon juice, and honey. Cover and blend until smooth. Serve over ice cubes.

NUTRITION FACTS PER SERVING: 120 cal., 1 g total fat (0 g sat. fat), 0 mg cho 6 mg sodium, 30 g carbo., 1 g fiber, 1 g pro.

Fizzy Kiwi Lemonade

PREP: 20 minutes **CHILL:** 2 to 24 hours **MAKES:** 6 servings

- 6 kiwifruits
- 1 cup sugar
- ¾ cup lemon juice
- 1 1-liter bottle carbonated water, chilled
- Ice cubes

one Peel kiwifruits. Place the peeled fruit in a blender; cover and blend until smooth. Strain mixture through a fine-mesh sieve placed over a bowl. Discard seeds (some may remain).

two In a large pitcher combine sugar and lemon juice, stirring to dissolve sugar. Stir in strained kiwifruit. Cover and chill for 2 to 24 hours.

three Before serving, slowly pour in carbonated water; stir gently. Serve over ice cubes.

NUTRITION FACTS PER SERVING: 196 cal., 1 g total fat (0 g sat. fat), 0 mg chol., 36 mg sodium, 48 g carbo.,0 g fiber, 1 g pro.

Honey-Mulled Apple Cider

PREP: 10 minutes **COOK:** Low 5 hours, High 2½ hours
MAKES: 10 servings

6	inches stick cinnamon, broken
1	teaspoon whole allspice
1	teaspoon whole cloves
10	cups pasteurized apple cider or apple juice (2½ quarts)
⅓	cup honey or packed light brown sugar
	Cinnamon sticks (optional)

one For spice bag, cut a double thickness of 100-percent-cotton cheesecloth into a 6-inch square. Place the 6 inches stick cinnamon, the allspice, and cloves in center of cloth. Tie closed with clean kitchen string. In a 3½- to 5-quart slow cooker combine spice bag, apple cider, and honey.

two Cover and cook on low-heat setting for 5 to 6 hours or on high-heat setting for 2½ to 3 hours. Discard spice bag.

three Ladle into mugs. If desired, garnish each serving with an additional cinnamon stick.

NUTRITION FACTS PER SERVING: 150 cal., 0 g total fat (0 g sat. fat), 0 mg chol., 8 mg sodium, 38 g carbo., 0 g fiber, 0 g pro.

Hot Strawberry Cider

START TO FINISH: 20 minutes **MAKES:** 8 servings

8	cups apple cider or apple juice
1	10-ounce package frozen strawberries in syrup
4	inches stick cinnamon
1	teaspoon whole cloves
	Fresh strawberry slices, apple slices, or stick cinnamon (optional)

one In a large saucepan combine apple cider, frozen strawberries, the 4 inches stick cinnamon, and the cloves. Bring to boiling; reduce heat. Simmer, covered, for 10 minutes.

two Pour strawberry mixture through a sieve lined with a double thickness of 100-percent-cotton cheesecloth. Discard seeds. Ladle into mugs. If desired, garnish each serving with fresh strawberries.

NUTRITION FACTS PER SERVING: 158 cal., 0 g total fat (0 g sat. fat), 0 mg chol., 9 mg sodium, 43 g carbo., 3 g fiber, 0 g pro.

Minted Iced Tea *See photo on page 276.*

PREP: 25 minutes **CHILL:** 4 hours **MAKES:** 16 to 18 servings

- 7   cups water
- 2   cups sugar
- 8   bags orange pekoe tea
- 8   sprigs fresh mint
- 8   cups cold water
- 2   cups orange juice
- ¾   cup lemon juice
      Ice cubes
      Fresh mint sprigs and/or orange slices (optional)

one In a large saucepan combine the 7 cups water and the sugar. Bring to boiling, stirring to dissolve sugar; reduce heat. Simmer, uncovered, for 5 minutes. Remove from heat.

two Add tea bags and the 8 mint sprigs; cover and let stand for 5 minutes. Using a slotted spoon, remove tea bags and mint sprigs.

three Transfer tea to a heatproof 1½- to 2-gallon container. Add the 8 cups cold water, the orange juice, and lemon juice. Cover and chill for at least 4 hours. Serve tea in 16 to 18 tall glasses over ice cubes. If desired, garnish each serving with an additional mint sprig and/or orange slice.

NUTRITION FACTS PER SERVING: 110 cal., 0 g total fat (0 g sat. fat), 0 mg chol., 3 mg sodium, 28 g carbo., 0 g fiber, 0 g pro.

Ginger-Lemon Tea

START TO FINISH: 20 minutes **MAKES:** 6 servings

- 6   cups water
- 4   teaspoons sugar
- 8   lemon peel strips (2½ ×1 inches each)
- 1   1-inch piece fresh ginger, thinly sliced
- 8   green tea bags

one In a large saucepan combine water, sugar, lemon peel strips, and ginger. Bring to boiling; reduce heat. Simmer, covered, for 10 minutes. Using a slotted spoon, remove lemon peel strips and ginger.

two Add tea bags to saucepan. Cover and let stand for 3 to 5 minutes. Remove tea bags.

NUTRITION FACTS PER SERVING: 13 cal., 0 g total fat (0 g sat. fat), 0 mg chol., 7 mg sodium, 3 g carbo., 0 g fiber, 0 g pro.

Mocha au Lait

START TO FINISH: 10 minutes **MAKES:** 12 servings

1½   cups nonfat dry milk powder
⅔   cup miniature semisweet chocolate pieces
½   cup instant coffee crystals
⅓   cup packed brown sugar

one For mix, in a storage container combine dry milk powder, chocolate pieces, coffee crystals, and brown sugar. Store, tightly covered, at room temperature.

two For each serving, pour ⅔ cup boiling water into a blender. Add ¼ cup of the mix. Cover and blend until frothy.

NUTRITION FACTS PER SERVING: 109 cal., 3 g total fat (1 g sat. fat), 2 mg chol., 55 mg sodium, 15 g carbo., 1 g fiber, 3 g pro.

Raspberry-Coffee Frappé

START TO FINISH: 10 minutes **MAKES:** 6 servings

2   cups strong brewed coffee, chilled
½   cup half-and-half or light cream
¼   cup raspberry-flavor syrup
1½   cups ice cubes
6   scoops coffee ice cream

one In a blender combine 1 cup of the coffee, the half-and-half, and raspberry syrup; add ice cubes. Cover and blend until ice cubes are finely crushed. Add the remaining 1 cup coffee. Cover and blend on the lowest speed until combined.

two Pour into 6 glasses. Top each serving with a scoop of coffee ice cream.

NUTRITION FACTS PER SERVING: 243 cal., 14 g total fat (9 g sat. fat), 87 mg chol., 69 mg sodium, 24 g carbo., 0 g fiber, 4 g pro.

Peanut Butter Cocoa

PREP: 10 minutes **COOK:** Low 3 hours, High 1½ hours
MAKES: 9 servings

1   cup instant milk chocolate or chocolate fudge
       cocoa mix
8   cups hot water
¾   cup chocolate-flavor syrup
¼   cup creamy peanut butter
1½   teaspoons vanilla

one Place cocoa mix in a 3½- or 4-quart slow cooker. Stir i
hot water and chocolate-flavor syrup.

two Cover and cook on low-heat setting for 3 to 4 hours or
on high-heat setting for 1½ to 2 hours. Whisk in peanut butt
and vanilla until smooth.

NUTRITION FACTS PER SERVING: 176 cal., 4 g total fat (1 g sat. fat),
1 mg chol., 115 mg sodium, 32 g carbo., 1 g fiber, 3 g pro.

Hot Caramel Chocolate

START TO FINISH: 15 minutes **MAKES:** 6 servings

⅓   cup sugar
⅓   cup unsweetened cocoa powder
⅓   cup water
6   milk chocolate-covered round caramels
6   cups milk, half-and-half, or light cream

one In a large saucepan combine sugar, cocoa powder,
and water. Heat over medium heat, stirring to dissolve sugar

two Add chocolate-covered caramels; stir until caramels
melt. Stir in milk; heat through.

NUTRITION FACTS PER SERVING: 213 cal., 7 g total fat (4 g sat. fat),
19 mg chol., 133 mg sodium, 29 g carbo., 0 g fiber, 10 g pro.

The Magic Pancake

4   eggs, slightly beaten

⅔   cup all-purpose flour

⅔   cup milk

1   cup finely shredded Swiss, cheddar, or Monterey Jack
      cheese (4 ounces)

2   tablespoons cooked bacon pieces

one Grease a 10-inch ovenproof skillet with shortening. Heat skillet in a 400°F oven.

two Meanwhile, in a medium bowl combine eggs, flour, and milk. Pour batter into hot skillet. Bake, uncovered, about 20 minutes or until pancake is puffed and golden brown.

three Sprinkle pancake with cheese and bacon pieces. Cut into wedges.

NUTRITION FACTS PER SERVING: 289 cal., 15 g total fat (8 g sat. fat), 244 mg chol., 207 mg sodium, 18 g carbo., 1 g fiber, 19 g pro.

Fancy Stack Pancakes

START TO FINISH: 15 minutes MAKES: 4 servings

8   frozen pancakes

½   cup cream cheese spread

3   tablespoons apricot, raspberry, blackberry, or
      blueberry spreadable fruit

one Spread each frozen pancake with 1 tablespoon of the cream cheese. Spoon about 1 teaspoon of the spreadable fruit on top of each pancake.

two Make 4 stacks of pancakes, using 2 pancakes for each stack. Place stacks on a large microwave-safe platter.

three Microwave, uncovered, on 50 percent power (medium) for 3½ to 4½ minutes or until pancakes are heated through. Serve warm.

NUTRITION FACTS PER SERVING: 296 cal., 12 g total fat (8 g sat. fat), 36 mg chol., 466 mg sodium, 41 g carbo., 1 g fiber, 6 g pro.

Baked Parmesan Chicken

PREP: 10 minutes **BAKE:** 25 minutes **MAKES:** 4 servings

- ½   cup crushed cornflakes
- 2   tablespoons grated Parmesan cheese
- ¼   teaspoon dried Italian seasoning, crushed
- 4   skinless, boneless chicken breast halves (1¼ pounds)
- 3   tablespoons butter or margarine, melted

one In a shallow dish combine cornflakes, cheese, and Italian seasoning. Dip chicken into melted butter, then roll in cornflake mixture to coat. Place chicken on a rack in a shallow baking pan.

two Bake, uncovered, in a 375°F oven about 25 minutes or until chicken is tender and no longer pink (170°F).

NUTRITION FACTS PER SERVING: 287 cal., 12 g total fat (7 g sat. fat), 109 mg chol., 318 mg sodium, 9 g carbo., 0 g fiber, 35 g pro.

Little Chicken Dippers

START TO FINISH: 15 minutes **MAKES:** 3 servings

- 1   10-ounce package frozen breaded chicken breast chunks
- ¼   cup bottled barbecue sauce
- 2   tablespoons grape jelly

one Bake chicken chunks according to package directions

two Meanwhile, for dipping sauce, in a small saucepan combine barbecue sauce and grape jelly. Cook and stir just until jelly melts. Serve chicken with dipping sauce.

NUTRITION FACTS PER SERVING: 366 cal., 23 g total fat (6 g sat. fat), 56 mg chol., 725 mg sodium, 27 g carbo., 0 g fiber, 13 g pro.

Chicken Salad Stacks

START TO FINISH: 15 minutes MAKES: 3 servings

4   7- to 8-inch flour tortillas

½   cup cream cheese spread

1   cup deli chicken salad or tuna salad

3   lettuce leaves

    Pimiento-stuffed green olives, pitted ripe olives, or
        cherry tomatoes (optional)

one Spread 3 of the tortillas with cream cheese. Top with chicken salad and lettuce leaves. Stack tortillas; top with the remaining tortilla.

two Cut tortilla stack into wedges. If desired, pierce each wedge with a decorative pick or a toothpick topped with olives or cherry tomatoes.

NUTRITION FACTS PER SERVING: 392 cal., 27 g total fat (12 g sat. fat), 75 mg chol., 391 mg sodium, 22 g carbo., 1 g fiber, 15 g pro.

Sausage-Corn Chowder

START TO FINISH: 20 minutes MAKES: 4 servings

12   ounces cooked smoked turkey sausage or
        turkey hot dogs

1   10¾-ounce can condensed cream of potato soup

⅓   cups milk

1   8½-ounce can cream-style corn

3   slices American cheese (3 ounces),
        torn into pieces

one Halve turkey sausage lengthwise; cut into ½-inch slices. Set aside.

two In a medium saucepan combine soup, milk, and cream-style corn. Stir in sausage and cheese. Cook and stir over medium heat until heated through.

NUTRITION FACTS PER SERVING: 342 cal., 18 g total fat (8 g sat. fat), 85 mg chol., 1,836 mg sodium, 27 g carbo., 1 g fiber, 23 g pro.

Cheeseburger and Fries Casserole

PREP: 15 minutes **BAKE:** 45 minutes **MAKES:** 8 to 10 servings

- 2 pounds lean ground beef
- 1 10¾-ounce can condensed golden mushroom soup
- 1 10¾-ounce can condensed cheddar cheese soup
- 1 20-ounce package frozen french-fried crinkle-cut potatoes

  Assorted toppings (such as ketchup, pickles, mustard, and/or chopped tomato) (optional)

one In a large skillet cook ground beef, half at a time, over medium-high heat until brown. Drain off fat. Spread meat in a ungreased 3-quart rectangular baking dish.

two In a medium bowl combine mushroom soup and cheese soup. Spread soup mixture over meat. Sprinkle with potatoes

three Bake, uncovered, in a 350°F oven for 45 to 55 minute or until potatoes are golden brown. If desired, serve with toppin

NUTRITION FACTS PER SERVING: 348 cal., 18 g total fat (6 g sat. fat), 78 mg chol., 654 mg sodium, 24 g carbo.,2 g fiber, 24 g pro.

Ready-Right-Now Sloppy Joes

START TO FINISH: 15 minutes **MAKES:** 6 servings

- 1 pound lean ground beef, ground pork, or uncooked ground turkey
- 1 8-ounce can tomato sauce
- ⅓ cup bottled barbecue sauce
- 1 teaspoon dried minced onion
- 6 hamburger buns, split

one In a large skillet cook ground meat over medium-high heat until brown. Drain off fat.

two Stir in tomato sauce, barbecue sauce, and dried onion Bring to boiling. Serve meat mixture on buns.

NUTRITION FACTS PER SERVING: 289 cal., 12 g total fat (4 g sat. fat), 48 mg chol., 556 mg sodium, 26 g carbo., 2 g fiber, 19 g pro.

Two Pizzas in One

8   ounces bulk Italian sausage or lean ground beef
2   15- to 15½-ounce frozen cheese pizzas
1   4-ounce can (drained weight) mushroom stems and
     pieces, drained
½   cup chopped sweet pepper
1   cup shredded co-jack cheese (4 ounces)

one In a medum skillet cook sausage over medium-high heat until brown. Drain off fat.

two Place a cheese pizza on a greased baking sheet. Top with cooked sausage, mushrooms , and sweet pepper. Top with the remaining pizza, crust side up. Cover pizza with foil.

three Bake in a 375°F oven for 30 minutes. Remove foil. Bake for 10 minutes more. Sprinkle with cheese. Bake, uncovered, about 5 minutes more or until cheese melts.

NUTRITION FACTS PER SERVING: 505 cal., 22 g total fat (11 g sat. fat), 64 mg chol., 1,131 mg sodium, 50 g carbo., 0 g fiber, 27 g pro.

Chili Dogs

START TO FINISH: 15 minutes **MAKES:** 4 servings

1   15-ounce can chili with beans, undrained
2   tablespoons bottled barbecue sauce
1   teaspoon yellow mustard
4   hot dogs
4   hot dog buns, split

one In a medium saucepan combine undrained chili, barbecue sauce, and mustard. Place hot dogs on top of chili mixture.

two Cook, covered, over medium heat until mixture is heated through, stirring occasionally. Place hot dogs on buns. Top with chili mixture.

NUTRITION FACTS PER SERVING: 389 cal., 20 g total fat (8 g sat. fat), 41 mg chol., 1,367 mg sodium, 38 g carbo., 6 g fiber, 15 g pro.

Snowflake Sandwiches

PREP: 35 minutes **RISE:** 30 minutes **BAKE:** 10 minutes
MAKES: 8 servings

- 8 frozen white or whole wheat Texas-style rolls, thawed
- 1 pound thinly sliced cooked ham or turkey
- 8 slices American cheese (6 to 8 ounces)
     Bottled ranch or creamy Italian salad dressing

one Flatten a roll into a 4-inch round. Using kitchen shears, make five or six 1-inch, V-shape cuts toward center of round about 1½ inches apart; discard triangular dough pieces. Make 2 small diagonal cuts in dough on each side of each V, creating a snowflake design. Repeat with the remaining rolls.

two Place rolls 2 inches apart on a greased large baking sheet. Cover and let rise in a warm place until nearly double in size (30 to 40 minutes). Bake, uncovered, in a 350°F oven for 10 to 12 minutes or until golden brown. Cool on a wire rack.

three Split rolls in half. Layer ham and cheese on bottoms of rolls. Add dressing; replace tops of rolls.

NUTRITION FACTS PER SERVING: 396 cal., 22 g total fat (8 g sat. fat), 59 mg chol., 1,462 mg sodium, 30 g carbo., 1 g fiber, 21 g pro.

Ham and Cheese Pizza Tortillas

PREP: 15 minutes **BAKE:** 12 minutes **MAKES:** 8 servings

- 12 7- to 8-inch flour tortillas
- ¼ cup purchased pesto
- 2 cups shredded mozzarella cheese (8 ounces)
- 8 ounces diced cooked ham (1½ cups)
- 1 8-ounce can pizza sauce or ½ cup purchased Alfredo pasta sauce

one Spread 4 of the tortillas with pesto. Top with 4 more tortillas. In a small bowl combine 1 cup of the cheese and the ham. Sprinkle ham mixture over tops of the stacked tortillas. Top with the remaining tortillas. Spread pizza sauce over tops of stacked tortillas; sprinkle with the remaining 1 cup cheese.

two Place tortilla stacks on an ungreased baking sheet. Bake, uncovered, in a 425°F oven for 12 to 15 minutes or until cheese melts. Cut each stack into wedges.

NUTRITION FACTS PER SERVING: 315 cal., 16 g total fat (6 g sat. fat), 32 mg chol., 772 mg sodium, 26 g carbo., 1 g fiber, 16 g pro.

Pepperoni-Pizza Potatoes

START TO FINISH: 25 minutes **MAKES:** 4 servings

- 4   medium baking potatoes (6 to 8 ounces each)
- 1   8-ounce jar pizza sauce
- 3½   ounces sliced pepperoni
- ¾   cup shredded mozzarella cheese (3 ounces)

one Scrub potatoes; pat dry. Pierce potatoes with a fork. Arrange about 1 inch apart on a microwave-safe plate. Microwave on 100 percent power (high) for 14 to 17 minutes or until tender, turning after 6 minutes. Remove from oven. Cover potatoes with foil; let stand for 6 minutes.

two Meanwhile, in a microwave-safe 2-cup measuring cup combine pizza sauce and pepperoni. Cover with vented microwave-safe plastic wrap. Microwave on high for 3 to 4 minutes or until heated through, stirring after 2 minutes.

three Cut each potato open. Spoon pepperoni mixture over potatoes. Sprinkle with cheese. Microwave, uncovered, on high for 2 to 3 minutes more or until cheese melts.

NUTRITION FACTS PER SERVING: 366 cal., 16 g total fat (7 g sat. fat), 32 mg chol., 611 mg sodium, 42 g carbo., 5 g fiber, 16 g pro.

Spuds with Broccoli Topper

START TO FINISH: 20 minutes **MAKES:** 4 servings

- 4   medium baking potatoes (6 to 8 ounces each)
- 1   cup frozen cut broccoli
- 1   tablespoon water
- ½   of an 8-ounce tub cream cheese spread
- ½   teaspoon Worcestershire sauce

one Scrub potatoes; pat dry. Pierce potatoes with a fork. Arrange about 1 inch apart on a microwave-safe plate. Microwave on 100 percent power (high) for 14 to 17 minutes or until tender, turning after 6 minutes. Remove from oven. Cover potatoes with foil; let stand for 6 minutes.

two Meanwhile, in a microwave-safe 1-quart casserole combine frozen broccoli and water. Microwave, uncovered, on high for 3 to 4 minutes or until broccoli is tender. Cut up any large pieces. Stir in cream cheese and Worcestershire sauce. Microwave, covered, on high for 1 to 2 minutes more or until heated through.

three Cut each potato open. Spoon cream cheese mixture over potatoes.

NUTRITION FACTS PER SERVING: 231 cal., 10 g total fat (7 g sat. fat), 28 mg chol., 118 mg sodium, 30 g carbo., 4 g fiber, 7 g pro.

Lip-Smackin' Mac 'n' Cheese

START TO FINISH: 25 minutes **MAKES:** 3 servings

- 2 cups dried corkscrew or elbow macaroni
- ¼ cup chopped onion
- 6 to 8 slices American cheese (6 ounces), torn into pieces
- ½ cup milk

  Dash black pepper

one In a large saucepan cook macaroni and onion according to macaroni package directions; drain. Return to saucepan.

two Stir in cheese, milk, and pepper. Cook and stir for 4 to 5 minutes or until cheese melts.

NUTRITION FACTS PER SERVING: 397 cal., 14 g total fat (10 g sat. fat), 42 mg chol., 791 mg sodium, 46 g carbo., 2 g fiber, 18 g pro.

Cheese and Bean Quesadillas

START TO FINISH: 20 minutes **MAKES:** 4 servings

- 4 7- to 8-inch flour tortillas
- ¼ cup refried beans
- ⅔ cup shredded co-jack cheese

  Bottled salsa (optional)

one Spread 2 of the tortillas with refried beans; sprinkle with cheese. Top with the remaining tortillas; press gently.

two In a medium skillet or griddle cook quesadillas, one at a time, over medium heat about 5 minutes or until cheese melts, turning once. Cut quesadillas into wedges. If desired, serve with salsa.

NUTRITION FACTS PER SERVING: 191 cal., 8 g total fat (5 g sat. fat), 18 mg chol., 326 mg sodium, 21 g carbo., 2 g fiber, 8 g pro.

Cheese Calzone

PREP: 15 minutes **BAKE:** 18 minutes **MAKES:** 4 servings

Nonstick cooking spray

1   13.8-ounce package refrigerated pizza dough

2   cups shredded cheddar cheese (8 ounces)

½   cup ricotta cheese

¼   grated Parmesan cheese

1   cup bottled thick-style spaghetti sauce or
     one 8-ounce can pizza sauce

one Line a 12-inch pizza pan with foil; coat with cooking spray. Press dough onto foil in the prepared pan, forming a 12-inch circle.

two In a large bowl combine cheddar cheese, ricotta cheese, and Parmesan cheese. Spoon cheese mixture onto half of the pizza dough. Fold dough over filling to form a half-circle; pinch edges to seal. Cut slits in top of dough to allow steam to escape.

three Bake, uncovered, in a 400°F oven for 18 to 20 minutes or until cheese melts, covering with foil after 10 minutes to prevent overbrowning. Cool in pan on a wire rack for 5 minutes. Cut calzone into wedges.

four Meanwhile, in a small saucepan heat spaghetti sauce until bubbly. Serve calzone with sauce.

NUTRITION FACTS PER SERVING: 520 cal., 28 g total fat (16 g sat. fat), 80 mg chol., 1,194 mg sodium, 40 g carbo., 3 g fiber, 27 g pro.

Carrot, Raisin, and Peanut Butter Sandwiches

START TO FINISH: 15 minutes **MAKES:** 4 servings

8   slices white, whole wheat, or
     cinnamon-raisin bread

½   to ⅔ cup peanut butter

¼   cup raisins

¼   cup shredded carrot

one Spread half of the bread slices with peanut butter. Top with raisins, carrot, and the remaining bread slices.

two Broil about 4 inches from the heat for 2 to 4 minutes or until bread is toasted, turning once.

NUTRITION FACTS PER SERVING: 354 cal., 18 g total fat (4 g sat. fat), 1 mg chol., 422 mg sodium, 39 g carbo., 4 g fiber, 13 g pro.

Arizona Corn Bread Cacti *See photo on page 277.*

PREP: 10 minutes **BAKE:** 12 minutes **MAKES:** 8 servings

- 1   11½-ounce package (8) refrigerated corn bread twists
- 2   teaspoons sunflower kernels
- ¾   cup bottled salsa

one Unroll and separate corn bread dough into 16 strips. Arrange 8 of the strips 3 inches apart on a greased large baking sheet. Cut each remaining strip in half crosswise.

two For each cactus, arrange 2 short strips on the sides of a longer strip on baking sheet to form a cactus, placing the ends of the shorter strips underneath the longer piece. Press gently together to seal. Sprinkle with sunflower kernels; press gently into dough.

three Bake, uncovered, in a 375°F oven about 12 minutes or until golden brown. Using a wide spatula, transfer to wire racks; cool. Serve corn bread with salsa.

NUTRITION FACTS PER SERVING: 150 cal., 6 g total fat (2 g sat. fat), 0 mg chol., 485 mg sodium, 20 g carbo., 0 g fiber, 3 g pro.

Cinnamon Snails

PREP: 15 minutes **BAKE:** 15 minutes **MAKES:** 4 servings

- ¼   cup finely chopped nuts
- 3   tablespoons sugar
- ½   teaspoon ground cinnamon
- 1   11-ounce package (8) refrigerated breadsticks

one In a small bowl combine nuts, sugar, and cinnamon. Sprinkle sugar mixture on a rolling surface.

two For each snail, unroll a breadstick; shape into a tight coil. Wrap another breadstick around the coil, forming a larger coil. Place on the sugared surface. Roll dough until ⅛ inch thick. Place, sugared side up, on a greased large baking sheet.

three Bake, uncovered, in a 375°F oven about 15 minutes or until golden brown. Serve warm.

NUTRITION FACTS PER SERVING: 305 cal., 10 g total fat (1 g sat. fat), 0 mg chol., 580 mg sodium, 46 g carbo., 2 g fiber, 7 g pro.

Flip-Flop Cake *See photo on page 278.*

PREP: 30 minutes **FREEZE:** 2 hours **MAKES:** 6 servings

1   10¾-ounce loaf frozen pound cake

¾   to 1 cup favorite ice cream

½   of an 8-ounce container frozen whipped dessert
      topping, thawed

2   pull-apart licorice twists

      Bright-color candy wafers and/or round candies

      Graham cracker crumbs (optional)

one Using a serrated knife, cut off the rounded top of the cake to make level. Cut cake in half horizontally. Cut each half into a flip-flop shape.*

two In a chilled small bowl stir ice cream just enough to soften. Spread over one of the cake halves. Top with the other cake half. Place on a baking sheet. Cover and freeze for at least 2 hours or until firm. Frost top and side with whipped topping.

three For flip-flop strap, cut ends of licorice twists diagonally. Insert a toothpick under each twist. Arrange twists with cut ends together to form a V-shape; insert toothpicks into cake. Decorate side of cake with candy wafers.

four Loosely cover cake and freeze until ready to serve. If desired, sprinkle cracker crumbs around cake for sand.

NUTRITION FACTS PER SERVING: 355 cal., 18 g total fat (12 g sat. fat), 137 mg chol., 238 mg sodium, 44 g carbo., 0 g fiber, 4 g pro.

Note: For a large crowd, double the recipe to make a pair of flip-flop cakes.

Note: To cut a flip-flop shape, trace the bottom of a child-size flip-flop (needs to be 7 to 7½ inches long) on a piece of paper. Cut out shape. Place paper, clean side down, on a piece of clean cardboard or sturdy paper; trace shape. Cut out shape. Place cardboard shape on top of one cake half and use a sharp knife to cut around shape and through cake. Repeat with the other cake half.

Chocolate-Dipped Waffles

PREP: 20 minutes **CHILL:** 30 minutes **MAKES:** 10 servings

1   cup semisweet chocolate pieces (6 ounces)

1   cup milk chocolate pieces (6 ounces)

2   teaspoons shortening

5   frozen buttermilk waffles or Belgian waffles

      Assorted toppings (such as toffee pieces, colorful
      sprinkles, and/or toasted coconut)

one In a small saucepan combine semisweet chocolate, milk chocolate, and shortening. Cook and stir over low heat until chocolate melts. Meanwhile, place frozen waffles on an ungreased baking sheet. Toast in oven according to package directions. Cut each waffle in half.

two Dip waffle halves into chocolate or spoon chocolate over halves to coat. Insert a wooden stick into side of each half. Place on a baking sheet lined with waxed paper. Sprinkle with toppings. Chill about 30 minutes or until chocolate is set.

NUTRITION FACTS PER SERVING: 289 cal., 16 g total fat (8 g sat. fat), 11 mg chol., 169 mg sodium, 35 g carbo., 1 g fiber, 3 g pro.

Spare-Me Sugar Cookies *See photo on page 278.*

PREP: 30 minutes **BAKE:** 6 minutes per batch
MAKES: about 24 servings

- 1   18-ounce roll refrigerated sugar cookie dough
- ¼   cup all-purpose flour
       Red, orange, green, or blue food coloring
       Coarse sugar (optional)

one In a large resealable plastic bag combine cookie dough and flour; knead until mixed. Add desired food coloring; knead just until dough appears marbled (do not overmix).*

two On a well-floured surface, roll dough until ¼ inch thick. Using a round 2½-inch cookie cutter, cut out dough. Place cutouts 2 inches apart on an ungreased cookie sheet. Reroll dough as needed. Using a drinking straw, cut 3 circles from each cookie to resemble bowling ball holes, making one large than the others. If desired, sprinkle cookies with coarse suga

three Bake, uncovered, in a 375°F oven for 6 to 8 minutes or until edges are firm. While still on baking sheet, use the straw to reshape bowling ball holes. Transfer cookies to wire racks; cool.

NUTRITION FACTS PER SERVING: 97 cal., 4 g total fat (1 g sat. fat), 6 mg chol 90 mg sodium, 14 g carbo., 0 g fiber, 1 g pro.

*Note: *If you like, divide the dough among four small resealable plastic bags or bowls and add a different color of food coloring to each bag.*

Crispy Chocolate Cutout Cookies

PREP: 15 minutes **CHILL:** 20 minutes **MAKES:** 8 or 9 servings

- 1   cup semisweet chocolate pieces (6 ounces)
- ¼   cup light-color corn syrup
- 2   tablespoons butter or margarine
- 3   cups crisp rice cereal

one Line a baking sheet with waxed paper. Grease waxed paper with butter; set aside.

two In a medium heavy saucepan combine chocolate pieces corn syrup, and the 2 tablespoons butter. Cook and stir over low heat until chocolate and butter melt. Stir in cereal.

three Transfer cereal mixture to the prepared baking sheet. Press into a 12×6-inch rectangle. Cover and chill about 20 minutes or until slightly firm. Using desired 3-inch cookie cutters, cut out shapes. Cover and chill until ready to serve.

NUTRITION FACTS PER HEART: 197 cal., 10 g total fat (6 g sat. fat), 9 mg cho 153 mg sodium, 30 g carbo., 1 g fiber, 2 g pro.

Chewy Granola Goodies

START TO FINISH: 20 minutes **MAKES:** 24 servings

1   10-ounce package marshmallows

¼   cup butter or margarine

4   cups granola with raisins

1½   cups crisp rice cereal

½   cup sunflower kernels

one Line a 13×9×2-inch pan with foil. Grease foil with butter; set aside. In a large saucepan combine marshmallows and the ¼ cup butter. Cook and stir until marshmallows melt. Stir in granola, rice cereal, and sunflower kernels.

two Press mixture into the prepared pan. Cool. Lift mixture from pan using edges of foil; peel off foil. Cut mixture into bars.

NUTRITION FACTS PER SERVING: 154 cal., 7 g total fat (3 g sat. fat), 6 mg chol., 50 mg sodium, 23 g carbo., 1 g fiber, 3 g pro.

Puzzle Cookies

PREP: 30 minutes **BAKE:** 7 minutes
MAKES: 6 cookies (24 servings)

1   18-ounce roll refrigerated sugar
     cookie dough

¼   cup all-purpose flour

2   egg yolks

2   teaspoons water
     Desired food coloring

one In a large resealable plastic bag combine cookie dough and flour; knead until mixed. Divide dough into 6 portions.

two On an ungreased large cookie sheet, pat each portion into a 5-inch square. Press a well-floured 3- to 4-inch cookie cutter into square (use smaller cutters, if desired). Carefully remove cookie cutter without removing dough. Using a table knife, cut outside portion of square into large puzzle pieces.

three In a small bowl combine egg yolks and water. Divide mixture among 3 or 4 small bowls. Add a different color of food coloring to each bowl; mix well.

four Using a small clean paintbrush, brush dough puzzle pieces with the different colors of egg yolk mixture. If mixture thickens while standing, stir in water, 1 drop at a time.

five Bake, uncovered, in a 350°F oven for 7 to 8 minutes or just until bottoms start to brown and centers are set. While still warm, carefully recut pieces with cookie cutter and knife. Trim edges as needed. Transfer cookies to a wire rack; cool.

NUTRITION FACTS PER SERVING: 102 cal., 5 g total fat (1 g sat. fat), 24 mg chol., 90 mg sodium, 13 g carbo., 0 g fiber, 1 g pro.

Frozen Chocolate-Peanut Dessert

PREP: 25 minutes **FREEZE:** 15 minutes plus 4 hours
STAND: 10 minutes **MAKES:** 15 servings

- 30 chocolate sandwich cookies with white filling, coarsely crushed
- ¼ cup butter or margarine, melted
- ½ gallon vanilla or chocolate ice cream
- 1 cup peanuts
- 1 12-ounce jar chocolate fudge ice cream topping
- 1 banana, sliced (optional)
- Maraschino cherries (optional)

one Freeze a large bowl and a 3-quart rectangular baking dish about 15 minutes or until very cold. Meanwhile, in a medium bowl combine crushed cookies and melted butter; set aside.

two Place ice cream in the cold bowl and stir just enough to soften. Spoon softened ice cream into the cold baking dish; press ice cream into an even layer. Sprinkle with cookie mixture and peanuts.

three Drizzle fudge topping over layers in baking dish. Cover and freeze for at least 4 hours or until firm.

four To serve, let stand at room temperature for 10 minutes to soften slightly. If desired, top with banana slices and cherries. Cut and serve immediately.

NUTRITION FACTS PER SERVING: 457 cal., 26 g total fat (12 g sat. fat), 81 mg chol., 406 mg sodium, 51 g carbo., 1 g fiber, 6 g pro.

GRILLING

Banana Split Kabobs

PREP: 20 minutes **GRILL:** 5 minutes **MAKES:** 4 servings

- 3 medium bananas, cut into 1-inch chunks
- 1½ cups large strawberries, halved
- 1½ cups fresh pineapple chunks
- 1 pint vanilla ice cream
- ½ cup caramel and/or chocolate ice cream topping
- Chopped nuts (optional)
- Whipped cream (optional)
- Maraschino cherries (optional)

one On eight 6- to 8-inch metal skewers, alternately thread bananas, strawberries, and pineapple, leaving ¼ inch between each piece.

two For a charcoal grill, grill kabobs on the rack of an uncovered grill directly over medium coals about 5 minutes or until fruit is warm and bananas are lightly browned, turning occasionally during grilling. (For a gas grill, preheat grill. Reduce heat to medium. Place kabobs on grill rack over heat. Cover and grill as above.)

three To serve, place a scoop of ice cream and 2 fruit skewers in each of 4 dessert dishes. Drizzle with caramel and/or chocolate topping and, if desired, sprinkle with nuts. If desired, garnish with whipped cream and cherries.

NUTRITION FACTS PER SERVING: 434 cal., 13 g total fat (8 g sat. fat), 45 mg chol., 153 mg sodium, 79 g carbo., 5 g fiber, 4 g pro.

Something More S'more *See photo on page 278.*

PREP: 10 minutes GRILL: 1 minute MAKES: 1 serving

1   large marshmallow

½   of a 1.45-ounce bar milk chocolate

2   cinnamon, chocolate, or regular graham crackers

one Place the marshmallow on the end of a long skewer. Roast marshmallow 3 to 4 inches from a campfire or hot coals about 1 minute or until golden brown, turning frequently.

two Place chocolate on one of the graham crackers. Place skewered marshmallow on top of chocolate. Place the remaining graham cracker on top of marshmallow; remove skewer. Let stand until chocolate melts.

NUTRITION FACTS PER SERVING: 186 cal., 8 g total fat (4 g sat. fat), 5 mg chol., 110 mg sodium, 27 g carbo., 1 g fiber, 3 g pro.

Chocolate-Banana S'more: Prepare as directed, except top the chocolate with 4 thin banana slices before adding marshmallow.

NUTRITION FACTS PER SERVING: 213 cal., 8 g total fat (5 g sat. fat), 5 mg chol., 110 mg sodium, 34 g carbo., 2 g fiber, 3 g pro.

Chocolate-Cherry S'more: Prepare as directed, except top the chocolate with 1 tablespoon chopped maraschino cherries before adding marshmallow.

NUTRITION FACTS PER SERVING: 203 cal., 8 g total fat (4 g sat. fat), 5 mg chol., 110 mg sodium, 31 g carbo., 1 g fiber, 3 g pro.

Chocolate-Mint S'more: Prepare as directed, except substitute one 1.5-ounce chocolate-covered cream-filled mint patty for the milk chocolate bar.

NUTRITION FACTS PER SERVING: 241 cal., 4 g total fat (2 g sat. fat), 0 mg chol., 103 mg sodium, 50 g carbo., 1 g fiber, 2 g pro.

Chocolate-Peanut Butter S'more: Prepare as directed, except spread the bottom graham cracker with 1 tablespoon peanut butter before adding the chocolate.

NUTRITION FACTS PER SERVING: 280 cal., 16 g total fat (6 g sat. fat), 5 mg chol., 183 mg sodium, 30 g carbo., 2 g fiber, 7 g pro.

Chocolate-Mint Treats

START TO FINISH: 20 minutes MAKES: 22 servings

½   cup canned vanilla frosting

3   tablespoons finely crushed striped round peppermint candies

44   chocolate wafer cookies

one In a small bowl combine frosting and crushed candies.

two Spread 1 teaspoon of the frosting mixture over the flat side of half of the chocolate wafer cookies. Top with the remaining chocolate wafer cookies, flat sides down.

NUTRITION FACTS PER SERVING: 88 cal., 3 g total fat (1 g sat. fat), 1 mg chol., 104 mg sodium, 15 g carbo., 0 g fiber, 1 g pro.

Berry Parfaits

START TO FINISH: 12 minutes **MAKES:** 2 servings

1   4-ounce container vanilla ready-to-eat pudding
¼   cup whipped cream or frozen whipped dessert topping, thawed
1   drop red food coloring (optional)
2   1-inch slices angel food cake, cut into 1-inch cubes
¾   cup strawberries, sliced, and/or raspberries

one In a small bowl gently fold together vanilla pudding and whipped cream. If desired, stir in red food coloring.

two Place one-fourth of the cake cubes in the bottoms of 2 parfait glasses. Add one-fourth of the berries and one-fourth of the pudding mixture. Repeat layers three more times. Serve immediately.

NUTRITION FACTS PER SERVING: 270 cal., 8 g total fat (4 g sat. fat), 25 mg chol., 337 mg sodium, 46 g carbo.,1 g fiber, 5 g pro.

Chocolate Brownie Pudding

START TO FINISH: 15 minutes **MAKES:** 2 servings

⅓   cup whipping cream
2   purchased chocolate brownies (about 2-inch squares)
2   4-ounce containers chocolate ready-to-eat pudding, chilled
¼   cup toffee pieces
¼   cup chopped pecans, toasted (see tip, page 280)

one In a medium bowl beat whipping cream with an electric mixer on medium speed until soft peaks form (tips curl).

two Crumble one of the brownies; divide evenly between 2 dessert dishes. Divide one container of pudding between dishes. Top with half of the whipped cream, half of the toffee pieces, and half of the pecans. Repeat layers. If desired, cover and chill for up to 1 hour.

NUTRITION FACTS PER SERVING: 661 cal., 45 g total fat (18 g sat. fat), 82 mg chol., 407 mg sodium, 61 g carbo., 2 g fiber, 7 g pro.

Banana-Raisin Trail Mix

START TO FINISH: 10 minutes MAKES: 14 servings

2 cups raisins

2 cups dried banana chips

2 cups unsalted dry roasted peanuts

1 6-ounce package mixed dried fruit bits (1⅓ cups)

one In a large bowl combine raisins, dried banana chips, peanuts, and mixed dried fruit bits. Store, tightly covered, at room temperature.

NUTRITION FACTS PER SERVING: 172 cal., 9 g total fat (4 g sat. fat), 0 mg chol., 6 mg sodium, 22 g carbo., 1 g fiber, 3 g pro.

Blaze-a-Trail Mix

START TO FINISH: 10 minutes MAKES: 10 servings

2 cups honey graham cereal

1 cup tiny marshmallows

1 cup peanuts

½ cup semisweet chocolate pieces

½ cup raisins

one In a medium bowl combine honey graham cereal, tiny marshmallows, peanuts, chocolate pieces, and raisins. Store, tightly covered, at room temperature.

NUTRITION FACTS PER SERVING: 199 cal., 10 g total fat (3 g sat. fat), 0 mg chol., 81 mg sodium, 26 g carbo., 2 g fiber, 5 g pro.

Dive-In Party Mix *See photo on page 277.*

START TO FINISH: 10 minutes MAKES: 8 to 10 servings

4 cups popped popcorn

3 cups bite-size, assorted-shape pretzel, cheese, and/or plain crackers

1 cup chewy fruit snacks

1 cup chocolate-covered raisins

one In a large bowl combine popcorn, bite-size crackers, chewy fruit snacks, and chocolate-covered raisins. Store, tightly covered, at room temperature.

NUTRITION FACTS PER SERVING: 228 cal., 5 g total fat (3 g sat. fat), 1 mg chol., 338 mg sodium, 45 g carbo., 2 g fiber, 4 g pro.

Caramel Corn and Peanuts

PREP: 10 minutes **BAKE:** 15 minutes **MAKES:** 8 servings

6	cups popped popcorn
3	tablespoons butter or margarine
¼	cup corn syrup
1	tablespoon molasses
1	cup dry roasted peanuts

one Place popcorn in an ungreased 13×9×2-inch baking pan. In a small saucepan melt butter; remove from heat. Stir in corn syrup and molasses. Drizzle molasses mixture over popcorn; toss gently to coat.

two Bake, uncovered, in a 325°F oven for 15 minutes, stirring twice. Transfer mixture to a serving bowl. Stir in peanuts. Store, tightly covered, at room temperature.

NUTRITION FACTS PER SERVING: 205 cal., 14 g total fat (4 g sat. fat), 12 mg chol., 61 mg sodium, 18 g carbo., 2 g fiber, 5 g pro.

Tasty Wheels

PREP: 20 minutes **CHILL:** 2 hours **MAKES:** about 24 servings

6	7- to 8-inch flour tortillas, warmed (see tip, page 16)
1	8-ounce tub cream cheese spread
6	lettuce leaves
6	thin slices cooked ham or deli roast beef

one Spread one side of each tortilla with 1 tablespoon of the cream cheese. Top with lettuce and ham. Spread each with another 1 tablespoon of the cream cheese. Roll up tightly.

two Using a serrated knife, cut tortilla rolls into 1-inch slices. Cover and chill for 2 hours.

NUTRITION FACTS PER SERVING: 66 cal., 4 g total fat (2 g sat. fat), 12 mg chol., 137 mg sodium, 5 g carbo., 0 g fiber, 2 g pro.

Peanutty Dip

START TO FINISH: 10 minutes MAKES: about 16 servings

½   cup peanut butter

½   cup plain yogurt

2   to 3 tablespoons honey

Assorted dippers (such as apple wedges, celery sticks, cucumber sticks, sliced carrots, and/or crackers)

one In a small bowl stir together peanut butter and yogurt until combined. Stir in honey to taste. Serve with assorted dippers.

NUTRITION FACTS PER SERVING DIP: 60 cal., 4 g total fat (1 g sat. fat), 1 mg chol., 41 mg sodium, 4 g carbo., 0 g fiber, 2 g pro.

Veggie Dip

START TO FINISH: 10 minutes MAKES: about 32 servings

1   8-ounce carton fat-free dairy sour cream or one 8-ounce tub cream cheese spread

1   6-ounce carton plain fat-free yogurt

1   0.4-ounce envelope ranch dry salad dressing mix

Assorted vegetable dippers

one In a medium bowl stir together sour cream, yogurt, and dry salad dressing mix. (If using cream cheese, beat with an electric mixer on medium speed until smooth.) Serve with assorted vegetable dippers.

NUTRITION FACTS PER SERVING DIP: 10 cal., 0 g total fat (0 g sat. fat), 1 mg chol., 40 mg sodium, 2 g carbo., 0 g fiber, 1 g pro.

Creamy Peanut Butter Spread

START TO FINISH: 10 minutes MAKES: about 24 servings

1   cup light-color corn syrup

½   cup creamy peanut butter

¼   cup marshmallow creme

Assorted crackers or apple slices

one In a small bowl stir together corn syrup, peanut butter, and marshmallow creme. Serve on assorted crackers.

NUTRITION FACTS PER SERVING SPREAD: 73 cal., 3 g total fat (1 g sat. fat), 0 mg chol., 42 mg sodium, 12 g carbo., 0 g fiber, 1 g pro.

All-American Fruit Smoothies See photo on page 277.

PREP: 10 minutes **CHILL:** 4 hours **MAKES:** 6 servings

3 medium bananas, cut up

1 cup sliced strawberries or mango chunks

2 cups apricot nectar

1 6-ounce carton plain yogurt

2 tablespoons honey

one In a blender combine banana pieces and strawberry slices. Add apricot nectar, yogurt, and honey. Cover and blend until smooth.

two Transfer to a glass pitcher. Cover and chill for at least 4 hours. Stir before serving.

NUTRITION FACTS PER SERVING: 153 cal., 2 g total fat (1 g sat. fat), 5 mg chol., 21 mg sodium, 35 g carbo., 2 g fiber, 2 g pro.

Sangria for Kids

START TO FINISH: 15 minutes **MAKES:** 20 servings

4 cups orange juice, chilled

1½ cups unsweetened purple or white grape juice, chilled

1 1-liter bottle ginger ale, chilled

2 cups assorted fruit (such as orange wedges, thinly sliced lemons or limes, pineapple wedges, peach slices, and/or halved strawberries)

2 cups ice cubes

one In a punch bowl or large pitcher stir together orange juice and grape juice. Slowly pour in ginger ale; stir gently. Stir in fruit and ice cubes.

NUTRITION FACTS PER SERVING: 57 cal., 0 g total fat (0 g sat. fat), 0 mg ch 5 mg sodium, 14 g carbo., 0 g fiber, 0 g pro.

398   5-ingredient favorites

Index

Note: **Boldfaced** page numbers indicate photographs.

A

All-American Apple Pie Bars, 333
All-American Fruit Smoothies, **277, 398**
Almonds
    Almond-Brie Spread, 350
    Almond-Butter Crunch, 336
    Almond Walleye, 133
    Toasted Almonds with Rosemary, 368
Angel Shortcake with Cream, 305
Appetizers and snacks. See also **Dips and spreads**
    Banana-Raisin Trail Mix, 395
    Blaze-a-Trail Mix, 395
    B.L.T. Bruschetta, 358
    Bread and Cheddar Wedges, 360
    Buffalo Wings, 353
    Caramel Corn and Peanuts, 396
    Cheese-Stuffed Pecans, 368
    Cheesy Pecan Quesadillas, 356
    Cheesy Potato Wedges, 365
    Chicken and Rice Spring Rolls, 358
    Chicken Wings with Barbecue Sauce, 353
    Cranberry-Sauced Franks, 355
    Crispy Onion Rings, **274,** 365
    Crunchy Trail Mix, 342
    Dive-In Party Mix, **277,** 395
    Easy Artichoke Roll, 362
    Feta-Stuffed Mushrooms, 364
    Five-Spice Drummies, 352
    Fruit and Peanut Snack Mix, 342
    Goat Cheese Pastry Rounds, **275,** 361
    Hoisin-Garlic Mushroom Appetizers, 364
    Hot Honeyed Spareribs, 355
    Italian-Style Chips, 367
    Olive Bread, 366
    Olive-Tomato Tarts, 361
    Plum Good Sausage and Meatballs, 354
    Polynesian Glazed Wings, **275,** 352
    Prosciutto-Arugula Roll-Ups, 362
    Puff Pastry Cheese Straws, 360
    Soft Pretzels, 366
    Spicy Chicken Fajita Bites, **275,** 356
    Spinach Pizza Bread, 363
    Strawberry and Cheese Bites, 359
    Sweet Spiced Popcorn, 343
    Tangy Cranberry Meatballs, 354
    Tasty Wheels, 396
    Toasted Almonds with Rosemary, 368
    Toasted Cheese Pita Crisps, 367
    Toasted Ravioli, 357
    Tomato-Pesto Toast, 359
    Tortellini in Ratatouille Sauce, 357
    Zucchini Bites, 363
Apple Butter Barbecue Sauce, 249
Apple-Buttered Sweet Potatoes, 211
Apple Butter–Sauced Pork Chops, 88

Apple cider
    Apple-Cranberry Punch, 369
    Honey-Mulled Apple Cider, 375
    Hot Strawberry Cider, 375
Apples
    All-American Apple Pie Bars, 333
    Apple-Buttered Sweet Potatoes, 211
    Apple Butter–Sauced Pork Chops, 88
    Apple-Pear Sauce, 297
    best, for cooking, 203
    Cider Peas and Apples, 205
    Cranberry-Apple-Orange Relish, 257
    Creamy Apple Salad, 232
    Curried Beans and Apples, 192, **263**
    Fruit and Broccoli Salad, 234
    Glazed Parsnips and Apples, 203
    Gorgonzola-Walnut-Stuffed Apples, 285
    Pork, Lentil, and Apple Soup, 175
    Pork Medallions with Apples, 75
    Praline Baked Apples, 285
    Slow-Cooked Apple Betty, 283
    Upside-Down Caramel Apple Cake, 309
    Veal Chops with Apples, 71
Apricot Nectar Dressing, 246
Apricots
    Apricot-Cranberry Chicken, 13
    Apricot-Peach Cobbler, 282
    Apricot-Peach Dessert Soup, 292
    Apricot Pulled Pork, 79
    Fruit and Peanut Snack Mix, 342
    Fruity Rice Pudding, 324
Arizona Corn Bread Cacti, **277,** 388
Artichokes
    Artichoke Dip with Pretzels, 347
    Canadian Bacon Pizza, 105
    Easy Artichoke Roll, 362
    Mediterranean Salad, 238, **269**
Arugula-Prosciutto Roll-Ups, 362
Asian Apricot-Glazed Chops, 84
Asian Beef Short Ribs, 56
Asian Chicken and Vegetables, 19
Asian Noodle Bowl, 160
Asian Pea Pod Salad, 235
Asparagus
    Asparagus in Dill Butter, 188
    Asparagus with Cheese and Chives, 188
    Asparagus with Citrus Mayonnaise, 189
    Baby Greens with Veggies, 237
    Chicken and Rice Spring Rolls, 358
    Foil-Wrapped Salmon Dinner, 131
    Ham and Asparagus Pasta, 103
    Peppy Asparagus-Shrimp Toss, 143
    Steamed Fish with Veggies, 134
Avocado-Lime Dip, Creamy, 344
Avocado-Turkey Quesadillas, 37

B

Baby Greens with Veggies, 237
Bacon
    Bacon Cheeseburgers, 65
    B.L.T. Bruschetta, 358
    BLT Salad, 105
    BLT Steaks, 50
    Canadian Bacon Pizza, 105
    precooked, buying, 105
Baked Beets in Gingered Syrup, 195

Baked Cheese, 351
Baked Cheese Fondue, 348
Baked Parmesan Chicken, 380
Baked Sweet Potato Fries, 210
Balsamic-Glazed Lamb and Greens, 107
Balsamic-Mustard Marinade, 260
Bananas
    Banana-Raisin Trail Mix, 395
    Banana Split Kabobs, 392
    Banana Split Trifles, 289
    Berry-Banana Smoothies, 373
    Cherry-Bananas Foster, 296
    Chocolate-Banana S'more, 393
    Dessert Burritos, 287
    Tropical Fruit Dip, **274,** 343
Barbecue Beans and Hot Dogs over Corn
    Bread, 36
Barbecued Pork Chop Sandwiches, 84, **121**
Barbecued Turkey Tenderloin
    Sandwiches, 32, **114**
Barbecue Rub, 259
Barley and Beef Soup, 171
Basic Moppin' Sauce, 250
Basil-Beef Sirloin, 42
Beans. See also **Green beans**
    Barbecue Beans and Hot Dogs over Corn
        Bread, 36
    Bean-and-Rice-Stuffed Peppers, 152
    Bean-Stuffed Cabbage Rolls, 158
    Beer-Simmered Beans, 193
    Black Bean and Corn Quesadillas, 150
    Cajun-Seasoned Vegetarian Gumbo, 185
    canned, rinsing salt from, 151
    Cheese and Bean Quesadillas, 386
    Cheesy Potato-Bean Soup, 183
    Cheesy Succotash, 212
    Chicken and Bean Burritos, 16
    Chicken Taco Salad, 25
    Chipotle-Bean Enchiladas, 152
    Curried Beans and Apples, 192, **263**
    dry, slow-cooking, 153
    Easy Burgoo, 177
    Greek-Seasoned Lentils, 163
    Layered Black Bean Dip, 345
    Lentil-Vegetable Turnovers, 155
    Marinated Bean Salad, 238
    Mediterranean Salad, 238, **269**
    Polenta and Black Beans, **124,** 151
    Pork, Lentil, and Apple Soup, 175
    Pork and Black Bean Potage, 176
    Red Beans over Spanish Rice, 153
    Savory Black Beans, 193
    Spicy Ham-and-Garbanzo Bean
        Soup, 178
    Spicy Simmered Beans and
        Vegetables, 154
    Taco Chili, 170
    Taco-Style Black Beans and Hominy, 154
    Texas Two-Step Stew, 180
    Tortilla Lasagna, 162
    Tostadas, 66
    Tuscan Bean and Sausage Stew, 179
    Vegetable and Rice Casserole, 157
    Vegetable Chili Medley, 185
    Western Beans, 194
    White Beans with Dried Tomatoes, 155

INDEX

Beef. *See also* **Meatballs; Veal;** *specific cuts below*
Asian Beef Short Ribs, 56
Beef Burgundy, **125,** 173
Beef in Red Wine Gravy, 57
Cheesy Reuben Potatoes, 62
Corned Beef and Cabbage, 48
Deli Roast Beef Sandwiches, 60
Fruited Beef Stew, 173
grass-fed, about, 46
Greek-Style Pitas, 62
Middle Eastern Pitas, 61
Old-Fashioned Beef Stew, 174
Reuben Loaves, 61
Reubens from a Crock, 48
Simple Short Rib Stew, 172
Sweet-and-Sour Beef Stew, 174
Thai Beef Stir-Fry, 56
Vegetable and Pastrami Panini, 60
Beef (ground)
Bacon Cheeseburgers, 65
Beefy Shepherd's Pie, 67
Beer and Pretzel Burgers, 64
Bunless Burgers, 63, **115**
Cacciatore-Style Penne, 67
Cheeseburger and Fries Casserole, 382
Cheesy Sloppy Joes, 68
Easy Goulash, 65
Gorgonzola- and Garlic-Stuffed Burgers, 64
Hamburgers with Squished Tomato Topper, 63
Mexican-Stuffed Sweet Peppers, 68
Ready-Right-Now Sloppy Joes, 382
Taco Chili, 170
Taco Pizza, 69
Tostadas, 66
Upside-Down Pizza Casserole, 66
Beef (roasts)
Basil-Beef Sirloin, 42
Beef and Barley Soup, 171
Chili-Rubbed Prime Rib, 42
Cola Pot Roast, 45
Creamy Beef-and-Potato Stew, 171
Five-Spice Tri-Tip Roast, 44
French Dips with Mushrooms, 47
German-Style Beef Roast, 43
Homestyle Beef and Vegetables, 44
Oven-Barbecued Beef Sandwiches, 47
Pot Roast with Chipotle-Fruit Sauce, 46
Pot Roast with Mushroom Sauce, 45
Stroganoff-Sauced Beef Roast, 43
Beef (steaks)
Beef Kabobs with Blue Cheese Dipping Sauce, 58
Beef Tenderloin with Blue Cheese, 53
Bloody Mary Steak, 54, **116**
BLT Steaks, 50
Deviled Steaks, 52
Flat-Iron Steaks, 52, **117**
flat-iron steaks, about, 52
Honey-Bourbon Steaks, 49
Mustard-Marinated Flank Steak, 55
Pepper Steak, 55, **117**
Prosciutto-Wrapped Tenderloin, 51
Round Steak with Herbs, 57
Saucy Strip Steaks, 50

Southwestern Steak Roll-Ups, 59
Spinach-Stuffed Flank Steak, 51
Steak and Mushrooms, 49
Steaks with Tarragon Butter, 54
Steak with Tuscan Tomato Sauce, 53, **118**
Thai Beef, 58
Beer and Pretzel Burgers, 64
Beer-Glazed Pork Chops, 83
Beer Marinade, 260
Beer-Salsa Dip, Cheesy, 346
Beer-Simmered Beans, 193
Beet Greens with Walnuts and Blue Cheese, 229, **270**
Beets, Baked, in Gingered Syrup, 195
Beets, Cranberry-Apple Spiced, 194
Berries. *See also specific berries*
Berry-Banana Smoothies, 373
Berry-Melon Vinaigrette, 245
Berry Parfaits, 394
Cheesecake-Fruit Parfaits, 289
Mixed Berry Cobbler, 280
Beverages (cold)
All-American Fruit Smoothies, **277,** 398
Apple-Cranberry Punch, 369
Berry-Banana Smoothies, 373
Champagne Fruit Punch, 370
Fancy Fruit Float, 372
Fizzy Kiwi Lemonade, 374
Fizzy Mint-Chocolate Soda, 372
Minted Iced Tea, **276,** 376
Orange Cream Punch, 370
Peach Nectar Punch, 369
Quick Ice Cream Shake, 372
Raspberry-Coffee Frappé, 377
Sangria for Kids, 398
Strawberry Smoothies, 373
Watermelon Lemonade, 374
Beverages (hot)
Ginger-Lemon Tea, 376
Honey-Mulled Apple Cider, 375
Hot and Spicy Cranberry Punch, **276,** 371
Hot Caramel Chocolate, 378
Hot Strawberry Cider, 375
Mocha au Lait, 377
Peanut Butter Cocoa, 378
Tomato Sipper, 371
Biscuits
Flaky Biscuits, 227
Green Onion Parker House Biscuits, 227, **266**
Pepper-Cheese Biscuits, 227
Bittersweet Chocolate Soufflé, **273,** 326
Black Bean and Corn Quesadillas, 150
Blackberry-Glazed Ham, 101
Black Cherry–Cranberry Supreme, 233
Blaze-a-Trail Mix, 395
Bloody Mary Steak, 54, **116**
B.L.T. Bruschetta, 358
BLT Salad, 105
BLT Steaks, 50
Blueberries
Blueberry-Kiwi Fool, 290
Double Berry Soup, 292
Easy Blueberry Sauce, 297
Red, White, and Blue Parfaits, 290

Watermelon-Berry Ice, 301
Blue Cheese Butter, 262
Bow Ties with Sausage and Sweet Peppers, 9
Bratwurst
Bratwurst with Kickin' Cranberry Ketchup, 100
Potato and Bratwurst Stew, 180
Bread pudding
drying bread cubes for, 322
Pumpkin Custard Bread Pudding, 323
Semisweet-Chocolate Bread Pudding, 322
Breads. *See also* **Tortillas**
Arizona Corn Bread Cacti, **277,** 388
B.L.T. Bruschetta, 358
Bread and Cheddar Wedges, 360
Broccoli Corn Bread, 225
Cheddary Corn Bread Rolls, 225, **266**
Cheese and Garlic Crescents, 228
Cinnamon Granola Loaf, 228
Cinnamon Snails, 388
Flaky Biscuits, 227
Focaccia Breadsticks, 221, **266**
Garlic and Cheese Focaccia, 226
Garlic Croutons, 224
Green Onion Parker House Biscuits, 227, **266**
Grilled French Bread, 222
Have-a-Ball Rolls, 224
Herbed Baguette, 223
Herbed Crouton Sticks, 221
Italian Breadsticks, 222
Olive Bread, 366
Pepper-Cheese Biscuits, 227
Reuben Loaves, 61
Rosemary and Swiss Buns, 226
Soft Pretzels, 366
Spinach Pizza Bread, 363
Strawberry and Cheese Bites, 359
Toasty-Hot French Bread Slices, 223
Tomato-Pesto Toast, 359
Tomato Sauce with Garlic Cheese Bread, 347
Brie Sandwiches with Greens, 148
Broccoli
Broccoli and Peppers, 195
Broccoli Corn Bread, 225
Creamy Tomato-Broccoli Sauce with Pasta, 164
Fruit and Broccoli Salad, 234
Hot-and-Sweet Pineapple Slaw, 239, **269**
Mexican Cauliflower and Broccoli Chowder, 186
Simply Ramen Chicken Soup, **126,** 166
Skillet Chicken Alfredo, 13
Spicy Pasta and Broccoli, 160
Spuds with Broccoli Topper, 385
Veggie Mash, 214
Brownie Pudding, Chocolate, 394
Brownie Pudding Cake, 309
Brownie Surprise Cupcakes, 312
Bruschetta, B.L.T., 358
Brussels sprouts
Brussels Sprouts with Prosciutto, 196
Glazed Brussels Sprouts, 196
Buffalo Wings, 353

...unless Burgers, 63, **115**
...uns, Rosemary and Swiss, 226
...urgers
  Bacon Cheeseburgers, 65
  Beer and Pretzel Burgers, 64
  Bunless Burgers, 63, **115**
  Gorgonzola- and Garlic-Stuffed
    Burgers, 64
  Hamburgers with Squished Tomato
    Topper, 63
  Italian-Stuffed Sausage Burgers, 97
  Mediterranean Lamb Burgers, 109, **118**
  Pork Patties with Honey Barbecue
    Sauce, 95
  Southwest Chicken Burgers, 22
  Sweet and Spicy Pork Burgers, 95
  testing for doneness, 22
...rritos, Chicken and Bean, 16
...rritos, Dessert, 287
...ttered Rosemary New Potatoes, 209
...tters, flavored
  Blue Cheese Butter, 262
  Citrus Butter, 262
  Tomato-Garlic Butter, 262
...tterscotch-Caramel Sauce, 328
...ttery Bay Scallops, 144

...c

...bbage or slaw mix. *See also* **Sauerkraut**
  Bean-Stuffed Cabbage Rolls, 158
  Corned Beef and Cabbage, 48
  Cranberry Coleslaw, 241
  Greek Cabbage Rolls, 110
  Napa Cabbage Slaw, 240
  Quick and Crunchy Turkey Salad, 39
  Really Red Coleslaw, 240, **268**
...cciatore-Style Penne, 67
...ajun Pork, 90
...ajun-Seasoned Vegetarian Gumbo, 185
...kes. *See also* **Cupcakes**
  Angel Shortcake with Cream, 305
  Brownie Pudding Cake, 309
  Cherry Trifle Cake, 310
  Chocolate-Covered Strawberry
    Cakes, 308
  Chocolate-Raspberry Cake, 303
  Coffee Angel Dessert, 306
  Crunchy Pound Cake Slices, 308
  Dipped Chocolate Angel Cake, 306
  Easy Crème de Menthe Cake, 305
  Flip-Flop Cake, **278,** 389
  Fruit Ribbon Cake, 302
  Gingerbread Pudding Cake, 310
  Gooey Chocolate-Caramel Cake, 304
  Little Peppermint Cakes, 307
  Passion Fruit and Strawberry Sorbet
    Cake, 315
  Shortcut Malted Chocolate Cake, 304
  Strawberry-Chocolate Cake, **271,** 302
  Tropical Angel Cake, 307
  Upside-Down Caramel Apple Cake, 309
...lzones
  Cheese Calzone, 387
  Ham and Cheese Calzones, 104
  Turkey Calzones, 38
...anadian Bacon Pizza, 105

Candy
  Almond-Butter Crunch, 336
  Double-Dipped Caramels, 338
  Haystacks, 339
  Macadamia-Vanilla Bark, 340
  Milk Chocolate-Caramel Clusters, 339
  Molded Peppermint Bark, 340
  Peanut Butter Balls, 338
  Peanut Butter Cups, 337
  White Chocolate–Cereal Drops, 340
  White Citrus Fudge, 336
Capellini with Shrimp and Pesto, 140
Caramel Clementines, 295
Caramel Corn and Peanuts, 396
Caramel–Milk Chocolate Clusters, 339
Caramels, Double-Dipped, 338
Carrots
  Carrot, Raisin, and Peanut Butter
    Sandwiches, 387
  Glazed Carrot Coins, 199
  Honey-Ginger Carrots, 198
  Honey-Glazed Carrots, 197, **264**
  Minted Snap Peas and Carrots, 206
  Sweet Baby Carrots, 198
  Sweet Saucy Carrots and Pecans, 197
  Veggie Mash, 214
Cashew-Toffee Cookies, 334
Cashew-Vegetable Stir-Fry, 157
Catfish and Zucchini, Crunchy, 135
Cauliflower, Cheesy, for a Crowd, 199
Cauliflower and Broccoli Chowder,
  Mexican, 186
Champagne Fruit Punch, 370
Cheddar
  Bread and Cheddar Wedges, 360
  Cheddary Corn Bread Rolls, 225, **266**
  Cheese Calzone, 387
  Chiles Rellenos, 146
  Foil-Grilled Cheese Sandwiches, 150
  Mock Cheese Soufflé, **124,** 146
  Smoky Chicken and Cheesy Potato
    Casserole, 26
Cheese. *See also* **Cheddar**
  Almond-Brie Spread, 350
  Bacon Cheeseburgers, 65
  Baked Cheese, 351
  Baked Cheese Fondue, 348
  Baked Parmesan Chicken, 380
  Beef Kabobs with Blue Cheese Dipping
    Sauce, 58
  Beef Tenderloin with Blue Cheese, 53
  Blue Cheese Butter, 262
  Brie Sandwiches with Greens, 148
  Cheese and Bean Quesadillas, 386
  Cheese and Garlic Crescents, 228
  Cheeseburger and Fries Casserole, 382
  Cheese Calzone, 387
  Cheese-Stuffed Pecans, 368
  Cheesy Beer-Salsa Dip, 346
  Cheesy Cauliflower for a Crowd, 199
  Cheesy Garlic Potato Gratin, 209
  Cheesy Peas and Potatoes, 205
  Cheesy Pecan Quesadillas, 356
  Cheesy Potato-Bean Soup, 183
  Cheesy Potato Wedges, 365
  Cheesy Reuben Potatoes, 62
  Cheesy Sloppy Joes, 68

  Cheesy Succotash, 212
  Cheesy Tortellini Casserole, 162
  Cheesy Vegetable Chowder, 184
  Chipotle Con Queso Dip, 345
  Creamy Cheese Spread, 350
  Feta-Stuffed Mushrooms, 364
  Feta-Tomato Pasta Salad, 243
  Fresh Mozzarella Salad, 234
  Fresh Tomato Pizza with Pesto, 149
  Garlic and Cheese Focaccia, 226
  Goat Cheese Pastry Rounds, **275,** 361
  Gorgonzola- and Garlic-Stuffed
    Burgers, 64
  Gorgonzola-Walnut-Stuffed Apples, 285
  Ham and Cheese Calzones, 104
  Ham and Cheese Pizza Tortillas, 384
  Herbed Feta Spread, 348
  Lip-Smackin' Mac 'n' Cheese, 386
  Mexican Lasagna, 98
  Mock Cheese Soufflé, **124,** 146
  Pepper-Cheese Biscuits, 227
  Pesto and Cheese Tomato Melts, 148
  Pesto Macaroni Salad, 243
  Pizza by the Yard, 99
  Pizza Margherita, 149
  Puff Pastry Cheese Straws, 360
  Reuben Loaves, 61
  Rosemary and Swiss Buns, 226
  Sausage-Cheese Dip, 346
  Snowflake Sandwiches, 384
  Spinach and Feta Omelet, 147
  Strawberry and Cheese Bites, 359
  Sweet Peppers Stuffed with Goat Cheese
    and Herbs, 207
  Taco Pizza, 69
  Toasted Cheese Pita Crisps, 367
  Tortilla Lasagna, 162
  Triple-Cheesy Pasta, 217
  Upside-Down Pizza Casserole, 66
  Veal Rolls Stuffed with Herb
    Cheese, 70, **118**
  Warm Brie, 351
Cheeseburger and Fries Casserole, 382
Cheesecake-Fruit Parfaits, 289
Cheesecakes, Chocolate Cookie, 314
Cherries
  Cherried Chicken, 21
  Cherry-Bananas Foster, 296
  Cherry-Chocolate Pastries, 321
  Cherry Trifle Cake, 310
  Chocolate-Cherry S'more, 393
  Frosty Chocolate-Cherry Yogurt, 298
  Fruity Rice Pudding, 324
  Ham Slice with Basil-Cherry Sauce, 102
  Peaches with Quick Cherry Sauce, 294
  Pork Medallions with Cherry Sauce, 74
Chewy Granola Goodies, 391
Chicken. *See also specific parts below*
  Buffalo Wings, 353
  Chicken Salad Stacks, 381
  Chicken Wings with Barbecue Sauce, 353
  Five-Spice Drummies, 352
  Garlicky Grilled Chicken, 7
  Honey-Mustard Baked Chicken, 7
  Kickin' Chicken, 8
  Oven-Fried Coconut Chicken, 9
  Polynesian Glazed Wings, **275,** 352

Chicken (continued)
Roast Chicken with Fruit and Pesto, 6
Southwest Chicken Burgers, 22
Sweet and Spicy Chicken, 9
Tuscan Chicken, 8
Chicken (breasts)
Apricot-Cranberry Chicken, 13
Baked Parmesan Chicken, 380
Chicken and Bean Burritos, 16
Chicken and Wild Rice Soup, 167
Chicken Burgundy, 12
Chicken Curry Soup, 167
Chicken Kabobs with Thai Brushing
Sauce, 14, **112**
Chicken with Pineapple-Hoisin Glaze, 10
Fast Chicken Fettuccine, 17
Florentine Chicken, 12
Greek Chicken with Couscous, 15
Little Chicken Dippers, 380
Pepper and Peach Fajita Chicken, 11
Ranch-Style Chicken Strips, 17
Skillet Chicken Alfredo, 13
Spicy Chicken Fajita Bites, **275,** 356
Sweet Ginger Stir-Fry, 15, **111**
Tangy Lemon Chicken, 11, **111**
Chicken (cooked)
Chicken Alfredo Potpies, 25
Chicken and Rice Spring Rolls, 358
Chicken Taco Salad, 25
Chicken Tortilla Soup, **126,** 166
Coconut-Chicken Pasta, 23
Homestyle Chicken and Stuffing, 24
Mandarin Chicken Salad, 26, **113**
Mushroom-Tomato-Pesto Pizza, 27
Quick Chicken Fajitas, 27, **113**
Quick Chicken Tortilla Bake, 23
Simply Ramen Chicken Soup, **126,** 166
Smoky Chicken and Cheesy Potato
Casserole, 26
Sweet Chicken Tostadas, 24
Chicken (drumsticks or thighs)
Asian Chicken and Vegetables, 19
Cherried Chicken, 21
Chicken and Corn Chowder, 168
Chicken Curry Soup, 167
Chipotle-Peach-Glazed Chicken
Thighs, 18
Coq au Vin Stew, 169
Cranberry Chicken, 19, **113**
Finger Lickin' Barbecue Chicken, 21
French-Onion Baked Chicken, 20
Honey-Glazed Chicken Drumsticks, 18
Honey-Mustard Chicken with Sweet
Potatoes, 20
Oriental-Style Chicken Stew, 168
Sausage and Chicken Gumbo, 169
Sweet Ginger Stir-Fry, 15, **111**
Chiles. See also **Chipotle peppers**
Chiles Rellenos, 146
Mango-Habañero Mojo, 257
Mustard-Jalapeño Glaze, 252
working with, 59
Chili, Taco, 170
Chili Dogs, 383
Chili Medley, Vegetable, 185
Chili-Rubbed Prime Rib, 42

Chipotle peppers
about, 152
Chipotle-Bean Enchiladas, 152
Chipotle Con Queso Dip, 345
Chipotle-Peach-Glazed Chicken
Thighs, 18
Cranberry-Chipotle Pork Chops, 81, **119**
Cranberry-Chipotle Sauce, 250
Chive Dressing, Creamy, 248
Chocolate
Bittersweet Chocolate Soufflé, **273,** 326
Brownie Pudding Cake, 309
Brownie Surprise Cupcakes, 312
Cherry-Chocolate Pastries, 321
Chocolate Brownie Pudding, 394
Chocolate-Caramel Fondue, 327
Chocolate Chip Thumbprints, 330
Chocolate Cookie Cheesecakes, 314
Chocolate-Covered Strawberry Cakes, 308
Chocolate-Dipped Waffles, 389
Chocolate-Mint Treats, 393
Chocolate Pots de Crème, 324
Chocolate-Raspberry Cake, 303
Chocolaty Candy Cane Cups, 337
Crispy Chocolate Cutout Cookies, 390
Crunchy Nut-Caramel Cupcakes, 314
Crunchy Pound Cake Slices, 308
Dipped Chocolate Angel Cake, 306
Easy Crème de Menthe Cake, 305
Five-Layer Bars, 332
Fizzy Mint-Chocolate Soda, 372
Frosty Chocolate-Cherry Yogurt, 298
Frozen Chocolate-Peanut Dessert, 392
Fudgy Peanut Butter Bites, 335
Gooey Chocolate-Caramel Cake, 304
Haystacks, 339
Hot Caramel Chocolate, 378
Hot Fudge Sauce, 328
Milk Chocolate–Caramel Clusters, 339
Mint Surprise Cupcakes, 312
Mocha au Lait, 377
Mocha Pears, 286
Peanut Butter and Chocolate
Pinwheels, 331
Peanut Butter Balls, 338
Peanut Butter Cocoa, 378
Peanut Butter Cups, 337
Peanut Butter S'more Tarts, 319
Praline Crunch Bars, 332
Raspberry and Chocolate Tulips, 320
Semisweet-Chocolate Bread
Pudding, 322
Shortcut Malted Chocolate Cake, 304
S'mores Bars, 333
Something More S'more;
variations, **278,** 393
Strawberry-Chocolate Cake, **271,** 302
Strawberry-Chocolate Pie, 316
Sunflower Chip Cookies, 330
Surprise Chocolate Bites, 329
Choucroute Garni, 86
Chowder
Cheesy Vegetable Chowder, 184
Chicken and Corn Chowder, 168
Corn and Sausage Chowder, 179
Creamy Clam Chowder, 182

Mexican Cauliflower and Broccoli
Chowder, 186
Mexican-Style Fish Chowder, 182
Sausage-Corn Chowder, 381
Chutney Salad Dressing, 247
Cider Peas and Apples, 205
Cilantro Shrimp, 139
Cinnamon Granola Loaf, 228
Cinnamon Snails, 388
Citrus Butter, 262
Citrus-Honey Marinade, 260
Clam Chowder, Creamy, 182
Clementines, Caramel, 295
Coconut
Crunchy Nut-Caramel Cupcakes, 314
Oven-Fried Coconut Chicken, 9
Parfait Pie with Coconut Shell, 318
Roasted Mango with Coconut, 284
Sunflower Chip Cookies, 330
toasting, 280
Coconut milk
Chicken Curry Soup, 167
Coconut-Chicken Pasta, 23
Curried Coconut Shrimp, 141
Thai Beef, 58
Coffee
Coffee Angel Dessert, 306
Coffee Custards, 325
Mocha au Lait, 377
Mocha Pears, 286
Raspberry-Coffee Frappé, 377
Cola Pot Roast, 45
Cookies and bars
All-American Apple Pie Bars, 333
Cashew-Toffee Cookies, 334
Chewy Granola Goodies, 391
Chocolate Chip Thumbprints, 330
Crispy Chocolate Cutout Cookies, 390
Easy Peanut Butter Cookies, 331
Five-Layer Bars, 332
Fudgy Peanut Butter Bites, 335
Gingersnap Dips, 335
Macadamia Nut Shortbread, 334
Peanut Butter and Chocolate
Pinwheels, 331
Pine Nut Cookies, 329
Praline Crunch Bars, 332
Puzzle Cookies, 391
S'mores Bars, 333
Spare-Me Sugar Cookies, **278,** 390
Sunflower Chip Cookies, 330
Surprise Chocolate Bites, 329
Cookies-and-Cream Cupcakes, **271,** 312
Coq au Vin Stew, 169
Corn
Cheesy Succotash, 212
Chicken and Corn Chowder, 168
Corn and Sausage Chowder, 179
Creamy Corn and Roasted Red
Peppers, 200
Creamy Crunchy Corn, 200
Easy Burgoo, 177
Fresh Corn and Tomato Salad, 236, **27**
Fresh Corn-Rice Salad, 244
Herbed Sweet Corn, 201
removing kernels from cob, 244
Sausage-Corn Chowder, 381

orn bread
  Arizona Corn Bread Cacti, **277,** 388
  Barbecue Beans and Hot Dogs over Corn
      Bread, 36
  Broccoli Corn Bread, 225
  Cheddary Corn Bread Rolls, 225, **266**
orned Beef and Cabbage, 48
ountry Chops and Peppers, 82
ountry-Style Smoked Sausage and
    Sauerkraut, 35
ouscous
  Couscous- and Pine Nut–Stuffed
      Peppers, 159
  Curried Couscous with Vegetables, 159
  Greek Chicken with Couscous, 15
  Mediterranean Shrimp and
      Couscous, 141
ranberries. *See also* **Cranberry sauce**
  Apricot-Cranberry Chicken, 13
  Bratwurst with Kickin' Cranberry
      Ketchup, 100
  Cranberry-Apple-Orange Relish, 257
  Cranberry Coleslaw, 241
  Fruit and Peanut Snack Mix, 342
  Fruity Wild Rice Salad, 244
  Hot and Spicy Cranberry
      Punch, **276,** 371
  Poached Pears in Cran-Amaretto
      Sauce, 287
  Winter Fruit Bowl, 232
ranberry-Apple Spiced Beets, 194
ranberry sauce
  Black Cherry–Cranberry Supreme, 233
  Cranberry Chicken, 19, **113**
  Cranberry-Chipotle Pork Chops, 81, **119**
  Cranberry-Chipotle Sauce, 250
  Cranberry-Glazed Pork Ribs, 94
  Cranberry Pork Roast, 77
  Cranberry-Sauced Franks, 355
  Frozen Cranberry Pie, 318
  Tangy Cranberry Meatballs, 354
eam-Topped Pears in Orange Sauce, 286
eamy Apple Salad, 232
eamy Avocado-Lime Dip, 344
eamy Beef-and-Potato Stew, 171
eamy Cheese Spread, 350
eamy Chive Dressing, 248
eamy Clam Chowder, 182
eamy Corn and Roasted Red Peppers, 200
eamy Crunchy Corn, 200
eamy Cucumbers, 239
eamy Garlic Dressing, 248
eamy Peanut Butter Spread, 397
eamy Potato Wedges, 208
eamy Tomato-Broccoli Sauce with
    Pasta, 164
ispy Chocolate Cutout Cookies, 390
ispy Onion Rings, **274,** 365
unchy Catfish and Zucchini, 135
unchy Nut-Caramel Cupcakes, 314
unchy Pound Cake Slices, 308
unchy Trail Mix, 342
ucumbers
  Creamy Cucumbers, 239
  Cucumber-Dill Sauce, 252
  Iceberg Lettuce with Cucumber-Mint
      Dressing, 230

Cupcakes
  Brownie Surprise Cupcakes, 312
  Cookies-and-Cream Cupcakes, **271,** 312
  Crunchy Nut-Caramel Cupcakes, 314
  Icy Orange-Filled Cupcakes, 313
  Mint Surprise Cupcakes, 312
  preparing, from cake recipes, 311
  Rosemary Mini Cupcakes, 311
Currant Sauce, 254
Curried Beans and Apples, 192, **263**
Curried Coconut Shrimp, 141
Curried Couscous with Vegetables, 159
Curry, Lamb, 109
Curry Chicken Soup, 167
Curry Rub, 259
Custards
  Chocolate Pots de Crème, 324
  Coffee Custards, 325
  Flan, 325

D

Daiquiri Sorbet, 300
Deli Roast Beef Sandwiches, 60
Desserts. *See also* **Cakes; Candy; Cookies
    and bars**
  Apple-Pear Sauce, 297
  Apricot-Peach Cobbler, 282
  Apricot-Peach Dessert Soup, 292
  Banana Split Kabobs, 392
  Banana Split Trifles, 289
  Berry Parfaits, 394
  Bittersweet Chocolate Soufflé, **273,** 326
  Blueberry-Kiwi Fool, 290
  Butterscotch-Caramel Sauce, 328
  Caramel Clementines, 295
  Cheesecake-Fruit Parfaits, 289
  Cherry-Bananas Foster, 296
  Cherry-Chocolate Pastries, 321
  Chocolate Brownie Pudding, 394
  Chocolate-Caramel Fondue, 327
  Chocolate Cookie Cheesecakes, 314
  Chocolate-Dipped Waffles, 389
  Chocolate-Mint Treats, 393
  Chocolate Pots de Crème, 324
  Chocolaty Candy Cane Cups, 337
  Coffee Angel Dessert, 306
  Coffee Custards, 325
  Cream-Topped Pears in Orange
      Sauce, 286
  Daiquiri Sorbet, 300
  Dessert Burritos, 287
  Dessert Waffles with Raspberry
      Sauce, 295
  Double Berry Soup, 292
  Easy Blueberry Sauce, 297
  Easy Fruit Cobbler, 282
  Easy Fruit Crisp, 283
  Fill-the-Grill Nectarine Toss, **272,** 296
  Flan, 325
  Frosty Chocolate-Cherry Yogurt, 298
  Frozen Berry Yogurt, 299
  Frozen Chocolate-Peanut Dessert, 392
  Frozen Cranberry Pie, 318
  Fruit-Filled Napoleons, 321
  Fruit-Topped Phyllo Cups, 320
  Fruity Rice Pudding, 324

  Ginger Fruit with Pineapple Sherbet, 294
  Glazed Nut Topping, 327
  Gorgonzola-Walnut-Stuffed Apples, 285
  Granola-Nectarine Gratin, 281
  Honeyed Figs and Yogurt, 293
  Hot Fudge Sauce, 328
  Juicy Raspberry Pie, 317
  Lemonade Ice Cream, **273,** 298
  Mango Cream, 291
  Mango-Papaya Fool, 290
  Mango-Raspberry Granita, 301
  Mint-Ginger Fruit Sorbet, 300
  Mixed Berry Cobbler, 280
  Mocha Pears, 286
  Parfait Pie with Coconut Shell, 318
  Peaches with Quick Cherry Sauce, 294
  Peanut Butter S'more Tarts, 319
  Pineapple Fries with Raspberry
      Ketchup, **273,** 288
  Pineapple-Peach Cobbler, 281
  Poached Pears in Cran-Amaretto
      Sauce, 287
  Praline Baked Apples, 285
  Pumpkin Custard Bread Pudding, 323
  Quick and Creamy Rice Pudding, 323
  Quick Strawberry Shortcake, 284
  Raspberries and Lemon Cream, 293
  Raspberry and Chocolate Tulips, 320
  Raspberry Whip, 291
  Red, White, and Blue Parfaits, 290
  Roasted Mango with Coconut, 284
  Rustic Pear Tart, 319
  Semisweet-Chocolate Bread
      Pudding, 322
  Shimmering Strawberry Pie, 316
  Slow-Cooked Apple Betty, 283
  Something More S'more;
      variations, **278,** 393
  Strawberries with Lime Dip, 288
  Strawberry-Chocolate Pie, 316
  Strawberry Gelato, 299
  Strawberry-Lime Fool, 290
  Watermelon-Berry Ice, 301
Deviled Steaks, 52
Dilled Peas and Walnuts, 204
Dipped Chocolate Angel Cake, 306
Dips and spreads
  Almond-Brie Spread, 350
  Artichoke Dip with Pretzels, 347
  Baked Cheese, 351
  Baked Cheese Fondue, 348
  Cheesy Beer-Salsa Dip, 346
  Chipotle Con Queso Dip, 345
  Chocolate-Caramel Fondue, 327
  Creamy Avocado-Lime Dip, 344
  Creamy Cheese Spread, 350
  Creamy Peanut Butter Spread, 397
  Eggplant-Garlic Spread, 349
  Herbed Feta Spread, 348
  Layered Black Bean Dip, 345
  Peanutty Dip, 397
  Sausage-Cheese Dip, 346
  Spiced Yogurt Dip, 344
  Sweet Onion Spread, 349
  Tomato Sauce with Garlic Cheese
      Bread, 347
  Tropical Fruit Dip, **274,** 343

Dips and spreads (continued)
Veggie Dip, 397
Warm Brie, 351
Dive-In Party Mix, **277,** 395
Double Berry Soup, 292
Double-Dipped Caramels, 338

E

Easy Artichoke Roll, 362
Easy Blueberry Sauce, 297
Easy Burgoo, 177
Easy Crème de Menthe Cake, 305
Easy Fruit Cobbler, 282
Easy Fruit Crisp, 283
Easy Goulash, 65
Easy Oven Risotto, 219
Easy Peanut Butter Cookies, 331
Easy Plum-Mustard Sauce, 254
Easy Pork Chops Supreme, 86
Easy Spanish Rice, 218
Easy Turkey-Pesto Potpies, 34
Easy Vegetable Minestrone, 186
Eggplant
Eggplant-Garlic Spread, 349
Eggplant Sauce with Whole Wheat
Pasta, 164
Tortellini in Ratatouille Sauce, 357
Eggs
Oven Omelets with Pesto, 147
Spinach and Feta Omelet, 147
Espresso Marinade, 261

F

Fajitas, Quick Chicken, 27, **113**
Fancy Fruit Float, 372
Fancy Stack Pancakes, 379
Farm-Style Green Beans, 190
Fast Chicken Fettuccine, 17
Feta-Stuffed Mushrooms, 364
Feta-Tomato Pasta Salad, 243
Figs and Yogurt, Honeyed, 293
Fill-the-Grill Nectarine Toss, **272,** 296
Finger Lickin' Barbecue Chicken, 21
Firecracker Foot-Longs, 100, **121**
Fire-Roasted Acorn Squash, 211
Fish. See also **Salmon; Tuna**
Almond Walleye, 133
Crunchy Catfish and Zucchini, 135
Lemon-Dill Fish Fillets, 136
Lime-Poached Mahi Mahi, 133
Mexican-Style Fish Chowder, 182
Mustard-Glazed Halibut Steaks, 136
Rocky Mountain Trout, 135
Snapper Veracruz, 134
Steamed Fish with Veggies, 134
Five-Layer Bars, 332
Five-Spice Drummies, 352
Five-Spice Tri-Tip Roast, 44
Fizzy Kiwi Lemonade, 374
Fizzy Mint-Chocolate Soda, 372
Flaky Biscuits, 227
Flan, 325
Flat-Iron Steaks, 52, **117**
Flip-Flop Cake, **278,** 389

Florentine Chicken, 12
Focaccia, Garlic and Cheese, 226
Focaccia Breadsticks, 221, **266**
Foil-Grilled Cheese Sandwiches, 150
Foil-Wrapped Salmon Dinner, 131
Fondue, Baked Cheese, 348
Fondue, Chocolate-Caramel, 327
food safety, 10
French-Onion Baked Chicken, 20
Fresh Corn and Tomato Salad, 236, **270**
Fresh Corn-Rice Salad, 244
Fresh Mozzarella Salad, 234
Fresh Tomato Pizza with Pesto, 149
Frosty Chocolate-Cherry Yogurt, 298
Frozen Berry Yogurt, 299
Frozen Chocolate-Peanut Dessert, 392
Frozen Cranberry Pie, 318
Fruit (dried). See also specific dried fruits
Banana-Raisin Trail Mix, 395
Fruit and Peanut Snack Mix, 342
Fruited Beef Stew, 173
Fruity Rice Pudding, 324
Fruity Wild Rice Salad, 244
Pot Roast with Chipotle-Fruit Sauce, 46
Roast Chicken with Fruit and Pesto, 6
Fruited Baked Ham, 101
Fruit (fresh). See also specific fruits
All-American Fruit Smoothies, **277,** 398
Curried Coconut Shrimp, 141
Easy Fruit Cobbler, 282
Easy Fruit Crisp, 283
Fancy Fruit Float, 372
Fruit and Broccoli Salad, 234
Fruit-Filled Napoleons, 321
Fruit-Topped Phyllo Cups, 320
Shrimp with Fruit Salsa, **123,** 138
Winter Fruit Bowl, 232
Fruit Ribbon Cake, 302
Fudge, White Citrus, 336
Fudgy Peanut Butter Bites, 335

G

Game hens
Hoisin-Sauced Cornish Hens, 40
Maple-Cranberry Game Hens, 40
Garden Bounty Tomato Soup, 183
Gardener's Pie, 156
Garlic
Creamy Garlic Dressing, 248
Eggplant-Garlic Spread, 349
Garlic and Cheese Focaccia, 226
Garlic-Buttered Shrimp Kabobs, 139
Garlic Croutons, 224
Garlicky Grilled Chicken, 7
Garlicky Grilled Portobellos, 202
Garlic-Roasted Red Potatoes, 207
Gremolata, 72
Gelato, Strawberry, 299
German-Style Beef Roast, 43
German-Style Pork Stew, 177
Ginger
Baked Beets in Gingered Syrup, 195
Ginger-Allspice Rub, 258
Ginger Fruit with Pineapple Sherbet, 294
Ginger-Lemon Pork Chops, 85
Ginger-Lemon Tea, 376

Ginger-Orange Brush-On, 251
Ginger Pea Pods and Noodles, 206
Ginger-Sesame Slaw, 241
Mint-Ginger Fruit Sorbet, 300
Gingerbread Pudding Cake, 310
Gingersnap Dips, 335
Glaze, Mustard-Jalapeño, 252
Glaze, Teriyaki, 251
Glazed Brussels Sprouts, 196
Glazed Carrot Coins, 199
Glazed Nut Topping, 327
Glazed Parsnips and Apples, 203
Glazed Prosciutto-Wrapped Shrimp, 137
Goat Cheese Pastry Rounds, **275,** 361
Golden Green Bean Crunch, 191
Gooey Chocolate-Caramel Cake, 304
Gorgonzola- and Garlic-Stuffed Burgers, 64
Gorgonzola-Walnut-Stuffed Apples, 285
Goulash, Easy, 65
Granita, Mango-Raspberry, 301
Granola
Chewy Granola Goodies, 391
Cinnamon Granola Loaf, 228
Easy Fruit Crisp, 283
Granola-Nectarine Gratin, 281
Grapes
Fruit and Broccoli Salad, 234
Fruit-Topped Phyllo Cups, 320
Orange Dream Fruit Salad, 233
Poppy Seed-Dressed Pasta
Salad, 242, **270**
Greek Cabbage Rolls, 110
Greek Chicken with Couscous, 15
Greek-Seasoned Lentils, 163
Greek-Style Pitas, 62
Green beans
Creamy Beef-and-Potato Stew, 171
Easy Vegetable Minestrone, 186
Farm-Style Green Beans, 190
Golden Green Bean Crunch, 191
Green Beans with Shallot Sauce, 191
Grilled Green Beans, 190, **263**
Marinated Bean Salad, 238
Pesto Macaroni Salad, 243
Saucy Green Beans and Potatoes, 192
Smoked Pork Chop Skillet, 89
Veal Rolls Stuffed with Herb
Cheese, 70, **118**
Green Onion Parker House Biscuits, 227, **266**
Greens. See also **Spinach**
Asian Pea Pod Salad, 235
Baby Greens with Veggies, 237
Balsamic-Glazed Lamb and Greens, 107
Beet Greens with Walnuts and Blue
Cheese, 229, **270**
BLT Salad, 105
Iceberg Lettuce with Cucumber-Mint
Dressing, 230
Mandarin Chicken Salad, 26, **113**
Mixed Greens with Pears, 230, **267**
Prosciutto-Arugula Roll-Ups, 362
Salmon Caesar Salad, 132
Gremolata, 72
Grilled recipes (desserts)
Banana Split Kabobs, 392
Dessert Burritos, 287
Fill-the-Grill Nectarine Toss, **272,** 296

Gorgonzola-Walnut-Stuffed
    Apples, 285
Peaches with Quick Cherry Sauce, 294
Pineapple Fries with Raspberry
    Ketchup, **273,** 288
Rustic Pear Tart, 319
Something More S'more;
    variations, **278,** 393
Grilled recipes (meat entrées)
Asian Apricot-Glazed Chops, 84
Barbecued Pork Chop
    Sandwiches, 84, **121**
Beef Kabobs with Blue Cheese Dipping
    Sauce, 58
Beer and Pretzel Burgers, 64
Beer-Glazed Pork Chops, 83
Blackberry-Glazed Ham, 101
BLT Steaks, 50
Bratwurst with Kickin' Cranberry
    Ketchup, 100
Bunless Burgers, 63, **115**
Chili-Rubbed Prime Rib, 42
Cranberry-Chipotle Pork
    Chops, 81, **119**
Cranberry-Glazed Pork Ribs, 94
Deviled Steaks, 52
Firecracker Foot-Longs, 100, **121**
Five-Spice Tri-Tip Roast, 44
Flat-Iron Steaks, 52, **117**
Ginger-Lemon Pork Chops, 85
Gorgonzola- and Garlic-Stuffed
    Burgers, 64
Hamburgers with Squished Tomato
    Topper, 63
Herbed Lamb Chops, 108
Honey-Bourbon Steaks, 49
Honey-Mustard Lamb Chops, 106
Honey-Mustard Pork Tenderloin
    Sandwiches, 80
Italian Rolled Pork Roast, 78
Italian-Stuffed Sausage Burgers, 97
Lamb Chops with Mint Marinade, 107
Lemon-and-Herb-Rubbed Pork Chops, 82
Lemon-Pepper Lamb, 106
Maple-and-Mustard-Glazed Ham
    Steak, 102
Margarita-Glazed Pork Chops, 85
Mediterranean Lamb Burgers, 109, **118**
Mustard-Marinated Flank Steak, 55
Peachy Pork Tenderloin, 73
Pineapple-Mustard Country-Style
    Ribs, 92
Pork Patties with Honey Barbecue
    Sauce, 95
Rhubarb-Glazed Pork Roast, 76
Saucy Strip Steaks, 50
Stout-Glazed Ribs, 93, **119**
Sweet and Spicy Pork Burgers, 95
Veal Chops with Apples, 71
Veal Chops with Ginger Butter, 71
Veal Rolls Stuffed with Herb
    Cheese, 70, **118**
Grilled recipes (poultry entrées)
Barbecued Turkey Tenderloin
    Sandwiches, 32, **114**
Chicken Burgundy, 12

Chicken Kabobs with Thai Brushing
    Sauce, 14, **112**
Chicken with Pineapple-Hoisin Glaze, 10
Chipotle-Peach-Glazed Chicken
    Thighs, 18
Garlicky Grilled Chicken, 7
Kickin' Chicken, 8
Maple-Cranberry Game Hens, 40
Southwest Chicken Burgers, 22
Turkey Breast with Raspberry Salsa, 30
Turkey on the Grill, 28
Turkey with Dried Tomato Pesto, 29, **114**
Grilled recipes (seafood entrées)
Cilantro Shrimp, 139
Foil-Wrapped Salmon Dinner, 131
Garlic-Buttered Shrimp Kabobs, 139
Glazed Prosciutto-Wrapped Shrimp, 137
Grilled Salmon with Mustard
    Glaze, **122,** 130
Lemon-Dill Fish Fillets, 136
Lobster Tails with Chive Butter, 145
Mustard-Glazed Halibut Steaks, 136
Orange-Marinated Salmon Steaks, 130
Rocky Mountain Trout, 135
Shrimp and Scallop Skewers, 142
Shrimp with Fruit Salsa, **123,** 138
Stuffed Tuna Steaks, **123,** 128
Thai-Spiced Scallop Kabobs, 145
Grilled recipes (sides and sandwiches)
Asparagus in Dill Butter, 188
Asparagus with Cheese and Chives, 188
Buttered Rosemary New Potatoes, 209
Cheesy Peas and Potatoes, 205
Fire-Roasted Acorn Squash, 211
Foil-Grilled Cheese Sandwiches, 150
Fresh Corn and Tomato Salad, 236, **270**
Garlicky Grilled Portobellos, 202
Grilled French Bread, 222
Grilled Green Beans, 190, **263**
Grilled Sweet Onions, 202
Grilled Sweet Pepper Relish, 256
Herbed Baguette, 223
Herbed Sweet Corn, 201
Herb-Grilled Tomatoes, 213, **264**
Italian Breadsticks, 222
Smoked Mushrooms, 201
Sweet Peppers Stuffed with Goat Cheese
    and Herbs, 207
Toasty-Hot French Bread Slices, 223
Grills
charcoal grills, about, 70
foil packet grilling, 205
gas grills, buying, 138
gas grills, safety checks for, 78
Gumbo, Cajun-Seasoned Vegetarian, 185
Gumbo, Sausage and Chicken, 169

H

Halibut Steaks, Mustard-Glazed, 136
Ham. *See also* **Prosciutto**
    Blackberry-Glazed Ham, 101
    Fruited Baked Ham, 101
    Ham, Melon, and Spinach Salad, 104
    Ham and Asparagus Pasta, 103
    Ham and Cheese Calzones, 104

Ham and Cheese Pizza Tor
Ham and Potatoes au Gra
Ham Slice with Basil-Che
Hearty Ham Stew, **126,**
Maple-and-Mustard-Glazed
    Steak, 102
Poppy Seed–Dressed Pasta
    Salad, 242, **270**
Snowflake Sandwiches, 384
Spicy Ham-and-Garbanzo Bean
    Soup, 178
Tasty Wheels, 396
Hamburgers with Squished Tomato Topper, 63
Have-a-Ball Rolls, 224
Haystacks, 339
Hearty Ham Stew, **126,** 178
Herbed Baguette, 223
Herbed Crouton Sticks, 221
Herbed Feta Spread, 348
Herbed Lamb Chops, 108
Herbed Sweet Corn, 201
Herbed Zucchini, 214
Herbs. *See also specific herbs*
    fresh, snipping, 215
    Gremolata, 72
    Herb-Buttermilk Dressing, 248
    Herb-Grilled Tomatoes, 213, **264**
    Herb Rub, 258
    herb substitutions, 236
    substituting dried for fresh, 236
Hoisin-Garlic Mushroom Appetizers, 364
Hoisin-Sauced Cornish Hens, 40
Homestyle Beef and Vegetables, 44
Homestyle Chicken and Stuffing, 24
Hominy
    Taco-Style Black Beans and Hominy, 154
    Texas Two-Step Stew, 180
Honey-Bourbon Steaks, 49
Honeyed Figs and Yogurt, 293
Honey-Ginger Carrots, 198
Honey-Glazed Carrots, 197, **264**
Honey-Glazed Chicken Drumsticks, 18
Honey-Mulled Apple Cider, 375
Honey-Mustard Baked Chicken, 7
Honey-Mustard Barbecue Pork Ribs, 91
Honey-Mustard Chicken with Sweet
    Potatoes, 20
Honey-Mustard Dressing, 247
Honey-Mustard Lamb Chops, 106
Honey-Mustard Pork Tenderloin
    Sandwiches, 80
Honey-Peach Sauce, 253
Hot and Spicy Cranberry Punch, **276,** 371
Hot-and-Sweet Pineapple Slaw, 239, **269**
Hot Caramel Chocolate, 378
Hot dogs
    Barbecue Beans and Hot Dogs over Corn
        Bread, 36
    Chili Dogs, 383
    Cranberry-Sauced Franks, 355
    Firecracker Foot-Longs, 100, **121**
Hot Fudge Sauce, 328
Hot Honeyed Spareribs, 355
Hot Strawberry Cider, 375
Iceberg Lettuce with Cucumber-Mint
    Dressing, 230

Ice cream
Banana Split Kabobs, 392
Banana Split Trifles, 289
Crunchy Pound Cake Slices, 308
Dessert Waffles with Raspberry
Sauce, 295
Fill-the-Grill Nectarine Toss, **272,** 296
Fizzy Mint-Chocolate Soda, 372
Frozen Chocolate-Peanut Dessert, 392
Frozen Cranberry Pie, 318
homemade, ripening, 298
Lemonade Ice Cream, **273,** 298
Parfait Pie with Coconut Shell, 318
Quick Ice Cream Shake, 372
Raspberry-Coffee Frappé, 377
Icy Orange-Filled Cupcakes, 313
Indian Lamb and Potato Stew, 181
Italian Breadsticks, 222
Italian Rolled Pork Roast, 78
Italian-Stuffed Sausage Burgers, 97
Italian-Style Chips, 367

J

Juicy Raspberry Pie, 317

K

Kickin' Chicken, 8
Kid-friendly recipes
All-American Fruit Smoothies, **277,** 398
Arizona Corn Bread Cacti, **277,** 388
Baked Parmesan Chicken, 380
Banana-Raisin Trail Mix, 395
Banana Split Kabobs, 392
Berry Parfaits, 394
Blaze-a-Trail Mix, 395
Caramel Corn and Peanuts, 396
Carrot, Raisin, and Peanut Butter
Sandwiches, 387
Cheese and Bean Quesadillas, 386
Cheeseburger and Fries Casserole, 382
Cheese Calzone, 387
Chewy Granola Goodies, 391
Chicken Salad Stacks, 381
Chili Dogs, 383
Chocolate Brownie Pudding, 394
Chocolate-Dipped Waffles, 389
Chocolate-Mint Treats, 393
Cinnamon Snails, 388
Creamy Peanut Butter Spread, 397
Crispy Chocolate Cutout Cookies, 390
Dive-In Party Mix, **277,** 395
Fancy Stack Pancakes, 379
Flip-Flop Cake, **278,** 389
Frozen Chocolate-Peanut Dessert, 392
Ham and Cheese Pizza Tortillas, 384
Lip-Smackin' Mac 'n' Cheese, 386
Little Chicken Dippers, 380
The Magic Pancake, 379
Peanutty Dip, 397
Pepperoni-Pizza Potatoes, 385
Puzzle Cookies, 391
Ready-Right-Now Sloppy Joes, 382
Sangria for Kids, 398
Sausage-Corn Chowder, 381

Snowflake Sandwiches, 384
Something More S'more; variations, **278,**
393
Spare-Me Sugar Cookies, **278,** 390
Spuds with Broccoli Topper, 385
Tasty Wheels, 396
Two Pizzas in One, 383
Veggie Dip, 397
Kiwi-Blueberry Fool, 290
Kiwi Lemonade, Fuzzy, 374

L

Lamb
Balsamic-Glazed Lamb and Greens, 107
Greek Cabbage Rolls, 110
Herbed Lamb Chops, 108
Honey-Mustard Lamb Chops, 106
Indian Lamb and Potato Stew, 181
Lamb Chops with Mint Marinade, 107
Lamb Curry, 109
Lamb Shanks with Basil Pesto, 108
Lemon-Pepper Lamb, 106
Mediterranean Lamb Burgers, 109, **118**
North African Lamb Stew, 181
Lasagna, Mexican, 98
Lasagna, Tortilla, 162
Layered Black Bean Dip, 345
Lemonade, Fizzy Kiwi, 374
Lemonade, Watermelon, 374
Lemonade Ice Cream, **273,** 298
Lemon-Pepper Lamb, 106
Lemons
Citrus Butter, 262
Gremolata, 72
Lemon-and-Herb-Rubbed Pork Chops, 82
Lemon-Dill Fish Fillets, 136
Lemon-Herb Brush-On, 250
Lemon-Nut Vinaigrette, 245
Lemon-Rosemary Marinade, 261
Lemon Sauce, 253
Lemon Sunshine Salad, 242
Lemony Herbed Asparagus, 189
Spicy Citrus Dressing, 246
Tangy Lemon Chicken, 11, **111**
Lentils
Greek-Seasoned Lentils, 163
Lentil-Vegetable Turnovers, 155
Pork, Lentil, and Apple Soup, 175
Pork and Black Bean Potage, 176
Light and Lemony Fettuccine, 216
Limes
Lime-Poached Mahi Mahi, 133
Spicy Citrus Dressing, 246
Strawberries with Lime Dip, 288
Strawberry-Lime Fool, 290
White Citrus Fudge, 336
Lip-Smackin' Mac 'n' Cheese, 386
Little Chicken Dippers, 380
Little Peppermint Cakes, 307
Lobster Tails with Chive Butter, 145

M

Macadamia nuts
Macadamia Nut Shortbread, 334

Macadamia-Vanilla Bark, 340
White Citrus Fudge, 336
The Magic Pancake, 379
Mahi Mahi, Lime-Poached, 133
Malted Chocolate Cake, Shortcut, 304
Mandarin Chicken Salad, 26, **113**
Mangoes
Mango Cream, 291
Mango-Habañero Mojo, 257
Mango-Papaya Fool, 290
Mango-Raspberry Granita, 301
Orange Dream Fruit Salad, 233
Roasted Mango with Coconut, 284
Maple-and-Mustard-Glazed Ham Steak, 102
Maple- and Mustard-Sauced Turkey Thighs, 3
Maple-Cranberry Game Hens, 40
Maple-Pecan Pork Chops, 81
Margarita-Glazed Pork Chops, 85
Marinades
Balsamic-Mustard Marinade, 260
Beer Marinade, 260
Citrus-Honey Marinade, 260
Espresso Marinade, 261
Lemon-Rosemary Marinade, 261
Sherry Marinade, 261
working with, 11
Marinara-Sauced Pasta, 215, **265**
Marinated Bean Salad, 238
Marshmallow(s)
Blaze-a-Trail Mix, 395
Chewy Granola Goodies, 391
Peanut Butter S'more Tarts, 319
S'mores Bars, 333
Something More S'more;
variations, **278,** 393
White Chocolate–Cereal Drops, 340
Meat. See **Beef; Lamb; Pork; Veal**
Meatballs
Meatball-Vegetable Stew, **125,** 170
Plum Good Sausage and Meatballs, 35
Saucy Meatball Sandwiches, 69, **115**
Tangy Cranberry Meatballs, 354
Meatless entrées
Asian Noodle Bowl, 160
Bean-and-Rice-Stuffed Peppers, 152
Bean-Stuffed Cabbage Rolls, 158
Black Bean and Corn Quesadillas, 150
Brie Sandwiches with Greens, 148
Cashew-Vegetable Stir-Fry, 157
Cheesy Tortellini Casserole, 162
Chiles Rellenos, 146
Chipotle-Bean Enchiladas, 152
Couscous- and Pine Nut-Stuffed
Peppers, 159
Creamy Tomato-Broccoli Sauce with
Pasta, 164
Curried Couscous with Vegetables, 159
Eggplant Sauce with Whole Wheat
Pasta, 164
Foil-Grilled Cheese Sandwiches, 150
Fresh Tomato Pizza with Pesto, 149
Gardener's Pie, 156
Greek-Seasoned Lentils, 163
Lentil-Vegetable Turnovers, 155
Mock Cheese Soufflé, **124,** 146
Oven Omelets with Pesto, 147
Pasta Stir-Fry, 161

Pesto and Cheese Tomato Melts, 148
Pizza Margherita, 149
Polenta and Black Beans, **124,** 151
Portobellos Florentine, 156
Red Beans over Spanish Rice, 153
Spicy Pasta and Broccoli, 160
Spicy Simmered Beans and
    Vegetables, 154
Spinach and Feta Omelet, 147
Summer Spaghetti, 161
Sweet-and-Sour Tofu, 163
Taco-Style Black Beans and Hominy, 154
Tortilla Lasagna, 162
Vegetable and Rice Casserole, 157
White Beans with Dried Tomatoes, 155
editerranean Lamb Burgers, 109, **118**
editerranean Parsnips, 204
editerranean Salad, 238, **269**
editerranean Shrimp and Couscous, 141
elon
    Berry-Melon Vinaigrette, 245
    Ham, Melon, and Spinach Salad, 104
    Tangy Melon Salad, 231
    Watermelon-Berry Ice, 301
    Watermelon Lemonade, 374
    Watermelon Salad with
        Watercress, 231, **267**
exican Cauliflower and Broccoli
    Chowder, 186
exican Lasagna, 98
exican-Stuffed Sweet Peppers, 68
exican-Style Fish Chowder, 182
ddle Eastern Pitas, 61
lk Chocolate–Caramel Clusters, 339
nt
    Chocolate-Mint S'more, 393
    Chocolate-Mint Treats, 393
    Chocolaty Candy Cane Cups, 337
    Easy Crème de Menthe Cake, 305
    Fizzy Mint-Chocolate Soda, 372
    Lamb Chops with Mint Marinade, 107
    Little Peppermint Cakes, 307
    Minted Iced Tea, **276,** 376
    Minted Snap Peas and Carrots, 206
    Mint-Ginger Fruit Sorbet, 300
    Mint Surprise Cupcakes, 312
    Molded Peppermint Bark, 340
xed Berry Cobbler, 280
xed Greens with Pears, 230, **267**
xed Pastas with Fresh Herbs, 216
ocha au Lait, 377
ocha Pears, 286
ck Cheese Soufflé, **124,** 146
olasses Barbecue Sauce, 249
olded Peppermint Bark, 340
ushrooms
    Feta-Stuffed Mushrooms, 364
    French Dips with Mushrooms, 47
    Garlicky Grilled Portobellos, 202
    Hoisin-Garlic Mushroom Appetizers, 364
    Mushroom-Tomato-Pesto Pizza, 27
    Pork and Mushroom Stew, 176
    Portobello Sauce, 253
    Portobellos Florentine, 156
    Smoked Mushrooms, 201
    Steak and Mushrooms, 49
u Shu–Style Pork Roll-Ups, 89

Mustard. *See also* **Honey-Mustard**
    Balsamic-Mustard Marinade, 260
    Maple- and Mustard-Sauced Turkey
        Thighs, 34
    Mustard-Glazed Halibut Steaks, 136
    Mustard-Horseradish Sauce, 252
    Mustard-Jalapeño Glaze, 252
    Mustard-Marinated Flank Steak, 55
    Mustard-Peppercorn Rub, 258
    Pork Chops Dijon, 87

N

Napa Cabbage Slaw, 240
Nectarine-Granola Gratin, 281
Nectarine Toss, Fill-the-Grill, **272,** 296
No-Bake Tuna Noodle Casserole, **122,** 129
Noodles
    Asian Noodle Bowl, 160
    Haystacks, 339
    Quick and Crunchy Turkey Salad, 39
    Simply Ramen Chicken Soup, **126,** 166
    Thai Beef Stir-Fry, 56
North African Lamb Stew, 181
Nuts. *See also* **Almonds; Peanut butter;**
        Peanuts; Pecans
    Cashew-Toffee Cookies, 334
    Cashew-Vegetable Stir-Fry, 157
    Chocolate Chip Thumbprints, 330
    Crunchy Pound Cake Slices, 308
    Glazed Nut Topping, 327
    Gorgonzola-Walnut-Stuffed Apples, 285
    Lemon-Nut Vinaigrette, 245
    Macadamia Nut Shortbread, 334
    Macadamia-Vanilla Bark, 340
    Nutty Turkey Tenderloins, 30
    Pine Nut Cookies, 329
    toasting, 280
    White Chocolate–Cereal Drops, 340
    White Citrus Fudge, 336

O

Okra
    Cajun Pork, 90
    Cajun-Seasoned Vegetarian Gumbo, 185
    Sausage and Chicken Gumbo, 169
Old-Fashioned Beef Stew, 174
Olives
    Olive Bread, 366
    Olive-Tomato Tarts, 361
    Spanish Olive Rub, 259
Omelet, Spinach and Feta, 147
Omelets with Pesto, Oven, 147
One-Pot Pesto Pasta, 97
Onions
    Crispy Onion Rings, **274,** 365
    Grilled Sweet Onions, 202
    sweet, varieties of, 202
    Sweet-and-Sour Onions, 203
    Sweet Onion Spread, 349
Oranges
    Citrus Butter, 262
    Citrus-Honey Marinade, 260
    Cranberry-Apple-Orange Relish, 257
    Ginger Fruit with Pineapple Sherbet, 294

Icy Orange-Filled Cupcakes, 313
Lemon Sunshine Salad, 242
Mandarin Chicken Salad, 26, **113**
Mango Cream, 291
Orange Cream Punch, 370
Orange Dream Fruit Salad, 233
Orange-Marinated Salmon Steaks, 130
Orange–Poppy Seed Dressing, 246
Orange Sesame Ribs, 92
Quick and Crunchy Turkey Salad, 39
Sangria for Kids,
Oriental-Style Chicken Stew, 168
Osso Buco, Veal, 72
Oven-Barbecued Beef Sandwiches, 47
Oven-Fried Coconut Chicken, 9
Oven Omelets with Pesto, 147

P

Pancake, The Magic, 379
Pancakes, Fancy Stack, 379
Papaya-Mango Fool, 290
Papaya Salsa, 255
Parfait Pie with Coconut Shell, 318
Parsnips
    Glazed Parsnips and Apples, 203
    Honey-Glazed Carrots, 197, **264**
    Mediterranean Parsnips, 204
Passion Fruit and Strawberry Sorbet Cake, 315
Pasta. *See also* **Couscous; Noodles**
    Bow Ties with Sausage and Sweet
        Peppers, 96
    Cacciatore-Style Penne, 67
    Capellini with Shrimp and Pesto, 140
    Cheesy Tortellini Casserole, 162
    Coconut-Chicken Pasta, 23
    combining types of, 216
    Creamy Tomato-Broccoli Sauce with
        Pasta, 164
    Easy Vegetable Minestrone, 186
    Eggplant Sauce with Whole Wheat
        Pasta, 164
    Fast Chicken Fettuccine, 17
    Feta-Tomato Pasta Salad, 243
    Ginger Pea Pods and Noodles, 206
    Ham and Asparagus Pasta, 103
    Lemon Sunshine Salad, 242
    Light and Lemony Fettuccine, 216
    Lip-Smackin' Mac 'n' Cheese, 386
    Marinara-Sauced Pasta, 215, **265**
    Mexican Lasagna, 98
    Mixed Pastas with Fresh Herbs, 216
    No-Bake Tuna Noodle Casserole, **122,** 129
    One-Pot Pesto Pasta, 97
    Pasta-Salami Salad, 99
    Pasta Stir-Fry, 161
    Pasta with Basil-Shrimp for
        Two, **123,** 140
    Pesto Macaroni Salad, 243
    Poppy Seed–Dressed Pasta
        Salad, 242, **270**
    Quick Turkey Tetrazzini, 37
    Saucy Sweet Pepper Pasta, 217
    Smoked Salmon Pasta, 132
    Smoked Sausage Pasta Bake, 96
    Spicy Pasta and Broccoli, 160
    Summer Spaghetti, 161

Pasta (continued)
    Toasted Ravioli, 357
    Tortellini in Ratatouille Sauce, 357
    Tortellini Soup Alfredo, 184
    Triple-Cheesy Pasta, 217
    Turkey and Pasta Primavera, 31
Pastrami and Vegetable Panini, 60
Peaches
    Apricot-Peach Cobbler, 282
    Apricot-Peach Dessert Soup, 292
    Daiquiri Sorbet, 300
    Honey-Peach Sauce, 253
    Lemon Sunshine Salad, 242
    Peaches with Quick Cherry Sauce, 294
    Peach Nectar Punch, 369
    Pepper and Peach Fajita Chicken, 11
    Pineapple-Peach Cobbler, 281
Peachy Pork Tenderloin, 73
Peanut butter
    Carrot, Raisin, and Peanut Butter
        Sandwiches, 387
    Chocolate–Peanut Butter S'more, 393
    Creamy Peanut Butter Spread, 397
    Easy Peanut Butter Cookies, 331
    Fudgy Peanut Butter Bites, 335
    Peanut Butter and Chocolate
        Pinwheels, 331
    Peanut Butter Balls, 338
    Peanut Butter Cocoa, 378
    Peanut Butter Cups, 337
    Peanut Butter S'more Tarts, 319
    Peanutty Dip, 397
    Surprise Chocolate Bites, 329
Peanuts
    Banana-Raisin Trail Mix, 395
    Blaze-a-Trail Mix, 395
    Caramel Corn and Peanuts, 396
    Crunchy Trail Mix, 342
    Five-Layer Bars, 332
    Frozen Chocolate-Peanut Dessert, 392
    Fruit and Peanut Snack Mix, 342
    Haystacks, 339
    Milk Chocolate–Caramel Clusters, 339
    Pea and Peanut Salad, 235
    Peanut Butter S'more Tarts, 319
    Sweet Spiced Popcorn, 343
Pears
    Apple-Pear Sauce, 297
    Cream-Topped Pears in Orange
        Sauce, 286
    Mixed Greens with Pears, 230, **267**
    Mocha Pears, 286
    Pear-Chutney Salsa, 256
    Poached Pears in Cran-Amaretto
        Sauce, 287
    Rustic Pear Tart, 319
Peas
    Asian Pea Pod Salad, 235
    Balsamic-Glazed Lamb and Greens, 107
    Cheesy Peas and Potatoes, 205
    Cider Peas and Apples, 205
    Dilled Peas and Walnuts, 204
    Ginger Pea Pods and Noodles, 206
    Minted Snap Peas and Carrots, 206
    Pea and Peanut Salad, 235
Pecans
    Cheese-Stuffed Pecans, 368

Crunchy Nut-Caramel Cupcakes, 314
    Maple-Pecan Pork Chops, 81
    Nutty Turkey Tenderloins, 30
    Praline Crunch Bars, 332
Pepper-Cheese Biscuits, 227
Pepperoni-Pizza Potatoes, 385
Peppers. See also **Chiles**
    Bean-and-Rice-Stuffed Peppers, 152
    Bow Ties with Sausage and Sweet
        Peppers, 96
    Broccoli and Peppers, 195
    Country Chops and Peppers, 82
    Couscous- and Pine Nut–Stuffed
        Peppers, 159
    Creamy Corn and Roasted Red
        Peppers, 200
    Grilled Sweet Pepper Relish, 256
    Mexican-Stuffed Sweet Peppers, 68
    Pepper and Peach Fajita Chicken, 11
    Pepper Steak, 55, **117**
    Pizza by the Yard, 99
    Salmon with Roasted Pepper Cream, 131
    Saucy Sweet Pepper Pasta, 217
    Summer Squash with Peppers, 212
    Sweet Peppers Stuffed with Goat Cheese
        and Herbs, 207
Peppy Asparagus-Shrimp Toss, 143
Pesto
    Capellini with Shrimp and Pesto, 140
    Easy Turkey-Pesto Potpies, 34
    Fresh Tomato Pizza with Pesto, 149
    Lamb Shanks with Basil Pesto, 108
    Mushroom-Tomato-Pesto Pizza, 27
    One-Pot Pesto Pasta, 97
    Oven Omelets with Pesto, 147
    Pesto and Cheese Tomato Melts, 148
    Pesto Macaroni Salad, 243
    Roast Chicken with Fruit and Pesto, 6
    serving ideas, 29
    Tomato-Pesto Toast, 359
    Turkey with Dried Tomato Pesto, 29, **114**
Pico de Gallo, 255
Pies (dessert)
    Frozen Cranberry Pie, 318
    Juicy Raspberry Pie, 317
    Parfait Pie with Coconut Shell, 318
    quick lattice tops for, 317
    Shimmering Strawberry Pie, 316
    Strawberry-Chocolate Pie, 316
Pies (savory)
    Beefy Shepherd's Pie, 67
    Chicken Alfredo Potpies, 25
    Easy Turkey-Pesto Potpies, 34
    Gardener's Pie, 156
Pineapple
    Banana Split Kabobs, 392
    Chicken Kabobs with Thai Brushing
        Sauce, 14, **112**
    Chicken with Pineapple-Hoisin Glaze, 10
    Creamy Apple Salad, 232
    Ginger Fruit with Pineapple Sherbet, 294
    Hot-and-Sweet Pineapple
        Slaw, 239, **269**
    Pineapple Fries with Raspberry
        Ketchup, **273,** 288
    Pineapple-Mustard Country-Style
        Ribs, 92

Pineapple-Peach Cobbler, 281
    Pineapple Relish, 255
    Tropical Fruit Dip, **274,** 343
    Tuna Salad with a Twist, 129
Pine Nut Cookies, 329
Pizza. See also **Calzones**
    Canadian Bacon Pizza, 105
    Fresh Tomato Pizza with Pesto, 149
    Mushroom-Tomato-Pesto Pizza, 27
    Pizza by the Yard, 99
    Pizza Margherita, 149
    Taco Pizza, 69
    Two Pizzas in One, 383
Plum Good Sausage and Meatballs, 354
Plum-Mustard Sauce, Easy, 254
Poached Pears in Cran-Amaretto Sauce, 287
Polenta
    Polenta and Black Beans, **124,** 151
    Polenta with Turkey Sausage
        Florentine, 35
    Sausage-Sauced Polenta, 98
Polynesian Glazed Wings, **275,** 352
Popcorn
    Caramel Corn and Peanuts, 396
    Dive-In Party Mix, **277,** 395
    Sweet Spiced Popcorn, 343
Poppy Seed–Dressed Pasta Salad, 242, **270**
Pork. See also **Bacon; Ham; Pork (sausages),**
        specific cuts below
    Easy Burgoo, 177
    Mu Shu–Style Pork Roll-Ups, 89
    Pork, Lentil, and Apple Soup, 175
    Pork and Black Bean Potage, 176
    Pork and Mushroom Stew, 176
    Pork Patties with Honey Barbecue
        Sauce, 95
    Sweet and Spicy Pork Burgers, 95
Pork (chops)
    Apple Butter–Sauced Pork Chops, 88
    Asian Apricot-Glazed Chops, 84
    Barbecued Pork Chop
        Sandwiches, 84, **121**
    Beer-Glazed Pork Chops, 83
    Choucroute Garni, 86
    Country Chops and Peppers, 82
    Cranberry-Chipotle Pork Chops, 81, **11**
    Easy Pork Chops Supreme, 86
    Ginger-Lemon Pork Chops, 85
    Lemon-and-Herb-Rubbed Pork Chops, 8
    Maple-Pecan Pork Chops, 81
    Margarita-Glazed Pork Chops, 85
    Pork Chops and Corn Bread Stuffing, 87
    Pork Chops Dijon, 87
    Pork Chops with Orange-Dijon Sauce, 8
    Smoked Chops and Potatoes, 88
    Smoked Pork Chop Skillet, 89
Pork (ribs)
    Cranberry-Glazed Pork Ribs, 94
    grilling, tip for, 93
    Honey-Mustard Barbecue Pork Ribs, 91
    Hot Honeyed Spareribs, 355
    Orange Sesame Ribs, 92
    Pineapple-Mustard Country-Style Ribs, 9
    Ribs and Sauerkraut, 94
    Stout-Glazed Ribs, 93, **119**
    types of, 93

rk (roasts)
Apricot Pulled Pork, 79
Cajun Pork, 90
Cranberry Pork Roast, 77
German-Style Pork Stew, 177
Italian Rolled Pork Roast, 78
Pork and Winter Squash Stew, 175
Pork Roast with Apricot Glaze, 77
Ranch Pork Roast, 79
Rhubarb-Glazed Pork Roast, 76
Shredded Pork Barbecue Rolls, 80, **121**
Slow-Cooked Asian-Style Pork, 91

rk (sausages)
Bow Ties with Sausage and Sweet
    Peppers, 96
Bratwurst with Kickin' Cranberry
    Ketchup, 100
Bunless Burgers, 63, **115**
Choucroute Garni, 86
Firecracker Foot-Longs, 100, **121**
Italian-Stuffed Sausage Burgers, 97
Mexican Lasagna, 98
One-Pot Pesto Pasta, 97
Pasta-Salami Salad, 99
Pizza by the Yard, 99
Plum Good Sausage and Meatballs, 354
Potato and Bratwurst Stew, 180
Sausage and Chicken Gumbo, 169
Sausage and Corn Bread Stuffing, 220
Sausage-Cheese Dip, 346
Sausage-Sauced Polenta, 98
Smoked Sausage Pasta Bake, 96
Texas Two-Step Stew, 180
Tuscan Bean and Sausage Stew, 179
Two Pizzas in One, 383

rk (tenderloin)
Honey-Mustard Pork Tenderloin
    Sandwiches, 80
Peachy Pork Tenderloin, 73
Pork Loin with Vegetables, 75
Pork Medallions with Apples, 75
Pork Medallions with Cherry Sauce, 74
Pork Tenderloin with Sweet Potatoes, 74
Pork with Cider and Cream, 72
Soy and Sesame Pork, 73
rtobello Sauce, 253
rtobellos Florentine, 156
tatoes. *See also* **Sweet potatoes**
Beefy Shepherd's Pie, 67
Buttered Rosemary New Potatoes, 209
Cheeseburger and Fries Casserole, 382
Cheesy Garlic Potato Gratin, 209
Cheesy Peas and Potatoes, 205
Cheesy Potato-Bean Soup, 183
Cheesy Potato Wedges, 365
Cheesy Reuben Potatoes, 62
Creamy Beef-and-Potato Stew, 171
Creamy Potato Wedges, 208
Garlic-Roasted Red Potatoes, 207
Ham and Potatoes au Gratin, 103, **120**
Indian Lamb and Potato Stew, 181
Pepperoni-Pizza Potatoes, 385
Potato and Bratwurst Stew, 180
Saucy Green Beans and Potatoes, 192
Shredded Hash Browns, 210
Smoked Chops and Potatoes, 88

Smoky Chicken and Cheesy Potato
    Casserole, 26
Spuds with Broccoli Topper, 385
Super Creamy Mashed Potatoes, 208
Veggie Mash, 214
Pot Roast with Chipotle-Fruit Sauce, 46
Pot Roast with Mushroom Sauce, 45
Pots de Crème, Chocolate, 324
Poultry. *See* Chicken; Game hens; Turkey
Praline Baked Apples, 285
Praline Crunch Bars, 332
Pretzel and Beer Burgers, 64
Pretzels, Soft, 366
Prosciutto
Brussels Sprouts with Prosciutto, 196
Glazed Prosciutto-Wrapped
    Shrimp, 137
Prosciutto-Arugula Roll-Ups, 362
Prosciutto-Wrapped Tenderloin, 51
Veal Rolls Stuffed with Herb
    Cheese, 70, **118**
Puddings
Chocolate Brownie Pudding, 394
Fruity Rice Pudding, 324
Pumpkin Custard Bread Pudding, 323
Quick and Creamy Rice Pudding, 323
Semisweet-Chocolate Bread
    Pudding, 322
Puff Pastry Cheese Straws, 360
Pumpkin Custard Bread Pudding, 323
Puzzle Cookies, 391

Q
Quesadillas
Black Bean and Corn Quesadillas, 150
Cheesy Pecan Quesadillas, 356
Turkey-Avocado Quesadillas, 37
Quick and Creamy Rice Pudding, 323
Quick and Crunchy Turkey Salad, 39
Quick Chicken Fajitas, 27, **113**
Quick Chicken Tortilla Bake, 23
Quick Ice Cream Shake, 372
Quick Strawberry Shortcake, 284
Quick Turkey Tetrazzini, 37

R
Raisins
Banana-Raisin Trail Mix, 395
Blaze-a-Trail Mix, 395
Carrot, Raisin, and Peanut Butter
    Sandwiches, 387
Five-Layer Bars, 332
Raisin-Herb Seasoned Stuffing, 220
Ranch Pork Roast, 79
Ranch-Style Chicken Strips, 17
Raspberries
Berry Parfaits, 394
Dessert Waffles with Raspberry
    Sauce, 295
Frozen Berry Yogurt, 299
Juicy Raspberry Pie, 317
Mango-Raspberry Granita, 301
Parfait Pie with Coconut Shell, 318

Pineapple Fries with Raspberry
    Ketchup, **273,** 288
Raspberries and Lemon Cream, 293
Raspberry and Chocolate Tulips, 320
Raspberry-Coffee Frappé, 377
Raspberry–Smoked Turkey Pockets, 38
Raspberry Whip, 291
Red, White, and Blue Parfaits, 290
Watermelon-Berry Ice, 301
Raspberry jam
Fruit Ribbon Cake, 302
Raspberry Piquant Sauce, 254
Turkey Breast with Raspberry Salsa, 30
Ready-Right-Now Sloppy Joes, 382
Really Red Coleslaw, 240, **268**
Red, White, and Blue Parfaits, 290
Relish
Cranberry-Apple-Orange Relish, 257
Grilled Sweet Pepper Relish, 256
Pineapple Relish, 255
Zucchini-Tomato Relish, 257
Reuben Loaves, 61
Reubens from a Crock, 48
Rhubarb-Glazed Pork Roast, 76
Ribs and Sauerkraut, 94
Rice. *See also* **Wild rice**
arborio, about, 219
aromatic, types of, 133
Bean-and-Rice-Stuffed Peppers, 152
Bean-Stuffed Cabbage Rolls, 158
Chicken and Rice Spring Rolls, 358
Curried Coconut Shrimp, 141
Easy Oven Risotto, 219
Easy Spanish Rice, 218
Fresh Corn-Rice Salad, 244
Fruity Rice Pudding, 324
Greek Cabbage Rolls, 110
Mexican-Stuffed Sweet Peppers, 68
Peppy Asparagus-Shrimp Toss, 143
Quick and Creamy Rice Pudding, 323
Red Beans over Spanish Rice, 153
Saffron Rice–Baked Tomatoes, 213
Scallop Fried Rice, 144
Texas Two-Step Stew, 180
Vegetable and Rice Casserole, 157
Vegetable Rice Pilaf, 219
Risotto, Easy Oven, 219
Roast Chicken with Fruit and Pesto, 6
Roasted Mango with Coconut, 284
Rocky Mountain Trout, 135
Rolls
Cheddary Corn Bread Rolls, 225, **266**
Cheese and Garlic Crescents, 228
Have-a-Ball Rolls, 224
Rosemary and Swiss Buns, 226
Rosemary Mini Cupcakes, 311
Round Steak with Herbs, 57
Rubs
Barbecue Rub, 259
Curry Rub, 259
Ginger-Allspice Rub, 258
Herb Rub, 258
Mustard-Peppercorn Rub, 258
Spanish Olive Rub, 259
Rustic Pear Tart, 319

INDEX

S

Saffron Rice–Baked Tomatoes, 213
Salad dressings
  Apricot Nectar Dressing, 246
  Berry-Melon Vinaigrette, 245
  Chutney Salad Dressing, 247
  Creamy Chive Dressing, 248
  Creamy Garlic Dressing, 248
  Herb-Buttermilk Dressing, 248
  Honey-Mustard Dressing, 247
  Lemon-Nut Vinaigrette, 245
  Orange–Poppy Seed Dressing, 246
  Spicy Citrus Dressing, 246
  Strawberry Vinaigrette, 245
  Thousand Island Dressing, 247
Salads
  Asian Pea Pod Salad, 235
  Baby Greens with Veggies, 237
  Black Cherry–Cranberry Supreme, 233
  BLT Salad, 105
  Chicken Taco Salad, 25
  Cranberry Coleslaw, 241
  Creamy Apple Salad, 232
  Creamy Cucumbers, 239
  Feta-Tomato Pasta Salad, 243
  Fresh Corn and Tomato Salad, 236, **270**
  Fresh Corn-Rice Salad, 244
  Fresh Mozzarella Salad, 234
  Fruit and Broccoli Salad, 234
  Fruity Wild Rice Salad, 244
  Ginger-Sesame Slaw, 241
  Ham, Melon, and Spinach Salad, 104
  Hot-and-Sweet Pineapple
    Slaw, 239, **269**
  Iceberg Lettuce with Cucumber-Mint
    Dressing, 230
  Lemon Sunshine Salad, 242
  Mandarin Chicken Salad, 26, **113**
  Marinated Bean Salad, 238
  Mediterranean Salad, 238, **269**
  Mixed Greens with Pears, 230, **267**
  Napa Cabbage Slaw, 240
  Orange Dream Fruit Salad, 233
  Pasta-Salami Salad, 99
  Pea and Peanut Salad, 235
  Pesto Macaroni Salad, 243
  Poppy Seed–Dressed Pasta
    Salad, 242, **270**
  Quick and Crunchy Turkey Salad, 39
  Really Red Coleslaw, 240, **268**
  Salmon Caesar Salad, 132
  Strawberry-Spinach Salad, 229
  Tangy Melon Salad, 231
  Tomato and Zucchini Salad, 237
  Watermelon Salad with
    Watercress, 231, **267**
  Winter Fruit Bowl, 232
Salami-Pasta Salad, 99
Salmon
  Foil-Wrapped Salmon Dinner, 131
  Grilled Salmon with Mustard
    Glaze, **122**, 130
  Orange-Marinated Salmon Steaks, 130
  Salmon Caesar Salad, 132
  Salmon with Roasted Pepper Cream, 131
  Smoked Salmon Pasta, 132

Salsas
  Papaya Salsa, 255
  Pear-Chutney Salsa, 256
  Pico de Gallo, 255
  Strawberry Salsa, 256
Sandwiches and wraps
  Barbecued Pork Chop
    Sandwiches, 84, **121**
  Barbecued Turkey Tenderloin
    Sandwiches, 32, **114**
  Bratwurst with Kickin' Cranberry
    Ketchup, 100
  Brie Sandwiches with Greens, 148
  Carrot, Raisin, and Peanut Butter
    Sandwiches, 387
  Chicken and Bean Burritos, 16
  Deli Roast Beef Sandwiches, 60
  Foil-Grilled Cheese Sandwiches, 150
  French Dips with Mushrooms, 47
  Greek-Style Pitas, 62
  Middle Eastern Pitas, 61
  Mu Shu–Style Pork Roll-Ups, 89
  Oven-Barbecued Beef Sandwiches, 47
  Pesto and Cheese Tomato Melts, 148
  Raspberry–Smoked Turkey Pockets, 38
  Reubens from a Crock, 48
  Saucy Meatball Sandwiches, 69, **115**
  Sesame-Ginger Turkey Wraps, 33, **115**
  Shredded Pork Barbecue Rolls, 80, **121**
  Snowflake Sandwiches, 384
  Tuna Salad with a Twist, 129
  Turkey Subs with Orange
    Mayonnaise, 39
  Vegetable and Pastrami Panini, 60
Sangria for Kids, 398
Sauces. See also **Salsas**
  Apple Butter Barbecue Sauce, 249
  Apple-Pear Sauce, 297
  Basic Moppin' Sauce, 250
  Butterscotch-Caramel Sauce, 328
  Cranberry-Chipotle Sauce, 250
  Cucumber-Dill Sauce, 252
  Currant Sauce, 254
  Easy Blueberry Sauce, 297
  Easy Plum-Mustard Sauce, 254
  Ginger-Orange Brush-On, 251
  Honey-Peach Sauce, 253
  Hot Fudge Sauce, 328
  Lemon-Herb Brush-On, 250
  Lemon Sauce, 253
  Mango-Habañero Mojo, 257
  Molasses Barbecue Sauce, 249
  Mustard-Horseradish Sauce, 252
  Portobello Sauce, 253
  Raspberry Piquant Sauce, 254
  Tandoori-Style Brush-On, 251
  Tangy Barbecue Sauce, 249
Saucy Green Beans and Potatoes, 192
Saucy Meatball Sandwiches, 69, **115**
Saucy Strip Steaks, 50
Saucy Sweet Pepper Pasta, 217
Sauerkraut
  Cheesy Reuben Potatoes, 62
  Choucroute Garni, 86
  Country-Style Smoked Sausage and
    Sauerkraut, 35
  Reuben Loaves, 61

Reubens from a Crock, 48
Ribs and Sauerkraut, 94
Sausages. See **Pork (sausages); Turkey
  (sausages)**
Savory Black Beans, 193
Scallops
  Buttery Bay Scallops, 144
  Scallop Fried Rice, 144
  Shrimp and Scallop Skewers, 142
  Thai-Spiced Scallop Kabobs, 145
Seafood. See **Fish; Shellfish**
Seeds, toasting, 280
Semisweet-Chocolate Bread Pudding, 322
Sesame-Ginger Turkey Wraps, 33, **115**
Sesame-Seared Tuna, 128
Shallot Sauce, Green Beans with, 191
Shellfish. See also **Scallops; Shrimp**
  Creamy Clam Chowder, 182
  Lobster Tails with Chive Butter, 145
Shepherd's Pie, Beefy, 67
Sherry Marinade, 261
Shimmering Strawberry Pie, 316
Shortbread, Macadamia Nut, 334
Shortcut Malted Chocolate Cake, 304
Shredded Hash Browns, 210
Shredded Pork Barbecue Rolls, 80, **121**
Shrimp
  Capellini with Shrimp and Pesto, 140
  Cilantro Shrimp, 139
  Curried Coconut Shrimp, 141
  Garlic-Buttered Shrimp Kabobs, 139
  Glazed Prosciutto-Wrapped Shrimp, 13
  Mediterranean Shrimp and
    Couscous, 141
  Pasta with Basil-Shrimp for
    Two, **123**, 140
  peeling and deveining, 137
  Peppy Asparagus-Shrimp Toss, 143
  Shrimp and Scallop Skewers, 142
  Shrimp with Fruit Salsa, **123**, 138
  Shrimp with Honey-Ginger Sauce, 143
  Sweet-and-Sour Shrimp, 142
Simple Short Rib Stew, 172
Simply Ramen Chicken Soup, **126**, 166
Skillet Chicken Alfredo, 13
Slaws
  Cranberry Coleslaw, 241
  Ginger-Sesame Slaw, 241
  Hot-and-Sweet Pineapple
    Slaw, 239, **269**
  Napa Cabbage Slaw, 240
  Really Red Coleslaw, 240, **268**
Sloppy Joes, Cheesy, 68
Sloppy Joes, Ready-Right-Now, 382
Slow cooker basics
  lean meat and poultry for, 90
  lifting lid, note about, 69
  slow cooker sizes, note about, 172
Slow cooker recipes (appetizers)
  Cheesy Beer-Salsa Dip, 346
  Chicken Wings with Barbecue Sauce, 35
  Chipotle Con Queso Dip, 345
  Cranberry-Sauced Franks, 355
  Creamy Avocado-Lime Dip, 344
  Hoisin-Garlic Mushroom Appetizers, 36
  Hot Honeyed Spareribs, 355
  Plum Good Sausage and Meatballs, 354

Polynesian Glazed Wings, **275,** 352
Sausage-Cheese Dip, 346
Spicy Chicken Fajita Bites, **275,** 356
Tomato Sauce with Garlic Cheese
    Bread, 347
ow cooker recipes (beverages)
Honey-Mulled Apple Cider, 375
Hot and Spicy Cranberry
    Punch, **276,** 371
Peanut Butter Cocoa, 378
Tomato Sipper, 371
ow cooker recipes (desserts)
Apricot-Peach Dessert Soup, 292
Brownie Pudding Cake, 309
Chocolate-Caramel Fondue, 327
Cream-Topped Pears in Orange
    Sauce, 286
Fruity Rice Pudding, 324
Gingerbread Pudding Cake, 310
Mixed Berry Cobbler, 280
Pineapple-Peach Cobbler, 281
Poached Pears in Cran-Amaretto
    Sauce, 287
Pumpkin Custard Bread Pudding, 323
Semisweet-Chocolate Bread
    Pudding, 322
Slow-Cooked Apple Betty, 283
ow cooker recipes (meat entrées)
Apple Butter–Sauced Pork Chops, 88
Apricot Pulled Pork, 79
Asian Beef Short Ribs, 56
Beef Burgundy, **125,** 173
Beef in Red Wine Gravy, 57
Beefy Shepherd's Pie, 67
Bloody Mary Steak, 54, **116**
Cajun Pork, 90
Cheesy Sloppy Joes, 68
Choucroute Garni, 86
Cola Pot Roast, 45
Corned Beef and Cabbage, 48
Cranberry Pork Roast, 77
Easy Goulash, 65
French Dips with Mushrooms, 47
Greek Cabbage Rolls, 110
Ham and Potatoes au Gratin, 103, **120**
Homestyle Beef and Vegetables, 44
Honey-Mustard Barbecue Pork Ribs, 91
Lamb Curry, 109
Lamb Shanks with Basil Pesto, 108
Mexican Lasagna, 98
Mexican-Stuffed Sweet Peppers, 68
Orange Sesame Ribs, 92
Pepper Steak, 55, **117**
Pizza by the Yard, 99
Pork Chops and Corn Bread Stuffing, 87
Pork Chops with Orange-Dijon Sauce, 83
Pork Roast with Apricot Glaze, 77
Pot Roast with Chipotle-Fruit Sauce, 46
Pot Roast with Mushroom Sauce, 45
Ranch Pork Roast, 79
Reubens from a Crock, 48
Ribs and Sauerkraut, 94
Round Steak with Herbs, 57
Shredded Pork Barbecue Rolls, 80, **121**
Slow-Cooked Asian-Style Pork, 91
Southwestern Steak Roll-Ups, 59

Steak with Tuscan Tomato
    Sauce, 53, **118**
Thai Beef, 58
Tostadas, 66
Veal Osso Buco, 72
Slow cooker recipes (poultry entrées)
Barbecue Beans and Hot Dogs over Corn
    Bread, 36
Cherried Chicken, 21
Chicken and Bean Burritos, 16
Country-Style Smoked Sausage and
    Sauerkraut, 35
Cranberry Chicken, 19, **113**
Finger Lickin' Barbecue Chicken, 21
Greek Chicken with Couscous, 15
Homestyle Chicken and Stuffing, 24
Honey-Mustard Chicken with Sweet
    Potatoes, 20
Maple- and Mustard-Sauced Turkey
    Thighs, 34
preparing ingredients ahead for, 33
Sesame-Ginger Turkey Wraps, 33, **115**
Smoky Chicken and Cheesy Potato
    Casserole, 26
Turkey and Pasta Primavera, 31
Slow cooker recipes (side dishes)
Apple-Buttered Sweet Potatoes, 211
Cheesy Cauliflower for a Crowd, 199
Cheesy Succotash, 212
Cranberry-Apple Spiced Beets, 194
Creamy Corn and Roasted Red
    Peppers, 200
Creamy Potato Wedges, 208
Curried Beans and Apples, 192, **263**
Ginger Pea Pods and Noodles, 206
Raisin-Herb Seasoned Stuffing, 220
Saucy Green Beans and Potatoes, 192
Saucy Sweet Pepper Pasta, 217
Sausage and Corn Bread Stuffing, 220
Super Creamy Mashed Potatoes, 208
Sweet Baby Carrots, 198
Triple-Cheesy Pasta, 217
Western Beans, 194
Wild Rice Pilaf with Squash, 218
Slow cooker recipes (soups and stews)
Apricot-Peach Dessert Soup, 292
Bean-and-Rice-Stuffed Peppers, 152
Bean-Stuffed Cabbage Rolls, 158
Beef and Barley Soup, 171
Cajun-Seasoned Vegetarian
    Gumbo, 185
Cheesy Potato-Bean Soup, 183
Cheesy Tortellini Casserole, 162
Chicken and Corn Chowder, 168
Chicken and Wild Rice Soup, 167
Chicken Curry Soup, 167
Chicken Tortilla Soup, **126,** 166
Coq au Vin Stew, 169
Corn and Sausage Chowder, 179
Creamy Beef-and-Potato Stew, 171
Creamy Tomato-Broccoli Sauce with
    Pasta, 164
Curried Couscous with Vegetables, 159
Easy Burgoo, 177
Easy Vegetable Minestrone, 186
Eggplant Sauce with Whole Wheat
    Pasta, 164

Fruited Beef Stew, 173
Garden Bounty Tomato Soup, 183
German-Style Pork Stew, 177
Greek-Seasoned Lentils, 163
Indian Lamb and Potato Stew, 181
Meatball-Vegetable Stew, **125,** 170
Mexican Cauliflower and Broccoli
    Chowder, 186
Mexican-Style Fish Chowder, 182
North African Lamb Stew, 181
Old-Fashioned Beef Stew, 174
Oriental-Style Chicken Stew, 168
Pork, Lentil, and Apple Soup, 175
Pork and Black Bean Potage, 176
Pork and Mushroom Stew, 176
Pork and Winter Squash Stew, 175
Potato and Bratwurst Stew, 180
Red Beans over Spanish Rice, 153
Sausage and Chicken Gumbo, 169
Spicy Ham-and-Garbanzo Bean
    Soup, 178
Sweet-and-Sour Beef Stew, 174
Sweet-and-Sour Tofu, 163
Taco Chili, 170
Taco-Style Black Beans and Hominy, 154
Texas Two-Step Stew, 180
Tortellini Soup Alfredo, 184
Tuscan Bean and Sausage Stew, 179
Vegetable and Rice Casserole, 157
Vegetable Chili Medley, 185
White Beans with Dried Tomatoes, 155
Smoked Chops and Potatoes, 88
Smoked Mushrooms, 201
Smoked Pork Chop Skillet, 89
Smoked Salmon Pasta, 132
Smoked Sausage Pasta Bake, 96
Smoky Chicken and Cheesy Potato
    Casserole, 26
Smoothies, All-American Fruit, **277,** 398
Smoothies, Berry-Banana, 373
Smoothies, Strawberry, 373
S'mores, Something More (and
    variations), **278,** 393
S'mores Bars, 333
S'more Tarts, Peanut Butter, 319
Snacks. See Appetizers and snacks
Snapper Veracruz, 134
Snowflake Sandwiches, 384
Soft Pretzels, 366
Sorbet, Daiquiri, 300
Sorbet, Mint-Ginger Fruit, 300
Sorbet Cake, Passion Fruit and
    Strawberry, 315
Soufflé, Bittersweet Chocolate, **273,** 326
Soufflé, Mock Cheese, **124,** 146
Soups. See also Chowder; Stews
Apricot-Peach Dessert Soup, 292
Beef and Barley Soup, 171
Cajun-Seasoned Vegetarian Gumbo, 185
Cheesy Potato-Bean Soup, 183
Chicken and Wild Rice Soup, 167
Chicken Curry Soup, 167
Chicken Tortilla Soup, **126,** 166
Double Berry Soup, 292
Easy Vegetable Minestrone, 186
Garden Bounty Tomato Soup, 183
Pork, Lentil, and Apple Soup, 175

Soups (continued)

Pork and Black Bean Potage, 176
Sausage and Chicken Gumbo, 169
Simply Ramen Chicken Soup, **126,** 166
Spicy Ham-and-Garbanzo Bean
Soup, 178
Tortellini Soup Alfredo, 184
Southwest Chicken Burgers, 22
Southwestern Steak Roll-Ups, 59
Soy and Sesame Pork, 73
Spanish Olive Rub, 259
Spare-Me Sugar Cookies, **278,** 390
Spiced Yogurt Dip, 344
Spicy Chicken Fajita Bites, **275,** 356
Spicy Citrus Dressing, 246
Spicy Ham-and-Garbanzo Bean Soup, 178
Spicy Pasta and Broccoli, 160
Spicy Simmered Beans and Vegetables, 154

Spinach

Brie Sandwiches with Greens, 148
Florentine Chicken, 12
Ham, Melon, and Spinach Salad, 104
Polenta with Turkey Sausage
Florentine, 35
Portobellos Florentine, 156
Spinach and Feta Omelet, 147
Spinach Pizza Bread, 363
Spinach-Stuffed Flank Steak, 51
Strawberry-Spinach Salad, 229
Turkey and Spinach Muffins with
Hollandaise, 36
Turkey Calzones, 38

Spreads. See **Dips and spreads**

Squash. See also **Zucchini**

Baby Greens with Veggies, 237
Capellini with Shrimp and Pesto, 140
Curried Couscous with Vegetables, 159
Fire-Roasted Acorn Squash, 211
Pork and Winter Squash Stew, 175
Pumpkin Custard Bread Pudding, 323
Summer Squash with Peppers, 212
Wild Rice Pilaf with Squash, 218
Steak and Mushrooms, 49
Steaks with Tarragon Butter, 54
Steak with Tuscan Tomato Sauce, 53, **118**
Steamed Fish with Veggies, 134

Stews. See also **Chili**

Beef Burgundy, **125,** 173
Coq au Vin Stew, 169
Creamy Beef-and-Potato Stew, 171
Easy Burgoo, 177
Fruited Beef Stew, 173
German-Style Pork Stew, 177
Hearty Ham Stew, **126,** 178
Indian Lamb and Potato Stew, 181
Meatball-Vegetable Stew, **125,** 170
North African Lamb Stew, 181
Old-Fashioned Beef Stew, 174
Oriental-Style Chicken Stew, 168
Pork and Mushroom Stew, 176
Pork and Winter Squash Stew, 175
Potato and Bratwurst Stew, 180
Simple Short Rib Stew, 172
Sweet-and-Sour Beef Stew, 174
Texas Two-Step Stew, 180
Tuscan Bean and Sausage Stew, 179
stir-fries, preparing, 56

Stout-Glazed Ribs, 93, **119**

Strawberries

All-American Fruit Smoothies, **277,** 398
Angel Shortcake with Cream, 305
Banana Split Kabobs, 392
Berry-Melon Vinaigrette, 245
Berry Parfaits, 394
Champagne Fruit Punch, 370
Chocolate-Covered Strawberry
Cakes, 308
Dipped Chocolate Angel Cake, 306
Double Berry Soup, 292
Frozen Berry Yogurt, 299
Hot Strawberry Cider, 375
Passion Fruit and Strawberry Sorbet
Cake, 315
Quick Strawberry Shortcake, 284
Red, White, and Blue Parfaits, 290
Shimmering Strawberry Pie, 316
Strawberries with Lime Dip, 288
Strawberry and Cheese Bites, 359
Strawberry-Chocolate Cake, **271,** 302
Strawberry-Chocolate Pie, 316
Strawberry Gelato, 299
Strawberry-Lime Fool, 290
Strawberry Salsa, 256
Strawberry Smoothies, 373
Strawberry-Spinach Salad, 229
Strawberry Vinaigrette, 245
Watermelon-Berry Ice, 301
Stroganoff-Sauced Beef Roast, 43
Stuffed Tuna Steaks, **123,** 128

Stuffing mix

Homestyle Chicken and Stuffing, 24
Nutty Turkey Tenderloins, 30
Pork Chops and Corn Bread Stuffing, 87
Raisin-Herb Seasoned Stuffing, 220
Sausage and Corn Bread Stuffing, 220
Succotash, Cheesy, 212
Summer Spaghetti, 161
Summer Squash with Peppers, 212
Sunflower Chip Cookies, 330
Super Creamy Mashed Potatoes, 208
Surprise Chocolate Bites, 329
Sweet-and-Sour Beef Stew, 174
Sweet-and-Sour Onions, 203
Sweet-and-Sour Shrimp, 142
Sweet-and-Sour Tofu, 163
Sweet and Spicy Chicken, 9
Sweet and Spicy Pork Burgers, 95
Sweet Baby Carrots, 198
Sweet Chicken Tostadas, 24
Sweet Ginger Stir-Fry, 15, **111**
Sweet Onion Spread, 349
Sweet Peppers Stuffed with Goat Cheese and
Herbs, 207

Sweet potatoes

Apple-Buttered Sweet Potatoes, 211
Baked Sweet Potato Fries, 210
Honey-Mustard Chicken with Sweet
Potatoes, 20
Pork Tenderloin with Sweet Potatoes, 74
Turkey Nuggets and Sweet Potatoes, 32
Sweet Saucy Carrots and Pecans, 197
Sweet Spiced Popcorn, 343

T

Taco Chili, 170
Taco Pizza, 69
Taco Salad, Chicken, 25
Taco-Style Black Beans and Hominy, 154
Tandoori-Style Brush-On, 251
Tangy Barbecue Sauce, 249
Tangy Cranberry Meatballs, 354
Tangy Lemon Chicken, 11, **111**
Tangy Melon Salad, 231

Tarts

Olive-Tomato Tarts, 361
Peanut Butter S'more Tarts, 319
Rustic Pear Tart, 319
Tasty Wheels, 396
Tea, Ginger-Lemon, 376
Tea, Iced Minted, **276,** 376
Teriyaki Glaze, 251
Texas Two-Step Stew, 180
Thai Beef, 58
Thai Beef Stir-Fry, 56
Thai-Spiced Scallop Kabobs, 145
thermometers, types of, 76
Thousand Island Dressing, 247
Toasted Almonds with Rosemary, 368
Toasted Cheese Pita Crisps, 367
Toasted Ravioli, 357
Toasty-Hot French Bread Slices, 223

Toffee pieces

Cashew-Toffee Cookies, 334
Double-Dipped Caramels, 338
Praline Crunch Bars, 332
Tofu, Sweet-and-Sour, 163

Tomatoes

B.L.T. Bruschetta, 358
BLT Salad, 105
BLT Steaks, 50
Creamy Tomato-Broccoli Sauce with
Pasta, 164
dried, about, 221
Farm-Style Green Beans, 190
Feta-Tomato Pasta Salad, 243
Fresh Corn and Tomato Salad, 236, **27**
Fresh Mozzarella Salad, 234
Fresh Tomato Pizza with Pesto, 149
Garden Bounty Tomato Soup, 183
Hamburgers with Squished Tomato
Topper, 63
Herb-Grilled Tomatoes, 213, **264**
Marinara-Sauced Pasta, 215, **265**
Mushroom-Tomato-Pesto Pizza, 27
Olive-Tomato Tarts, 361
Pesto and Cheese Tomato Melts, 148
Pico de Gallo, 255
Pizza Margherita, 149
Saffron Rice-Baked Tomatoes, 213
Steak with Tuscan Tomato Sauce, 53, **1.**
Tomato and Zucchini Salad, 237
Tomato-Garlic Butter, 262
Tomato-Pesto Toast, 359
Tomato Sauce with Garlic Cheese
Bread, 347
Tomato Sipper, 371
Turkey with Dried Tomato Pesto, 29, **11**
White Beans with Dried Tomatoes, 155
Zucchini-Tomato Relish, 257

rtellini
Cheesy Tortellini Casserole, 162
Tortellini in Ratatouille Sauce, 357
Tortellini Soup Alfredo, 184

rtillas
Black Bean and Corn Quesadillas, 150
Cheese and Bean Quesadillas, 386
Cheesy Pecan Quesadillas, 356
Chicken and Bean Burritos, 16
Chicken Salad Stacks, 381
Chipotle-Bean Enchiladas, 152
Dessert Burritos, 287
Ham and Cheese Pizza Tortillas, 384
Italian-Style Chips, 367
Mexican Lasagna, 98
Mu Shu–Style Pork Roll-Ups, 89
Quick Chicken Fajitas, 27, **113**
Quick Chicken Tortilla Bake, 23
Sesame-Ginger Turkey Wraps, 33, **115**
Southwestern Steak Roll-Ups, 59
Spicy Chicken Fajita Bites, **275,** 356
Tasty Wheels, 396
Tortilla Lasagna, 162
Turkey-Avocado Quesadillas, 37
warming, 16
stadas, 66
stadas, Sweet Chicken, 24
ple-Cheesy Pasta, 217
pical Angel Cake, 307
pical Fruit Dip, **274,** 343
ut, Rocky Mountain, 135
na
No-Bake Tuna Noodle
Casserole, **122,** 129
Sesame-Seared Tuna, 128
Stuffed Tuna Steaks, **123,** 128
Tuna Salad with a Twist, 129
rkey
Barbecued Turkey Tenderloin
Sandwiches, 32, **114**
Easy Turkey-Pesto Potpies, 34
Maple- and Mustard-Sauced Turkey
Thighs, 34
Nutty Turkey Tenderloins, 30
Quick and Crunchy Turkey Salad, 39
Quick Turkey Tetrazzini, 37
Raspberry–Smoked Turkey Pockets, 38
Sesame-Ginger Turkey Wraps, 33, **115**
Turkey and Pasta Primavera, 31
Turkey and Spinach Muffins with
Hollandaise, 36
Turkey-Avocado Quesadillas, 37
Turkey Breast with Raspberry Salsa, 30
Turkey Calzones, 38
Turkey Nuggets and Sweet Potatoes, 32
Turkey on the Grill, 28
Turkey Subs with Orange Mayonnaise, 39
Turkey Tenderloin with Black Bean and
Corn Salsa, 31
Turkey with Dried Tomato Pesto, 29, **114**
rkey (hot dogs)
BBQ Beans and Hot Dogs over Corn
Bread, 36
rkey (sausages)
Corn and Sausage Chowder, 179
Country-Style Smoked Sausage and
Sauerkraut, 35

Polenta with Turkey Sausage
Florentine, 35
Sausage-Corn Chowder, 381
Tuscan Bean and Sausage Stew, 179
Tuscan Chicken, 8
Two Pizzas in One, 383

U
Upside-Down Caramel Apple Cake, 309
Upside-Down Pizza Casserole, 66

V
Veal
Veal Chops with Apples, 71
Veal Chops with Ginger Butter, 71
Veal Osso Buco, 72
Veal Rolls Stuffed with Herb
Cheese, 70, **118**
Vegetables. *See also specific vegetables*
Asian Chicken and Vegetables, 19
Asian Noodle Bowl, 160
Beef Burgundy, **125,** 173
Cajun-Seasoned Vegetarian Gumbo, 185
Cashew-Vegetable Stir-Fry, 157
Cheesy Vegetable Chowder, 184
Chicken Alfredo Potpies, 25
Cola Pot Roast, 45
Fruited Beef Stew, 173
Garden Bounty Tomato Soup, 183
Gardener's Pie, 156
Hearty Ham Stew, **126,** 178
Homestyle Beef and Vegetables, 44
Lamb Curry, 109
Lamb Shanks with Basil Pesto, 108
Lentil-Vegetable Turnovers, 155
Meatball-Vegetable Stew, **125,** 170
Mu Shu–Style Pork Roll-Ups, 89
Oven Omelets with Pesto, 147
Pasta Stir-Fry, 161
Slow-Cooked Asian-Style Pork, 91
Spicy Simmered Beans and Vegetables, 154
Summer Spaghetti, 161
Sweet-and-Sour Beef Stew, 174
Sweet-and-Sour Shrimp, 142
Sweet Ginger Stir-Fry, 15, **111**
Thai Beef Stir-Fry, 56
Turkey and Pasta Primavera, 31
Vegetable and Pastrami Panini, 60
Vegetable and Rice Casserole, 157
Vegetable Chili Medley, 185
Vegetable Rice Pilaf, 219
Veggie Dip, 397
Veggie Mash, 214
Vinaigrettes
Berry-Melon Vinaigrette, 245
Lemon-Nut Vinaigrette, 245
Strawberry Vinaigrette, 245

W
Waffles, Chocolate-Dipped, 389
Waffles, Dessert, with Raspberry Sauce, 295
Walleye, Almond, 133
Walnut-Gorgonzola-Stuffed Apples, 285

Warm Brie, 351
Watercress, Watermelon Salad with, 231, **267**
Watermelon
Berry-Melon Vinaigrette, 245
Tangy Melon Salad, 231
Watermelon-Berry Ice, 301
Watermelon Lemonade, 374
Watermelon Salad with
Watercress, 231, **267**
Western Beans, 194
White Beans with Dried Tomatoes, 155
White Chocolate–Cereal Drops, 340
White Citrus Fudge, 336
Wild rice
Chicken and Wild Rice Soup, 167
Fruity Wild Rice Salad, 244
Wild Rice Pilaf with Squash, 218
Winter Fruit Bowl, 232

Y
Yogurt
All-American Fruit Smoothies, **277,** 398
Frosty Chocolate-Cherry Yogurt, 298
Frozen Berry Yogurt, 299
Honeyed Figs and Yogurt, 293
Peanutty Dip, 397
Raspberries and Lemon Cream, 293
Raspberry Whip, 291
Red, White, and Blue Parfaits, 290
Spiced Yogurt Dip, 344
Tropical Fruit Dip, **274,** 343

Z
Zucchini
Crunchy Catfish and Zucchini, 135
Fast Chicken Fettuccine, 17
Herbed Zucchini, 214
Honey-Mustard Lamb Chops, 106
Tomato and Zucchini Salad, 237
Tortellini in Ratatouille Sauce, 357
Zucchini Bites, 363
Zucchini-Tomato Relish, 257

Metric Information

The charts on this page provide a guide for converting measurements from the U.S. customary system, which is used throughout this book, to the metric system.

Product Differences

Most of the ingredients called for in the recipes in this book are available in most countries. However, some are known by different names. Here are some common American ingredients and their possible counterparts:

- Sugar (white) is granulated, fine granulated, or castor sugar.
- Powdered sugar is icing sugar.
- All-purpose flour is enriched, bleached or unbleached white household flour. When self-rising flour is used in place of all-purpose flour in a recipe that calls for leavening, omit the leavening agent (baking soda or baking powder) and salt.
- Light-colored corn syrup is golden syrup.
- Cornstarch is cornflour.
- Baking soda is bicarbonate of soda.
- Vanilla or vanilla extract is vanilla essence.
- Green, red, or yellow sweet peppers are capsicums or bell peppers.
- Golden raisins are sultanas.

Volume and Weight

The United States traditionally uses cup measures for liquid and solid ingredients. The chart below shows the approximate imperial and metric equivalents. If you are accustomed to weighing solid ingredients, the following approximate equivalents will be helpful.

- 1 cup butter, castor sugar, or rice = 8 ounces = ½ pound = 250 grams
- 1 cup flour = 4 ounces = ¼ pound = 125 grams
- 1 cup icing sugar = 5 ounces = 150 grams

Canadian and U.S. volume for a cup measure is 8 fluid ounces (237 ml), but the standard metric equivalent is 250 ml.

1 British imperial cup is 10 fluid ounces.

In Australia, 1 tablespoon equals 20 ml, and there are 4 teaspoons in the Australian tablespoon.

Spoon measures are used for smaller amounts of ingredients. Although the size of the tablespoon varies slightly in different countries, for practical purposes and for recipes in this book, a straight substitution is all that's necessary. Measurements made using cups or spoons always should be level unless stated otherwise.

Common Weight Range Replacements

Imperial / U.S.	Metric
½ ounce	15 g
1 ounce	25 g or 30 g
4 ounces (¼ pound)	115 g or 125 g
8 ounces (½ pound)	225 g or 250 g
16 ounces (1 pound)	450 g or 500 g
1¼ pounds	625 g
1½ pounds	750 g
2 pounds or 2¼ pounds	1,000 g or 1 Kg

Oven Temperature Equivalents

Fahrenheit Setting	Celsius Setting*	Gas Setting
300°F	150°C	Gas Mark 2 (very low)
325°F	160°C	Gas Mark 3 (low)
350°F	180°C	Gas Mark 4 (moderate)
375°F	190°C	Gas Mark 5 (moderate)
400°F	200°C	Gas Mark 6 (hot)
425°F	220°C	Gas Mark 7 (hot)
450°F	230°C	Gas Mark 8 (very hot)
475°F	240°C	Gas Mark 9 (very hot)
500°F	260°C	Gas Mark 10 (extremely hot)
Broil	Broil	Grill

*Electric and gas ovens may be calibrated using celsius. However, for an electric ove increase celsius setting 10 to 20 degrees when cooking above 160°C. For convectio or forced air ovens (gas or electric) lower the temperature setting 25°F/10°C when cooking at all heat levels.

Baking Pan Sizes

Imperial / U.S.	Metric
9×1½-inch round cake pan	22- or 23×4-cm (1.5 L)
9×1½-inch pie plate	22- or 23×4-cm (1 L)
8×8×2-inch square cake pan	20×5-cm (2 L)
9×9×2-inch square cake pan	22- or 23×4.5-cm (2.5 L)
11×7×1½-inch baking pan	28×17×4-cm (2 L)
2-quart rectangular baking pan	30×19×4.5-cm (3 L)
13×9×2-inch baking pan	34×22×4.5-cm (3.5 L)
15×10×1-inch jelly roll pan	40×25×2-cm
9×5×3-inch loaf pan	23×13×8-cm (2 L)
2-quart casserole	2 L

U.S. / Standard Metric Equivalents

⅛ teaspoon = 0.5 ml	
¼ teaspoon = 1 ml	
½ teaspoon = 2 ml	
1 teaspoon = 5 ml	
1 tablespoon = 15 ml	
2 tablespoons = 25 ml	
¼ cup = 2 fluid ounces = 50 ml	
⅓ cup = 3 fluid ounces = 75 ml	
½ cup = 4 fluid ounces = 125 ml	
⅔ cup = 5 fluid ounces = 150 ml	
¾ cup = 6 fluid ounces = 175 ml	
1 cup = 8 fluid ounces = 250 ml	
2 cups = 1 pint = 500 ml	
1 quart = 1 litre	